ARNOLD BENNETT

Photograph by Howard Coster

ARNOLD BENNETT: THE LAST YEARS

ARNOLD BENNETT

A Biography

by

REGINALD POUND

NEW YORK
HARCOURT, BRACE AND COMPANY

LIBRARY OF CONGRESS CATALOG CARD NUMBER: 52-9859

PRINTED IN THE UNITED STATES OF AMERICA

"Most folk are nobodies, but I
am somebody". — *These Twain.*

LIST OF ILLUSTRATIONS

LIST OF ILLUSTRATIONS—*contd.*

AUTHOR'S PREFACE

ARNOLD BENNETT'S work as a novelist has been the subject of a number of books. There has been no full account, until now, of his rise from small beginnings in the Six Towns of fact which became the Five Towns of his fiction to eminence in the literary and social scene of the 1920s, a decade in which he was as prominent as Shaw and Wells.

As the reader will be quick to realise, this book could not have been written without the help of Arnold Bennett himself in terms of diaries and letters, the result of his remarkable and sometimes incredible industry. I have been fortunate, too, in having the goodwill of his relatives, his friends and admirers, and of contemporaries who had dealings with or knowledge of him. Their readiness to assist has been a demonstration of the esteem, respect and affection with which he continues to be remembered.

It has not been my chief interest or business to endorse his disclaimers of familiar legends which grew up about his name. Five years before he died, in 1931, he wrote for his own satisfaction in some notes which he was making apart from his regular daily journal practice:

> I have not had a clear and fixed ambition. I began to write novels because my friends said I could. The same for plays. But I always had a strong feeling for journalism, which feeling is as strong as ever it was. I seldom ask myself what gives me most happiness or unhappiness. It is only on the rare occasions when I deliberately enquire into it that I realise that nothing gives me a purer pleasure than the first half of a fine cigar. I am not interested in money.

Since that was written, critical attitudes to his character and work have given often unjust weight to the subject of another written repudiation of his:

> . . . a great journalistic legend, still growing yearly, credits me with being the 'business man of letters' and also with being the man

who always succeeded in doing what he said he would do. I am not a man of business. If I were I should not pay somebody else a large annual sum for managing my affairs. As for succeeding in my carefully laid designs, the less said the better about that.

Hoping to have done not less than help finally to disperse such false notions of his character as may remain, I have tried to do a little more— to establish him in the mind of the reader not only as a personage but as a person.

R.P.

CHAPTER ONE

(1)

"A PAVEMENT artist has done you, sir, very lifelike. I saw it myself this morning at Hyde Park Corner."

Arnold Bennett's man Fred told him, March 29, 1927. He noted it in his private journal, adding the comment: "New manifestation of fame." There was a touch of poetic fitness in it, for he had written some years before that to him the word 'pavement' was one of the most beautiful in the English language.

The glow of satisfaction was warrantable in that his was a kind of celebrity rarely if ever acknowledged in that itinerant branch of popular art. His qualification for so unusual a form of recognition was that he had become a public figure such as no author in this country had been before or has been since. Richard Sickert, the painter, meeting him casually at the Garrick Club one evening at about that time, had raised a point which possibly the pavement artist in his own fashion was raising too: "I'm so glad to see you again, Bennett, because everywhere I hear you spoken of as a marvel of the modern world. Why is it?"

The question was asked through one of the most provocative beards of the era in a voice soft with insinuation. Sickert had just invited him to join a dinner party which had already begun in a private room at the club. Several other noted artists were there as guests. Arnold Bennett had looked him in the eye and declined. The invitation was too much of an afterthought for his liking.

He could look them all in the eye, anyone and everyone. He was now not only the eminently successful writing man. He had enlarged himself into a personality of magisterial importance in the life of the community. Like one of his Five Towns characters, "at forty his fame was assured; at fifty he was an institution; and at sixty an oracle." He had acquired that air of being "august within" which sometimes owes little to experience and yet always suggests an intimidating profundity of it. He was not only a senator of the republic of letters, one of literature's lawgivers. Like a man of the Renaissance, he seemed to be greater than his work. Baudelaire said of the menials in Balzac's

[1]

novels that they had an intensity of will to be themselves. It is a characteristic of the Five Towns people. Having become a writer, Arnold Bennett went on to be himself.

He had been a figure of the London literary and journalistic scene since the beginning of the century. He had become a personage of it, a sudden and dramatic rise in rank, in 1909–10 with the publication of his novel *The Old Wives' Tale.*

In that work he had succeeded in an enterprise which not many writers have had the nerve to attempt, far less the will to persevere in, that of making ordinary things inspiring and dullness seem romantic. Take some china clay, some crushed stone and flint, fine it down with water into the smooth creamy stuff known in the Potteries as 'slip', and out of it will be whirled and turned and shaped a bowl or a vase or some other object to please the eye or meet a need. Arnold Bennett took other Potteries raw materials not less commonplace and made out of them lasting works of literature.

For him the deepest satisfaction was not in winning the recognition which he had predicted long before would one day be his. It was in proving that he, too, was a master of his medium, like the craftsmen among whom he was born and brought up and to whom he had heard his father grumble: "Poor Arnold, he'll never be able to make a living. I don't know what we're going to *do* with poor Arnold."

A reading generation separated from his personality and time by twenty years will not easily understand the quite exceptional position which Arnold Bennett held in English life during his last decade. Hardy and Kipling were alive, though high accomplishment for both was of the past. Wells, Conrad, Shaw, Belloc, Chesterton, Galsworthy were not only alive but kicking, the last-named wearing the white spats of his superior social station. Arnold Bennett was a contemporary in a way that none of the others was. He was more completely of his time than any of them.

The brains of Wells and Shaw would have responded, not necessarily antiphonally, to the stimulus of some other age. Wells could have talked to Rousseau, Shaw no doubt to Voltaire. "Not every man fits every hour," Goethe said, perceiving the dynamic inequalities of human fortune. Arnold Bennett perfectly fitted his hour. It is impossible to imagine his being produced by any other period or any other environment. He reacted with the competence of the craftsman, if not unfailingly with the conscience of the artist, to the governing impulse towards personal fulfilment, with its indispensable proviso of material

[2]

security, which was the active principle of his class and generation. "I should like to see a more sustained effort," his father had remarked begrudgingly on being shown a short story which his son had contributed to *The Yellow Book*, the magazine epitome of the '90s. It was to become a family joke: sustained effort, indeed! Arnold Bennett produced more than eighty published volumes. There was, in addition, his journal of a million words, only a part of which has appeared in print. For most members of the journalistic profession his mass of miscellaneous article-writing alone would have been a career.

Marshalled behind *The Old Wives' Tale* were other novels, plays, the so-called "pocket philosophies", essays, criticism, reviews, serial stories, short stories, collaborations, a formidable amount of accomplishment, much of it distinguished. It was the outflow of a mind which might have found expression in quite other realms of concentration. Arnold Bennett's mental organisation, which had prompted H. G. Wells to write to him in 1911: "You have the best mind in Europe (in many respects)", a compliment rather than a judgment, was of a quality to encourage the view that his attachment to the business of writing may have been as fortuitous in the first instance as he had hinted in his book, *The Truth about an Author*.

He had wanted to be an architect. It needs no special effort of the imagination to place him as a likely success in almost any of the professions. He had the hands and the keen objective attention of a surgeon. He would have made a good college president. Taking a more modest view of himself, he said: "I am a writer, just as I might be a hotel-keeper, a solicitor, a doctor, a grocer, or an earthenware manufacturer."

Between 1911 and 1930 his position was outstanding among British writers, although his books rarely touched the 'best-seller' peaks and his consistently large income was derived mainly from his enormous journalistic industry. The solid and enduring part of his reputation rested on two important novels, *The Old Wives' Tale* and *Clayhanger*. He had found a new public for himself in the theatre. *Milestones*, his play of three generations written in partnership with Edward Knoblock, was a success, and so was his own stage version of his novel *Buried Alive*, dramatised as *The Great Adventure*.

There had been his immensely successful American tour of 1911–12. "I had an indescribably triumphant time," he wrote to Mrs. Belloc Lowndes on his return. "In fact the calm and unenthusiastic-minded editors said privately that no English author—neither Dickens nor Kipling—had ever been so well received. The financial side of the affair is (for a modest realist) *fantastique*." Summing up the year's work and takings on the last page of his journal for 1912, he recorded having made about £16,000, "which may be called success by any worldly-minded author." He added: "It is apparently about as much as I have earned during all the previous part of my life." He was forty-five.

On April 21, 1913, he noted in the same place: "Exhibition of Max Beerbohm's cartoons at the Leicester Galleries. Crowd. I was at once recognised—with a certain lack of politeness—by two men," but although his reputation had expanded into fame he had no conceits about it. He wrote on August 8, 1914, that his secretary had told him that while some of the residents of the Essex village where he had lately come to live were reading a Central News Agency war service telegram sent to him and displayed for public information in the post office window, a man remarked: "Let's see, who is Arnold Bennett?' The reply was: "He's the War Minister." Then in correction: "Oh, no, he isn't—he's the actor chap that lives down the road."

On March 23, 1915, he had the felicity of "being greeted by cries from the pit" at the first night of J. M. Barrie's *Rosy Rapture*, a form of acknowledgment that was to become a recurring phenomenon (favourite word) of his West End appearances in the years of his social eminence after the war. His arrival in the stalls was often marked by hand-clapping that was sufficient testimony to his public status to justify his often elaborate pretence, in what may sometimes have been the best acting of the evening, of not noticing it at all. He was "loudly cheered" as he entered a box at the Lyric Theatre, Hammersmith, for the first night of *Riverside Nights* in April, 1926. And there was the gratifying moment when, also at the theatre, he felt his arm being touched from behind and heard a memorable voice say over his shoulder: "You don't know me, Mr. Bennett, but I know you. I'm Ellen Terry."

An incident that for him was an event. He blushed, not knowing why he did so. "The great legendary figures," he wrote afterwards, "really should not make such remarks to their juniors," a reproof which scarcely hides his satisfaction at having been chosen for just such a lapse.

On a journey to the North of England: "An acquaintance stepped into my compartment and said: 'Forbes Robertson is on this train and would like to come and see you.' I was touched; I could hardly believe it. But I would not agree to the proposition, which seemed to me monstrous; my extremely illustrious senior approaching *me*! 'No,' I

[4]

said. 'I will go and see him.' But Sir Johnston and I met in the corridor, he being on his way to me." As he gives it, the episode is like a passage from *The Diary of a Nobody* and the self-satisfaction implicit in the throw-away line, 'he being on his way to me ' is not the only hint of an underlying affinity between the Arnold Bennett of the frilled evening shirts and Mr. Pooter. Like him, Arnold Bennett at times seemed to be a burlesque of his class.

Then there was the remarkable afternoon in the coffee-room at the Reform Club in London when a figure of stately deportment advanced towards him saying: "You probably don't remember me. I'm Henry James." This was a signal of distinction for a writing person of any rank, not ignoring the likelihood that it was a reflection also of Henry James' innate good manners. Bennett blushed then too. "He asked me if I was alone. I blushed again. It seemed to me incredible that Henry James should actually be asking to join my party." Some of the self-mistrust may have been due to the fact that he had cast up the James account for posterity in the *New Age* and had drawn attention to certain debit items. "His attitude towards the spectacle of life is at bottom conventional, timid, and undecided," a not imprecise statement of Arnold Bennett's attitude to the spectacle of Henry James, who referred to him in a letter to H. G. Wells as "the eminent Arnold Bennett", sending him through Wells "cordial and rueful greetings".

Like George Moore, James had been impressed by Arnold Bennett's earning power as a writer. He had spoken in one of the club conversations about his "grovelling poverty". At a dinner party on October 10, 1912, George Moore turned to Arnold Bennett and said: "You've made a very great deal of money." Bennett's answer was that it was not his fault: "I couldn't help it." Whereupon, Bennett noted, "he emerged from his *gaffe* with a certain grace by saying with a serious air that he wished *he* could do it."

The money-making prowess of Arnold Bennett is not likely to have contributed much to his wider reputation, though his boasted half-a-crown-a-word rate of payment from editors gained him notoriety, not to say envy, in Fleet Street. The pit at the theatre would hardly have saluted it, whatever respect it might and probably did elicit from the stalls, and the pavement artist, one may safely assume, was not paying homage to his subject's standing at the bank.

He liked receiving, as he often did receive, the hat-raising acknowledgments of passers-by in the street. What he did not care so much about was being recognised by strangers who on seeing him reacted immediately with the exclamation: "There's Arnold Bennett!" He often complained of it. Noting instances during a trip to Norway in 1929, he added: "Manners! Manners!" Read in the privacy of his journal it suggests that public emphasis on his identity made him feel uncomfortable. Returning from St. Malo by a night boat, he wrote: " 'My' steward offered me his excuses for having recognised me from my photographs. I am surprised that anybody can recognise me from my photographs. But people do. Often I see them leaning towards each other and I hear them say in a whisper audible a hundred yards off: 'There's Arnold Bennett!' Which I think not the best manners on their part."

An up-and-coming novelist, Louis Golding, who later wrote *Magnolia Street*, called on Arnold Bennett at his house in Cadogan Square, London. Towards the end of their talk, the eager young author, relishing the time and attention Bennett was giving him, exclaimed: "It must be an extraordinary experience, Mr. Bennett, to be as well-known as you are, to hear people say 'There's Arnold Bennett', to be recognised wherever you go." Arnold Bennett looked at him with a faint trace of a smile. "It *is* rather wonderful," he admitted, "—a—in—a—a—disgusting sort of way."

The "unsurpassable courtesy" of the Italian Customs chief who came out of his office in the high Alps to pay his respects ceremonially to Bennett the writer was a pleasurably different kind of experience, a tribute as well as a gesture. But his reiterated dislike of being stared at and pointed out has to be equated with his cultivation of personal idiosyncrasies designed to fix him in the public mind. It can only be accounted for by a fundamental awkwardness in his social stance. A man of the lower-middle class, he was absorbed not so much in dissociating himself from that *milieu* as in establishing himself in another more congenial. To those spared its circumstances by the accidents of life this is a situation which can be either amusing or boring, depending on the compensatory behaviour of the victim, as he often supposes himself to be. Writing a valedictory note on their friendship as an intro- duction to an American edition of *The Old Wives' Tale*, Somerset Maugham said: "For all his assurance and his knowing air, I feel he was, here among men, impressed, delighted, but a little afraid of doing the wrong thing and never entirely at his ease."

Mr. Maugham was surprised to see how patronising were the obituary notices after Arnold Bennett's death. "A certain amount of fun was made of his obsession with grandeur and luxury, and the pleasure he took in trains-de-luxe and first-class hotels. He never quite grew accustomed to the appurtenances of wealth. Once he said to me: 'If you've ever really been poor you remain poor at heart all your life. I've often walked,' he added, 'when I could very well afford to take a taxi simply because I couldn't bring myself to waste the shilling it would cost.' " He made the remark, 'Once poor, always poor,' to his friend Dr. Griffin, after going round a room switching off needless lights in his house in Cadogan Square. Mr. James Bone, of the *Manchester Guardian*, took Don Marquis, the American humorist, to tea with Bennett. Handing round a plate of *petits fours*, Bennett upset them on the floor. Continuing to talk, he groped under chairs and divans until the last little cake had been recovered and put back on the plate, which he then resumed handing round. For all the luxury he came to know, the shadow of poverty went with him through the years. He could never finally divest himself of the poverty-consciousness of his beginnings.

(2)

While he was objecting to the discomforts of public recognition, he was also taking care to be recognised by embellishing his appearance with the amiable vanities of a well-barbered quiff riding high above his brow and glittering gold fobs in his waistcoat pockets. The cartoonists, busy at their immemorial preoccupation with personality at the expense of character, seized on these affectations and, in doing so, much assisted the processes by which he became famous. More often than most of his fellow authors, he was a subject of their attentions, as congenial to the witty line of Max Beerbohm as to the rugged purposefulness of Sir Bernard Partridge of *Punch*. There is an instinct in cartoonists to disregard the sublime if not invariably to overstate the ridiculous. In depicting Arnold Bennett they rarely missed the provincial in him, the man who, as Chesterton may not have said, looked as if he had come up to London for the Cup Tie and never gone back, and who, according to George Bernard Shaw in one of his less generous moods, had the air of "a fourth-rate clerk from the Potteries and out of work at that".

The quiff, curling like votive smoke and balancing, by design, the deep indented chin; the clustered discoloured front teeth and the morbidly pendant lower lip; the drooping eyelids and the always half-open mouth; the absurdly heavy fobs and the pleated evening shirts, over the making and fitting of which he presided with feminine watch-

[7]

fulness; the stiff aldermanic presence—these were an incitement to the cartoonists to excel themselves at their trade of subordinating dignity to impudence. When someone was accused in Arnold Bennett's presence of having too great a lust for publicity, he pointed upward in silence at his quiff, then downward to the fobs—which Wells had spoken of as "Arnold's gastric jewellery"—and, with a smile, indicated that he was to be classed with the offender. Vanities they were, but components, also, of a notably successful attempt to integrate the deficiencies of his appearance into his personality, converting them from liabilities into assets, a process which he had applied to his often distracting speech defect with equally successful results.

The spectacular part of his life was set against a background of journalism rather than of literature. As a much advertised writer on books in a London evening newspaper and a regular contributor of articles to the Sunday newspapers, he was known to broader masses of the public than those to which his novels and plays had given him access. He had written regularly and notably for the *Daily News* (now *News Chronicle*) and the *New Statesman* during the First World War and for magazines on both sides of the Atlantic, including *The Strand Magazine* and *The Saturday Evening Post*. His Sunday newspaper writing in the middle and late 'twenties vastly increased his reading audience. There was a period when his photograph, distended to poster-size for bus-top display and brutally amplifying the heavy-eyed effects of the insomnia which harassed him for most of his life, was among the familiar details of the London traffic momentum. "Arnold Bennett on Manners." "Arnold Bennett on Doctors." "Arnold Bennett on Tipping." "Arnold Bennett on Servants." A Sunday newspaper editor invited him to write an article to be headed "My God by Arnold Bennett", a proposal refused and scathingly dealt with in his journal.

This relentless concentration of publicity fixed the name of Arnold Bennett more surely in the mass mind than it had been before. Mention of it in speech or print required no identifying clause or footnote. He could stand in front of his shaving-mirror like the heads of certain Five Towns households of whom he had written in *These Twain* and say with them: "Most folk are nobodies, but I am somebody."

(3)

He was somebody; and what was the answer to Sickert's pertinent if not impertinent question? He was the writer of the day who was most

[8]

read on the subject of books and on topics of general interest arising out of books, but what of it, though no one since has had anything like the same commanding position or influence? He was active in the theatre, but no longer very successful there. He was being consulted, expensively, by the new race of producers which the application of sound to films was bringing into prominence, and that impressed him more than it did anyone else.

He was constantly being encouraged by newspaper and magazine editors to be oracular on matters of national interest and was paid handsomely for his utterances, and the chief effect of this, as has been noted, was to extend the width rather than to increase the depth of his reputation. He was not the most admired of English writers, though among the most successful and though time had confirmed the right of at least one of his works to a place in the grand edifice of English literature. Nor did he have the attributes which, privately exploited, often lead to public gain—the gift of after-dinner speaking, of anecdotal resource, of epigrammatic *finesse*.

Yet he was somebody, and everybody seemed to be aware of it, like the lady of whom he wrote in the journal, July 22, 1927: "As I came home on the bus a woman who had climbed up after me said: 'I'm on the wrong bus and I got on to it so that I could travel by the same bus as Arnold Bennett. She was a lady and seemed quite serious. She got off the bus before Hyde Park Corner. I was quite touched. I talked to her for a bit." A little while before that he had gone out into the streets to observe advertising of his political novel, *Lord Raingo*, in which Lord Birkenhead had feared that he was the central character and in which Winston Churchill recognised himself thinly disguised as Tom Hogarth. "The poster of me on the motor-buses is artistically ineffective," Bennett noted. "The portrait of myself is merely offensive." Writing to his nephew from Milan in 1926, he mentioned: "Everybody seems to know me." And in the journal for February 4, 1930: "Yesterday two men accosted me in the street. One said he was the greatest admirer of my work in England. The other was a military sergeant whom I had not seen for thirteen years. I didn't know him. He insisted on shaking hands and then tried to borrow £2. He failed." Travelling to Manchester by train in October, 1927, "a man came along and introduced himself on the ground that his wife had said I was I and he wasn't sure, though he had seen me before and his wife had not. Good God!"

At Cannes, "we went into the American bar at the Café de Paris.

[9]

As I went in the bartender called out, 'Good evening, Mr. Bennett.' He said he had seen me at the *cercle* at Nice, into which *cercle* I have never been; so I can't think how he did come to know me. There is an immense proud satisfaction in being recognised at sight by bartenders." In London, October 20, 1924: "Dined at the Savoy grill-room. Four photographs of me had been circulated among the staff so that there could be no mistake about recognising me." To be known at sight to bartenders and yet not to head-waiters might not have been a blemish on the career of Denry Machin, hero of *The Card*, but in the context of his creator's social activities of the post-Armistice period it was a little strange, remembering his emphasis on the enchantments of life in the best hotels.

Despite the anomaly, somehow made more unseemly by the fobs, not even omniscience was denied him. During a walk through Harrods' Stores, one of the directors approached him with the suggestion that he should write an article "to stop the rot of bad trade caused here by the New York slump". He had already refused an invitation to stand for Parliament. And he had experienced a satisfaction unique in the profession of letters. When his bank manager requested him to call, he replied: "On the contrary, you call and see me."

Dining out, he was put next to Winston Churchill, "who said I was 'down in the mouth', and hoped it wasn't because I didn't like him." Edgar Wallace told him that *The Great Adventure* had influenced him as a playwright "more than anything". He dined with Lord Birkenhead, sometime Lord Chancellor of England, "who, to my surprise, paid me the £10 he owed me, but only by borrowing it from the hotel." J. L. Garvin, editor of *The Observer*, "was delighted by my article on Keyserling; he said that after reading it he stood up in his office and cried 'Hoorah!' " Mrs. Thomas Hardy called to ask his advice about her late husband's literary contracts and to state, also, her dissatisfaction with the arrangements for his funeral. "I advised her to sell Max Gate. We parted with reluctance. She thanked me again." J. M. Keynes (later Lord Keynes) called to discuss amalgamating the *New Statesman* and *The Nation*. Speaking for the *New Statesman*, of which he was a director, Arnold Bennett turned down a hard-pressed proposition of Keynes'. "I told him I would not agree. The matter dropped and we talked at large. He stayed till 6 p.m. and was very agreeable and most acutely intelligent."

The directors of the Great Western Railway invited him to meet them at lunch so that they might thank him for "a handsome laudatory

[10]

picture of the G.W. line I gave in an article of mine called 'The Reek' ''. The Savoy Hotel named a dish after him. Frank Swinnerton, newly returned from lecturing in the United States, assured him of a continuing interest in his works and personality there, although H. L. Mencken had written of him as a declining force in literature. 'And how about this for being in the swim?' he seems to be asking as he notes that Tallulah Bankhead, met at the Ivy Restaurant in London, had said: '' 'Come into the telephone box with me.' So I did and listened to lots of 'darlings', etc. I thought she would kiss me in the box, but she didn't. I said to Noel: 'I shall see you in your new play on Wednesday night.' He said: 'How I envy you!' '' Writing it down in the ever-receptive journal, he might have fancied himself composing another sequel to *The Card*, that light-hearted novel of his which A. J. Balfour had mentioned by name in the House of Commons.

The Prince of Wales (now the Duke of Windsor), met at dinner, "spoke with approval of my soft shirt." Lloyd George rang up to ask him to lunch. "I refused." He did not like Lloyd George: "I always feel uncomfortable when I am near him," an antipathy with implications to be discussed later. Word was passed to him that Sir Arthur Quiller-Couch, the 'Q' of many novels and King Edward VII Professor of English Literature at Cambridge, had spoken of him as "the most accomplished living craftsman of letters". André Gide called. Hugh Walpole called. John Buchan called: The Sitwells called. Michael Arlen called. Noel Coward called. The B.B.C. called: "They want me to fill a two-hour programme with items entirely of my own choosing. They will let me have symphony orchestras, comedians, anything I want."

At Le Touquet, July, 1928: "I was accosted by a young American who began: 'Will you allow a lifelong admirer of your work——'. " The principal Norwegian newspaper proposed celebrating his sixtieth birthday by a "richly illustrated article" which was to have in it a message from him to the Norwegian people. "I bet no English paper will celebrate my *soixantième* in this way," and none did.

"The buses were full of my next Sunday's article on doctors and medicine. Also advertisements of the *Faust* film at the Albert Hall with my name prominent on the big poster of the same. In fact it was about the best advertising day I ever had."

In 1901 he had written with Calvinistic assurance of his future to a friend: "Although I am thirty-three and have not made a name, I infallibly know that I *shall* make a name and that soon. But I should like to be a legend."

[11]

Now, nearly thirty years after, he was casting before him the shadow of the legend he had hoped to be.

(4)

He wanted to become a legend, and it is like a backhander from fate, whose ironies he so diligently reported, that there has gathered about his name a legend as unjust as it is unattractive. "I am not interested in money," he wrote in the additional journal he was keeping between 1926 and 1930; whereas the belief that money was one of his prime and even obsessional interests has been fixed with plaque-like rigidity in the critical thought of the last two decades. Nearly twenty years after his death a writer in *The Times Literary Supplement* quoted with the feeling for which the Germans have the word *schadenfreude* an unwarranted story of Arnold Bennett calling out in his last delirium for a hotel bill.

That he was capable of admirable generosities is known to those closest to him. They would agree that his nature also displayed a caution easily mistaken for parsimony. To a member of his household who had served him long and well his wedding present was a £2 tin clock. His first and hardly considered action on learning of the financial calamity of someone well known to him from early days was to write a cheque for £1,500 by way of relieving immediate stress. It was followed by a letter fixing what was thought a stiff rate of interest on the loan. Within a few days after the declaration of war in 1914 he had told his literary agent, J. B. Pinker, to use funds in hand for the help of writers likely to feel the pinch of events. Also, he arranged to be told of "any hard cases" in the village of Thorpe-le-Soken, Essex, where he had lately gone to live.

Here speaks his widow, Marguerite Bennett: "Arnold, wide-awake though he was, was pretty often deceived by people, and many took advantage of his kindness of heart—his impulsive moods making him promise money, help, and protection. He has helped many. He has for years given a big or a small pension to old people not related to him, as well as to members of his family. I did admire his generosity. He had, however, the pettiness that most intellectual people of his type have. He was so amusingly mean in trifles."

When an old friend of his in the Potteries was involved in a financial scandal, Bennett went to Stoke-on-Trent to see what help he could give. He invited another friend to meet him at the North Staffordshire

Hotel a few minutes before the relatives of the man who was in trouble were due to meet him there. A quick exchange of information took place. Bennett asked: "Is it a bad affair?" He was told that it was a very bad affair. "Can he be saved?" The answer was no. "How much to put things square?" Bennett asked. "Over five thousand pounds," was the reply. "Thanks. Goodbye—they're coming," Bennett said, as if he was rehearsing a scene from one of his Five Towns novels. Having met the relatives and said very little, he went to a local bank and did what was required to set things right.

Sending for a well-known author in the 1920s, he said: "Look here, I've made more money than I expected this year; here's a cheque for five hundred pounds for you to give away, as you think best, to younger writers and painters. There's only one condition: my name mustn't be mentioned." Quoting this in his memoirs, Sir Osbert Sitwell recalls other instances of Bennett's thought for the less successful and says that "it was in essence very typical of the character of a man who was seldom in his lifetime or afterwards given credit for possessing, as he did in an extraordinary degree, the quality these facts display". He gave financial help to writers still with us. Among those who are not, D. H. Lawrence was one who had money from him, duly repaid. He contributed regularly to the pension raised for W. N. P. Barbellion, author of *The Journal of a Disappointed Man*.

Sir Newman Flower, of Cassell & Company, who published several of Arnold Bennett's books, has referred to Bennett's generosities in his volume of reminiscences, *Just as it Happened:* "There are some who could tell a story—and I am one of them—about the unknown men whom Bennett helped—the little unknown people whom he made and strived to make. There are one or two people, well-known in letters now, whom Bennett made. . . . He is dead, but some of us know—and we would not rob them of their little pride by revealing what we know—since they will not admit it." Labouring under the stress of his feelings at what time and the detractors have done to Arnold Bennett's name and reputation, Sir Newman Flower deplores the absence of biographical references to what he calls "the extreme humanity of him". He refutes the prevailing belief that here was one "who knelt to the God of luxury and worshipped Self". He brands it as "a foul and false valuation".

By Frank Swinnerton, who had a closer intimacy of friendship with Arnold Bennett than most of those in their Reform Club circle, we are assured that his attitude to money has been "more painstakingly

misrepresented than any other characteristic. He did not love money",
and Mr. Swinnerton tells how Bennett helped others—"all sorts of
causes and all sorts of individuals; often on his own initiative and
without request being made, sometimes generously on appeal." He
carried a spare cheque in his pocket to be ready for any emergency of
need in others. When Frank Swinnerton mentioned the difficulties of a
writer not known personally to Bennett, the latter said at once: "What
shall you send? I'd like to do the same," producing the spare cheque
from his wallet. "Always, it was: 'That chap. . . . He has to be helped. [1]
His solicitor and fellow clubman, Geoffrey W. Russell, insists: "It is an
erroneous belief that Arnold Bennett cared excessively about money,"
and adds as advice to Bennett's biographer: "Take your chance of
getting rid of that notion."

The beginnings, in part, of an unfair judgment may be traced to
Arnold Bennett's early book, *The Truth about an Author*, which struck
a bounderish note in the ears of critics of forty years ago because it
linked the sanctities of authorship with the crudities of commerce.
Some of the more sensitive reviewers had not recovered from the shock
of learning from the autobiography of Anthony Trollope that successful
authorship, like successful stockbroking, can be a matter of catching
the 9.15 and of arriving at a desk at a fixed time every morning. Or
possibly they thought it perverse of Arnold Bennett to imply that while
he was aware of the claims of art he was unwilling to forgo his meals
on that account. He put it on record in *The New Age* that in his opinion
"genuine artists" produce their best work when they are in need of cash,
a view of creativeness capable of upsetting more sensibilities then than
now. We owe about half the *Comédie Humaine* of Balzac, he said, to
that writer's "extravagant imprudence". Scott's "mania for landed
estate" was brought into the same argument. And when *The Times*
objected to Trollope's "clock-work methods" he was roused to make a
sharp rejoinder. "It appears that this horrid secret ought to have been
for ever concealed. 'Fatal admission!' exclaims *The Times*. Fatal
fiddlesticks. His reputation rests on the value of his novels, and not
in the least on the manner in which he chose to write them. And his
reputation is secure. Moreover, there is no reason why great literature
should not be produced to time, with a watch on the desk. Persons
who chatter about the necessity of awaiting inspirational hypersthenia
don't know what the business of being an artist is. They have only
read about it sentimentally."

[1] Preface to *Arnold Bennett's Letters to his Nephew* (Heinemann, 1936).

[14]

The author of *The Old Wives' Tale* was the author, also, of *Teresa of Watling Street* and should not be allowed to forget it. *The Gates of Wrath* appeared in the same list of works as *Anna of the Five Towns*. The hand that wrote *A Letter Home* in *The Yellow Book* could write articles for *Tit-Bits*. "In a blinding flash I saw that an author was in essence the same thing as a grocer or a duke," and critical eyebrows twitched at the double affront.

"It is glorious to sell all that you have and give it to Art, but I want my books and my pictures and to mix with the fellows whose names shine on the foreheads of the magazines. Disgusting, isn't it? I think so sometimes. . . ." [1] Written when he was twenty-seven, it reads like the expression of a wish rather than a declaration of policy. "The most curious thing that has happened to me is that I have practically lost all my ambition except the ambition to be allowed to work quietly," he wrote to the same friend a few years later. "I have never had a clear and fixed ambition," he states in the extra-journal of 1926–30, where he testifies to some of the guiding principles of his life. It is true that in *The Truth about an Author* he had remarked, not more than half seriously, that he was engaged in the "manufacture of a dazzling reputation". But the source of the energy which was to produce that result was not in an excess of ambition. He regarded mere ambition as "an inferior motive" for effort and achievement.

The mainspring of Arnold Bennett's career was a desire to emulate, not an intention to excel. It is to be looked for in his adolescent identification with Balzac, Zola, Dumas, those tribal story-tellers of the French who enjoyed so eminent a prestige, so affluent a fame. To write books and to be able to live like *that*: to write books and to conquer the social heights and command the homage of cities, to live in grand hotels and to own a yacht, to have a flat and a life of one's own in Paris! What there was of single-minded ambition in this consisted of a powerful wish to escape from uncongenial early surroundings and, still more decisive as a propellent, to secure himself against the chances of ever again enduring the miseries of being poor.

His nervous dread of poverty was troubling him in practical as well as emotional terms up to his fortieth year or so, to recur twenty years further on when all the world supposed him to be impregnable. In 1908 he was worrying because his outgoings exceeded his income by a margin of as little as a pound a week. He recorded in the journal that he was bothered about his finances at Fontainebleau shortly after he had set

[1] To George Sturt ("George Bourne"), of Farnham.

[15]

up house there with his French wife. For several years he was living on money borrowed at five per cent from his literary agent.

"He was extravagant in nothing, but the humiliations of his penurious youth and early manhood had implanted in him a morbid fear of being short of money," is one of the autobiographical touches in his novel *Clayhanger*, in which the chief character is a substantial projection of himself. And the recurrence of his old poverty dreads in his last years undoubtedly added to his interior distress. He arrived at his sixties still not in sight of security and his position was serious in that for all his astonishing earning capacity he had been unable to provide either for his old age or for his dependants. Dorothy Cheston Bennett has said: "Arnold was more generous than the average person. He was indeed most rarely generous, and together with his reputation for business acumen and common-sense, his generosity lent support to the legend of his riches. I was myself deceived by this conflicting point for quite some time."

He had written in the journal for September 12, 1898: "A certain chronic poverty had forced upon me the fact that I was giving no attention to money-making, and in order to be happy I must have a fair supply of money." Writing saleable fiction was the answer, the only practical solution for him of the problem confronting many conscientious writers, how to live without private resources. For the view, so long persisting, that Arnold Bennett was preoccupied with thoughts of money in the grossest sense it is indeed impossible to find any support that can be respected.

"I find that I am much less interested in money than Phillpotts or Wells," he wrote after casting up his accounts for 1905. Commenting on "a most unsatisfactory contract" received from his literary agent, Pinker, for a story called *The Statue*, he noted: "I flatter myself that this almost certain loss of money, at a time when I particularly want it, did not disturb me for more than a few minutes." Reading the fourth volume of Taine's Letters: ". . . the portrait of the man gradually grew clear to me, and inspired me with ideals similar to his own: the doing simply of the work which one believes to be best, and the neglect of all gross and vain considerations. Why should I worry after fame and money, knowing as I do that these will not increase my happiness?"

The criticism that idealism and grand hotels bracket uneasily together assumes that Arnold Bennett was taken in by luxury as well as attracted by it, a proposition to which none who knew him well enough is likely to assent. "My dear H. G.," he wrote to Wells in 1905, "surely the irony of my descriptions of leading hotels is not too fine for you?"

The intensity of his mundane interests and activities has likewise been used to challenge his sense of the higher values. He spoke of himself as being doctrinally irreligious and "instinctively opposed" to the dogma of the Churches. Intellectually, he had long been in revolt against the faith of his fathers and of his upbringing and had taken his place with the Victorian agnostics. Dogmatically unanchored, his view was that only right living could make life worth living. "In London you cannot walk far or ride long before your eye meets quotations from the Bible displayed by religious societies or individuals. The latter usually chalk their admonitions on pavements or walls. Thus you read: 'Prepare to meet thy God.' I cannot recall ever having seen advertised the words: 'Blessed are they that do hunger and thirst after righteousness.' Yet here is no religious dogma to offend or to chill. Here for every conscience is a reminder to which no dialectical or emotional exception can be taken, an appeal likely to arouse some response from the dormant or semi-dormant motive power that actuates right living. Next in importance to that Beatitude I should put, not another Beatitude, but a later passage from the Sermon: 'All things whatsoever ye would that men should do to you, do ye even so to them.' No religious dogma here either! But an injunction, independent of religious dogma, which must be persuasive to all temperaments, and which should invigorate the very root of the individual instinct for justice and goodwill."

His main religious difficulty, he said, lay in his conviction that the human brain was not constructed to exercise itself in the realms of the infinite. This shuts out poetry as it shuts out mysticism. But Arnold Bennett's humility in these matters was genuine, and he also thought it important for mental hygiene that the mind should not be required to function at too high altitudes. "I marvel at the minds of unquestionably great men who have come to definite decisions as to what God is, what He thinks, how He acts. The daring of the doctrine of the Trinity staggers me," and he insisted, "quite honestly and without false modesty," that he was too humble to approach such mysteries. "I should not object to having a religious creed. I should rather like to have one." But he added that he had never felt within himself "the operation of a religious instinct", and that, if he had, his naturally cautious and self-sufficient cast of mind would have impeded it.

[17]

Persisting in the tentative attitude, he turned in his later years to Eastern philosophy and to the Bible, finding meditative satisfaction in 'Be still, and know that I *am* God', from the 46th Psalm. The mystical emotion of the Bible, he wrote in his journal for 1929, is "perhaps the deepest source of private comfort". The works of Troward, author of the *Edinburgh Lectures on Mental Science*, confirmed his belief in the possibilities of creative personal development, a subject on which he had declaimed with brisk assurance in the 'pocket philosophies'. He took a private course of instruction in Christian Science, primarily in the hope of mastering his speech trouble and afterwards because it seemed to supply a technique for dealing with the larger ills of existence. He could not decide whether he had profited in the wider sense; as for the speech difficulty, it was obdurate and remained. Speculating in 1928 on the possibility of survival after death, he claimed that the theory of the transmigration of souls is "not utterly inconceivable". He wrote to a reader of his in New York that while he had never "rejected quite definitely" the idea of personal immortality, it did not commend itself to his intelligence.

His religion, like his politics, was humanist and distinguished by a fine tolerance of opinion. Not everyone would agree that it lacked spirituality because it insisted that human personality can be cultivated and that it is the duty of the individual to live up to the best that is in him. An article of his faith is set out in *Things that have Interested Me*, where he is writing about life's greatest satisfactions:

There is one major satisfaction—and it may well be the greatest of all—which is equally open to all. I mean the exercise of bene-volence. I do not necessarily mean what are called 'good works', which by the way are often bad works, regrettable in their subtly sinister influence on the doer as well as on the receiver, and which in any case many people have neither the time nor the ability to perform.

Let those who can, do good works; the best cure for worry, depression, melancholy brooding, is to go deliberately forth and try to lift with one's sympathy the gloom of somebody else. And let both those who can and those who can't do good works make a practice of benevolent *thought*. Let all think kindly of others; never criticise them, never condemn, never judge; on the contrary, let all condone, excuse, justify, seek to comprehend, seek to put themselves in the place of others. The mental attitude has to be perseveringly cultivated. It cannot be adopted by a mere good resolution. (Some—exceedingly few—are born with it, and all I have to say of them is, that they do not know their luck, for something within them is always mysteriously manufacturing happiness for them.) We must ask ourselves about a thousand times a day, 'Who am I to sit in judgment?' We must learn to perceive the absurdity, the impudence, and the preposterousness of sitting in judgment. To err is human, to forgive ought to be. Here is the finest form of benevolence, and it will produce the finest form of satisfaction—a satisfaction which increases from year to year and only reaches its maximum when life ends.

His deepest political prejudice was a dislike of Tory ideas, associated in Potteries history with the Church of England and its enmity towards the Radicals of a century ago who voiced the people's discontents and stirred up the movements of protest which swelled into the terrible riots that became part of the local folk-memory. When he was writing *Clayhanger* in a top bedroom at the Royal York Hotel, Brighton, in 1910, a General Election year, he made this journal note:

> *January 11.*—Grand rolling weather. Foamy sea, boisterous wind, sun, pageant of clouds, and Brighton full of wealthy imperative persons dashing about in furs and cars. I walked with joy to and fro on this unequalled promenade. And yet, at this election time, when all wealth and all snobbery is leagued together against the poor, I could spit in the face of arrogant and unmerciful Brighton, sporting its damned Tory colours.
>
> Certainly this morning as I looked at all the splendid solidity of Brighton, symbol of a system that is built on the grinding of the faces of the poor, I had to admit that it would take a lot of demolishing, that I couldn't expect to overset it with a single manifesto and a single election, or with fifty. So that even if the elections are lost, or are not won, I don't care. Besides, things never turn out as badly as our fears. . . .

In an earlier and more historic General Election year, 1906, he had written an article for *T.P.'s Weekly* called 'Despising Politics'. The cultivated man, he said, was disgusted with "the whole prodigious and shameless theatricality, and with superb disdain washes his hands clean of politics". Such an attitude, he went on to insist, was wrong. "Politics can only be judged by comparison; there is no absolute standard. And by comparison the conduct of English politics is the most sagacious and the least corrupt that the world has yet seen in a great country of

[19]

complex interests. I do not think I overstate". And for that reason he counselled his readers to go to the polling-booth: "Politics are what they are by the inevitable and splendid movement of human evolution. They were worse. They will be better". Temperamentally he was non-Party, not disposed to 'join' anything, common sense not being an institutional quality. And what was for him the common sense of politics was necessarily unacceptable to most people. "One set of political opinions is just about as 'good' as the other—one makes for progress while the other makes for stability, both aims being perfectly laudable." State that to the politicians, "and they would freeze you with righteous disdain and accuse you of 'wanting the best of both worlds'. There is only one world."

If politically he makes a firmer outline against his early background of smoky streets than when seen against the dubious glitter of the London night clubs, his social conscience was not dimmed into compromise with the evils he had so scrupulously etched into his novels of the Five Towns. The more prosperous he became, the more sensitive he was about walking over the pavement gratings giving furtive light to workers below, especially the class personified by Elsie in *Riceyman Steps*. The "tremendous actuality" of injustice had to be faced, but he was not asking for a suspension of activities designed to abolish the exploitation which accounted for so much of it. Condemning the General Strike of 1926 as "a political crime" that had to be paid for, an attack aimed at the authority of the Government, when he heard that the vanmen employed by a leading London store were being offered the choice of taking their holidays at once or of being 'stood off' without pay because the volume of business had fallen, he wrote a letter of strong indignation to the head of the firm, who was one of his friends.

(5)

From the bundle-cluttered little pawnshop in Hope Street, Hanley, Staffordshire, to his "rather noble thing in houses", 75 Cadogan Square, London, once the home of a Viceroy of India, had been a forty years' progress. For all that he had achieved in those years, he did not look back upon them with the characteristic Victorian self-satisfaction. He was not disposed to measure his or any kind of personal success by the standards of Samuel Smiles and the other moralists of the age for whom life was an account rendered by yours faithfully, Time. For Arnold Bennett time was no servant. Time was the master, the tyrant, the dispossessor, and its operations had always a sombre masochistic fascination for him. Old Man Shushions in *Clayhanger* was "time's obscene victim", his decrepitude hateful, disgusting. Sir Desmond MacCarthy said that reading *The Old Wives' Tale* gave him his first insight into the verities of growing old. Arnold Bennett wrote of time in the mood of the monodist and we can see that this made him the frustrated poet: he was sensitive to the mystery of time but not to its magic. A nurse called at his house in 1928 about employment. As soon as she had gone he wrote down: "Seventeen years in one family. Said she was forty-three. I gave her fifty-two. Pathetic spectacle. The poor thing depressed me much." It was an endless theme, a saturating obsession that probably had its source in his childhood attendance at the big Wesleyan Methodist chapel on Swan Bank, Burslem, where there was no escaping the implacable reminders of human mortality in precept, sermon and hymn. *A few more years shall roll, A few more seasons come, And we shall be with those that rest, Asleep within the tomb.* . . . The sin-burdened congregations, come to the mercy seat in broadcloth, alpaca, and rustling silk, sang the fearful doggerel with the relish of connoisseurs of the morbid, filling his nervous organism with dreads that reappeared agonisingly in his dreams and giving the hour of five a significance for him now beyond our probing.

A critic[1] has wished us to consider time as the hero of Arnold Bennett's chief novels, presumably because it is the classic role of the hero to conquer. A hero is not necessarily 'heroic'; but it may be said with as much force that time is the villain of them. It stalks in the same ominous guise through the thirty or so journal volumes, where his dismay is constantly underlined by the severity of his observation in noting its effects upon himself and others. And had he not made time's brutalities the theme of *The Old Wives' Tale*? ". . . there is extreme pathos in the mere fact that every stout ageing woman was once a young girl with the unique charm of youth in her form and movements and in her mind. And the fact that the change from the young girl to the stout ageing woman is made up of an infinite number of infinitesimal changes, each unperceived by her, only intensifies the pathos," a pathos ever-present to Arnold Bennett's sensibilities. He dined, "Maida-Vailishly," as he put it, one evening in 1928 with George Arliss. "Later, in came Gerald Lawrence and his wife, once Fay Davis, and their daughter. I said to Mrs. Cullen, 'I haven't seen Fay Davis for twenty-five years.' 'Yes,' she said, 'it's very sad, isn't it?' She had the right

[1] Mr. E. M. Forster.

[21]

word there. It was sad to see the remains of a fine woman. It always is."

Soon after Arnold Bennett began keeping his journal, in 1896, he noted the approach of middle age in his father. "I felt acutely that he and I were of different generations; that parent and child, be they never so willing, can never come intellectually together, simply because one time of life differs crudely and harshly from another. He has now the physical and mental deliberateness which characterises the ageing. . . . A few nights ago when I laughingly referred to my 'aged parents', he quickly seized the phrase, repeated it, and recounted it to callers— jokingly, but I could see that it occupied his thoughts."

Time overtakes Arnold Bennett in his turn and he noted on April 14, 1913, just after his forty-sixth birthday: "Advance of age. I now sit down to brush my hair and put my collar and tie on." Another decade and a half goes by and time lies as heavily as always on the spirit of the author of *How to Live on* 24 *Hours a Day*. He is moved by the spectacle of its ascendancy over the bravest in our midst:

November 13, 1929.—On Sunday last I attended the special performance for V.C.s of *Journey's End*. . . The younger men excited admiring respect in me. But the old men, the ageing men, the portly men who had in the worldly sense 'succeeded', all the mature men with their dignity of presence—these excited in me more than admiring respect. They excited in me the tender feelings which pathos excites. They had once been young and adventurous and audacious. They had done marvels of audacity; but all that had happened a long time ago, and now they were sobered and a bit prim and conscious of experience, and deliberate in gesture. I say it was touching.

Yet now that he too was ageing and portly and almost extravagantly deliberate in gesture, he could not bring himself to face these truths about himself. At sixty he was giving his heart more to do than was sensible in one of his years. He had lately learnt to dance (and *Punch* had skittishly proposed that his novel *Helen with the High Hand* should be renamed *Helen with the High Kick*), and he had doubtless also learned to ignore, with high-crested disdain, the grins of those of the younger set who saw him ponderously involved in the intimacies of tango and foxtrot. Each day had its complex of professional and social obligations; almost no night its unbroken rest.

[22]

He had reduced his weight by adopting the Hornibrook system of exercises, and was having his jackets cut with a shade more waist than was required by strict fidelity to his figure. A recollection remains of him in his last year hurrying from the Strand into the Savoy Hotel, rounding the corner by the tailor's shop with the swerve of a schoolboy who fears being late for a treat, though one knew that in a few moments he would be advancing into the grill-room with a grave seignorial air intended to dispose of any idea that he was there except under duress of duty. Bowler hat tilted over the right ear, wrists thrust deeply into the pockets of the inevitable blue Melton overcoat swinging kiltishly from the waist, he looked, as was noted in another journal of the period, "a trifle absurd." There were absurdities in his nature, as perhaps there are in the nature of all lovable persons; and Arnold Bennett was 'adored' by his friends, says Sir John Squire. "Even his very oddities were endearing," says Somerset Maugham, who was doubtless unaware that eating rice pudding every day for several years was one of them and wearing boots, in preference to shoes, another. "It was impossible to know him without liking him," Mr. Maugham has said, and H. G. Wells wrote that Bennett "radiated and evoked affection to an unusual degree".

He was now squiring a beautiful young woman of less than half his years and, when walking behind her to meet the public gaze in restaurants or at the theatre, was given to straightening his shoulders with the pride of middle-aged conquest. "See that?" whispered a well-known artist to his wife as they walked behind Bennett and his lady into a West End hotel. Bennett had thrown back his shoulders as they approached the bowing waiters of the restaurant, precisely as the young man from the North, hero of his first novel, had done on his first walk in the streets of the metropolis. "Pathetic," whispered the artist's wife as they swept forward to take their place at Bennett's table. Here he was, the novelist of middle-aged emotions, flinching from the truth that this is a phase of life in which a man had better go without a good time than have to endure the rigours of getting over it.

His marriage, with its sequel of tension and breakdown, had been a disconcerting advertisement for one known to be a formidable enemy of disorder in personal affairs. He appears, from his letters, the journal, and the evidence of friends, to have faced his situation with propriety and good sense. How two married persons intimately react to one another is not necessarily the business of others, and there will be no trespass here on the private life of the lady who, having long since returned to live in her native country of France, continues to bear his name and to commemorate it by reproducing his signature as part of her own. Arnold Bennett explained the circumstances from his side, and his feelings about them, to a number of his friends, among them Mr. Raymond Needham, Q.C., and Professor Thomas Bodkin. His letter on the subject to his sister, Mrs. Kennerley, is eloquent of restrained grievance and also of magnanimity: "I hope she will continue to see you, as your influence is bound to be good. She is evidently very unhappy and I wish I could do something for her." He seems to have been perfectly clear in his mind that there was no other course open to them but separation. One of his oldest woman friends believed that he had made a mistake and wrote reproachfully to him. He replied: "I ought to tell you that your remarks on the subject, though prompted by a laudable and warm-hearted sympathy for an apparent victim, have done me some temporary prejudice. You were known as an old friend of mine, and accordingly the more weight was attached to your verdict against me; but even this cannot count for long."

The unconventional domestic arrangement which followed a few years after, and at which "all London" was supposed to have connived, brought him private felicities and public uneasiness. Though he had long since shrugged off its obvious restraints, his Methodist conscience had never been finally rebuffed and not all his exertions of will and intellect could reach down far enough to pluck out the roots of the mental discomforts of his situation. He sought with eagerness the rationalising aid of his friends, from most of whom he received the moral support he required. It did not dispel the chapel-organ echoes from the unforgiving past.

"Come on, Nocker!" the boys of his past, playing football among the pit-mounds of Burslem, had yelled when he made his rare appearances in their games. "Come on, Nocker!" Translated into the terms of a career, how Nocker had come on! He had long outgrown the *gauche* and not entirely likeable young E. A. Bennett who had edited a women's paper in London and written a novel that had made his mother "play nervously with her bread". He was now even out of touch with the author of *The Old Wives' Tale* and *Clayhanger*, those achievements in literature which had won him so great an esteem. Human character at its highest, it has been said, is a specific perspective of the universe. As a novelist, Arnold Bennett created some memorable characters, but his greatest character creation was himself.

And, in the language of the pavement artist, it was all his own work.

[24]

From the cartoon by Sir Max Beerbohm in "Observations" (Heinemann, 1927)

THE OLD AND THE YOUNG SELF

OLD SELF: "ALL GONE ACCORDING TO PLAN, YOU SEE"
YOUNG SELF: "*MY* PLAN, YOU KNOW"

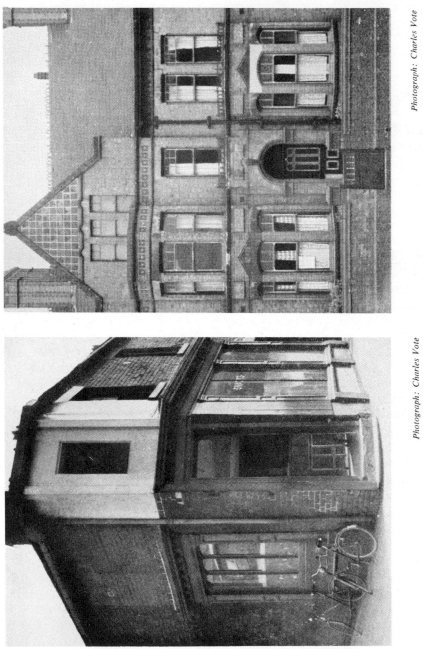

Photograph: Charles Vote

205 WATERLOO ROAD, BURSLEM

Photograph: Charles Vote

90 HOPE STREET, HANLEY, BENNETT'S BIRTHPLACE

CHAPTER TWO

(1)

SUPPOSING he had written the autobiography for which handsome monetary inducements were being put before him in 1924, how much more would he have told us about himself than was already known from his first novel, *A Man from the North*, from *The Truth about an Author*, and from *Clayhanger*, in which some of the dreariest domestic material was taken from his Potteries childhood and youth? "What a celestial rumpus there would be!" he had exclaimed in print when a critic proposed that novelists should write more autobiography into their work, a suggestion which he later considered in *The Author's Craft* and applied, with far from distinguished effect, in a novel called *The Glimpse*. His idea about his autobiography was that "it might be something remarkable".

In the end no one believed that it would be. Various editorial and publishing personalities appeared in the letter and cable exchanges across the Atlantic (the sum of £7,000 having been mentioned for the serial rights alone), conspicuous among them the astute and showy grand-scale buyer of literary material for the Hearst papers and magazines of America, Ray Long, whose star of good fortune, high shining for many years, was soon to move down the sky, leaving him stranded and suicidal in an unsympathetic world.

The bargaining at no time became pressing. The correspondence dragged on. There was a point at which Bennett was asked to submit some specimen chapters, a professional indignity against which he made no protest but which he certainly had not experienced since his freelance journalist days so theatrically deplored in *The Truth about an Author* ("call it my purgatorio"). And presently his American publisher and friend, George Doran, had to tell him in the jauntiest tone he could summon for the occasion that the negotiations had faded out.

It was too late for one-dimensional autobiography and the odd thing is that he had not seen that it would be. The 'celestial rumpus' effect had already been produced by Margot Asquith's memoirs and by the diaries of Colonel Repington and Colonel House. Booksellers

[25]

were being left with stocks of discretion on their shelves. The era of unrestrained self-revelation was at hand, speeded by the new cult of the unconscious which, with the goat-footed D. H. Lawrence as its prophet, was undermining the pillars of convention in literature as in mental science. The organised idleness which is a large part of modern war had stimulated in 1914–18 new reading tastes and habits, a social change repeated in the greater war that was to follow. The Hemingway school of writers, which specialised in growing beards in place of chins, would soon be jeering the romantic tradition into the limbo. Psychological interpretations were affecting creative effort as well as critical opinion.

Arnold Bennett by no means ignored the unconscious. He was afraid of it. He was sufficiently aware of its potency to have reminded us, in one of the early 'pocket philosophies', that a may man be sentimentally involved with his wife while at the same time hating her, and he had not required to read the French and Russian novelists to understand the power of instincts suppressed, the silent havoc they can do. Georges Lafourcade wrote in his study of Bennett that while he shows penetration in illustrating "the discontinuity of our sentimental life", in depicting the human tendency to think in one way and act in another, giving his characters two voices, "the unspoken one being often more important than the one that actually speaks," he does not reveal the mainsprings of action.[1] Miss Rebecca West said in *The Strange Necessity* that he disdained the "little presents" of the unconscious, the promptings which tell the artist that his theme has its sanction and co-operation, 'the passing madness' which Schiller said is the mark of the best creative effort. His psychological insight falters when he is himself the subject of it. Referring to his youthful habit of idle boastings about what he would do when older, he said: "I think now that something subconscious must have prompted them," and he wrote naïvely in the journal in 1923: "My punctuality is exaggerated to a point of being almost a neurosis."

The slowing down and final collapse of the autobiography negotiations started at the American end, just when he was ready to comply with the unflattering request to send over the specimen chapters. "For several hours yesterday I was reading volume 8 and then re-reading volume 7 of my journal, and I very definitely thought it worth rehandling. I found scarcely any of it dull. This perusal arose out of *The Strand Magazine* request for my reminiscences and from *The Ladies' Home Journal's* interest in the American rights thereof."

[1] *Arnold Bennett: A Study*, by Georges Lafourcade (Muller, 1939).

The autobiography of Arnold Bennett was never written because he was one of those of whom De Quincey said "it is not in their power to lay aside reserve". He wrote in the unpublished extra-journal: "I scarcely ever analyse my own character or take the trouble imaginatively to see myself as others see me. Only in my fifty-ninth or sixtieth years have I done enough of this analysis even to enable me to perceive my own defects of demeanour. I doubt if I know what my chief qualities and chief defects are."

The Truth about an Author, which owed something of its inspiration to R. L. Stevenson's book on the art of writing, told only a small part of the truth about Arnold Bennett and that not the most relevant to a study of his character or to tracing the sources of his mental and moral development. It is a briskly written and sometimes witty description of his experiences as a London solicitor's clerk who is drawn by chance into literary and artistic circles and how he adapts himself to them. Its invigorating astringency has not evaporated with the years. Would-be writers who are quick at inferences might still find it profitable to read. It depicts an intellectual 'card' in the making. We are shown the reactions of a mind sensitive enough to be aware of the crudities of opportunism but compelled to resort to it, an eager and responsive brain engaged in acquiring the cultural principles and values denied it by early circumstances. Along with the cerebral swagger and the far from ingratiating style we see, also, the first signs of an integrity of mind which was to crown his great success with the respect as well as the affection of those who knew him best.

Wells, Shaw, Bennett: their names were more often linked than those of any other writers in the decade after the First World War. And just as Shaw was the greatest of the three in personality, so Bennett was the greatest in character. As for Wells, his personality was not publicly attractive, although it could infallibly charm its private circles. "And why is it," a young woman asked Arnold Bennett when he proposed she should meet Wells, "that one always has a feeling of his being caddish when one reads his books?" Arnold Bennett reflected as was his way before giving a possibly consequential opinion, and then replied: "I'm afraid because it's true," adding: "You see, if H. G.'s inclinations clash with his duty, his inclinations always win."

Arnold Bennett's inclinations were by no means sovereign in his affairs. In the last year of his life he went to Charing Cross Hospital with a letter written to him by a patient there, a man who was unknown to him. The then House Governor, Philip Inman (now Lord Inman) saw him unattended in the hall and asked if he could help. Bennett who was looking troubled, showed him the letter: "I have only a little while to live, the doctors tell me, and I should be so very grateful if you would give me the opportunity of thanking you personally for all the pleasure you have given me in your books." When Philip Inman offered to take him into the ward, Bennett said haltingly: "I've dreaded this, but I made myself come."

We seem to see working more explicitly in him the urge towards fullness of character which Freud, trespassing in the domain of philosophy, considered a "benevolent illusion", but which other authorities regard as a tropism, an unconscious persistence in the co-ordinating processes that lead to self-realisation and fulfilment; "a dynamic need within the self to realise itself as a harmonious whole".[1] In *These Twain* he made Edwin Clayhanger reflect: "Perfection was a desolating thought. Nevertheless, the struggle towards it was instinctive and had to go on." Arnold Bennett said: "I feel intensely that we are travelling from imperfection to perfection, and that here is the sole immediate answer to the enigma of the universe."

But, while he acknowledged the urge towards completion inherent in human character, he shrank from self-analysis. "He had always been averse from self-examination," he said of the chief male character in *Imperial Palace*, and into the characterisation of Evelyn Orcham he had put a good deal of his own. At the same time, he announced Rousseau's *Confessions* as an excitement of the soul. "What measured wisdom! What impartial truth! What close and intricate psychological observation!" This enthusiasm found no answering call from Arnold Bennett's soul when the prospect of writing his own life presented itself. There is no attempt of his in that *genre* which does not produce the flat effect of censorship. He could be genially communicative about his forebears and his unpromising beginnings. He could reveal in an article written for a newspaper with a very large circulation[2] that there was in his family a supposedly illegitimate strain which, if verifiable, would show his ancestry to have been buttressed by genius. He did not shrink from making it known that in his early surroundings there was little to encourage his growing sensibilities and much that outraged them. He did not take refuge in the social evasions or affectations which have long sustained the English comic spirit. Nor did he adopt the protective coloration of accent or amplify his foreground by way of obscuring

[1] *Nervous Disorders and Religion* by Dr. J. E. McKenzie (Allen & Unwin).
[2] *Daily Express* (London).

his background. The method of compensation he most often used consisted of remarking when some well-known name occurred in a conversation: "He's a *great* friend of mine."

Of the urgencies of his nature or the bias of his deeper feelings we should have been told suggestively little. It was as if he wanted it believed that he had quelled the interior commotion that is the common lot, that the mental training which he both practised and preached had achieved its purpose of freeing his attention for his appointment with success and the obligations that go with it.

However, it seems that all was not smooth functioning within. Embedded in the early pages of the journal are his closely-written notes of a dream he had in which a complex symbolism, woven into a fantasy about "a young girl with a snub nose, dressed in black, with a black apron", suggests that it indexed an agonising drama of unrealised tendencies played out in the depths of his being one night in his thirty-first year. She stepped out of the dream into the pages of his first novel, *A Man from the North*: "her nose was short and flattened but her mouth happened to be perfect, of exactly the classic form and size, with delectable lips half hiding the small white teeth." Interpreted by the technique which postulates dreams as the portal to the unconscious, this dream of Bennett's has been judged to contain perilous stuff, perilous, that is to say, for him. Set out as he set it out, its principal theme would be seen to link the uninhibited laughter of Diogenes with the involuted irony of James Joyce. He had evidently not succeeded in complying with scriptural injunction to put away childish things, and the resulting psychological handicap manifested itself in several ways, not least in the curious metallic quality of his writing. He wrote down the substance of the dream in livid detail as if trying to rid himself of a horrid clinging memory of evil. The moon-green brilliance of his recollection of its morbid nuances suggests that he was the victim of a sense of 'sin' which had generated enough energy to commit him to a lifelong thraldom of propitiation in the form of exaggerated punctuality and fastidiousness, and had helped to shape his oddly retracted physical personality much as the less elegant graining in wood may speak to us of storms of long ago. He carried himself rigidly, one shoulder a little higher than the other and each moving stiffly as he walked, his chin held inward as if he had once received a blow there and had ever since gone about on his guard against another. It was like a rehearsal for the sleep-walking performance which he would never give, for the energy behind the dream had sentenced him to often prostrating insomnia. The

[29]

insomnia of Arnold Bennett, its severities unguessed even by those close to him, was at times a martyrdom of the spirit. There is a glimpse, no more, but revealing, in the brief study of insomnia in *Things that have Interested Me*: "Powerful is the mind that can keep control of itself in such crises," though he knew, and wrote what he knew, that this is a form of suffering much subject to over-emphasis. In Bennett's case, exaggeration was not only unlikely but uncharacteristic.

Nor was this the only sign of the intrusion of the conflict of the dream into his physical being. Neuralgia was the scourge of his days as insomnia was of his nights He was constantly mauled by it, at times to the point of extreme exhaustion after bouts lasting a fortnight or more There is a monotonous number of entries in the journal about its recurrence, as there is also about the means by which he tried to procure himself relief. Like insomnia, neuralgia is an affliction apt to evoke the imperfect sympathies of the unafflicted He was given to trying curious forms of alleviation. Returning, sunk in gloom, from the funeral of Lady Beaverbrook in December, 1927, he flung off his hat and without waiting to be divested of his overcoat and wrap called for "the King's whisky", a brand of Scotch supplied only to Buckingham Palace, of which an influential friend had secured him a bottle. "Pour it in here," he ordered, holding out his cupped hands. Thus receiving it, he threw the whisky over his head and rubbed it desperately into his scalp and neck. His face was grey with pain.

Then there was the speech chaos, not stammer, not stutter, a paralysis which at its worst made him throw back his head epileptically and bite the air until release came from its capricious power, or press his hand over his mouth as if to check the garbled flow. His own diagnosis was that his brain gave him two orders at the same time, one dictating speech, the other not-speech. Eloquent, it may seem, of distress elsewhere, it is seen from the journal to have preoccupied him with remedial hopes and disappointments throughout his life. At thirty he was seeing a so-called mental healer in Bloomsbury in whose claims he had no faith but to whom he gave a cheque for a guinea lest he be wrong. Twenty years later he followed a French speech therapist to Aberdeen, of all places, in another pursuit of help. Later still he tried Couéism, and in the last two years of his life he was consulting yet one more speech expert, a Mr. Bawden of South Croydon, and was exploring also the scope of Christian Science in that connection.

Often the defect reduced him to silence when he wished to say something and caused him to give a wrong impression when he said it, for the sudden staccato recovery from the gaps of hesitancy was apt to be mistaken for self-assertion. Disjointed speech probably often means a short-circuiting in the nervous system. There is the theory that an overbearing father or schoolmaster may produce a fierce desire to retaliate and at the same time a fear to do so, with a resulting interference with the powers of expression. Arnold Bennett managed, some thought brilliantly, to transform his defect into an asset of his personality, using it when necessary to reinforce his more positive statements. He made one of his rarely expanded comments on the subject in a letter dated November 14, 1923:[1]

I used to discuss this matter with the late W. H. R. Rivers, one of the greatest specialists on nervous afflictions. He could never suggest anything better than to forget the trouble and leave it alone. As he stammered himself, he would be very likely to know all there is to be known. Also he was a very intimate friend of mine and a really great man. . . . Why the subject is not more generally studied than it is by the experts I have never understood, for the affection is very widespread (among males—it is very rare among females) and the nervous strain of it is of course continuous and severe—very severe. . . . It is always a marvel to me that I, with my acute general sensitiveness, have risen above this *enormous* handicap and am, even in spite of it, recognised as a great 'persuader' of people.

H. G. Wells wrote in *Experiment in Autobiography*: "The stammer he had never been able to conquer was utilised for a conversational method of pauses and explosions," and Wells concluded that it had its origin in an early sex complication involving emotional shock. The Bennett family explanation was more prosaic. It all began when Arnold crushed his fingers in the mangle, they said. Wells pursued the matter thus: "In some way that I find obscure and perplexing his sexual life did not flood into his general life. His personality, so to speak, never fused with a woman's. He never gave the effect of being welded, even temporarily, with the woman he was with. They did not seem really to have got together," and he added the opinion that there was "some hitch in his make-up, some early scar that . . . had robbed him of his normal confidence and set up a life-long awkwardness".

Mr. Somerset Maugham has said that "it was painful to watch the struggle he had sometimes to get the words out. It was torture to him.

[1] To Dorothy Cheston Bennett.

Few realised the exhaustion it caused him to speak. . . . It tore his nerves to pieces", and exposed him to humiliations and ridicule and impatience. Mr. J. B. Atkins, formerly editor of *The Spectator*, a friend over many years, says that everyone who knew Bennett admired his resolve not to come to terms with his speech weakness: "There was no surrender, no substitution of some synonym which would have come out more easily, and he prohibited by a look any mistaken attempt to help him." When he could not speak a difficult word he would sing it, having first reminded his hearers that no singer stammered.

In any attempt to understand his deeper emotional attitudes Miss Dorothy Cheston, who shared Arnold Bennett's last years and by his legally ratified wish added his name to hers, has suggested that it is vital to take into account the facts of his broken engagement to Miss Eleanor Green, the young American girl with whose family he became friendly in his early Paris days. "The breaking of this engagement was a hurt of which he bore marks to the end of his life."

The broken engagement was a disturbing occurrence: he wrote in the journal that he had had difficulty in finishing the novel he was working on at the time. That its after-effects were vitally important may be doubted. It seems to have repeated a pattern of frustration that had its origin in some much earlier dislocation of his emotions, as Wells thought. When he was a solicitor's clerk, not long arrived in London, a zestful colleague of the law inflamed his imagination with stories of the allurements of a young woman he knew in lodgings at Camberwell Green. They arranged to visit her on a Saturday afternoon. In fairness, the particulars should hardly be given the permanence of print; it is enough to say that the adventure had a Restoration comedy anti-climax, with jeering profanity from the young woman at Bennett's expense. The episode threw such a shadow of desperation across his face as he left the scene that his colleague remembered it with amusement long after. It seems clear that Bennett himself could not laugh it off, and another stage in the charade was acted out years later when he led Mrs. Belloc Lowndes to believe that he carried "a little book in which he kept careful note of his amorous adventures". This pretence to an extravagance of animal magnetism, this presenting himself in the role of a Casanova, complete with statistics, was all of a piece with the underlying dissonance of the dream, with his futile affection for Eleanor Green, eighteen to his thirty-nine, with his unregarded devotion to a famous beauty, in its fatuity worthy of Cervantes, with his disclosure to a woman friend in New York that he had never been in love until he met Miss Green, and with his journal confession, "I see that, at bottom, I have an intellectual scorn, or the scorn of an intellectual man, for all sexual-physical manifestations. They seem childish to me. . . I can feel myself despising them at the very moment of deriving satisfaction from them, as if I were playing at being a child." There was no woman, it seems, who could make him indifferent to the universe.

It was a dilemma not to be intellectually resolved and it tends to bear out Wells' belief that Bennett's sexual growth never came to fullness. That it was somewhere checked very early on we are the more inclined to agree when we find him recording the pleasures of Saturday, June 26, 1896:

> . . . In the afternoon we rowed lazily up the river, from Richmond to Kingston—Brown and I, and two little girls, Daisy and Georgie, whom Brown in a moment of inspiration had invited to complete the party. Tall little girls for their twelve or thirteen years, with wide straw hats, white blouses, and long foal-like legs showing below their short blue skirts; shy at first, but gradually expanding and unfolding before our efforts to be utterly, absurdly foolish, and laughing loyally at far-fetched allusive jokes which they could not possibly have understood; always in doubt whether or not to believe what we said and in any case accepting or rejecting it with cautious reservations. Georgie, the eldest (*sic*) was a spoilt girl, and both spoke with an alarming cockney accent, yet the unique charm characteristic of just their age, made their worst sins of behaviour delightful. They rowed till they were tired, labouring hard and willingly, anxious to do their best, and when questioned admitted without shame that they *were* tired—'a bit.' We camped and brewed tea on an island and Georgie ate so many sardines and strawberries that she was sick on the way home and had to lie quiet in the bows till the colour came back to her cheeks. In the evening at the corner of the street, Brown kisses them and I shake hands with a profound bow, and they make off sedately side by side to their home a few yards away. A quite new and tickling sensation, this intimate companionship with very young girls.

His gallantry, unlike his friend's, we observe, was inhibited; a charming picture which tells us more about the artist than about his subjects and reminding us that there are to be found in his novels some

[33]

of the best studies of young girlhood ever written. Of the child Edith in *The Glimpse*: "I had an extraordinary and exquisite sense of intimacy with her," he says in his role of narrator. He had achieved freedom from the menace of an environment that never ceased to hurt him with its reminder of old humiliations, but there remained a psychic link tethering him to a past haunted by a snub-nosed young girl in black.

(2)

He wrote the newspaper article sketching his childhood background and the characters of some of his nearest relatives at a time when he was at the zenith of his social renown. Not that it called for great moral courage. He had now arrived socially, as long before he had arrived professionally. He was prominent in circles in which he never felt wholly at home but always wished to be. He was constantly in the company of men and women of a class which had retained much of its former exclusiveness, though the war had blurred social differences and mown down many of the once rigid class prejudices. And if the contrasts of his rise in the world gave him an air of self-approval, exaggerated by his puffed-out shirt fronts, it was countered by an honesty about his origins that can still be admired. "Unconsciously I must always have had the take-me-or-leave-me attitude which is characteristic of the Five Towns."

The newspaper article was his contribution to a series written by well-known people and published under the title of 'Who I Am'. Accepting the editorial invitation, which came from the present writer, Arnold Bennett wrote: "The series ought to be a success, provided you can ensure a fair amount of honesty on the part of your authors." He intended to be candid, he said, as most of his relatives were dead.

Among those who survived were some who did not approve his publication of the story that an illegitimate strain ran through the family line. "It is said locally, with what truth I know not, that my family is descended on the paternal side from James Brindley, the eighteenth century canal engineer. Doubt has been cast on his morals," more recently by a leading Staffordshire genealogist who says that Brindley "had a reputation for producing illegitimate children".

The story persists in the Potteries, where at least one living member of the Bennett family can be found to support it. Arnold Bennett himself appears to have cherished the possibility. He used the name of Brindley for several of his characters. That the genes of a great man may have trespassed on his ancestry was part of the "hazardous strangeness of existence", nor did he apparently stop to think of the feelings of any direct Brindley descendants. He had written in the journal for May 13, 1901:

> We were talking of the neighbourhood of Macclesfield. . . . My mother said: 'We' (that is herself, sister and brother) 'were all baptised at Mellor Church, near Marple. Grandfather had a farm there. Father and his three brothers were all born there. There were four Longson brothers. 'All dead, I suppose,' I said. 'Eh, bless ye, yes. Long and long ago.' This evocation by my mother of these farming Puritanical ancestors just now was rather touching, in a way. It gave me larger ideas of the institution of 'the family'. When I thought also of my mother's side (the Claytons), my father's side (the Bennetts) descended illegitimately, as my Uncle John once told me, from 'Schemer' Brindley, the engineer, and my father's mother's side (the Vernons, of whom several I believe are living now in Burslem ignored by my father and us)—when I thought of all these four stocks gathered and combined to produce me, a writer, an artist pure and simple, yet with strong mercantile instincts, living on a farm after two generations of town life, I wondered. . . .

James Brindley, called 'Schemer' because he planned great engineering schemes, was of the stature of Stephenson, Talfourd and Rennie. As any study of him may be quite out of focus here we shall have little to say about him. Briefly, he linked Manchester with Liverpool and the sea by canal and so made them cities not only of our North but of the world. These were achievements of an unlettered imagination. Brindley owed nothing to the schools. Cradled in illiteracy, he was barely able to sign his name and right up to the last he was writing 'engon' for 'engine'.

Backed in his larger enterprises by a scarcely less illiterate Duke of Bridgwater, he began his working life as apprentice to a Derbyshire millwright named Abraham Bennett. This Bennett had a daughter and she and James Brindley begat a lusty rumour if nothing more. The story starts there and perhaps the name of Bennett in that distant context is the least significant part of it. Generically speaking, confirmation of the Brindley connection appears not to exist, though it is a fact that the present Bennett generation has thrown up a group of young engineers.

We conclude that it is one of those basically poetic fancies with which lower-middle-class families often sustain their morale. When there is no famous man to be invoked, there is a rich uncle in Australia or lawyers are investigating a will with missing heirs advertised for in the *News of the World*. Then we meet a close relative of Arnold Bennett's, a member of his own family and generation, and are baffled by a likeness that will not pair off in the memory until we see it again looking out from a portrait engraving in a Victorian work of reference, the face of James Brindley. The resemblance strikes the attention with the force of last-minute evidence for a crumbling defence, and lines of Thomas Hardy's echo solemnly from the past: "*I am the family face . . . projecting trait and trace . . . leaping from place to place . . . over oblivion. . . .*"

Arnold Bennett may have had no opportunity of noting the occurrence of this apparitional sequence in his family line, for it seems to have appeared late in the life of its transmitter. He would have been impressed. He would have seen in it proof of the "mysteriousness of all human existence" which was a constant of his thought.

(3)

There was an uncle who was a pottery artist in Lambeth; a maternal grandfather who was first a weaver, then a draper; a formidable aunt on his mother's side; and his mother, whose long suppressed true self was revealed, he said, on the death of his father, an autocrat whose gold ring rapping sharply on the glass of the front door was among his eldest son's abiding recollections. These were the characters with which he chose to illustrate his theme of 'Who I Am'. They were stated rather than drawn. The projection was outward, away from himself. He used the first person pronoun with remarkable restraint in this contribution to a series in which it was an imperative of the title. "I grew up in an atmosphere of sustained effort, of grim 'sticking it', of silent endurance, of never being beaten by circumstances. I am now glad of it," and one imagines the sepulchral figures of his elders closing in to hear this reaffirmation of principles that had ruled their lives.

Reading J. M. Barrie's *Margaret Ogilvy*, "a picture of a grave, mighty, passionate family of men and women," as he described them in a journal note, he found himself making comparisons with his own family, "and in particular comparing Margaret Ogilvy and

J. M. Barrie with my mother and myself. Again and again, I had to acknowledge inferiority—inferiority of essential 'character', apart from inessential talent—a lack of bigness, and a presence of certain littlenesses. Yet at the same time, I found us sturdy enough not to be ashamed of shortcomings What we are, we are! 'I exist as I am, that is enough'. To hold such a creed religiously is in one way to be great. A proud, self-unconscious self-esteem: that is what few people have. If at times it deserts me and mine, it always returns the stronger for having retreated. We are of the North, outwardly brusque, stoical, undemonstrative, scornful of the impulsive; inwardly, all sentiment and crushed tenderness. We are of the North, incredibly, ruthlessly independent; and eager to say 'Damn you' to all the deities at the least hint of condescension."

He lay bare the "pietistic posturings" of his remembered ancestors, "to me utterly exasperating." He recalled the boredom of his chapel-going, filing in behind his parents and sisters to the family pew; all that continuously enervating religious experience of his adolescence from which, in *Anna of the Five Towns* especially, he had pressed and squeezed and extracted with the smooth ruthlessness of a manufacturing process what there was in it of human passion and human truth.

"Many preached Christianity," he declared in the newspaper article, "but few practised it. I was depressed by the examples of this hypocrisy that I saw around me." It is made to sound like a personal grievance from which flowed decisive actions of his life. The Five Towns people were perhaps being asked to see in it not his excuse for running away from them but his reason for not going back. "I hated the thought of my youth," he wrote in 1926, returning from a Sunday morning walk in London in the course of which he had heard a congregation singing hymns.

From the generalising criticism of local religious behaviour he turned to particularising his father's. "In ceremonial religious matters he did not practise what he preached." He brings his father back in the psychologically fashionable role of a tyrant whose slippers were a symbol less of weary feet than of female servitude. "My chief recollection of him is of an auburn-haired man lounging in the armchair of the dining-room," which gives us a picture of Enoch Bennett, solicitor of Hanley, conducting himself like a bailiff in his own house, very much the man in possession. His personal style was apt to be intimidating, as the imperious rapping on the front door suggests, and his wife shrank to less than life-size in his presence.

[37]

Arnold Bennett said that his mother had no sense of humour, but it is clear that her quiet ways, contrasting with the sometimes violent self-projection of her husband, drew her children to her. In her Wesleyan Methodism she never wavered when Arnold and his brother Frank, in the arrogance of their growing opinions, probed her religious sensibilities. In this Arnold tried her severely. She believed what her forefathers had believed and because they believed it. Obstinacy of that order no doubt severely tried him. It did not shake their underlying affection for one another. "I would commit naughty witticisms and then, seeing her face, would walk round the table and kiss her."

"My mother during my father's lifetime was my father's wife. When he died, we discovered that she too had a most powerful individuality." It is an expedient and familiar formula when there is no pedigree to show. You have no difficulty in agreeing that the Chinese are wise in such matters and that what counts is virtue, not arms. Arnold Bennett discovered in his pottery-painting uncle and in his weaver-turned-draper grandfather the virtue most respected in lower-middle-class England, that of making money and keeping it. The uncle made enough to own a row of houses. "They brought him 18 per cent and he lived in vigorous retirement for some years." The grandfather, "by unending small economies, saved up a lot of money." His other grandfather "was said to be the best 'turner' in the pottery trade". An aunt was "a refined and forceful woman". His father "did what always seemed to me to be a marvellous thing—he decided to become a solicitor and at thirty-four he became one. This was something of a feat for a man of his age". Another of the aunts "possessed one of the most attractive and formidable personalities I have ever encountered", and there is the final compensatory assertion: "Beyond doubt my father's influence was the main factor in making a home in which the 'humanities' flourished more brightly than in any other home of my acquaintance. Entering the houses of his friends, wealthier or poorer, I always felt that I was going into something inferior intellectually, more confined and stuffy, places where the outlook was less wide and the dominant personalities less vigorous, original, and free."

(4)

He could not write about himself from within and, from the publishing point of view, another defect in him as autobiographer would have been his reticence about other people. The unpublished parts of the journal contain much interesting and often intimate information about his friends and acquaintances and about persons who were neither. But he professed in his published *1929 Journal* a keen dislike of gossip in print. By this time he had become vulnerable, for the young actress who had come into his life was now publicly sharing it and the author of *Mental Efficiency* had no prescription for the touchiness which that situation often produced.

His journal, however, was no longer being written on the Goncourt model, nor for its original purpose as a repository of material that might be absorbed into his novels. It was being used as a means of ministering to a growing obsession with his output of words per annum. "At the beginning of this year," he wrote in the extra-journal, April 16, 1926, "I resolved to average 1,000 words a day throughout the year. But I soon found that this record-breaking could not be done. I then said I would do 300,000 words in the year. I managed this up to the end of March and may manage it—just—up to the end of April, in spite of very grave interruptions and other obstacles. But I doubt if I shall go through the year successfully. I am now constantly thinking about the number of words I am writing. And there often comes into my mind such a phrase as: 'Well, that will make so many hundreds more. Good!' In my new Fantasia [*The Vanguard*] this passion for hundreds has led to me having to write a lot of stuff a second time."

The insecurity feelings bound up with this may have been primarily psychological: they were also economic. He was worrying more than he had needed to for many years about his overheads. He may have had signals of declining powers. An old impacted dread, Johnsonian in its capacity to affright the heart, was perhaps stirring in its subconscious recess. The cocksure I'm-telling-you tone of the mental training books had masked a secret cerebral disquiet which reason can disarm as a force and yet not dispel as a spectre. The Stoic thought of Epictetus and Marcus Aurelius with which he had long fortified himself could provide armour against fear but not delivery from the causes of it. And at sixty, when he feared that he had reached his critical year, the armour of Arnold Bennett, the distended grandiose *persona* of a fundamentally diffident and anxious man, was being tested by attack from too many points of existence. The later parts of the journal reflect his hopelessly divided attention and an almost morbid compulsion to write more words and yet still more. He had begun the journal back in the 'nineties as a palette on which he had daubed his first impressions of people and places to be worked up for subsequent use in the novels.

Often now it was being filled with the materials of social gossip, which he affected to despise.

Still, it is civilised gossip, precise, shrewd, good-natured, revealing what his old friend André Gide of France called his "vigilant generosity and his tireless curiosity". If he had lived to edit it for publication he would have shown a scrupulous care for the feelings of others. Unhappily, a false emphasis was given by legal proceedings which followed the appearance of possibly too hastily selected parts of the journal after his death. The unpublished parts, in particular, show that his sense of duty as a friend to whom others turned in their troubles was constantly sapping the energy needed for dealing with his own. And if the journal of the last years reflects what some might think a misguided enthusiasm for the pleasures of such resorts as Ciro's and the Embassy Club, it contains abundant evidence to show that in the more sober transactions of life his highly esteemed common sense had not left him, nor had his percipience failed.

He saw behind the jauntiness of Sir Gerald du Maurier "a deep constitutional gloom". He considered that "for all his great success, both here and in the U.S.A., there is something pathetic about Hugh Walpole". He observed that Mrs. Patrick Campbell had been "softened by misfortune". Sir Edward Elgar seemed to him to be "a disgruntled old man, full of affectations". James Joyce was "a very strong personality indeed: his interests are strictly limited and when he is not interested he does not hide the fact". Admiring Aldous Huxley, he adds: "But he is too narrow." T. S. Eliot, consulting him about the uncertain future of his magazine, *The Criterion*, struck him as being "a bit self-centred. Twice I told him I had another appointment, and at last I had to drag him out of the club and drop him on the pavement. Even there he continued". After the funeral of Mrs. H. G. Wells: "Number of really A.1 people present, very small; which shows how Wells kept out of the 'great' world and how the great world is practically not interested in Wells."

At the Garrick Club last night G. H. Mair [formerly of the *Manchester Guardian*] told us he was absolutely sure that Shaw has not been an ascetic. He knew that G.B.S. had had an affair with Florence Farr, if not with Mrs. Patrick Campbell. Also he said that, in reply to an American criticism to the effect that when talking about love G.B.S. did not know what he was talking about, G.B.S. wrote to the paper to say that few people could possess a greater practical experience as amorists than he possessed. This found us very startled, and Anthony Hope incredulous, but Mair reiterated that he was quite sure.

As to Shaw's amorousness, it occurs to me that only a practical man would have written the first act of 'Man and Superman'.

At a dinner given at the Savoy Hotel, London, Lord Birkenhead produced a letter which he showed to Bennett, who noted: "The letter was from Baldwin. An offer of the Lord Chancellorship; but an offer with a string to it. It was made on the condition that it would be refused. Birkenhead was very disappointed. He wanted the Woolsack again. The letter was soiled; he had evidently been carrying it about to show his friends."

An entry of March 22, 1920, presents a personality whose subsequent promotion in the hierarchy of professional criticism brought him a prominence and a regard which temper Arnold Bennett's trenchant exactitude:

J. E. Agate came early for tea in order to get counsel. He is a man of forty or so, rather coarse-looking and therefore rather coarse in some things. Fattish. Had reputation for sexual perversity. Married a beautiful young French girl (twenty-three or so), who has now evidently left him, after about a year or less of marriage. He was a dramatic critic of the *Manchester Guardian* for ten years. A.S.C. during war. Principal job: partner in some cotton trade concern. Has just sold out for (he says) £5,000 and decided to come to London to make a living. Wants to be in publishing, with sideshows as a novelist and dramatic critic. Has published two war books and a novel. All good. Some fine things in the novel. Made £100 out of it, and £120 out of the war books together. Writes with difficulty. Knows a deuce of a lot about French dramatic literature. Seems to understand acting. Has certain sensibilities. Yet his taste capricious and unreliable. Has various conventional prejudices against institutions. The man has points and refinements; but he is fundamentally unintelligent. . . . He wouldn't go. Stopped one hundred minutes and was dreadfully boring.

Often in the company of J. A. Spender, the influential Liberal editor and publicist, he noted him as "a wonderful, ageing man, so informed and judicious and sagacious and kindly, but with a tendency to bore people, a bit 'grey' in colour; there is a lack of vitality and fun in him". Spender had said he wished *he* could make enough to live on by writing an article a week. "Well, he can't and never will, because his really admirable articles are not exciting enough to read."

On holiday in Scotland with Lord Beaverbrook: "His interest in the Border chieftain robbers and their keeps and methods was very noticeable. He returned to the subject again and again." And after a week-end with the Galsworthys in Sussex:

John, always exact and quiet, always speaking with authority though saying little, always judicial, just, kindly, and broadminded, is the god of that house. The niece-in-law runs the house; Ada runs the garden (five gardeners). Ada also runs John (secretarially: he told me he could not stand a secretary) and John is God. And John deserves to be God too. He seems to do only about two or two and a half hours a day. He rides at 7.45. Breakfasts at 9.30. Then he deals with his mail, till about 11. Then writes till lunch at 1.30. Then gives the afternoon to exercise (tennis and croquet), pottering and reading. He looks quite as old as he is, sixty-one and three-quarters, but he can beat me (who looks younger) at games. I bet he can be grim at times, but always with urbanity. He is benevolence itself. But very reserved. He is now nearly bald with a forehead more terrifically domed than ever, tall, thin; not too well-dressed but well enough dressed.

Autobiography fails as literature when it does not exhibit to the reader more than one plane of its subject's existence; not only the processional sequence of happenings that composes his physical life, but the enlargements of experience that spring from his emotional responses. Arnold Bennett had supplied the answer to his own auto-biographical dilemma when in a consideration of James Joyce's *Portrait of the Artist as a Young Man* he wrote: "He had resources but could not use them."

CHAPTER THREE

(1)

"**I**'M going to get out of this," Arnold Bennett said to a friend, Frank Beardmore, as they strolled in a Burslem twilight of 1888. He had left the Middle School at Newcastle-under-Lyme four years before and had been working as a clerk in his father's law office at Hanley. Now in his twenty-first year he felt equal to facing the wrath that was sure to come. His father was still paying him no more than pocket money and had said that he would not increase it.

Arnold Bennett's intention to free himself of this uncomplimentary dependence had been growing in his thoughts since his return from London, where his father had taken him to sit for matriculation at London University. It was his first visit to the capital city and he gave himself up to it so thoroughly in his imagination that the return half of a ticket from the Potteries was of no interest to him thereafter. The homeward journey had been depressing, his gloom deepening as the train rolled on through what he would later describe as "England in little, lost in the heart of England", towards the potbanks, the pit-mounds, the smoking chimneys of the Six Towns which for euphony's sake he would reduce to five.

The elder Bennett, lolling tight-trousered in his corner, was well-satisfied to be going back to the scene of his growing local prestige, hardly indicated by the reference to him in the Burslem directory as legal adviser to "The Burslem Coffee House Company, Limited" and "The Cheshire and North Staffordshire Wesleyan Middle Class School Association, Limited", connections which were probably of little importance to his practice as a solicitor. His son, all moods and disaffection, sat staring at a far-spreading, flat panorama which had no hold on his attention. He could not get London out of his head.

"There grows in the North Country a certain kind of youth of whom it may be said that he is born to be a Londoner. The metropolis, and everything that pertains to it, that comes down from it, that goes up into it, has for him an imperious fascination." It is the opening paragraph of Bennett's first novel, *A Man from the North*.

[43]

He had discovered the power of London to relax him socially, to relieve him of the regret that is the emotional undertone of much lower-middle-class existence, to minister to his no less potent lower-middle-class wish to dissociate himself from his origins while not necessarily disowning them. He was obsessed by the spectacle of London, by its prodigious sights and sounds, by its wealth, by the opportunities it offered for self-indulgence, by its vast invigorating challenge to the begrudging we-knew-him-when spirit of the community that was about to receive him once more into its sooty embrace. Arnold Bennett, the provincial, was to become one of the great Londoners, an act of alienation which the Five Towns would not forgive.

The journey had widened the distance between him and his father, whose tyrannies now seemed still more intolerable. The terms of their uncomfortable relationship are stated in *Clayhanger*, from which it is clear that Enoch Bennett's attitude as a parent was largely answerable for the deterioration of his eldest son's regard for him. Seen as Darius Clayhanger, the steam-printer, Enoch Bennett was "an old man, who had always been old, generally harsh, often truculent, and seldom indulgent". It was not the final true epitaph for Enoch Bennett, but the eldest of the family wrote from disparagements to which his brothers and sisters were much less frequently exposed.

"Poor Arnold, I don't know what we're going to *do* with poor Arnold. He'll never get a *living*." Enoch Bennett's gibe, ending on its note of affected dismay, is recalled by a contemporary of Arnold Bennett's at Burslem as a wilful taunt, for other people were there at the time and the attention of the moment was wholly fixed on him. Adding to the cruelty of it, his father gulped and gobbled in imitation of his son's crippled speech, a form of humiliation capable of post-dating its effects in the life of the victim.

The clue to Enoch Bennett's outburst on that occasion was his disappointment at the failure of Arnold to pass the examination which was the first step into the profession of the law. Having matriculated, he had been thought capable of following up that success. No doubt Enoch Bennett had a sentiment for seeing "—& Son" on his practice plate. When word came by post that Arnold had failed, his father rose from the breakfast table and strode white-faced from the room.

One must be fair to Enoch Bennett's memory. His autocratic style had sanctions outside himself. He was conforming to a social pattern, not simply expressing a personal urge. Father-dominance being a keystone in the broad arch of Victorian social life, the Bennetts of the

Waterloo Road were as vulnerable to it as the Barretts of Wimpole Street. Enoch Bennett's surviving child, Mrs. Emilie Vernon, remembers him as a parent who was both forbidding and affectionate. Her recollection tells her that his affection was real but that he did not often show it conventionally. He had an overriding concern for the personal success of each of his children.

He and his wife in their later years seldom spoke to each other. Each had a natural reserve that grew to be unnatural. They never quarrelled. Mrs. Vernon remembers the surprise with which once she heard her father say to her and her sisters: "Always remember, your mother is a wonderful woman." The tone of his voice was as remarkable to her as the sentiment it expressed. Contrasting with it were fits of harsh temper, not seen then as possible precursors of the fate awaiting him. Enoch Bennett never lost his school-teacher stance and style. He was for ever "sending for" his sons. They had to stand before him to report progress in their lessons, to state their difficulties, to receive his criticisms. Sometimes, but not often, he would relax and join in their discussions and his shouted loud command, "Look it up!", ringing over their arguments, came to have the weight of a proverb in the household.

Enoch Bennett was a potter's son, born in one of the small and narrow houses of Pitt Street, Burslem, off the Waterloo Road, which alternates frequently between the two social levels of road and street in its functional course of linking the federated boroughs now known as the city of Stoke-on-Trent. It is the Trafalgar Road of the Bennett novels and it has a notable significance in the lives of a number of their leading characters, of Edwin Clayhanger and Hilda Lessways in particular. It is a dominant part of their environment, as it was of Arnold Bennett's in his early youth. The Waterloo Road is a classic example of ribbon development, stringing together a series of communities extending to a little under ten miles in length and covering no more than three miles at their greatest width.

We can travel the Waterloo Road, which commemorates the battle, with the narrator of *The Matador of the Five Towns*, "past all those strange little Indian-red houses, and ragged empty spaces, and poster-hoardings, and rounded kilns, and high, smoking chimneys, up hill, down hill, and up hill again, encountering and overtaking many electric trams that dipped and rose like ships at sea, into Crown Square, the centre of Hanbridge, the metropolis of the Five Towns. . . ." Or we can see it in another perspective in *Anna of the Five Towns*:

"Five contiguous towns—Turnhill, Bursley, Hanbridge, Knype

[45]

and Longshaw—united by a single winding thoroughfare some eight miles in length, have inundated the valley like a succession of great lakes. They are mean and forbidding of aspect—sombre, hard-featured, uncouth; and the vaporous poisons of their ovens and chimneys have soiled and shrivelled the surrounding country till there is no village lane within a league but what offers a gaunt and ludicrous travesty of rural charm. Nothing could be more prosaic than the huddled, red-brown streets; nothing more seemingly remote from romance."

Like many of Burslem's lesser streets, Pitt Street appears at first sight to embody the worst domestic evils of the industrial revolution, a street of narrow poky houses with dark entries giving access to the rows of cramped overlooked backyards. The Industrial Revolution has been succeeded by a social revolution. These mean-looking little numbered houses, repellent in their brick-and-tile uniformity, are the homes of people who while doubtless desiring better have replaced squalor with a self-respect expressed in amenities rather than manners. The smoke flow on firing days, though restrained by the use of gas on the potbanks, is still the enemy of the housewife, but the standard of comfort and of appearances is higher than it was when Pitt Street was new, and the impulse of the casual observer to stigmatise these streets of lowly homes as slums is both unreliable and unjust.

Arnold Bennett's paternal grandfather, John Bennett, is known to have been an apprentice turner, a journeyman potter, and a master potter with premises in Albert Street, at a time, this, when small pottery firms were springing up like mushrooms, a great many of them having as brief an existence. He was a prominent Sunday School superintendent, credited with having organised some of the largest attendances known in the towns' religious history. "A very respectable, good and useful man," was the tribute of a long-lived member of the well-known pottery manufacturing family of Wood, of Burslem. John Bennett's religious activities were prominent in a curious local episode. He was a member of a congregation which seceded from the Wesleyan Methodist connexion at Swan Bank, Burslem. The Wesleyans would not allow writing or arithmetic to be taught in Sunday School. Rejecting this ruling of the Wesleyan Methodist Conference through the connexional authorities, John Bennett and his colleagues were 'locked out'. They met where else they could, in the open air, in tents, in any building available for the purpose, until their own place of worship was built at Hill Top, Burslem. It is still there.

John Bennett is thought to have had some success as a pottery-maker, though nothing is known now about his ware. Arnold Bennett apparently did not know that he had ever been a master-man and was content to describe him as "the best turner in the pottery trade", a reputation passed down by hearsay. He owned a number of small properties; some of them in Pitt Street remain in the family. The neighbours there of long ago heard Enoch Bennett's screams coming from the backyard of number 41, when his father thrashed him for telling a lie. Enoch Bennett's account of the incident is noted in Arnold Bennett's journal: "My grandfather knelt down and prayed and then he thrashed the Pater with his braces till neither of them could very well stand," and the victim may have wished for once that his address had been bottomless Pitt Street.

Enoch Bennett left school at the age of twelve to be a potter like his father before him. There had been a time, not so very many years before, when "children were whipped from their beds at three in the morning to work till eight at night", as Arnold Bennett had recorded in *Whom God Hath Joined*. There is a grim picture of this child exploitation in *When I was a Child*, an old potter's reminiscences published in 1903: "Imagine a poor child getting home at nine or ten at night, having left between four and five in the morning—a child, too, under ten years of age. His mother takes him on her knee and salts his porridge with her tears. She then carries him to bed, and makes that bed shake with her sobs." Enoch Bennett was spared these depths, but he found the conditions of labour, and particularly the white occupational dust, unendurable and after a year or so he sought release by teaching. The fact that at his age he could do so is a hint of the state of education in mid-Victorian England. The pupil-teacher system had just been started. Suitable scholars between the ages of thirteen and eighteen could be apprenticed to a schoolmaster at £5 a year.

School attendance was voluntary. A central Education Department had only recently been set up and the clergy continued to be in charge of most of the schools. A majority of the children of the day grew up with no schooling because there were too few schools and because also the industrial developments were creating a market for child labour.[1] Illiteracy is not an asset of industrialism, if it is of politics or religion, for men at machines must be nimble mentally and manually, and if production could tolerate a certain degree of it the expanding processes

---

[1] In the 'sixties more than two thousand girls under ten years of age were at work in the Potteries.

of distribution could not. The Education Act of 1870, which made schooling compulsory, was formal recognition of the fact that the revolution in work which was being wrought in England was producing a need for mental services of unexpected new kinds.

This demand, and the limited number of trained brains capable of responding to it, contributed to the 'self-help' impetus which was one of the characteristic features of nineteenth-century morality. Enoch Bennett, Arnold's father, applied it with some success in his affairs. In his youth he had a notion of becoming a lawyer. His father objected. "The law is of the Devil!" John Bennett would say angrily. Frustrated there, Enoch turned again to teaching and his success in qualifying as a certificated teacher rounded off an impressive display of will-power. He taught for a time in a school that has so far not been identified. Details of his teaching career are scanty. It is believed, from family recollection, that he never found full employment as a teacher. Anyhow, he went back to the potbanks and became a partner in the Nile Street firm of Bennett & Hurd, which failed. He was described as a potter in the certificate of his marriage to Sarah Ann Longson in 1866.

The Longsons were farming folk from the Cheshire-Derbyshire border, and they too had been subjected to the stern character-moulding forces of Wesleyan Methodism. One of them, Arnold Bennett's mother's father, took up cottage weaving, working twelve hours a day for five days a week and on the sixth walking to market, twenty-five miles there and back, to sell his cloth. He had the habit of thrift and saved enough to start in business as a tailor in the small town with the limerick-inciting name of Glossop, thirteen miles south-east of Manchester. He married a young woman from there, Frances Clayton, a surname Arnold Bennett used in his stories, usually to denote a social grade above that of most of his Five Towns people. This may well have derived from his grandmother Clayton's frequent assertion that she had married beneath herself. Becoming quite blind, long crippled by rheumatism, complaining never, this grandmother of Arnold Bennett's was of the race of lace-capped invalids of the period whose role it was to be "an example", sweetly enduring, horridly resigned. Her surviving grand-daughter, Mrs. Vernon, remembers this grandmother running the fingers of blindness over her young face to discover what she was like, whether the family features had prevailed. The *retroussé* nose thus disclosed made the old lady call urgently for her "nose improver", a velvet-lined contraption which she clipped on to the child's face to correct a tendency opposed to the Grecian ideal which the paintings of Sir John Millais and Lord Leighton had taught the Victorians to admire.

When Enoch Bennett married her, Sarah Ann Longson, called 'S'ran' by her adult children, was living with her people over the draper's shop which Robert Longson, the former weaver, had opened in St. John's Square, Burslem, the St. Luke's Square of the novels. The great revolution of the times had moved him, as it moved many, to look further afield for opportunity. His two daughters served with him behind the counter, looking after the 'ladies' side'. The younger girl married a china manufacturer, Ezra Bourne, and became Auntie Bourne in Arnold Bennett's life and Mrs. Hamps in his novels, for many readers the most memorable of his characters, "bland, superb, morally immense," a magnificent old lady whose magnificence was "limited to herself", permeating her weakness and her strength, her hypocrisy and her ruthless hospitality.

Her sister, Sarah Ann, Arnold Bennett's mother, was conspicuously less assertive of herself but as strong in principle and will. People habitually thought of her as being "nice". She had a quiet, refined individuality and charm that brought custom to the shop when she took over the fashion showroom on the first floor. Her features were more delicate than her sister's and her smiling soft brown eyes had their own power of attraction. She was to appear from time to time in her son's journal, usually stepping forth from the shadow of illness or death. "I don't like that woman at all," she grumbled after seeing *Carmen* at Hanley, and her sons and daughters cherished the remark and quoted it with laughing remembrance long after.

Sarah Ann Bennett had nine children, three lost in infancy. It seems that her husband had overcome his father's objection to the law as a career and that he was reading for it at the time of their marriage. There are a good many blanks in his personal history at this time. Mrs. Vernon feels sure that there were times when her father was "almost desperate about money". She herself was sent to live for long periods with her Longson grandparents at the shop which is immortalised in *The Old Wives' Tale*, and her brother Arnold was often there with her. Sarah Ann Bennett more than once went back to work in the shop between her pregnancies. When she was not well enough to do that she took in work at home, re-modelling hats.

Failing as a pottery man, Enoch Bennett turned to pawnbroking, which had a connotation in the Potteries different from that in some other communities. Pawnbroking was looked on there as a social service, like banking. A fair supply of capital was needed to start and maintain a pawnbroker's business, which might have to deal with hundreds of customers every week. In the days of large families pawnbrokers in the Potteries were resorted to by mothers who had no room in their small houses for their children's best clothes between Monday and Saturday. The pawnbroker's neat oil-cloth bundles kept the garments clean and tidy for the Sabbath. "On my left a very long and mysterious passage all full of black bundles," is one of Arnold Bennett's childhood memories in *The Truth about an Author*.

Probably with financial help from his father, Enoch Bennett rented the wedge-shaped corner shop at 90, Hope Street, Shelton, a township since merged into Hanley. There he started a small drapery and pawnbroking business. And there Arnold Bennett, baptised Enoch Arnold, was born on May 27, 1867, the family Bible says at "$\frac{1}{2}$-past ten o'clock a.m." The address given on the birth certificate is Hanover Street, from which there was a door to the Hope Street premises; father's occupation 'Draper', changed to 'Pawnbroker' on the birth certificates of his next three children.

(2)

Before Enoch Bennett reached the point of qualifying as a solicitor the family lived in several different houses, their addresses apparently altering with their circumstances. For about a year they lived in a part of Burslem called Dalehall, after a property which appears in early records as Dale Hall. On the maps of today the streets are shown clustering there like the scabs of an old disease, though in the Bennetts' time the worst effects of industrialism had not touched them. There were green margins and open views and the smoke of the potbanks had not become the domestic nuisance of later years, when the housewives of Dalehall had to change their window curtains every few days or do without them, as many consequently did. Even so, for the Bennetts it was the atmosphere of social discouragement and economic struggle, temporarily defeating Enoch Bennett's purpose of attaining a better standard for himself and his family.

According to Arnold Bennett's solicitor brother Frank, Dalehall saw the family fortunes at their lowest. This brother was heard to speak of "that awful house", referring apparently to their brief time in John Street, a *cul-de-sac* of four-roomed houses opening directly on to the pavement. Remembering the blacking family episode in the life of Charles Dickens, it is tempting to speculate on what the humiliations of life in this mean street did to Bennett, who never mentioned it. We may equate the relative poverty with the luxury he coveted and subsequently enjoyed, the poky rooms with the spaciousness of grand hotels, the huddling propinquity with his compulsion to move on and out into the world, the all-pervading ugliness with his passion for beauty.

Life in small houses may have affected him in other ways. His mother had nine children in twelve years, three dying at birth, or soon after, during Arnold's boyhood. As the first child, he became the prefect of the family and it is a reasonable premise that this helped to fix in him his strong sense of law and order. It would have tended to balance the feeling of displacement which is sometimes the eldest child's experience, the resentment at the diversion of maternal attention, and so on.

The result of the quick succession of pregnancies and infant deaths on the imagination of the growing boy, whose religious upbringing hyphenated sex with sin, may have been emotionally distorting. A boy of his class whose mother was frequently with child might well have been made excessively self-conscious outside the home as well as in it. Nor very likely was his mother's child-bearing the only intrusion of sexual intimacies into his awareness in that restricted domesticity. Wells's guess that early in Bennett's life there was a sex complication involving emotional shock may have been near the truth. There were elements of profound disgust in the dream. And disgust, it seems, made him wish to put his Dalehall experiences beyond the reach of memory.

(3)

Law books were piled on the table in the little front room—the *Institutes of Justinian*, Maine's *Ancient Law*, Austin's *Lectures on General Jurisprudence*: for months on end Enoch Bennett sat on into the early morning hours, reading. There was little quiet in the house, no room in which he could read without interruption except at night. The mental effort must have been intense. It told on his temper. His irritations flared up in particular against his eldest boy, whose existence often seemed to make him uncomfortable.

There was some easing of the tensions when his father-in-law, the draper of St. John's Square, offered him the use of a house he owned in Newport Lane, number 175. This is a street which cuts through the western part of Burslem and has many smaller streets running off it on either side, some of them covering the grounds of the original Dale Hall and having names which commemorate local worthies, Brindley among them. There is also a Bennett Street, but no one knows why. Ellgreave Street may be a relevant reminder of Osmond Orgreave in *Clayhanger*.

Much of the property represented the Victorian virtues of thrift and self-help. Fountain Buildings used to be known as "Twopenny Row" because it was built under a scheme backed by the eighteenth-century potter Enoch Wood, who gave his workpeople a chance to buy the houses by very small weekly payments. A row of near-by houses called Freehold Terrace is renamed Freehold Villas in *Hilda Lessways*: "Freehold Villas symbolised the final triumph of Victorian economics, the apotheosis of the prudent and industrious artisan. It corresponded with a building society secretary's dream of paradise. And indeed it was a very real achievement."

As for 175 Newport Lane, Bennett made it Hilda Lessways' home. From her bedroom window she looked out on to a view which continues to retain various points of recognition familiar to her, including the flour mill "that sometimes made nearly as much smoke as the kilns and chimneys enclosing the prospect on either hand". Today the air of the neighbourhood is probably clearer than it has been for a hundred years, though a walk through its streets still exposes one to the discomfort of grits in the eye. When parts of Bennett's picaresque novel, *The Card*, were filmed in Bag Street, Dalehall, in 1951, Burslem Fire Brigade was called in to supply the smoke which was not issuing in sufficient density from the adjoining potbanks to suggest the atmosphere of Dalehall *circa* 1910.

Here, at Newport Lane, the Bennetts' affairs took a turn for the better, socially if not economically. Enoch Bennett had passed his first law examination and was serving his time as an articled clerk to a solicitor named Ellis, whose office in Market Place figures in *The Card* as that of Duncalf's. Now further heroic study took him on to his finals and to his admission as a solicitor. According to the Law Society's records he was admitted in November, 1876; he is named as 'solicitor' on one of his children's birth certificates in October of that year. It was indeed "something of a feat", as his son wrote many years after, not only for a man of his age, thirty-four, but considering his background and education.

He did not buy a practice. He put his name on the door of an office in Piccadilly, Hanley, and entered on what may have been a thin time while he was establishing himself in his profession. In 1879 there was seemingly some improvement in his position and the family moved to what is now 198 Waterloo Road, a better address than any they had lived at before. The house is one of a terrace of stone-ornamented houses having little iron first-floor balconies. In two years more Enoch Bennett had enough confidence in his future to build a house of his own. It cost £900, plus £200 for the land. He borrowed £800 on mortgage. The new house was number 205 Waterloo Road, in an exclusively small red-brick terrace situated where the road passes through Cobridge, between Hanley and Burslem. Cobridge is Bleakridge in *Clayhanger* and the setting of the new house is there described: "Bleakridge was the summit of the little billow of land between Bursley and Hanbridge. Trafalgar Road passed over the crest of the billow. Bleakridge was certainly not more than a hundred feet higher than Bursley; yet people were now talking a lot about the advantages of living 'up' at Bleakridge, 'above' the smoke, 'out' of the town. . . . To hear them one might have fancied that Bleakridge was away in the mountains somewhere."

For the Bennetts, moving into the new house was an experience full of inner excitements. Edwin Clayhanger's feelings were Arnold Bennett's own: "The new house inspired him. It was not paradise. But it was a temple . . . I say that the hot-water system of the new house, simple and primitive as it was, affected and inspired Edwin like a poem. . . . All this was marvellous . . . it was romantic." It had enough rooms to allow one to be set aside for Enoch Bennett's books, entitling the room to be spoken of in savoured moments as "the library". The house had been planned by an architect. Bricklayers, carpenters, joiners, plumbers, painters had put typically sound Victorian workmanship into its construction and finish. There was a wide staircase with a heavy pitch-pine balustrade capable of supporting the exuberances of youth and the infirmities of age. The coloured window lights reflected more than the changing moods of the day. Enoch Arnold Bennett had known the emotions of Edwin Clayhanger as he watched the house nearing completion. The sight of it had "thrilled him to fine impulses".

(4)

Before he was old enough for school his mother had given him lessons at home. From the house in Newport Lane he went daily to the Wesleyan Infants' School at Swan Bank until he was nine years old. He was then entered as a pupil at the Burslem Endowed School, housed in the Wedgwood Institute in Queen Street, Burslem, where later he attended evening classes. Harold Keates Hales, sometime Member of Parliament for Hanley and Bennett's original of 'the Card', was at the Endowed School at the same time. "I can see him now as he was in those days," Hales wrote in his autobiography. "He sat to my left and slightly in front of me. In his hands he held his wooden-framed slate complete with pencil and sponge. 'Spit' was our watchword as we laboured at our slates. . . . Poor Bennett hated spitting, yet he was forced to spit and spit again. . . ."

The Endowed School headmaster was Horace Byatt, M.A., and it was H. G. Wells, not Arnold Bennett, who conferred biographical significance on him, for he left Burslem to take charge of Midhurst Grammar School, Sussex, where Wells received part of his education. Wells described him in *Experiment in Autobiography* as "a not very brilliant graduate of Dublin University . . . a dark, semi-clerical man, plumply active, with bushy hair, sidewhiskers, a cleft chin, and a valiant rotund voice". The future would-be saviour of civilisation liked Byatt. So did Arnold Bennett, according to Hales, who himself saw the head-master as "a sallow-faced survival of the earliest Victorian days, with a scruffy moustache and sidewhiskers of baboon-like thickness". Byatt, M.A., was influential in the life of Bennett as he was in Wells's. At the Endowed School he introduced a curriculum which included French and it was from him that Bennett got his first knowledge of a language which he never mastered but which was unquestionably an asset to him in his development as a novelist. At the Endowed School the pupils were required to take French but not to speak it, an anomaly later reproduced at the Middle School at Newcastle-under-Lyme and there, oddly enough, under a headmaster, D. B. Hurley, whose linguistic powers were exceptional.

Wells's education was intrinsically more interesting to read about than Bennett's, perhaps because Wells' latent invalidism made him seem precocious, whereas Bennett "developed rather slowly", his own admission. Discussing Bennett in *Experiment in Autobiography*, Wells wrote: "Since I have been writing about educated and uneducated types, I perceive I am exposed to the question whether Bennett was an educated type. I would say that in my sense of the word he was absolutely immune to education and that he did not need it."

Arnold Bennett said that the first story he ever read alone was

The Ugly Duckling and that it filled him with a sense of "the deep sadness which pervades all romance, beauty, and adventure", a theme which provides sombre throbbing undertones in *Clayhanger* and *These Twain*. He was known at school for his moodiness and in his adult life he was attacked by despondencies deep enough to suggest, again, that he was the victim of some early psychological shock. Hales did not think that Bennett was happy at school. "Anyway, he was never outwardly and boisterously happy."

Clayhanger supplies various details of Arnold Bennett's school-days, among them that "he knew nothing of the mechanism of the body and the mind, through which his soul had to express and fulfil itself". Nor had any sentiment for nature been encouraged in Edwin; and Bennett himself was almost comically ignorant of some of the facts of natural history. When he was thirty-seven: "I always thought that a hen would only lay eggs with the assistance of a cock once to each egg. But today I came across a hen that was confined solitary in a court about seven feet square and had laid an egg every day for a week. If the thing had not actually been before my eyes I should not have believed it." He never learned to distinguish between a duck and a drake or a carrot leaf and a parsnip leaf. Walking in the forest of Fontainebleau: "I was astonished by the grandeur and multitude of the spiders' webs. I broke two to see what they would do, but they did nothing—just hung loose in the breeze."

In 1880 the Endowed School, having outgrown the Wedgwood Institute, moved to Longport Hall, former seat of one of the older pottery-making dynasties, the Davenports, between Burslem and its wealthy satellite, Porthill. In readiness for moving day, an appeal was made by the headmaster for as much string as the boys could produce for packing up books. Hales remembered Bennett's contribution— "it was a masterpiece." The order had gone forth: Bring every scrap of string you can find. Bennett laid the results of his diligence on the headmaster's desk. "Thick rope, thin rope, cord, twine, ragged little scraps, and stout hempen lengths. At first I thought it was a subtle joke, but I soon saw that it was not. He had laid hands on every scrap he could find and had made them up into one imposing piece." [1]

His father discouraged him from playing games with the local boys, lest he became as uncouth as they. Also, says Hales, he seemed to be much concerned about the state of his clothes, perhaps by way of making up for real or imagined physical inelegancies. Hales remem-

[1] *Autobiography of the Card* by H. K. Hales (Sampson Low, 1936).

bered Bennett's preference for wearing white-spotted blue ties. Forty years later Hales called on Bennett in Cadogan Square, London. "He wore a blue bow with white spots. I couldn't help thinking of the classroom at Longport where the embryo connoisseur in haberdashery had flaunted the same magnificence before us."

As a strolling Five Towns youth he had taken to the habit of wearing brown kid gloves on weekday evenings, conscious, it seems, of the family's new-found standing in the community. Hales remembered the gloves. He remembered Bennett peeling them off to play in one of the evening football games in which his father had forbidden him to join. The glove habit remained with him, fixed in his mind as one of the determinants of social respectability. Raymond Needham, Q.C., who knew Arnold Bennett when he was self-consciously sampling the pleasures of country life for the first time, in the early 1900s, recalls being privately amused by seeing Bennett arrayed in riding breeches and lavender gloves for a walk through the Bedfordshire fields.

About the football games, he wrote in *Mental Efficiency*, in mutinous deference as always to the passing of the years: "Astonishing! Once I could play left-wing forward for an hour and a half without dropping down dead." Hales gives an account in his book of one of the evening matches, quoted here not as a corrective of Bennett's claim to efficiency as a player but for the glimpse it gives of the raw material from which time and experience were to fashion a fastidious public personality:

A dusty wasteland in the twilight. A mob of shouting footballers. Two tin cans or two piles of coats for the goal. And Nocker, his ungainly figure screwing itself up for the big dash. No elegance. Coat and hat laid aside, long trousers tucked into boot tops for greater freedom, shirt-sleeves rolled up in fighting style. The ball comes towards him. He gets it, fumbles at first—and then is off. Bricks and rubble litter the uneven ground. His heavy feet plough their way through, dust spurting up as he runs. 'Come on, Nocker!' we yell from the centre of the pitch. 'Shoot!' The left foot swings back, the small ball flashes goalwards. Then the disdainful Nocker shuffles back to his place. He has scored a goal. He is no longer the despised, studious bookworm, but an athlete.

(5)

The most decisive of his educational experiences was the entry of his name in the register of the Middle School, Newcastle-under-Lyme,

By permission of Mr. Richard Bennett
ENOCH BENNETT, HIS FATHER

By permission of Mr. Richard Bennett
SARAH ANN BENNETT, HIS MOTHER

By permission of Mr. Richard Bennett
SARAH ANN BENNETT

By permission of Mr. W. W. Kennerley
TERTIA, ELDEST SISTER

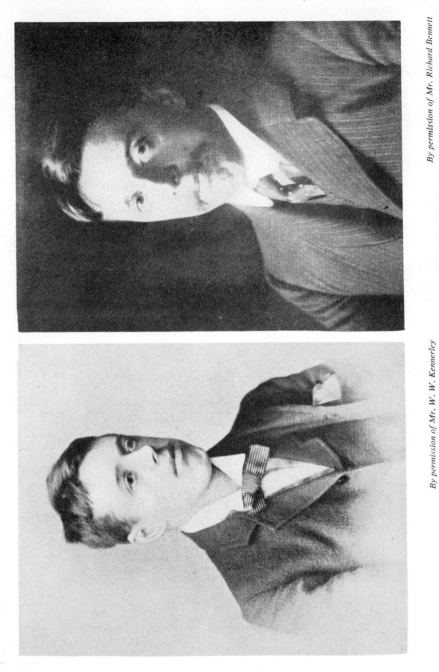

By permission of Mr. Richard Bennett

BENNETT, THE SOLICITOR'S CLERK

By permission of Mr. W. W. Kennerley

ARNOLD BENNETT, AGED 21

(since transferred to Wolstanton and now known as Wolstanton County Grammar School). This was in May, 1882: "age last birthday, fourteen." The Middle School was the historical legatee of a grammar school of Queen Elizabeth's time. It was endowed by several charity bequests and was for long known as Orme's School after one of them. In the 1870s it was decided to merge Newcastle-under-Lyme's several educational charities and the Middle School was the result, the "excellent institution" of a series of local directories published thereafter. The fee for pupils under fourteen, in Bennett's time, was four guineas a year.

The daily walk from Cobridge took him off the Waterloo Road through a no-man's land of brick-strewn pastures and brambly hollows, some with water in them, a neighbourhood in which there was always the risk of a clash with rougher boys. A sometimes adventurous walk of three miles and in certain matters more instructive than the lessons which came at the end of it. Clay barges moving with lazy explicitness through the landscape along the Trent and Mersey Canal gave him an idea of the romance of geography, a missing element of his education.

The short cut through the wastelands, under the railway line, over the canal in whose clay-whitened waters optimistic fishermen were often to be seen dropping their floats, across fields sagging from old mining operations, then over an iron bridge and up the slopes to Wolstanton, brought him and his brother and some cousins who joined in the daily journey through a street in Newcastle-under-Lyme where it was said that a Frenchwoman had come to live. When Arnold Bennett heard the rumour he insisted on dawdling past the house in the hope of an opportunity of speaking to her in her own tongue. One morning, there she was, cleaning the doorstep. Bennett went forward and greeted her in French, receiving a smiling response. The other boys stood on the pavement, watching. The greetings were exchanged on several mornings, Bennett always going forward to speak while the others remained behind, watching. One of them, a Bennett cousin, remembered the look of pleasure in Arnold's eyes as he joined them again. It was a success of the kind that Denry Machin, the Card, would have boasted about.

Not that one would be profitably employed in trying to trace the beginnings of Arnold Bennett's French sympathies. He said he recognised the existence of "a French thread" running through his life, but could not account for it. "Neither my forebears nor the friends of my youth displayed the slightest interest in France or the French."

[57]

He was sorry that he never went to a university. Doubtless he had a sharper sense of what he had missed because he had qualified not to miss it, the only Middle School boy of his year to pass the Cambridge Local Examination, and that in competition with more formidable entrants from the High School. His father wanted his services as a clerk, so no university for him.

"The best education is self-education," he wrote in *How to Make the Best of Life*, seeing it as a process of taking from life what "not even the universities have to give", and he declared that the only satisfaction that might reconcile him to being young again would be "the marvellous opportunity of starting quite fresh to educate myself". The education spectacle that moved him most, he said, was of "that immensely larger class leaving school who do not proceed to a university", the spare-time students engaged in self-education, 'self' in italics. "It palpitates with drama." He knew what he was writing about even if he over-wrote it. He had himself attended evening classes at the Wedgwood Institute (foundation-stone laid by Mr. Gladstone, 1863), taking a course of science lectures and also an art course, sitting among the apprentice potters studying to perfect themselves at their trade.

Surveying his mental equipment for the career of letters on which he proposed to embark, he noted when he was thirty: "A list of the master-pieces I have not read would fill a volume." His greatest appetite had been for the French novelists, among them Ouida. "Yes, Ouida was the unique fountain of romance for me." He devoured Ouida's novels, carried away by "the scenes of gilded vice into which she introduced me". It was from Ouida that he received his bias towards "liaisons under pink lampshades", which he said he could never indulge "owing to a puritanical ancestry and upbringing." His habit, later, of turning up a plate or a coffee cup to see if it bore a Potteries trade-mark as soon as he sat down at a restaurant table may have been inimical, anyhow, to the kind of romance he pictured for himself.

If Ouida did not directly inspire him to pack his bag for Paris when the time came, it is extremely likely that she was part-author of the remark he made to his friend Beardmore that summer's evening in Burslem: "Frank, I'm going to get out of this."

CHAPTER FOUR

(1)

WHILE it is clear from the journal, most especially from the unpublished parts, that Arnold Bennett possessed more delicate sensibilities than some of his critics have cared to believe, the social ignominies of his earliest years left in him no deposit of bitterness, no corrosion of the spirit. The stuff was almost certainly there, as in the childhood of Dickens, for the sustenance of one of the most banal of human resentments. Unlike Dickens, who had been affronted by the realisation that he came from the menial class, he did not discharge his youthful desolations into the public domain. Bennett kept a lifelong silence about the worst part of his childhood, at what price in psychic power it is impossible to assess.

In his concern to yoke space with time in defying his father's wish that he should stay on in the office at Hanley to succeed him professionally in the usual order of events it is possible to see more than the revolt of youth from uncongenial surroundings and prospects. None of his affections, it appears, was tied by his environment. The scenes of his most impressionable years put no spell of loyalty upon him. Returning from Manchester on October 20, 1927: "I took the 12.5 back to London, which went through the Potteries. The sight of this district gave me a shudder." It seems that he was under the compulsion of a congenital prejudice, a legacy of history, that he never felt any deep affinity with his background.

In Britain the chain-harrows of early history, tumbling unevenly over the human scene, left largely untouched various racial and social groups segregated from the main community existence by geographic or economic influences in valleys and dales and hill pockets and sleepy hollows. There they resisted change or survived in spite of it, community remnants never thoroughly mastered, converted, or absorbed.

This was the condition of some of the peoples of the north-west where the Roman wave, losing force, percolated rather than rolled on and where there resides a human type which received fewer alien elements than its more exposed neighbours. There undoubtedly persists among the people of the Potteries a difference readily noticed, not so readily defined, except in the physical terms of seeming to be smaller and more compact of build than the English average. Writing about them in his brief study of Arnold Bennett thirty years ago, Harvey Darton said:

Egotism, then, moral and social, is their predominant characteristic. It is a local condition, explained by local conditions. The Potteries refused railways at first. They had been engaged for countless generations in one single self-sufficing and prosperous craft. They preserved, therefore, without change, not merely their trade customs, but their personal manners. They were, until quite recent years, a piece of England walled off in the very heart of England. The motor and the railway have made great transformations; but until 1880 or a little later the Townsmen dwelt like the Albanians before the Turkish Revolution, who, when the Young Turks first prevailed, were observed to come down from their hill fortresses, blinking, curious, armed with strange weapons, into a world, a social order, they had never seen.

In his *English Journey* J. B. Priestley reported on the Five Towns as the embodiment of a kind of provincial life expressing the industrialism of the last century in "its dirtiest and most cynical aspect", and deemed it monstrous that fine craftsmen should be compelled to live and work in such surroundings. "The region is a clutter of small towns, but inside these towns everything is small too. . . . It is a marvel to me that the cups and saucers turn out to be the right size."

"These potters appeared to me to be undersized, and somewhat thin, too! But what elbows! What glaring egoistic eyes!" says the narrator in Arnold Bennett's best-known short story, *The Death of Simon Fuge*. Bennett gibed at them for their crassness in resisting the coming of the main-line railway and being satisfied with "their miserable loop-line" to connect them with the nation's arterial traffic. He made notes about their peculiar sexual nonconformities, about middle-aged women of the potbanks paying boys 'of thirteen or fourteen twopence for illicit pleasures, this on information given him by a local doctor, among other odd excesses. You were never quite certain what forms their lawlessness would take. In the 1870s Burslem citizens found it necessary for their peace of mind to organise a Society for the Prosecution of Garden Robbers. Arnold Bennett defended them against the slander that they gloried in man v. dog fights. He would not have that.

A stranger visiting the Potteries will not fare worse than in any other part of the country and he may receive impulsively generous attentions and hospitality of an expansiveness less often met with elsewhere. None the less, he is likely to be made aware of an unusual mental climate, and the idea may enter his head that the possibility exists of his running the risk of a peculiar kind of victimisation, that he might be enticed into thinking himself accepted only to suffer disillusionment from a people who remained pagan longer than their neighbours and who have seemed to some observers to be haunted by a *nibelung* past. It is a past stretching back far beyond the furious '40s when mobs of hungry potters swept through the district wrecking and looting until the Dragoon Guards had to be called out to scatter them with musket fire. A past in which work on the potbanks was liable to be followed by a train of diseases due to the prevailing use of lead—grim anæmias and toxic poisonings, tuberculosis, cataract, and various kinds of debility. A past longer than that of most industries. There are references to potters and throwers in the local court rolls of the fourteenth century. The local clay, baked by local coal, was the foundation of the Potteries. Less readily traced is the source of the local dialect. A historian of the region has pointed out that it differs from the dialects of the neighbouring counties and from the speech of all the other parts of Staffordshire: "it is a puzzle."

Recalling his personal style, some have conjectured that Arnold Bennett was himself of the old Roman stock, which might give the Brindley rumour new relevance. There was a touch of the conqueror about him, a hint of arrogance that made him unpopular with some of his contemporaries as a youth. As a novelist he could not keep the note of condescension out of his Five Towns books. He seemed to look at his characters from the height of Hanchurch Hill which gives a sweeping dramatic view of the Five Towns from end to end. Nor did he ever relinquish his opinion that the neighbouring Welsh were "an inferior people", a statement to which he would give verbal expression without apparently exerting himself to consider its worth as a theory or its point as a bred-in-the-bone presumption. Its roots may have gone too deeply for that. "The Welsh are about five hundred years behind civilisation," he wrote after seeing the Portmadoc Players in London in 1924.

Bound up with these attitudes, it seems most likely, is the reason why in the Potteries his memory is faintly respected but not cherished except by an admiring few, why one has to tell, not ask, the taxi-drivers where Arnold Bennett was born, why there has been no move to commemorate him in statue form. It was largely one man's perseverance, Sir Francis Joseph's, and not a community's interest, which placed a plaque on Bennett's birthplace. A cynical view has it that things might have been different had he allowed his reputation to be topped off by the knighthood proposed to him at the end of the First World War. His presentation of the Five Towns character as being powerfully materialistic encourages if it does not wholly excuse the presumption that a title would have obtained him a local esteem which his work never did. A statue to him might then have been placed alongside Wedgwood's in the station square at Stoke. Meanwhile, the polite suburb of Porthill has paid its own tribute to his memory by giving some of its new roads names familiar to readers of the novels—Bursley Way, Tellwright Avenue, Denry Crescent, The Cardway, among them.

Not even the widely acclaimed success of *The Old Wives' Tale* bestirred the people of the then newly federated boroughs to pay him the compliment of reading what he wrote. In the journal for August 23, 1912, he entered without comment a statement of *The Staffordshire Sentinel* about the favourite authors of local library users: "Strange to say, Arnold Bennett is placed nineteenth on the list."

In more recent times, at a committee meeting called to discuss business which included a scheme to acquire pictures of well-known Potteries personages for permanent exhibition, the mention of Arnold Bennett's name called forth the question from a member: "Bennett? Which firm did he belong to?"

(2)

"If you want to see the Potteries of Arnold Bennett's novels you'd better hurry; the scene is changing very rapidly." So the readers of *Punch* were told in 1950. It is undeniably a changing scene in some of its aspects, though hardly in the large organic sense there implied. Much that is indigenous and characteristic remains: the smoke flow over the roof lines, diminished though it is by the increasing use of gas ovens in place of coal, the bottle-shaped kilns stuck about like funnels originally designed to carry off the exudations of a malice operating in the nether depths, the gaping earth-wounds cauterised by the fires of long extinct enterprises, the mine-gear rising above the landscape like armatures for sculptural colossi never begun, the tumultuous accretion of the labours of generations of slip makers, jolliers, saggar makers, bottom knockers, mould-runners, thimble pickers, gloss sorters, strippers, and others whose craft names likewise suggest that here exists an order of beings not quite of our context, secretive, eccentric and apart. One is not in the least surprised to hear that a witch is buried in the ghastly churchyard of St. John's, Burslem, or that her coffin was once dug up and turned round to placate the fears of the populace.

While there is a possibility of error in overstating Potteries separateness—industry there was experimenting with progressive schemes like co-partnership and profit-sharing well ahead of some other parts of the country—today, still, there is a suggestion of entirely private activities being conducted under the smoke waves. Component processes of pottery manufacture, detached from the chain of cause and effect, are apt to startle the imagination. You unexpectedly come upon women workers sitting splay-legged in a half-circle in the middle of the floor of a warehouse stacked to the rafters with dishes and plates. The women seem to be intent on smashing the lot. They hammer at them with gleaming chisel-like sorting tools, chipping off the flecks left after the firing in the kilns, and the din they make is loud with atavistic echoes as if this were a group reversion to an uninhibited past. And when the Five Towns hooters and sirens mark the more urgent hours of the working day you will not be the first to think that the fluting and cooing and whistling have a gnomish sound.

Arnold Bennett would recognise, also, the ancillary local trades; the grinding mills, the glaze and colour works, the cask and crate makers' yards. Mining in the district has been concentrated since his day and there is a pit-mound, looking like a pyramid of Egypt, which he may not have known although it towers in the sky behind his old home in the Waterloo Road. He would know the brewery between Regent Street and Pitt Street, and the covered market between Queen Street and the Market Place, its stonework, new when he was a boy, crumbling now from smoke pollution and its mouldings removed as a public danger. The Fountain Works of the famous Enoch Wood are still there, converted to other uses, built in 1789 and imposing in their day, a landmark most familiar to him, with the Wedgwood Institute, all terracotta and mosaics, the Old Town Hall and its 'Golden Angel' weathervane (the city of Stoke-on-Trent now has seven town halls), Swan Bank Methodist Church, almost exactly as he knew it externally, but changed inside, the big house of the Wedgwood family, now the

Midland Bank's Burslem branch, the Shambles or Meat Market, which he said was one of the town's best architectural features, deteriorated into a relic on which steamship companies and British Railways display posters intended to entice the people of the Five Towns temporarily away from the smoke. From the Waterloo Road he would see, today, the old building on its triangular site by Scotia Road that was known as Barracks Bank after the 1840 riots and before then was the poorhouse, forerunner of the 'Bastille' at Chell with its painful memories for Edwin Clayhanger's father, a victim of the brutal Poor Laws of the time. Now the pottery of Alcock, Lyndley & Bloor, its oven chimneys stood out prominently against the sunset sky through Bennett's youth. Indeed, the buildings of Burslem have not changed so much as those of the other Potteries towns. Hanley, the shopping centre of the region, and Stoke, its administrative heart, both have many street frontages that Arnold Bennett never knew. Once the most advanced of the Five Towns, and mother of them all, Burslem has dropped behind the others, holding fast to its essential Georgian and Victorian character.

The Waterloo Road would not confound Arnold Bennett with overwhelming differences: there have been few marked changes since his day, though progress has swept away the horse and steam trams of his boyhood and the electric trams that replaced them. For him it had many intimate associations: his mother lived out her widowhood at 179; his younger brother Septimus the sculptor and modeller who figures as Cyril Povey in *The Old Wives' Tale*, lived at 182 after his marriage; number 81 was the shop and house (with its side door, which Bennett used in preference to the shop door) of Samuel Barlow, the musical plumber who married Bennett's Aunt Sarah. His brother Frank lived at the house on the corner of Hill Street and the Waterloo Road: it is the house of Brindley in *The Death of Simon Fuge*. One of the more imposing houses in Waterloo Road, of the kind that used to be dignified as "a residence", is Bleak Hill House, home of Dr. Russell, who was the Dr. Stirling of the novels, and this was the address also of Fearns, the solicitor, in *Whom God Hath Joined*. At number 181 Waterloo Road there lived for some years Robert Longson, Bennett's grandfather, who had kept the shop of *The Old Wives' Tale*.

Macintyre's Works with the clock tower is another of the older landmarks Bennett knew well. Of the seventy-nine pottery firms listed in the early '80s, when he was running about those streets, no more than twenty survive, and some of them are differently situated and no

ENOCH BENNETT (ARNOLD BENNETT'S FATHER) DURING HIS LAST ILLNESS, WITH SARAH ANN BENNETT, SEATED LEFT, ARNOLD BENNETT AND HIS SISTER TERTIA AT BACK, AND FRANK BENNETT, SEATED RIGHT

FAMILY GROUP IN THE GARDEN AT 205 WATERLOO ROAD, BURSLEM. ARNOLD BENNETT'S MOTHER IS IN THE CENTRE, WITH TERTIA BENNETT AT BACK. ON THE RIGHT IS HIS UNCLE JOHN BENNETT

Photograph: Charles Vote

WATERLOO ROAD, BURSLEM, THE 'TRAFALGAR ROAD' OF THE NOVELS

By permission of Mrs. Wainwright Morgan

THE ONE HUNDREDTH MUSICAL EVENING AT THE MARRIOTTS'. ARNOLD BENNETT IS
FIFTH FROM THE LEFT IN THE GROUP ON THE STAIRS

doubt their names, familiar to him, hide different owners. The Hill Pottery, which appears in *Clayhanger* as the Sytch Pottery, still exists, described to Edwin Clayhanger by Orgreave, the architect, as having the town's best window. Alcock, Brindley, Maddock, Hammersley, Wood, Keeling, Furnival, Massey, Boulton, Eardley, Malkin, Wilshaw, Boote, Wade, Hancock: these are Five Towns names which continue to appear in the local directories, from which Bennett took the names of many if not most of his characters. The name of Leicester, chemist, who was a neighbour of the Bennetts at 203 Waterloo Road, is another that persists from his time and before, and so do Pidduck & Beardmore, ironmongers; Swinnerton, caterers; Cliffs, butcher; Calvert, grocer; Norris, wines and spirits; Savage, printer; Heaton, solicitor; Steele, auctioneer.

He would know Ye Olde French Horn inn in Fountain Square, Hanley, where his father had his office when more prosperous times came; and the Hope Sunday School, "Erected 1835" says the inscription on its front. It is part of the nineteenth-century undergrowth which is still so thick among these streets that our century has as yet made only a limited impression on them.

True, lines of prefabricated dwellings, looking like pathetic improvisations of cardboard, serrate the slope of Hanover Street behind the house where Bennett was born; the effect is to point the grim durability of their surroundings. The 240s of the Waterloo Road have glazed tiles in their porches and leaded panes of stained glass in their lower windows, refinements of the once prosperous terrace-dwellers who had bells instead of knockers and undersized general servants to answer them. Across the way from the Bennett's old home at 205 Waterloo Road is a large new red-brick Army establishment, and there is a television aerial on its high roof, signs of our times that make the Victorian perspective seem still more remote. But in this residue of his era Arnold Bennett could still go poking about and find even now more of the known and familiar than of the new and strange. Time is changing Potteries processes and techniques. It has done little to soften the harsh, incisive impressions of the Five Towns and their people which he bequeathed to us:

> Melancholy, familiar, inexplicable, and piteous—the melancholy of existence itself—rose like a vapour out of the sodden ground, ennobling all the scene. The lofty disc of the Town Hall clock solitary in the sky was somehow so heartrending, and the lives of the

people both within and without the houses seemed to be so woven of futility and sorrow, that the menace of eternity grew intolerable. [1]

(3)

H. G. Wells found "the clay-whitened potbanks and the marvellous effects of its dust and smoke-laden atmosphere very stimulating". He was referring in his autobiography to his first visit to the Potteries, where he stayed with a fellow science student who had a job at Wedgwood's. His inventory of the local scene took in its "blazing ironfoundries, its steaming canals", and he reminded himself that as he went about Burslem during that holiday in the late '80s he may have jostled in the streets another young man, "that friendly rival of my middle years, Arnold Bennett."

In *The New Machiavelli*, published in 1911, Wells had used his recollections of this Potteries visit to point the moral of capitalistic exploitation as part of the argument of the book. As Remington, the hero, he visited a wealthy uncle at Newcastle (Arnold Bennett's Oldcastle) and had "prowled alone, curious and interested, through shabby back streets of mean little homes . . . followed canals, sometimes canals of mysteriously heated waters with ghostly wisps of steam rising against blackened walls or a distant prospect of dustbin-fed vegetable gardens, saw women pouring out from the potbanks, heard the hooters summoning idle toilers to work, lost my way among slag heaps as big as the hills of the south country, dodged trains at manifestly dangerous level crossings, and surveyed across dark intervening spaces, the flaming uproar, the gnome-like activities of the iron-foundries". He heard talk of strikes by desperate men and of the horrors of lead poisoning "that was in those days one of the normal risks of certain sorts of pottery workers". An uncle of Remington's is the typical Potteries master-man. "There are hordes of such men as he throughout all the modern industrial world. . . . Yet it is only in Arnold Bennett's novels that I have ever found a picture of them. These men have raised themselves up from the general mass of untrained, uncultured, poorish people in a hard industrious selfish struggle. To drive others they had first to drive themselves."

The ugliness imprinted itself on the more recent mind of George Orwell: "Right in among the rows of tiny blackened houses, part of

[1] *These Twain.*

the street as it were, are the 'potbanks'—conical brick chimneys like gigantic burgundy bottles buried in the soil and belching their smoke almost in your face. . . . I passed that way in snowy weather and even the snow was black. The best thing one can say for the pottery towns is that they are fairly small and stop abruptly. Less than ten miles away you can stand in undefiled country, on the almost naked hills, and the pottery towns are only a smudge in the distance. It would probably be quite easy to extract a sort of beauty, as Arnold Bennett did, from the blackness of the industrial towns; one can easily imagine Baudelaire, for instance, writing a poem about a slag-heap." [1]

In the journal, September 7, 1910, Bennett wrote: "Yesterday I finished the third or fourth perusal of *A Mummer's Wife*. This book is original and fine and beautiful. . . . You have squalor and sordidness turned into poetry. . . ." George Moore's novel showed him what was to be done with the Potteries as a setting for a tale of human passion and he later agreed that it had disclosed to him possibilities which he had not seen before. He wrote to Moore on December 24, 1920: ". . . and I wish also to tell you that it was the first chapters of *A Mummer's Wife* which opened my eyes to the romantic nature of the district that I had blindly inhabited for over twenty years. You are indeed the father of all my Five Towns books." And he noted in the journal of his last year, on March 10, 1930:

> Jimmy Glover, a fat man, formerly chief musical conductor at Drury Lane and a great theatrical celebrity, introduced himself to me at the Savoy last night, saying that he had given to George Moore, at G.M.'s request, all the details and the chief facts and general scenario for the opening chapter (Potteries) of *A Mummer's Wife*. He said he thought this would interest me. It very much did. I had thought that G.M. had studied the whole matter for himself. Glover said he was the original of Montgomery in the novel.

(4)

Soon he would be leaving Burslem for good, setting out on the great adventure of being himself which is youth's dream and birthright, of escaping from the embarrassments of "the obscure mutual antipathy which separates one generation from the next," of disclaiming a debt he never owed, of living his own life instead of having it lived

[1] *The Road to Wigan Pier.*

for him. With this momentous act of change before him, Arnold Bennett had been preparing to better his chances in the market where bargains are made with destiny as well as with men.

Pitman's shorthand—that was the talisman of the new times that were coming! For him it was more than a professional aid; it was a romantic accomplishment. "It's going to be the great thing of the future!" he made George Cannon say in *Hilda Lessways*. "There never was anything like it! It leads to everything! There's nothing it won't lead to! It's the key of the future. It's a thing that'll revolutionise all business and secretarial work and so on—revolutionise it!" The gospel according to St. Isaac was never expounded more fervently and almost certainly never with more exclamation marks.

The excitement of learning shorthand had to be restrained in Arnold Bennett's case. It was important that his father should not find out. Studying the "mysterious strokes and curves and dots" was an investment which he meant should pay him dividends in London, not in Hanley. The system invented by Isaac Pitman had been making headway as one of the new office techniques, and an increasing number of young men, and with them a few progressive young women, were learning it at evening classes and by correspondence. Apart from improving his chances in the labour market, it may have had an additional attraction for Bennett.

His father had been asked by a small group of local business-men to join them in reviving a paper to challenge *The Staffordshire Sentinel*, then as now the leading organ of Potteries news and opinion. Enoch Bennett acted as the paper's legal adviser and according to *The Truth about an Author* he put up some of the money and had the mortification of losing it. The idea was to take over a moribund journal formerly known as *The Staffordshire Knot & Potteries Examiner*, founded in 1843 as *The Potteries Examiner*, and to give it a new lease of life as *The Staffordshire Knot*.

The prime mover was William Owen, who had started his working life as an apprentice at Doulton's and who had broken away to become founder-editor of a series of local papers. He started a *Daily Mail* some years before the future Northcliffe made that name renowned in daily journalism. Owen was descended from the line of Robert Owen, the pioneering Christian Socialist whose theories swept the country after the Reform Bill of 1832. William Owen deserved, it seems, more good fortune than came his way. Two of his sons were to make names in the journalism of our time, Harold Owen, who also wrote the celebrated melodrama *Mr. Wu*, and Collinson Owen, newspaper special correspondent and author of many books.

Talks about the new paper were carried on at Enoch Bennett's house, where the eldest son could hardly have been unaware of the thrill of the project. Starting a new paper is a gamble, whatever the auspices, and if there are games of chance more impetuously played few are more exhilarating in the expectation of success or in its fulfilment. This was a game fated to be lost. Arnold Bennett was not directly implicated, but he may have caught his enthusiasm for shorthand from it and he wrote something of the spirit of the venture into *Hilda Lessways*: "The *Chronicle* was an organ! It was the courageous rival of the ineffable *Signal*, its natural enemy. One day it would trample on the *Signal*!"

The paper lasted only a few months, long enough, it may well have been, to give him the notion of journalism as a career. More particularly, he gained from the opportunity it gave him of making contact with the mature minds of two men, A. W. Wood, architect, and Joseph Dawson, printer and stationer. Absalom Wood may be seen as the original of Osmond Orgreave, that "fine, joyous, superior, luxurious, companionable man", the architect who put such a spell on young Edwin Clayhanger when he showed him the unregarded merits of the Sytch Pottery from the architectural standpoint and spoke the word 'beautiful' in a way that the boy had never heard it spoken before. He is shown as a man of creative intelligence and in time Arnold Bennett and he reached terms of close friendship.

So did Bennett and Joseph Dawson, whose printing office was in Newcastle Street. Dawson had been sub-editor of the new paper under Owen. The son of a Wesleyan minister, he had gathered to himself an exceptional knowledge of English literature. Members of the Bennett family remembered seeing Arnold in earnest conversation with him in the shop, the centre-piece of which was a showcase of artists' materials which figures in *Clayhanger* as "a cabinet . . . magnificent, complicated and complete, like a monument".

Of Dawson, Bennett later wrote: "He was as young at sixty as I was at forty. I remember once when I made some sarcastic remark to him about Tennyson's *Idylls of the King* tears came into his eyes. 'Don't say such a thing! Don't say such a thing!' he protested. The book had meant so much to him. He was sixty-three then. Fancy a man of sixty-three being so young that he could be moved about a book! I shall never forget this incident, which seemed to me to be very beautiful."

Arnold Bennett's first attempts at professional writing were those of an amateur trying his hand in the local paper. A year or so before leaving for London he was sending occasional notes to *The Staffordshire Sentinel* office. Before that he had attempted serial story writing, perhaps on an impulse derived from Owen, who put a serial story in all his papers, often writing them himself; he was proud of the opening sentence of one of his stories: "And the ship was sinking fast. . . ." Bennett had no luck with his serial ideas, but the editor of the *Sentinel* liked something about the writing of them and in returning a specimen chapter suggested that Bennett should call. Their interview led to his writing notes which, being talked about in the town, gave him his first understanding of the power that resides in the pen of the journalist who treats facts with respect. His first published note was about the North Staffordshire Steam Tramways considered from the opposing local attitudes of convenience and nuisance.

Beneath this immature surface activity the urges of identification were busier still, committing the young E. A. Bennett to a career of self-expression of which paragraph writing was the first feeble intimation. In the depths of his consciousness there were evidently at work the polarising processes which merge dreams into reality, wishes into fulfilment, projecting youth's private world into the realm of the possible and perhaps of the inevitable. On one of his evening strolls in Burslem during his last year there he stopped behind his two or three companions to stand and stare into the fly-blown window of a little shop which sold vegetables and sweets and offered "Well-Aired Beds To Let." The others called to him to come on. He shouted back: "It's all right; you go on," and continued to stare into the window. One by one the others drifted back, curious to share his interest. Challenged, he said gravely: "I'm going to put all this down. I'm going to be a writer."

Zola's disciple, who had lately read that novel of the master's in which big-shop life is described with so much wealth of detail, was practising the concentration, the observation, the selection of the artist whose purpose it is not to embellish life but to see it as truly as he can. And how far Arnold Bennett would be carried by his identifying drives is shown by a number of striking examples of near-plagiarism from Zola to be found in one of his early novels, *The Price of Love*.[1]

There was another set of circumstances that may not have had much

---

[1] Traced by Miss M. Locherbie-Goff in *La Jeunesse d'Arnold Bennett.*

to do with forming his journalistic resolution but which tended to improve his technical facility as a writer. The Bennett family were keen followers of the competitions in the weekly papers in which prizes were given for various kinds of word play. One of the most successful was called 'Missing Words', inaugurated by *Pearson's Weekly*. Readers were given a verse, a phrase, or a limerick with a blank in it for the insertion of the correct missing word, usually represented by a number of synonyms. 'Missing Words' was worked up to so great a pitch of popular interest that there were alarms about national degeneration and finally the competition was banned by law, after proceedings at Bow Street, "bringing indignation and affliction into tens of thousands of respectable homes," according to *These Twain*.

Word competitions were a source of much mental ingenuity among weekly paper readers and the vocabularies of the more industrious were often pedantically extended. It is conceivable that this traffic with remote editorial judgments opened Arnold Bennett's mind to the attractions of journalism further afield. The practice of word-finding probably helped to give him a fluency of thought which he could not hope to reproduce in speech. Indubitably (as he would say) he became a connoisseur of the right word. It was one of his professional distinctions.

(6)

Unknown to his father, who was now senior partner in the firm of Bennett & Baddeley, of Hanley, he had been answering situations-vacant advertisements in a London newspaper and had arranged to take a shorthand clerkship in the offices of a firm of lawyers called Le Brasseur & Oakley, of New Court, Lincoln's Inn Fields. When the time of leaving came, Enoch Bennett went with him to Stoke station to see him into the London train. Bennett senior, angry at first, had subsided into a surprising and perhaps all too prophetic complacence, and he even tried to persuade the rest of the family that he had connived at the change. But it was Arnold Bennett's mother who paid the fare, having told her husband that the boy had saved it out of his office pay, which Enoch Bennett gladly believed.

"The future was his, to use as he liked. Magnificent, consoling thought! . . . If he chose to seek ruin, to abandon himself to the most ignoble impulses, there was none to restrain him," which is Arnold Bennett, in the character of Richard Larch in *A Man from the North*, making youth's primordial gesture of rebelling from without knowing what it is rebelling to. "Some achievement in literature certainly lay in the abyss of my desires," Bennett said in *The Truth about an Author*, "but I allowed it to remain there, vague and unnoticed."

He took with him to London a high-pitched accent which rhymed 'class' with 'gas', a habit of pronouncing either as 'eether', a tendency to drop his 'h's when his feelings were disturbed, and an oddly persistent inattention to the grammatical use of the personal pronoun: "If other people can hit the popular taste, why not me?" (June 5, 1899); "On Sunday Dr. Vallée took Mme and I to Fontainebleau," (March 23, 1904); "The officers of the Union Castle ships dreaded Kipling and prayed not to find themselves on the same ship as him," (February 20, 1909); "After looking myself up in *Chambers' Encyclopedia* I had to look up Galsworthy and was pleased to note that he is given less space than me." (April 19, 1926.) He took with him some of the harshness of the surroundings into which he had been born, the pride, the fortitude, the severity of judgment, which life had stamped into his Five Towns make-up. Also, a conceit of the intellect which was to offend many in the first years of his apprenticeship to letters. It was shared by other members of the family. Some of them have spoken of it as "the curse of the Bennetts", an arrogance of opinion which Arnold Bennett learned to control, though an assertive upward tilt of the head remained to mislead the unknowing.

In his mental luggage for the classic journey there was, too, an unwholesome fear of death, probably exaggerated by, if not directly traceable to, the infant mortality in the family during his most plastic years. It would never leave him, though he would try to rob it of its subjective force in his greatest novels—he would try and would fail, as is seen in *The Old Wives' Tale* where an apparently unconsciously inserted 'I' disfigures the immense context of objectivity with an abruptness that is capable of startling a sensitive reader. The extraordinary lapse occurs in a passage relating to the death of a leading character.

Many years afterwards he recalled in a letter of condolence to Mrs. Beardmore, with whose family the Bennetts had always been on the closest terms of neighbourliness at Burslem: 'When I first left home, in 1889, the Pater was rather shy of saying to me all those things that fathers are supposed to say to their sons in such circumstances, and he got Mr. Beardmore to do it. This is the scene in which I best remember him, standing on the hearthrug at 205 and talking to me while the Pater sat silent in the easy-chair.'

The journey he was making would involve him in the splendours and miseries of high success. It would ultimately sever him from his roots and shrivel his greatest powers as an artist. In his buttoned-up jacket and sagging bow tie, with the slobbery fullness of the mouth and his already tired eyes, he looked a bit oafish as he took his seat in the London train that March morning of 1889. The marks of the football he had kicked around in the outer office during his father's absences remained on the ceiling there for two or three years after he had gone.

CHAPTER FIVE

(1)

NEW COURT, Lincoln's Inn Fields, has changed little since Arnold Bennett arrived in London in his twenty-first year to take up his junior post in the office of Le Brasseur & Oakley. It is a red brick sanctuary just behind the Royal Courts of Justice in the Strand. Bennett called it New Serjeant's Inn in his first novel. He took the scene as he saw it and he took some of his office colleagues for his characters, notably Albert Jenkins, the Cockney junior shorthand clerk "who carried his hat either at the back of his head or tilted almost on the bridge of his nose". The original of Jenkins lives on into our time unreconciled to Bennett's appropriation of him for fiction use: "I don't think he should have done it." For the purposes of gathering information about this part of Bennett's career it was arranged with Jenkins (which is not his name) to be at a rendezvous near New Court. No plan of pre-recognition had been made for this meeting of strangers and, as it proved, none was required. Custom had survived to provide what was necessary, for Jenkins was being faithful to the characteristic by which Arnold Bennett had described him over sixty years before: he was wearing his hat tilted down over his nose.

Some years after the publication of the novel, *A Man from the North*, Bennett and Jenkins met by chance in the Strand. As Jenkins puts it, "there was a bit of a brush." Jenkins had seized the opportunity of "ticking Bennett off". Bennett was taken aback by the encounter and had little to say, being crippled by his speech trouble, as always in a crisis of the emotions. He managed to articulate a denial of Jenkins' charge of plagiarising the personality of an old colleague, but the disclaimer was not found acceptable then or after. Neither a life-time spent in the precincts of the Royal Courts of Justice nor a placatory autographed copy of the novel has persuaded Jenkins of the reality of Edwin Clayhanger's major discovery that "to reconcile oneself to injustice was the master achievement".

The early London experiences of Richard Larch in the novel, which was published by John Lane in 1898, were those of Arnold Bennett and one's assurance of this is confirmed by the fact that there was little that was remarkable about them. The novel was the first evidence of his urge towards self-expression and of his gifts as a conscious artist. Read today, *A Man from the North* is found to have something more than the faded charm of a pressed flower. If it is not technically a model for a first novel in any epoch, it is an example of good behaviour in a young novelist. There is no over-reaching in theme or treatment. It is simple, unaffected, unassertive. Though it has no tensions and though the drama is of the life around him rather than inherent in the central personality, it is beautifully nervous and the first intimations of competence are unmistakably there. The competence was doubtless instinctive, heritage of the race of craftsmen from which he came. Soon in the solicitor's office he was being promoted for his competence as a costs clerk. In the novel Richard Larch is asked: 'Do you feel equal to taking charge of the department?' We are told that he 'answered very decidedly in the affirmative', and that, we can believe, is how Arnold Bennett entered into his enjoyment of four pounds a week. He was twenty-three and paid in brilliant clinking gold.

Le Brasseur & Oakley had much to do with the legal work of the promotion and eastward extension of London's underground railway system. Parliamentary sanctions had to be obtained and between October and February over several years the staff was working long hours, far into the night, preparing business to be tabled at various House of Commons committees. Getting out what was called the book of reference was an indispensable part of the work. It meant house-to-house calls along the route of the proposed new underground section for details of ownership, rights, leases, rents, rates, and a lot of other matters. Everything had to be entered in the book of reference. The legal costs per mile were extremely heavy.

It was Arnold Bennett's job as senior costs clerk to keep and file the daily record of expenditure made by the firm for its clients and to note all other costs incurred. When the clients settled the bills the clerk who drew them normally received a commission of $1\frac{1}{2}$ per cent or, if a bill was particularly complicated, $2\frac{1}{2}$ per cent. After Arnold Bennett had left the firm his successor in the office found that he had drawn up a number of bills which were the business of another clerk and had pocketed the commission on them. It was long remembered against him. Jenkins continues to insist that it was "a nasty bit of work".

There was another matter which caused some hardening of office opinion against Bennett at that time. It was known that he did word competitions in the weeklies and it was understood that the family back in Burslem, who had formed their own syndicate, had more than once been successful in winning some of the smaller prizes of money. For this last reason his fellow clerks were surprised to discover that Bennett contemplated starting legal proceedings against the publishers of one of the more prominent competition journals. Apparently he saw himself profiting in the role of common informer, without whose activities, duly rewarded from the public purse, the police could not start action. The idea got round the office that this was another of Bennett's methods of proving himself as smart as the Londoners. Another possible explanation might have been more to the point. In *These Twain* the competitions are spoken as a "dubious activity". One wonders whether he privately deplored his people's addiction to an activity which identified them with the social and intellectual mediocrity of the neighbours. The Bennetts had moved up out of the *Tit-Bits* and *Pearson's Weekly* common run. If devotion to word competitions represented a longing for insurance against the economic pressures, the preoccupation could not insulate them from a risk which Arnold Bennett, wearing the brown kid gloves of their new estate, might have thought unworthy.

He was not popular at Le Brasseur & Oakley's: "too temperamental for the law and often gloomy; not easy to get on with," according to Jenkins's memory. Thought provincially raw by his seniors, he surprised them with his knowledge of French, though he never spoke it. One of the older clerks, John Eland, was fluent in French idiom, and Bennett and he became companions in excursions to the British Museum reading-room and to Booksellers' Row, otherwise Holywell Street, a bit of old London which vanished with the advent of the Aldwych improvement scheme of the early 1900s. Eland was a collector of books *qua* books, that is, in terms of colophons, registers, watermarks, and *fautes-d'impression*. "He was acquainted, I think, with every second-hand bookstall in the metropolis; and Saturday afternoons we visited most of them," and no doubt helped to build up in Bennett's mind the second-hand bookshop background of what some critics think a Bennett masterpiece, *Riceyman Steps*.

Drawing on Jenkins's memory again, we learn that Bennett had "fits of vegetarianism". More to Bennett's credit, Jenkins considers, was his swimming skill, exhibited during summer lunch hours at the Endell Street Baths, Long Acre. He had been taught to swim by Spencer Till, a clerk in his father's office at Hanley, where he learnt a trick, vulgarly known in the Potteries as a 'gutser', which commanded Jenkins's admiration. It consisted of falling flat on his stomach from a horizontal bar across the baths and presumably it could have been the cause of the undiagnosed stomach trouble from which he suffered through all the later years.

The Truth about an Author says: "The managing clerk of the office, a university man, autocratic, but kindly and sagacious, bought a country practice and left us. He called me into his room to say good-bye. 'You've no business to be here,' he said, sharply. 'You ought to be doing something else. If I find you here when I visit town next, I shall look on you as a d—d fool. Don't forget what I say'."

Bennett could not but be impressed. "A university man" had been impressed by him. "I was scarcely twenty-three. My self-esteem, always vigorous, was flattered into all sorts of new developments. I gradually perceived that, quite without intending it, I had acquired a reputation. As what? Well, as a learned youth not lacking brilliance. And this reputation had, I am convinced, sprung solely from the habit of buying books printed mainly in languages which neither myself nor my acquaintances could read."

All that the law could offer him for some years would be sub-sistence. He now saw that he wanted more than that. He wanted independence, the condition he most envied in others. He had come to London minus the sound foundation of apprenticeship that was the Victorian requirement for every young middle-class man of sense and virtue. But he had a good intelligence and it incited him to poses of a sometimes amusing kind. He said that he never met with disaster and gave this as the prize example of his success as an intellectual bam-boozler: "I remember feeling very shy one night in a drawing-room rather new to me. My host had just returned from Venice, and was describing the palace where Browning lived; but he could not remember the name of it. 'Rezzonico,' I said at once, and I chanced to intercept the look of astonishment that passed between host and hostess. I frequented that drawing-room a great deal afterwards, and was always expected to speak *ex cathedra* on English literature." It encourages the opinion that when he permitted Hales, M.P., to take inspirational credit for *The Card* he was being not simply co-operative but self-effacing.

As for London, he said that "as an entity" it was as good as his dreams of it had been, but he could form no high opinion of the people who reckoned themselves Londoners. "I was humble enough when I arrived, but they soon cured me of that—they were so ready to be impressed!" All those Londoners who were successfully performing the feat of 'getting on', he found, were provincials like himself. "I enrolled myself in their ranks. I said that I too would get on. The d—d fool phrase of the Chancery clerk rang in my ears like a bugle to march," and a remote but not wholly insignificant sequel is to be found in a London Library volume of theatre and literary reminiscences by a well-known contemporary in which, against each of the several admiring references to Bennett's personality and fame, is scrawled in the capital letters of an immense exasperation: VULGAR PROVINCIAL HOBBLEDEHOY.

Arnold Bennett to E. H. Beardmore:

> 46, Alexandra Road
> Hornsey, N.
>
> 4th September, '90.
>
> MY DEAR EDWARD,—I am writing to congratulate you on having reached the mature age of 21. . . . I find I have no particular suggestion to offer or advice to give, except this. A man in your position, with good settled prospects, and no cares worth a button, can only sail on one course, namely, the matrimonial. I maintain it is your imperative duty to get married, and I would suggest Miss Jones, who lives near you. £40,000 in her own right, my boy! Think of it. Another forty from her father! Ready and willing to consider any offer! Your father suggested her to me, but, as usual, I am willing to sacrifice myself. I make no charge whatever for imparting this magnificent idea to you.
>
> Yours,
> E. A. BENNETT

(2)

Tit-Bits, still thriving prototype of popular weekly periodicals, published a serial story called *What's Bred in the Bone* by Grant Allen, and offered twenty guineas for the best parody of it to be received after the last instalment had appeared. Arnold Bennett, taking pen in hand for his first attempt at producing something for the London literary market, settled down to six evenings' writing and re-writing, and won the twenty guineas. "My friends were delighted, but they declined to admit a particle of surprise." His friends were the Marriotts of 6 Victoria Grove (now Netherton Grove), Chelsea. Frederick

Marriott was art master at Goldsmiths' College, London. Bennett had first met him in the home of Joseph Hill, principal of the Blackheath School of Arts and Crafts, a Burslem man who had known Bennett's people.

Frederick Marriott wrote of Bennett in some unpublished notes: "He was about twenty-three but appeared to be younger, partly, I think, on account of his lavender-coloured voice and boyish high-pitched laugh." Marriott invited him to spend an evening at his studio and with that there began a friendship of forty years. It was given further impetus by the circumstances of Marriott's position as a householder. He had a £400 mortgage on 6 Victoria Grove and a thoroughly old-fashioned distaste for debt. When on another visit Bennett mentioned that he hoped to change his lodgings in Raphael Street, Knightsbridge, Marriott proposed that he should join his family as a paying guest. Frederick Marriott says in his notes that the term 'paying guest' had only lately been invented. It made it possible for people of the professional class to augment their incomes by letting rooms without risking their self-respect; and Arnold Bennett became a contributor to the Marriott mortgage redemption fund.

Hill's introduction of Bennett to Marriott was a consequential act, switching Bennett's future through to the main line of his development. He was at once stimulated and excited by the change. "My new intimates were not only keenly appreciative of beauty, they were bent on creating it. They dreamed of great art-works, lovely compositions, impassioned song. Music and painting they were familiar with, and from me they were serenely sure of literature. The glorious accent with which they clothed that word—literature!" When he won the *Tit-Bits* prize the Marriotts and their friends, perhaps to reassure themselves too, insisted that "caricature was a perfectly legitimate form of art, often leading to much original beauty". His father, receiving word of his success, begrudgingly remarked that it was "better than a jab in the eye with a burnt stick", a Cyclopean alternative which he was given to quoting on these occasions.

Arnold Bennett arrived at the Marriotts' in a four-wheeler loaded to the roof with books in the spring of 1891. The sight of the books, neatly bundled with string, troubled the Marriotts because they had no shelf room. He also brought along his own mantelpiece clock. On a panel under the dial was inscribed: DO IT NOW.

Chelsea enlivened his imagination and, judging by the dreams which he attributes to the hero of the fourth Clayhanger novel, who also lived in Chelsea, "legends of vanished resorts of pleasure and vice stirred his longings and his sense of romantic beauty". Raphael Street, Knightsbridge, had something to commend it but nothing so thrilling as this, and 46 Alexandra Road, Hornsey, London, N., the first of his London addresses, was but an outpost of the Puritan intolerance he had known at home, for his landlady objected to his utterance of the word 'theatre' in her hearing.

Soon after settling in at 6 Victoria Grove, he asked and was given the Marriotts' permission to conduct from that address a postal business in second-hand books which he had started in his Hornsey lodgings. He issued two catalogues from Chelsea, entitling them "Books for Bibliophiles", with items mostly priced at under ten shillings. One of his customers was the Right Honourable Augustine Birrell, sometime Secretary for Ireland and a notable essayist, who forgot to pay for his purchase until reminded of it by Bennett at a public banquet many years after.

Marriott, showing young Bennett round Chelsea, lighted up his mind with intriguing recollections of his own as a young man from the Potteries. He had seen Carlyle. He had seen Tennyson, "wearing a great black sombrero and carrying a churchwarden pipe." He had known a painter who had met Turner. "Turner told him he hadn't missed seeing a sunrise for thirty years." It was the custom of leading artists of the '90s to open their studios to the public on Sundays. Visitors were allowed to see not only finished pictures but work still on the easel. Marriott took Bennett into the studios of G. F. Watts and Burne-Jones. Coming away from one of these visits, Bennett stood on the pavement making notes on the flap of an envelope. Looking back on that moment years afterwards, Marriott took pleasure in claiming to have been present at the inception of a famous journal.

The London that he found so romantic was being electrically lighted and people were walking out in the summer dusk to look at the strings of new lamps that gave enchantment to the streets. In winter, boys with naphtha flares were still offering their services as guides through the fog. The talk was about Charles Stewart Parnell. The newspapers were printing details of company flotations covering what then seemed a bewildering range of new enterprises, a reflection of the accelerating industrial and commercial pace and implying immense untapped reserves of investing money. Bennett saw a woman cyclist stoned in the street. The antipathetic twins, capital and labour, were on the brink of imposing trials of strength. There was a growing fear

Photograph: Charles Vote

ST. JOHN'S SQUARE, BURSLEM. THE BAINES' SHOP OF "THE OLD WIVES' TALE" IS AT
THE RIGHT OF THE PICTURE

6 NETHERTON (FORMERLY VICTORIA) GROVE, CHELSEA

at the governing centre of the potential menace of Labour organised, of undisclosed union developments, of the power of the strike weapon confidently brandished. Society was feeling the first shivers of a nervousness that would roll in wave after wave over succeeding generations until today it divides the world.

(3)

Frederick Marriott was an important influence in Bennett's life through the opportunities he was able to provide for Bennett to enlarge his circle of friendship and acquaintance with the many-sided people who were constantly at the house. If it did not put the final polish on Bennett's corrugated personality it undoubtedly softened the edges of his provincialism by bringing before him a variety of human patterns on which a young man might model his manners and tastes. There were painters, musicians, civil servants, journalists, representatives of an intellectual society quite new to him. The occasions that brought them most often together were the Marriotts' musical evenings, which had started with a group of fewer than half a dozen friends meeting occasionally for music and discussion and had expanded into regular events attended by thirty or forty people.

They had been casual affairs until Bennett arrived. It was not long before he took charge of the arrangements and planned the programmes: two hours' serious music, refreshments, then some light-hearted entertainment. He caused the programmes to be printed. He insisted that evening dress should be worn. Soon the Marriott musical evenings began to be talked about. When Frederick Marriott went up to Burslem for Christmas with the Bennett family he found that Arnold Bennett imposed a similar routine on the festivities there. "You could hardly pull a cracker without first receiving a signal from Arnold."

Bennett's mother had given him some piano lessons when he was fourteen but he had never learned to play. Now, driven on by the desire to justify himself to the talented people around him, he resumed his piano study to such purpose that in a few months he was filling the morning air with Chopin and being regarded with new respect by his Chelsea friends. He almost certainly had the help of a well-known musician and brilliant pianist, Herbert Sharpe, who later became a professor at the Royal College of Music. *Anna of the Five Towns* is dedicated to him "with affection and admiration, as an artist whose individuality and achievement have continually inspired me". Granted that Herbert Sharpe assisted Bennett's musical education, it would have been interesting to know his opinion of the hysterical homage to music in *Sacred and Profane Love,* in which novel a revolving piano-stool is made to appear the indispensable item of a domestic interior lush with green rep, valances, fringes, tassels and lustres. Mrs. Herbert Sharpe is credited with having had a hand in Bennett's cultural development. She spoke French and showed the utmost in patience in encouraging him to talk to her in that language and in correcting his errors of pronunciation. He never became much good at conversational French but it was Mrs. Sharpe who gave him the confidence to attempt it in a drawing-room.

(4)

The faded four-page programme of the hundredth musical evening at 6 Victoria Grove commemorates an occasion dated April 20, 1901. It preserves the names of sixty invited guests, names among which Arnold Bennett's reached the greatest prominence but all of which have equal rank as those of the celebrants of a charming if sometimes over-earnest embellishment of the civilised life. We can picture the tinted coffee cups rising and falling on the tides of talk in the interval and imagine amusing scruples about the pose of the little finger in manipulating them. The music was the music of Liszt, Bach, Beethoven, Berlioz, Gluck, Saint-Saëns and Tschaikowski. Stanley Hazell, a popular member of the circle, sang his skittish song *In a Putney Garden,* parodying a Chelsea evening. There was more laughter when the studio was darkened for an illustrated humorous lecture entitled *Lantern Medley on One Sharpe.* Marriott told one of his customary parson stories in a voice suitably distorted for the purpose. Dr. John Farrar of Putney proposed someone's health. E. A. Bennett sang his 'Cider Song', remembered from schooldays and for which he provided his own vamping accompaniment on the piano. No one there would have believed that a day was to come when he would have the opportunity or the nerve to sing it from the stage of a London theatre, as he did in 1929. Miss Marriott, the host's sister, recited *The Armada* by Lord Macaulay, and Arnold Bennett's time phobia might be eased by the knowledge that Miss Marriott would be reciting and singing in the 1950s, and that the Turkish lantern which shed its soft diffused glow on them that evening of long ago still hangs in the studio. The programme, opened by Herbert Sharpe playing 'Caprice on Ballet Airs from *Alceste*', was rounded off by "General Entertainment by the Entire Company".

It was a wonderful evening, the best of all the Marriott evenings; everyone said so, the departing guests exchanging loud appreciative sentiments as the echoes of their footsteps trailed away into the night under which a spring of the new century was flushing its lamp-lit green.

CHAPTER SIX

(1)

ACKNOWLEDGING the cheque from *Tit-Bits*, Arnold Bennett took the opportunity of asking whether he could send in some articles. The answer was yes and in a few weeks he received a postal order for ten shillings for a short piece entitled 'How a Case is Prepared for Trial'. Next, "Mr. E. A. Bennett, 6 Victoria Grove, Chelsea," was announced in the same paper as the winner of a guinea for the week's prize short story. Writers who had six short stories printed in *Tit-Bits* were awarded a medallion specially struck for editorial presentation to favoured contributors. It was a distinction which Arnold Bennett did not earn and may not have coveted. The story by him which was published was tailored for the trade, down to the familiar old *rat-tat* cliché for the postman's knock. It showed deft appreciation of the importance of money and luxury as fiction ingredients appealing to readers not intimately acquainted with either. A certain facility is obvious and the story reads like the work of an amateur who has professionalism in view. He pretended to be more pleased with the guinea than with the story that had earned it, "despicably bad, a commercial product," and it ended his connection with the paper until his ascending fame presently inspired the editor to tell a new generation of readers that Arnold Bennett, "the famous playwright and novelist," had been one of his contributors.

Counselling the would-be writer in *How to Become an Author*, Bennett wrote: "He must not, if he happen to have a refined literary taste, despise the popular weekly. In nine cases out of ten, he may take it for granted that if he cannot please this class of paper he can please no other class." Practice at the *Tit-Bits* level was an apprenticeship served by many a proficient journalist, if only by one major novelist, Bennett himself. There was for him a residual satisfaction: "I wrote everything with a nice regard for English; I would lavish a night on a few paragraphs; and years of this penal servitude left me with a dexterity in the handling of sentences that still surprises the possessor of it." For the Methodists among whom he was brought up

[84]

it was in craftsmanship and not in the arts that men gave proof of their divinity.

Writing for a popular weekly was good practice in concise expression, for which his legal employment had already prepared him. It did not provide either the incentive or the scope for the better work he wished to do, and only by doing it could he hope to reach the higher flights of writing success and win the satisfactions and rewards which had made the lives of Balzac and Zola seem to him enviable above all others. The unconscious artist has to do things; the conscious artist wants to do them: he uses his medium, the other is used by it. Arnold Bennett had written to his friend Sturt of Farnham in 1894:

> In order that a man can sit down deliberately to be artistic, and be damned to every other consideration, he must have some inward assurance that there is a brilliant or at least a pleasant conclusion to the dark tunnel which he is entering. . . . I have no inward assurance that I could ever do anything more than mediocre, viewed strictly as art—very mediocre. On the other hand, I have a clear idea that by cultivating that 'lightness of touch' to which you refer and exercising it upon the topicalities of the hour, I could turn out things that could be read with zest . . . I would sooner succeed as a caricaturist of passing follies than fail as a producer of 'documents humains'. And you know if it came to an alternative between a semi-luxurious competence and fidelity to Art, Art would have my undiminished affection—and my back.

(2)

Just before he left the law for journalism he wrote a short story called *A Letter Home* which appeared under his full name of Enoch Arnold Bennett in *The Yellow Book*, where it received critical attention, the first of his writings to do so. It showed him writing at a higher level of proficiency and showed also that his French reading was beginning to influence his style. A good many better known writers would have been glad to see their work in *The Yellow Book*, which Holbrook Jackson tells us in *The Eighteen Nineties* was "newness *in excelsis*: novelty naked and unashamed. People were puzzled and shocked and delighted, and yellow became the colour of the hour, the symbol of the time-spirit. It was associated with all that was *bizarre* and queer in art and life, with all that was outrageously modern". According to Bennett, his story was singled out for praise by "several fiercely literary papers".

To have gained the applause of his talented Chelsea friends was an important satisfaction. To have merited the consideration of less impulsive and impassioned judges was even more exciting. He saw that he could *write*, he said, and the italics are his. "By heaven! I will write a novel!" Sturt, his candid friend for thirty years, wrote to him: "On me not the least pleasing result of your *Yellow Book* story is the chance it gives of saying pleasant things for a change. For it *is* distinctly pleasant, after doggedly slating a man, to be able at last to say honestly, Bravo!"

Among the other names in *The Yellow Book* index for that quarter, July, 1895, were Kenneth Grahame, Henry James, Edmund Gosse, Walter Sickert, and Laurence Housman. Bennett was twenty-eight. He had not yet assumed the role of the wilful extravert of *The Truth about an Author*. His essential diffidence, which he presently made an elaborate show of discarding, appears in the long letter he wrote to Sturt on November 11, 1895:

I find a novel the damnedest nerve-shattering experience as ever was. Nothing but my strong aversion to being beaten by anything on God's earth that I set myself to whip, prevents me from throwing up the present one. And this, mind you, in spite of the facts that I have all my material in hand, and that I am not short of inspiration—as I believe they call it! It is the *arrangement* that kills one, the mere arrangement of 'sensation and event' which—in a manner o' speaking—one knows by heart. Conversations are the very devil to me—at present I eschew them all I can, and when I can't avoid jaw, keep it short and *très select*. This is *à la* de Maupassant, who could, however, do conversations *à merveille*, when he felt that way. I have developed so strangely these last three years—my first attempt at fiction was made exactly two and a half years ago—that I don't know what may happen in the future, but at present I do 'sensations' best, leaving events alone.

With regard to the impression abroad that pages undiversified by dialogue are apt to be dull, I am persuaded that dullness, apparent dullness, can be done away with by a judicious arrangement of paragraphs. The effect of a separate line of four or five words in the middle of two longish paragraphs must be seen to be believed. The

French know this—they taught it to me. Probably you are aware of it, but unless you have consciously meditated upon it, I venture to think that you have not grasped (excuse my cheek) the tremendous effect, even on an educated and trained reader, of paragraph arrangement.

Of course a determined attempt to write for the eye (the eye which reads a whole page in a flash, as it were—am I clear?) influences materially the details of style which are meant to appeal to the intellect only. If you have a long paragraph, you can't offhandedly cut it in two, or shove a short line into the middle of it. You must deliberately, from the beginning of the par, work up to the short line, or the short par. (If, as is probable, you have thought out all this for yourself kindly excuse my exuberance, but I am interested in the little matter.)

In my new volume of the Edinburgh Stevenson, there is a luminous essay, reprinted for the first time from a *Fortnightly Review* of 1881, on 'Some technical elements of style in literature'. You must read it when you come up; it is profoundly interesting to a craftsman. He deals chiefly with the sweet uses of alliteration—subtle, concealed alliteration, of course—and he damn' well knows what he is talking about. The essential 'stylistic' (his word) differences between prose and verse are also finely set out. I read the thing last night in bed—after an evening at Chapman's—and was made to think thereby.

Curious. My style has altered (improved, I trust) so much during the progress of this bally novel, that one reason for writing the whole thing again is the difference between the earlier and later portions. I feel more sure than ever I did in my life before, that I *can* write in time, and 'make people care' too, as Hy. James says—though perhaps only a few people. Still, to have made fellow artists care—that is the thing! That is what will give ultimate peace of mind. Do you ever suddenly stand still and ponder: 'Suppose, after all, I am an artist, rather a fine one! But it can't be true. What am *I* that *I* should be an artist? Every dabbler thinks he is—till he learns better. And yet, and yet. . . .'

I have never been in love (wish to God I had, when I am struggling with a love scene!) but I imagine that the joy of the artist when he first *knows* that he is an artist, is similar to the joy of the lover when he first knows that he is in love and loved; and the thought of both, after the first scepticism has gone, is: 'What the hades have I done to deserve this ineffable happiness?'

I have boasted to at least one person (another of my indiscretions) that I know I am an artist. I know no such thing. When I have read my first novel in print, I think I shall know.

Yes, I am well aware that this farrago, coming from a youthful person who has nothing to show, nothing done, is absurdly self-conscious and egotistic. But my dear villager, one writes to please oneself, after all, not to please the correspondent addressed. Is not this a great truth?

A propos des bottes, have you got Roget's 'Thesaurus of English Words and Phrases'? It is the most wonderful machine for getting at words that you know but can't think of at the moment, that I have encountered. Even when you have only an adumbrated notion of the idea itself, this precious volume will help you to define it, and end up by giving you the word to describe the idea it has itself defined. I bought it about a year ago, and wonder now how I ever did without it. If I had to choose between Shakspere and Roget, I would let Billy go, upon my word. . . .

I must return to technics: I believe in short chapters, 2000 to 3000 words, and in making, as a rule, each chapter a complete scene, and detached—of course there are exceptions. I learnt this from the brothers de Goncourt. I must get you to read their 'Renée Mauperin'. To study the principles of its construction is both 'entertaining and instructive'.

My favourite masters and models: (1) Turgenev, a royal first (you must read 'On the Eve'—*flawless*, I tell you. Bring back such books of mine as you have; I have others you must read); (2) de Maupassant; (3) de Goncourts; (4) George Moore—the great author who can neither write nor spell!

Stevenson only helps me in minute details of style.

Excuse prolixity,

Yours ever,

ARNOLD BENNETT.

(3)

Prominent among the Chelsea personalities was Edwin Alfred Rickards, a young architect of high talent whom some thought touched with genius. A member of the Marriott circle, he was to share an acknowledgment from Bennett of being one of "the two most interesting, provocative, and stimulating men I have yet encountered", the other being H. G. Wells. They had met at one of the 'evenings' and their reaction to each other had been as smooth and as natural as a chemical conflux. It was made a bond for life, with subsequent adjustments, when they took a bus ride together and Bennett showed interest in some Georgian houses in the Brompton Road and, receiving Rickards's approval of his taste, reaffirmed his old regret that he had not 'gone in for' architecture as a career. Their social background was the same, their instincts about equally predatory. A draper's shop had been among the early scenes of Rickards's life, with the slight variation that he had served behind the counter and Bennett had not. Professor Sir Charles Reilly, the Liverpool architect, recalled Rickards as "a Cockney Kipps", a description which Rickards's innumerable self-caricatures tend to confirm. He had started as an office boy, "and then," says Reilly in his book, "by endless sketching and measuring in South Kensington Museum, he made himself not only one of the most effective and speedy draughtsmen of the day but a master of baroque detail such as this country had not before possessed. . . . The very spirit of the man was baroque in his zest for life, his vivid conversation, in his love of opera and the ballet, in his flamboyant worship of the opposite sex, but his poor little body, which was to succumb to the results of exposure in the war, was the reverse." [1]

From the same source comes testimony to the graphic expression which always impressed those who met Rickards professionally. "No one, not even Lutyens, could combine dignity and gaiety, richness and vividness, could in short put so much genuine emotion into a building as this Kipps-like creature we all learned to love." Reilly recalled "watching the ornament flow in a happy stream from the end of his BB pencil as he drew a half-inch detail for a part of the design for the Wesleyan Central Hall at Westminster. I watched great trophies of women and armour form themselves over the windows with amazement". Doubt interrupted Rickards's inspiration. He wondered aloud what a possibly censorious committee might have to say about the kind of ornamentation he was drawing. "They won't like to ask about the women," he said to Reilly, "but they're sure to ask about the shields and swords and helmets." Reilly suggested: " 'The complete armour of God.' " 'Right, man!' exclaimed Rickards, his pencil racing on again. 'What a thing it is to have been to Cambridge!' "

When he died in 1920 Rickards left substantial memorials of his creative exuberance: his share in the designing of the Central Hall,

[1] *Scaffolding in the Sky* by C. H. Reilly (Routledge, 1938).

Westminster, the Cardiff City Hall and Law Courts, Deptford Town Hall, the Third Church of Christ Scientist in Mayfair, among them. He was a gifted caricaturist whom Bennett thought might have become "one of the most famous caricaturists if not the supreme caricaturist of the age". His restless talent expressed itself incessantly on table-cloths, menu cards, backs of envelopes, and the total effect of looking through the hundreds of specimens of his talent that remain is of a vanished excellence. Some of his drawings for Arnold Bennett's book called *Paris Nights* show distinguished accomplishment, and his water-colour illustrations for Bennett's yachting diary of 1912–14, *The Log of the 'Velsa'*, can still please the eye with the light of distant days.

According to Bennett, Rickards had an enthusiasm for life such as he had seldom known in any person and he has left us with a mental silhouette of Rickards quixotically surveying the universe: "Riding a horse, any old horse, over a Bedfordshire common, with nothing in view but the sky and the common and the horse's ears, he could savour life with as much keenness, validity, and fairness, as amid the marvels of any continental city."

He would compare the quality of Rickards's conversation, he said, with that of Stendhal. Yet he reported Rickards's talk on their travels together as if the man was a neurasthenic egotist, whose thought grooves were tediously well worn on the sex theme. They went to Holland and the Baltic coast in Bennett's yacht, and Bennett was at pains to write down his friend's not invariably captivating remarks about the women. They had hardly tied up in the port of Copenhagen before Rickards was calling out joyfully: "This is a most exciting city— already I've seen lots of beautiful girls, some with tow-coloured hair!" Ashore, he was struck dumb by the appearance of a group of girls seen in an art gallery and by the interest they were showing "in the art of their own country". Approaching them hopefully, he found that they were English. At Aarhus he was "intensely disappointed by the women". In Amsterdam he at once decided that he would like to marry a Dutch girl. "They have such nice blue eyes and are so quiet." Pursuing the familiar topic, Bennett said: "With your description of the ugliness and unsexedness of the women there you've put me right off Munich." Rickards's reply made him laugh: "Well, they're all beautiful in Vienna and that can worry you just as much in another way."

Bennett said that Rickards savoured life rather than enjoyed it. He was often at the mercy of despondencies in which his morbid sensitivity would erect a mountain of grievance out of a molehill of misunderstanding. He told Bennett: "I wake up in the night and hear a door crack and I shake with fear." "What of?" Bennett asked. "I don't know. Well, the mere fact of being alive, for one thing." Descending the steps of "the architecturally treated precipice behind Helsingborg", Rickards remarked: "I shall fall down stairs some day . . . my glasses, you know. I shall make a wrong step and over I shall go. And that will be the end of me—if I'm lucky."

His partner for nearly thirty years, Dr. H. V. Lanchester, says a little caustically: "He was quite a personality in the pseudo-Bohemian circles of London in the early years of the century, a fluent talker who spared neither himself nor his friends in his conversation—a mixture of naïveté and satire." Dr. Lanchester thinks that Bennett's artistic development owed more to Rickards than to any other man. He does not tell us what strains and stresses he himself had to bear in his collaboration with a disposition quicksilvery in its responses, unreliable in its moods. Arnold Bennett sometimes found them too much and he noted in the journal that he had had to address stern remarks to Rickards on the deterioration of his manners.

The building of the Central Hall was a notable event in Rickards's professional life. Writing in the journal in 1909 after Rickards had shown him over the unfinished building, Bennett said: "He is now gradually getting hold of me again as a great artist." Bennett was writing *Clayhanger* and as the conscious artist he needed the incentive as well as the inspiration of great achievements to produce the "large, arresting and decisive" results he was aiming at. His visit to the unfinished but already imposing building sent his aspirations soaring. There is a clue to what it may have meant to him in the notes he made after an earlier visit with Rickards to the unfinished Roman Catholic Cathedral in Westminster, ". . . a work of great and monumental art. Bentley, the architect, was wandering under the dome, examining and enjoying his mighty production." The visit was lifted out of Bennett's journal and put into his novel, *The Roll Call*, in which Rickards as a young man appears as George Cannon, the architect:

On the highest floor, at the other extremity of the cathedral, in front of the apse, a figure had appeared in a frockcoat and a silk hat. The figure stood solitary, gazing around in the dying light.

'By Jove!' It's Bentley! It's the architect!'

George literally trembled. He literally gave a sob. The vision of

Bentley within his masterpiece . . . was too much for him. Renewed ambition rushed through him in electric currents. What completed the unbearable grandeur of the scene was that Bentley had cancer of the tongue.

He did not write in that high-pitched key when noting what he had seen of the building of the Central Hall. True, it is of another order of architecture, not so assertively disposed in the London sky. Built on the site of the old Royal Aquarium, a resort of the '70s, the Central Hall was designed by the firm of Lanchester & Rickards as the headquarters of the denomination from which Arnold Bennett had long since withdrawn his allegiance and to which it has been thought that he was often less than just in what he wrote about it, forgetting or ignoring the fact that it had assisted his secular as well as religious education. His impressions of the incomplete Central Hall do not suggest that he was moved by a vision of its fulfilment, of what it would mean to the staunch and vigorous community which it represents in Christendom. His notes were written rather as if the intimations he received of structural ideas being converted into timeless form were of no more than visual interest to him, as if they had not challenged his sympathies. It was to the great Byzantine cathedral to the south-west that he would turn when in later years his fatigue-ravaged powers cried out for renewal and refreshment.

Recently in a box of Rickards's sketches in Dr. Lanchester's possession there has been found part of a letter from Arnold Bennett apparently written by him to Rickards soon after the publication of *Clayhanger*: it is undated and may have survived only because under Bennett's gracefully inscribed initials Rickards had sketched an amusing profile of his Chelsea Arts Club crony and collaborator, Henry Poole, R.A.

. . . it is a pity that, having criticised it, you can't now read it. I mean for your sake. Because you make your first appearance in the last part of it, as an infant, and you may recognise one or two things. You will appear in the following two novels of the 'trilogy' (as the publishers and critics love to call it) and then you will be the hero of the fourth book, about London. You can't possibly understand yourself unless you begin at the beginning.

Summing up his friendship with Rickards, whose precariously

poised temperament sometimes unsettled it, Arnold Bennett said in a written address spoken for him at a dinner celebrating the success of the firm of Lanchester & Rickards in the Cardiff competition: "I used to say that Rickards the man had influenced my view of life more than any other person I have ever met. In my sublime simplicity I thought I was paying Rickards a compliment. Then one night, while I was lying awake thinking about the boy, it occurred to me like a clap of thunder that such a statement might not raise Rickards in the esteem of many eminently respectable people. So I decided not to repeat it any more. Nevertheless, it's true."

(4)

The artists and musicians and journalists around him were engrossed in their careers, having careers to be engrossed in. He had as yet no career, only a wish to shine as they shone. Dr. Farrar, the Putney general practitioner, after giving Bennett a physical overhaul, administered a mental tonic that had the summary effect of stimulating his patient's self-esteem and probably aggravating temporarily the sleeplessness which was one of the subjects of their consultation. The doctor had said, sitting back with his stethoscope round his neck and his finger-tips together: "You know, you're one of the most highly-strung men I've ever met."

Arnold Bennett makes much of this in *The Truth about an Author*. "I thought better of myself . . . I perceived that I must begin life again," and when some of his Chelsea friends accused him of being as temperamental as they were themselves it produced in him "a state of ferment". Despite the facetiousness, it is the stuff of autobiography, this revelation that was vouchsafed to him in Putney and set him on the road to Parnassus. The doctor's pronouncement identified him gratifyingly with his new environment, stamping him as being of the same fine grain and temper as his friends of the Marriott circle, encouraging him to assert himself as equally sensitive and gifted; in short, an artist. "On a certain memorable day I saw tears in the eyes of a woman as she read some verses which, with journalistic versatility, I had written to the order of a musical composer. I walked straight out into the street, my heart beating like a horrid metronome. Am I an artist? I demanded; and the egotist replied: Can you doubt it?"

The cliché of the consulting-room marked an abrupt decisive change in his attitude to himself. It had the dynamic effect of convincing him

[93]

that he too was of the elect, that he could walk the pavements of Chelsea with the proud step of those whose eyes are on the stars. The sombre work-for-the-night-is-coming compulsion of his Methodist upbringing gave him assurance of the economic salvation rewarding tasks well done and of avoiding the fate of those victims of London who, according to the rhetorical flourish with which he closed Chapter One of his first novel, "lacking boldness and resolution, are trampled underfoot and do not often rise again."

CHAPTER SEVEN

(1)

IN his fourth year as a London clerk Arnold Bennett went back to Burslem for part of his summer holiday. Some of the neighbours in the Waterloo Road did not immediately recognise this young fellow with the downy moustache as Enoch Bennett's awkward eldest boy. Spruce and confident, he was talking and carrying himself as if he had made his dispositions for the future and had no doubt about the ultimate success of his strategy in doing so. Assertively emphasising the ancient interaction of industry and art in the Potteries, he was identifying himself as a kindred spirit of the artists whose genius for design and decoration had contributed to the fame of the local wares in the markets of the world. He showed a surprising knowledge of music and was authoritatively inquisitive about the Hanley Festival, a recent visit to the town by Madam Clara Butt, 'the human cello', and the performances of the North Staffordshire Festival Choir.

Even his father was impressed. That was the practical object of the visit. Their old tensions had been relaxed by Enoch Bennett's acceptance of the inevitable, as by his son's manifest self-development. Another smoothing circumstance was that Frank, the second boy, had taken up his law studies and was expected to step into Arnold's place in the office at Hanley, as in time he did, with results that his brother was to note forty years after: "Most of Frank's troubles—and they have been severe—come from the Pater's forcing him into a profession for which he felt and expressed a marked distaste."

Arnold had seen an advertisement in a London newspaper for an assistant editor of a weekly journal. He had found out that the journal was named *Woman* and that whoever was appointed would have to produce £300 for shares in addition to journalistic qualifications. It was about the £300 that Bennett had travelled to Burslem to see his father. The matter was talked over for three days before "the old man" gave his decision in favour of the scheme. On the strength of it Arnold Bennett handed in his notice at Le Brasseur & Oakley's. When the partner who handled staff matters asked the reason, Bennett replied: "I'm going on a paper." Recalling that moment of his life, he said: "My pride must have been disgusting. This was the last time I ever said 'sir' to any man under the rank of knight." Did he remember that Balzac had known a moment like it? He too had summarily renounced the law for literature.

Woman was a penny paper bidding for the support of the intelligent part of the growing circulation potential of women readers. Its Number One, out January 3, 1890, announced: "Our *raison d'être* is neither politics, dress, the doings of the 'society' of reality or imagination, the ventilation of imaginary grievances of the sex, the school of sickly sentimentality nor the advertisement of vice and the vicious, but simply to inform and entertain modern woman—not as she might be, but as we find her." Ships have been launched without champagne: few new journals have been started without a good dose of editorial unction, a custom with an old if hypocritical pedigree. *Woman* had a motto on its front cover: "Forward! But not too fast," an incitement to lively comment in the clubs and bars of the town.

There was a "Woman" Publishing Company with offices at various times at 90, Shaftesbury Avenue; Cecil Court, St. Martin's Lane; Fetter Lane, Fleet Street; of but the company itself the Registrar of Companies reports 'no trace', possibly a comment on the less strict company laws of the period, though the name is given in Kelly's directories. The managing editor and part proprietor was Fitzroy Gardner, sometime manager for Sir Herbert Beerbohm Tree during his Haymarket Theatre régime and later with Pélissier of "The Follies".

Gardner was the son of a London surgeon. On leaving Rugby, he became a clerk in the Old Court of Exchequer when the law courts were at Westminster as part of the Parliament buildings. At the age of thirty-three he was retired on pension, which became a subject of inquiry in the House of Commons. He claimed the credit, all of it, for first bringing forward the idea of the office of Public Trustee. He cherished his remembrance of being the last member of the public to leave the once-notorious Cremorne Gardens, at 6 a.m., when they were finally closed in 1876. Another of the satisfactions of his lifetime was to be able to say that he had founded the winter season at the Swiss resort of Grindelwald. He was the familiar if not typical product of our English public school system, the uninspired amateur.

To Bennett, persisting in his provincial pleasure at being near the centre of things, Gardner was the polished man of the world, intimidatingly aloof when the mood was on him, knowledgeable about the comforts of existence and, judging by Bennett's notes, about such out-of-the-way manifestations of the life force as Lesbianism, and free with the names of contemporary devotees of that cult. He was sixty when war came in 1914 and his first instinct was to have his face massaged and to present himself at the nearest recruiting office. After some setbacks, depressing for one of his type who finds in war more opportunities of self-expression than in peace, he was given a commission and events thereafter bore him on to provost duties with the British Army of the Rhine.

His father's £300, besides acquiring debentures in the paper, had procured for Arnold Bennett a salary of £150 a year for working one full day and four half-days a week, with the courtesy title of assistant editor. In point of fact he was the sub-editor, the only others on the staff being Gardner and a secretary. The £50 drop in income worried him, but the chance of renouncing the routine of the legal life was not to be lost. He shut his books at Le Brasseur & Oakley's on the last day of 1893 and in the first hours of the New Year walked briskly into the offices of *Woman* at 90, Shaftesbury Avenue.

There is the question whether Enoch Bennett's acquiescence in all this was pathological in origin, though the onset of his terrible depreciating illness was not yet. Viewed as business, buying shares in *Woman* had little to commend it. The paper was hardly two years old. It was having to fight for circulation. It showed no sign of being a money-maker. Prominent names had been used as window-dressing for the early issues—Sarah Bernhardt and Marie Corelli—but there was not enough finance available to sustain a campaign of publicity and promotion. *Woman* was certainly not the kind of investing possibility to appeal to a Midlander who had seen at close quarters the collapse of a publishing venture for want of capital. Enoch Bennett decided to overlook the risk and why he did so we shall not know. He was investing perhaps in his son's abilities, making amends for his old detracting attitude to them.

Looking back on this editorial phase, Arnold Bennett said he felt that he was in his element: "I lived." His exhilaration came from oddly mixed sources. He was 'Barbara' who wrote on books. He shared with Gardner the pseudonym of 'Marjorie' who did 'Town Talk'. He wrote 'Answers to Correspondents' and, no doubt, most of the questions. That 'Cecile' and 'Lady Vain', writing comments on music and beauty culture respectively, hid other activities of his there is no evidence except a suspicious competence of style. He corrected proofs of articles on 'Should Women Ride Astride?' 'Is Human Nature Improving?' 'Men's Women' and (naturally) 'Women's Men'. On pages dominated by the ugly black-letter advertising of subsequently celebrated trade names—Scrubb's Ammonia, Scott's Emulsion, W. D. & H. O. Wills' Cigarettes (only 'advanced' women smoked them), Mazawattee Tea, Jaeger Pure Wool Clothing, Hine's Hair Curlers, The Patent Busk Protector, and Chivers's Jellies—we read that "over five hundred ladies in Washington are wearing divided skirts", that knitted corsets were being worn, that a company was being promoted to establish "restaurants for ladies", that the wife of "a well-known bicyclist" had died of laudanum taking, that "sexual love had undergone a glorifying transformation from a universal brute instinct to (very commonly) an exalting ideal passion".

Writing the caption for an illustration of a layette, Bennett added conscientiously: "Cut-to-measure patterns supplied", and laughter was heard outside as well as inside the office. For a young man exposed to the titillations of a paper written and edited for women there was always the chance of a sex *contretemps* brightening the day's work. "I was talking to Mrs. Gardner about a *risqué* line which had appeared in a notice of some underclothing in *Woman*. I said: 'A man can get himself into such a state of nervous apprehension that he sees indecency in the most innocent and harmless phrase.' " His lunch-time acquaintances at the Temple Bar Restaurant were agitating him by quoting examples of the printed *gaffes* that had made Fleet Street laugh, the gossip paragraph about a well-known woman philanthropist which read: "Mrs. X——, famous for her chastity," the report which stated: "Mr. Y——, the rising young politician, made his first pubic speech at——."

Helping to run a women's paper was a more liberal education than he had expected. "I learnt a good deal about frocks, household management, and the secret nature of women, especially the secret nature of women," some of whom made him uncomfortable by crying when he told them they could not write. "I could tolerate anything but tears. When they cried, I would beg them to leave the presence." Recalling the background of this editorial time, he wrote: "To earn her own living was a daring adventure for a girl, and many parents forbade it. Skirts trailed in the dust and mud of pavements. Three guineas was a monstrous price for a hat, and twenty guineas for a frock. Really imitative imitation furs had scarcely been invented. Stockings were cheap. Scent was cheap. Women never used unprintable oaths. Bicycles for ladies had only recently become respectable."

When Fitzroy Gardner left *Woman* to try his luck as a theatre *impresario* (and he did not have any), Arnold Bennett moved into his chair as editor. "I seemed to resemble Louis the Fifteenth beginning to reign after the death of the Regent, but with no troublesome Fleury in the background. 'Now', I cried, 'up goes the circulation! But circulations cannot be bullied into ascension. They will rise only on the pinions of a carefully constructed policy." Soon he was having to admit that he knew too little about journalism for women. One of his contributors, Mrs. Roy Devereux, author of *The Ascent of Woman*, an attempt to carry feminism into the realm of metaphysics, encouraged him to believe that to succeed editorially he must above all be a competent judge of women's clothes' styles. He said that thereafter he practised the habit of "always glancing first at a woman's skirt and then at her shoes". He became censoriously interested in women's clothes and boasted that he never lost the habit of thus appraising a woman when he met her for the first time, as for example Miss Rebecca West, twenty-five years after: "Very carelessly and very badly dressed." In Paris he "looked instinctively at the hang of the skirts with the eye of a man who had sat for years in the editorial chair of a women's paper". Passing the bedroom of his hostess on a week-end visit with his wife, he noted: "Very poor nightdress lying on the bed." The journal contains some charming vignettes of the fashions of his early days in London:

June 29, 1897.—Mrs. May came to see me at the office, a woman of forty, spare, with a wise, sad, restrained, benevolent look on her thin features. She was dressed with perfect taste, simplicity and appositeness, in yellow piqué, with white kid gloves, and seemed with her quiet, calm, half-weary voice, to be the incarnation of utter coolness. Her jacket hung limp where it had play, like sails in the tropics, and the skirt, too, fell away in straight lines of studied severity. It was a distinctively English dress, of the finest type, depending for its effects, not on costliness, elaboration or artistic blendings, but on simplicity, severity and suitability.

I wonder if women realise the acute pleasure which men derive from the sight of them in their fresh, cool, clean summer toilettes—openwork stockings, diaphanous sleeves, and general impression of *musliness*.

Yet he was not notably successful in dressing the women of his novels, some of whom are supposed to be of the first degree of smartness, and it may be relevant to recall, too, his singular incapacity to convince us that any of them made the final surrender of their sex. Meanwhile, in the pre-eminently female context of this part of his career he experimented with his own appearance and is r~membered by a Fleet Street acquaintance walking away from the Fetter Lane offices of his paper wearing a brand-new white bowler hat, "looking as if he had just received it for review."

He saw women as in a glass darkly. They were mysterious, baffling, eternally uncomprehended, "suggesting the infinite," a riddle of existence, "remoter than the stars, unattainable as the moon." An early critic of his work noted that he appeared to be "obsessed by the formidableness of the female". Clayhanger's throes of passion for Hilda Lessways agitate his creator into using a telegraphese of dots, interrogation marks, marks of exclamation. ". . . the upper part of her flushed face was caged behind the bars of the veil; behind those bars her eyes mysteriously gleamed. . . . Spanish! . . . No exaggeration in all this! . . . Was she the most wondrous? Or was she commonplace? Was she deceiving him? Or did she alone possess the true insight? . . . Useless! He was baffled." He makes Clayhanger see women "as a foreign race encamped among us men", and of the transfiguring moment in which the love of Edwin and Hilda fuses in their overwhelming realisation of what each means to the other, he says feebly: "They kissed." He believed that "the two sexes must for ever remain distant, antagonistic, and mutually inexplicable".

Few of his women characters exist in their own right. The Baines sisters and Auntie Hamps are exceptions, because he had known them as personalities within his experience. The others serve the purpose of foils and contrasts, throwing their male complements into sharper relief. Bennett wrote a great many 'popular' articles and one book which gained him a reputation for understanding women. It was as doubtful as his other reputation for "always doing what he said he would do". Wells said of him that he never knew the "egoism expanded out of sight", the eclipsing self-forgetfulness of the lover. He wrote to Mrs. Hilda Hellman, of New York, in acknowledgment of a parting present on his leaving for home after his memorable American tour of 1911: ". . . I am very much obliged, and indeed tickled, by this gift from one who prefers women to men. The explanation of the phenomenon is that I am partly a woman."

He involved the women of his novels in situations and incidents from his own life, as if he was engaged less in the act of creating them as characters than in indulging imaginatively in intimacies of emotional contact which were denied him in reality. His women, mostly, seem to be projections rather than creations.

(2)

After all, it was his notes on books that proved to be his most successful journalistic work at that time. Apart from *Woman*, he had been writing reviews for a small paper called *Hearth and Home*, in which his father also had some shares. They brought him reviewing work for *The Academy*, a high-class weekly dealing with the arts. *The Academy* was edited by C. Lewis Hind, champion of the post-Impressionists who was given to weeping at the sight of Matisse's 'Girl with the Green Eyes'. Before that Hind had been sub-editor of the *Art Journal* and editor of the *Pall Mall Budget*. E. V. Lucas was on the staff of *The Academy* and remembered Bennett visiting the office: "He was wearing a white bowler hat, and was assertive and dogmatic in a high-pitched voice, liable at any moment to stop suddenly and struggle for life." When Hind heard that Bennett was at work on a novel, he warned him: "Fiction will be the rock on which you will split. You are a critic. All you critics are the same. You want to write novels and you never write good ones." His sound judgment in choosing Bennett to review books was at any rate never in dispute. Years later Bennett said it was he who chose *The Academy* in which to review them. The point became a needless public argument, with Bennett having the last word: "Ever amiable, ever enthusiastic about something or other, Lewis Hind showed little comprehension of literature at any time."

His prestige as a reviewer for *The Academy* gave Arnold Bennett new assurance that he could tackle a novel. "I sat at my oaken bureau . . . under the sweet influence of the de Goncourts, Turgenev, Flaubert, and de Maupassant," especially the last-named, whose unadorned vocabulary and modulated style were for Bennett the marks of fine craftsmanship. Strict accuracy would have enjoined him to say that it was Marriott's oaken bureau, which remains in the drawing-room adjoining the studio at what used to be 6 Victoria Grove, awaiting its next important assignment through nearly sixty years.

Arnold Bennett to George Sturt:

December 11, 1895

I was working all Saturday till 10.30, all Sunday till 6.30 (after which I rewrote an article on Art) all yesterday till 9.30: about 6,000 words in three days, and pretty good so far as I can make out. In fact I *know* that it is good. . . . I gave three hours yesterday morning (staying away from the office, having pleaded a chill on the liver) to about 300 words. There is a marmoreal undeniable beauty about 'em which persuades me to suspend the rule of striking out every sentence that is 'fine'. I am looking forward to another three hours tonight. D'you know, I think I am going to improve in dialogue, a conclusion not arrived at from anything actually done, but from intimations, premonitions.

His fluency as a reviewer played tricks with him as a novelist. Again and again it receded, leaving him staring in dismay at the sheets of paper before him. "Immediately the fundamental brainwork began, I lost nearly all my confidence." He lost it intermittently for six months, but plodded on in the "grim sticking it" spirit of his upbringing. When the spirit weakened he turned to his *Yellow Book* short story as to a secret tipple. "It heartened me, restored my faith in the existence of art and suggested the comfortable belief that things were not as bad as they seemed."

He fell into Stevenson's way of acting the gestures and mannerisms of his characters, with the difference that Stevenson did not know that he did it and Bennett did. ". . . it needs a constant, or at least a repeated, mental effort to grasp the fact that certain stories which I have written, and the novel I am now finishing, aren't really true. I frequently have to say to myself, as it were: 'But of course it's not true, really !' " He was capable of being "carried away" even towards the end of his career as a novelist. Writing *Accident* in 1927, he caused one of the characters to lose his temper. "I did it with such heat that I felt as if I had lost my own temper when I went down to see Miss Nerney and I felt called upon to explain to her the cause of my demeanour."

It was to be a novel of purpose, this first novel of his; it was to teach as experience teaches. "My novels will all have a purpose. The purpose of *A Man from the North* is to 'expose' a few of the hardships and evils of the life of the young celibate clerk in London."

The autobiographical interest of *A Man from the North* is chiefly environmental. The young Richard Larch is sent from Bursley to

London as a result of a long deferred marriage between two people whose engagement had been broken. This had been a happening in the Bennett family history. His father's sister Sarah had quarrelled with her fiancé, Sam Barlow, a plumber, and had married him after an estrangement lasting twelve years.

The novel was finished on May 15, 1896, "at noon precisely." He feared that it was strained in tone if not hysterical. "Still, I should not be surprised if it impressed many respectable people. The worst parts of it seem to me to be in front of my *Yellow Book* story, which came in for a full share of laudation."

His labour of more than a year had become a brown paper parcel sent to John Lane at the Bodley Head, in Vigo Street, Piccadilly. Lane's reader was John Buchan, described in Bennett's journal after their first meeting in June, 1896:

A very young, fair man; charmingly shy; 'varsity' in every tone and gesture. He talks quietly in a feminine, exiguous voice, with the accent of Kensington tempered perhaps by a shadow or a shade of Scotch (or was that my imagination?) Already—he cannot be more than twenty-three—he is a favourite of publishers, who actually seek after him, and has published one book. He told me that his second novel, a long Scotch romance, was just finished, and that he had practically sold the serial rights. . . . A most modest, retiring man, yet obviously sane and shrewd. Well-disposed too, and anxious to be just; a man to compel respect; one who 'counts'.

Reporting on *A Man from the North*, Buchan said it was written "with great knowledge and a good deal of insight", that the style was good, the characterisation distinguished by "a succession of rare and subtle touches". Lane read out the report to Bennett, who had called on him at his office, "which resembled a small drawing-room." He did not fail to pass on Buchan's final opinion: "I do not think it is likely to be a striking success." This drew from Bennett the pained exclamation: "Oh!" Lane took a chance on Bennett as he had on other young writers of the day and published the book. Discussing it many years after, a critic wrote:

The book was a product of the eighteen-nineties—of that strenuous and now dim period of deliberate artistic hypertrophy when the British Barbarians were smitten from the hill-tops, when *The Yellow Book* was born and died and *The Savoy* rose from its ashes, itself a phœnix burnt untimely, when Wilde and Dowson and Beardsley were thought shocking, and Whistler not quite respectable. . . . *A Man from the North* was in the movement, but most distinctly not of it. It was before the movement, in one sense. It wore the literary air of the newer æsthetic evolution. It is far the most 'literary' of Arnold Bennett's books. . . . It marks its author at once as a conscious, even a self-conscious, literary artist, striving after a certain objective effect. [1]

This discerning student of Bennett's early work apparently did not discern the shadow of *The Old Wives' Tale* which lies across that part of *A Man from the North* in which there is a passing view of life in a busy market square as it was seen by a young girl through the windows of the shop over which she lived.

The novel did not sell. "My profits from this book with the exceptional style and the exceptional knowledge of human nature, exceeded the cost of having it typewritten by the sum of one sovereign. Nor was I, nor am I, disposed to grumble at this. Many a first book has cost its author a hundred pounds. I got a new hat out of mine."

He deplored much more "the dishonour of the prophet in his own country", recalling that his novel was naturalistic, without 'realism' in the vulgar sense, "but desperately exact in places." The effect on readers brought up on the works of Dickens and Mrs. Henry Wood was "appalling, frightful, tragical". Some of his readers, he fancied, had not read a novel for ten years before reading his. "For months I hestitated to visit the town which had the foresight to bear me, and which is going to be famous on that score. I was castigated in the local paper."

The novel did not sell but it was far from neglected critically, considering that it was a first novel. Referring to the reviews, forty-one, proudly counted, he wrote: "The fact to be asserted is that I, quite obscure and defenceless, was treated very well. I could afford to smile from a high altitude at the remark of *The New York Observer* that 'the story and characters are commonplace in the extreme'. I felt that I had not lived in vain, and that kindred spirits were abroad in the land." One of them wrote to him:

10 March, 1902.

MY DEAR SIR,—The reading of *A Man from the North* has inspired me with the greatest respect for your artistic conscience. I am

[1] F. J. Harvey Darton: *Arnold Bennett* (Nisbet, 1915).

profoundly impressed with the achievement of style. The root of the matter—which is expression—is there, and the sacred fire, too. I hope you will give me the credit for understanding what you have tried for there. My dear Sir, I do envy you the power of coming so near to your desire.

The thing as written is undeniable. To read it was to me quite a new experience of the language; and the delight was great enough to make me completely disregard the subject.

This at first; but as you may suppose I've read the book more than once. Unfortunately, I don't know how to criticise; to discuss, however, I am ready. Now the book (as a novel, not as a piece of writing) *is* disputable.

Generally, however, I may say that the die has not been struck hard enough. Here's a piece of pure metal scrupulously shaped, with a true—and more—a beautiful ring: but the die has not been struck hard enough. I admit that the outlines of the design are sharp enough. What it wants is more emphatic modelling; more relief. And one could even quarrel with the design itself.

Nothing would give me greater pleasure than to have it out with you, the book there on the table, to be thumbed and caressed. I would quarrel not with the truth of your conception but with the realism thereof. You stop just short of being absolutely real because you are faithful to your dogmas of realism. Now realism in art will never approach reality. And your art, your gift, should be put to the service of a larger and freer faith.

Yours sincerely,
JOSEPH CONRAD.

P.S.—Of course I may have misunderstood your standpoint utterly. I want to hear what you have to say, if you think it worth while to say anything to me. Only let it be *viva voce*. Come when you can spare a day.[1]

(3)

Before the publication of the novel he had received an encouraging personal acknowledgment of his standing as a reviewer of books. It came about as a result of a letter he had written:

[1] G. Jean-Aubry: *Joseph Conrad, Life and Letters* (Heinemann 1927)

WOMAN
St. Dunstan's Chambers,
10 and 11 Fetter Lane,
Fleet Street, London, E.C.

30 Sept. 1897.

DEAR SIR,—For a long time I have been intending to write to you, and express my appreciation of your work, and also to ask what is your connection with Burslem and the Potteries. Burslem (where I come from) is mentioned at the beginning of 'The Time Machine' and one of your short stories runs over the entire Pottery district—I forget the title of it.

I enclose my review of your latest book.

Believe me, dear Sir,

Faithfully yours,

E. A. BENNETT
(Editor of 'Woman')

H. G. Wells, Esq.

The recipient of the letter answered that, oddly enough, he had just overcome a strong impulse to write his thanks to the editor of *Woman* for the notice that had appeared there. He went on to explain that he had spent a holiday with an old friend who worked in the Potteries. He added his appreciation of the support which *Woman* had always given him.

Arnold Bennett to H. G. Wells:

6, Victoria Grove,
Chelsea, S.W.

10 Oct. 1897.

MY DEAR SIR,—I am very glad to have your letter, and very glad to find that the Potteries made such an impression on you. I lived there till I was 21, and have been away from it 9 years, and only during the last few years have I begun to see its possibilities. Particularly this year I have been deeply impressed by it. It seems to me that there are immense possibilities in the very romance of manufacture—not wonders of machinery and that sort of stuff—but in the tremendous altercation with nature that is continually going on—and in various other matters. Anyhow, I am trying to shove the notions into my

[106]

next novel. Only it wants doing on a Zolaesque scale. I would send you a rough sketch of my somewhat vague ideas in this direction, but fear to bore you. To my mind it is just your field. As for the people, I know 'em inside out, and if you are a Northern man you would grasp them instinctively.

I am quite sure there is an aspect of these industrial districts which is really *grandiose*, full of dark splendours, and which has been absolutely missed by all the novelists up to date.

I have troubled you with all this because you are the first man I have come across whom the Potteries has impressed, emotionally. There are a number of good men in the Potteries, but I have never yet met one who could be got to see what I saw; they were all inclined to scoff.

Sincerely yours,
E. A. Bennett.

(4)

He added to his income from *Woman* by taking pupils for private tuition in journalism. The first of them, a solicitor from Canada who wanted to write saleable fiction, appealed to him for professional advice. "I named a fee that might have frightened him, but it did not. And so it fell out that I taught journalism to him, and to others, for a year or two." He was himself writing short stories for *Woman*, using the curious pen-name of 'Sal Volatile', though the stories were not so flippant as it suggests. Presumably as editor he was paying himself for them. He needed the money. His expenses were going up. The Marriotts had decided to retire domestically to the studio adjoining the house, Bennett becoming the householder in their place. He went to Burslem to fetch his sister Tertia to keep house for him. A fatality in which she had been a central figure had recently cast its shadow over the family. The young Burslem man to whom it was expected she would become engaged had been drowned while on holiday at Barmouth with Enoch and Sarah Bennett and the younger members of their family. There were in the tragedy elements of psychological strangeness. "We both always knew that something like this would happen," Tertia Bennett told Arnold. "We sometimes referred to it. We knew we should never be married. Before W—— went away he said to Minnie: 'I'm going to die, Min.' He had parted from his mother with the words: 'Goodbye, Mother—meet you in heaven.' On the morning of the accident he sang continually

[107]

the refrain of a comic song, 'There's nothing to do but die.' " And in the journal for September 15, 1897, there is the pathetic sequel note:

I brought Tertia to London. As we drove up to 6, Victoria Grove, Marriott came to the front door and stood on the steps. His face was working.

'Well,' Tertia exclaimed, with a desperate pitiful effort at self-control and cheerfulness, 'here I am—bicycle and all.' Marriott burst into tears, but not Tertia.

The fatality is a recurring theme in the journal over several days. He sets out the details of the drowning, the attempted rescue, the desolation that fell on the holiday-makers, the funeral scenes at Burslem. He records a tribute to his brother Frank: "F—B—said to me that our Frank's coolness at a moment when his chance of life was the slenderest was a magnificent sight—something to remember." Drowning tragedies haunted several of Arnold Bennett's subsequent holidays: he seemed to be fated to witness them. The tragedy at Barmouth touched him perhaps more deeply than he knew. He writes about his defaulting nerves. Out cycling with Marriott: "I imagined every possible sort of accident in each case following out a train of circumstances to the direst possible climax. In particular I dreaded a puncture, and that I might take cold, to be followed by rheumatic fever." And: "Lately I have been depressed by apprehensions as to the future. I have imagined all possible misfortunes and calamities." Office crises found him singularly lacking in the courage to face them. "A few years of such misery (the lot of many men), even a year of it, even a month, would drive me, I fancy, to clerkhood again, just for the sake of being free from responsibility and worry." His stomach malady reappeared violently and he had to see a doctor, who told him that he must be prepared to suffer indefinitely from the same obscure cause; "my stomach would always be a trouble to me." He could not eat an apple without paying the price for days after. A glass of beer was liable to exact a severe penalty of derangement. His physician friend, Farrar, told another old friend of them both, Frederick Alcock, the chief Customs officer of Newhaven and Tilbury, that Bennett was so highly strung that "his spirit knew no respite".

His passionate fastidiousness in household matters greatly tried his sister in her housekeeper role. Everything had to be in its place. He abominated dust. No one must touch his books. And his silences could be shattering. Tertia Bennett failed in lighting the sitting-room fire on a freezing morning; she was still on her knees, trying to light it with numbed fingers, when he returned for lunch. Not attempting to help, he went back to the hall, put on his overcoat, cap, and muffler, and in silence took his place at table. His sister afterwards said that in these moods he could be "terrible". Perhaps it was from her insight into the tenebrous side of his nature that she felt impelled to intercede with him on behalf of his wife when their marital relationship came to an end. His sister said that there were times when she was afraid to go near him, or to make any sound in his hearing, so bedevilled with gloom was he.

Dried figs were among his indulgences at this time; he kept boxes of them in different parts of the house, so that he could help himself at his fancy. He was upset at finding that someone else had the same taste. Suspecting a 'char', who was reliable in all other ways, he hit on the idea of checking her light-fingered impulses by putting in each box a card inscribed 'Thou, God, seest me', and was almost too pleased with himself when the trick succeeded.

(5)

He went to Paris that autumn for his first visit. Rickards went with him and Rickards's midnight loquacity probably contributed to the fatigue of which Bennett was soon complaining in the journal. In three days he was writing as if out of a cloud of disillusionment, reporting that the visitor to Paris, however virginal in his enthusiasm, "does not enjoy unbroken ecstasy." The restraints of money and language weighed upon him. So perhaps did those of his puritanical upbringing, which may have had more to do with his depression than he realised. An opportunity of witnessing the *danse du ventre* at the Casino de Paris refreshed his knowledge of anatomy while confirming his doubts whether he was "seeing the right things". His doubts were in part corrected by his first view of the Pantheon, with its "wonderfully moving legend" in gold letters stretching across the face of the building. "It breathes piety in the true sense."

He resented his inability to fix Paris in a phrase, a literary conceit which remained ungratified. "I search for a formula which should express Paris—in vain." He found it impossible to seize "the great central difference" between Latin and Teuton, and recorded treading on a dead cat in the Place de la Concorde, "its limbs all spread abroad and its cheek on the roadway," with no sign that he was aware of its possible relevancy to the besetting question. Continuing to seek the final felicitous phrase, he wrote after walking in the gardens of the Luxembourg: "Here is some Doing . . . the people are less self-conscious and more purposeful; more truly lighthearted and yet more earnest."

He noted "the frequency of *maisons d'accouchement* of vast size", in a city with a population said to be static if not in decline. One of them had a large pictorial sign showing a young woman, "in modern costume," gazing at an opening bush from which a beautiful baby looked out. Fountain spray, the lights by the river, evening mists, the "gaslit resounding monotony" of the rue St. Martin by night, young women, "carelessly *chic*," giving him looks and Rickards giving them looks, scolding nursemaids with children trailing coloured balloons, the devils of Notre Dame gazing out "with a certain benign satisfaction" over Zola's Paris: he filled the journal with notes of a "thousand mere trifles", trying diligently "to get behind and below them, but without success".

For Sunday, October 31, 1897, we find: "I left Paris. None of my deepest impressions about it seems to have been set down at all." It is as if he had been made painfully aware of his intellectual rawness, as if he had been patronised and was in no position to protest. He had new forebodings for the future, "which seems to be one of narrow possibilities."

CHAPTER EIGHT

(1)

RED brick, baked in the furnace of the industrial revolution, marked significant stages in Arnold Bennett's life. His father's new red brick house at Cobridge represented a change for the better in the family fortunes. His first fiction hero had for his boyhood background "The Red House", Bursley (Bennett for Burslem). New Court's "very red brick" signified escape and independence. And, apart from the mellow masterpieces of Tudor times, it would be hard to find red brick more sumptuously employed than in the design and fabrication of Cadogan Square, London, where at Number 75 he reached the summit of his great middle class success.

Soon after returning from Paris he went to live at 9 Fulham Park Gardens, in a red brick suburb dominated by the Fulham Road. The move was one more step towards social self-sufficiency. At the same time he admitted to shrinking from new cares and was nervously bothered about the chances of his being called for jury duty, so much so that he seriously thought of renting the house in his brother's name. Then, deciding that jury service might yield experience useful to him as a writer, he signed the lease and became tenant of the house for three years, from 1897 to 1900.

Keeping him company there was Gregory Hill, son of the one-time principal of the Blackheath School of Art who had introduced him to Marriott. Gregory Hill, whose mother kept house for them, found the Bennett household routine exacting: "he was not an easy man to live with." The bathroom had to be vacated for him at eight o'clock sharp every morning. Meals were strictly punctual. The grandfather clock was always kept a quarter of an hour fast, no more, no less, as a mark of Bennett's scorn for most people's casual attitude to time-keeping. He revenged himself for the untidiness of others by hiding things not put in their places and Gregory Hill was compelled to hunt long and exasperatingly for books which he had not put back on their shelves. He also had to endure Bennett's enthusiasm for rice pudding, practically the staple dish of the household. It appeared at almost every evening meal throughout his time in Fulham Park Gardens. With it

[111]

Bennett took extraordinary quantities of salt, heaped spoons of it at a time, a taste medically interpreted as a symptom of low blood pressure. This predilection remained with him. He noted with amusement the remark of a waitress when in 1928 he ordered more salt to be put on the table at tea in a Winchelsea café: "More salt—whatever *for*?"

For many months at Fulham Park Gardens a stranger constantly visited the house. His name was Godfrey and Bennett was mysterious about him, referring to him as "Mister God——, my pup——" meaning pupil. Godfrey was in fact not a pupil but a speech specialist. The order was that there must be "no interruption on any account" when he called. His visits occurred over more than a year, Bennett keeping up the pupil pretence all through.

He was experimenting with his appearance by wearing flowing 'arty' ties, Rickards having established agreement with him on the proposition that clothes have a deterministic effect on personality and therefore on prospects, though Balzac's views on that matter may not have escaped Bennett's attention. Very soon we find him writing: "Most men who succeed are well-dressed." Fussiness over clothes may sometimes be seen as a sign of something more than a desire for social approval. Arnold Bennett went on to rationalise it as a sense of duty. "No one can be the worse, and the vast majority will be the better, for dressing as well as their means, their leisure, and their taste will allow." The clothes rivalry between Bennett and Rickards often diverted the Marriott group of friends, but never more than when in 1928 Arnold Bennett was proclaimed the best dressed man of the year by the chief organ of the British tailoring trade, *The Tailor and Cutter*. Gregory Hill remembers Bennett laughing as he came home one evening because a navvy, passing him in the Fulham Road, had glared malevolently at the unusually bright flowing tie he was wearing and had muttered down his clay pipe stem: "O Christ!"

Early in 1899 his friends received a printed card of invitation: '*E. A. Bennett, At Home, Thursday, March 2nd, 7.30. To celebrate the tenth anniversary of his advent in the metropolis. Music, pork pies, and other attractions. R.S.V.P.*'

9 Fulham Park Gardens,
London, S. W.

24 Sep. '99

MY DEAR WELLS,—A year or two ago we exchanged a few letters, and since then I have heard nothing from you, though I often hear *of*

[112]

you from common friends—Roche, Lewis Hind, Eden Phillpotts, etc. I am writing now because I must—to congratulate you on the short stories in the 'Pall Mall Magazine', which seem to improve as they go on, and which certainly strike me as being fine and in a very special sense *original* work. I like this 'prophetic' line of fiction. I will not say that I know nothing else so *strongly* imagined, but I will say that I know nothing else where the imagination is used with such virtuosity in the manipulation of material, or where the invention is so fresh, adroit and convincing. (And this despite the fact that I disagree (ferociously) with your general vision of the future of the race. Nor do I think that the changes you describe or any changes equally radical could occur in that fraction of time called a century.)

Among the 200-odd books that I have pretended to review this year 'The Sleeper Awakes' has not found a place. But I shall be coming across it sooner or later, and shall expect it to be very excellent. If it is on the plane of the stories, I can't understand why it is only in its 8th thousand. (Or rather I *can* understand.)

I have heard of your illnesses in a vague way from time to time. I remember one lunch with J. N. Dunn when he was awfully depressed about your bodily condition. I hope this business is now all over, and that you are able to work fair and square, unhandicapped.

Believe me,

Sincerely yours,

E. A. BENNETT.

(2)

He had begun a new novel, his second, published presently as *Anna of the Five Towns*, though as before a different title stood at the top of the page when he began writing it. He was bothered by "a lack of sustained determination", he told Sturt, seeing it as the cardinal defect of his character, the weakness of his first fiction hero, Richard Larch. "I know I haven't got the creative impulse for a big theme, but I fancy I can by sheer force of concentration and monotony do something effective in a small way." Force of monotony stamped the novel with truth and the inexorable flow of the commonplace gave it an integrity recognised by critics and readers alike. In *Anna of the Five Towns* he displayed a specialised knowledge which did not inform *A Man from the North*, and his sketches of pottery processes, complete with footnotes, mark the novel off from others in the Five Towns series.

[113]

Writing it presented him with the practical problem of meeting his overheads at the same time. "I must have brass and writing novels isn't the way to do it," he wrote to Sturt. He could not afford to write novels, he said, and when Lever Tillotson, representing the Bolton literary syndicate which bought serials and short stories and resold them to the provincial press and to some of the smaller weeklies, among them *Woman*, called to offer him new material he asked himself the question: Why should all the buying be on one side? Tillotson, a typical young man from the North, keen, efficient, hard, and a victim of the family affliction of deafness, was one of three brothers whose father had founded a substantial business, which included an evening newspaper and the literary syndicate, on money he had made out of jobbing printing. After one of Tillotson's calls in 1898, Bennett noted:

I was struck, as I have been before, by the man's perfect ignorance of what constitutes literature, and by the accord which exists between his own literary tastes and those of the baser portion of the general public. He gave some interesting details as to the current prices per thousand. Thomas Hardy is being outstripped by some of the younger men. He stands now equal only with H. G. Wells at 12 guineas per thousand, which is also the price of the blood-and-thunder of William Le Queux. Stanley Weyman, because of his larger following in America, can only be bought at 16 to 18 guineas per thousand. Kipling stands solitary and terrible at £50 per thousand words, £200 being his minimum for the shortest short story. What surprised me most was a statement that W. W. Jacobs (quite a new man, who has published only two small books of a quietly humorous nature, but about whom an inordinate amount of fuss has been made) recently refused an offer of £500 for six short stories. I asked about Eden Phillpotts. The reply was: 'He has recently put up his price and we think it is too high. Besides, the sound of his name is against his success with us—Phill-potts!' A curious criticism. But in another year, if I mistake not, Tillotsons' will be glad to pay him more than his present price—the comparatively small figure of five guineas a thousand words.

Coveting some of the cash which Tillotsons were ready to pay for "the right stuff", Arnold Bennett hinted as much to their representative, sitting in the office of *Woman* with the proofs of serials and short stories draped across his knees. Lever Tillotson said: "We never buy stories from editors." Proceeding to the demolition of this policy,

Bennett ascribed the successful outcome of his assault to "the great and sublime truth" that business is business, "the foundations of England's glory." Capitulating, Tillotson sounded the warning: "Nothing supernatural. And nothing against the trade unions."

He wrote the serial in twelve days, mentally working out each instalment while walking along the Thames Embankment on his way to the editorial chair. "I put in generous quantities of wealth, luxury, feminine beauty, surprise, catastrophe, and genial incurable optimism." Tillotsons paid him £75 and having savoured the pleasure of "earning the money of shame" he immediately contracted to do another serial at a better price. "I said that my drawing-room wanted new furniture; I said that I might lift the sensational serial to a higher plane, thus serving the cause of art; I said—I don't know what I said, all to my conscience. But I began the serial."

Hearing that "sensational fiction" was now earnestly engaging his friend's energies, Sturt, his best critic of the early days, required reassurances about his artistic intentions. Bennett wrote to him, June 5, 1899:

> I began this serial partly because I had a notion that my position was not founded on a rock . . . and partly because I didn't see why I shouldn't write as good exciting fiction as anyone else. My ambition is to earn enough apart from my editorial salary. I am sick of editing *Woman* and of being bound to go to a blasted office every day. I want to work when I feel inclined, to travel more. I saw only one way of freeing myself of official ties, namely fiction. . . . I have to report an immense increase in facility, not only for rotten but for decent stuff . . . but I have loftier heights yet to conquer.

So, he embarked on the professional dualism, the compromise between "glory and something more edible and warmer at nights", which was to disturb his admirers and confuse his critics, some to the point of diagnosing schizophrenia, for the rest of his days.

as from 9, Fulham Park Gardens,

MY DEAR WELLS,   2 Aug, 1900.

I should immensely like to come down and have a day or so with you. I oughtn't to, but I think I will. I am extended just now over a Tillotson serial. I have been laid aside for a month with an abscess, and am already late with the delivery, but the benevolent syndicate has granted me an extension of 6 weeks, bless it.

I write this letter from Burslem, whence I depart tonight, and where I have been observing the effect of the Wesleyan Methodist Conference on the community. I came down specially to observe the same, and have been well rewarded. The public examinations of candidates for ordination, the other night at Longton, was one of the most genuinely *interesting* things that I have ever watched.

It is enough for me that you and Mrs. Wells were interested in 'Man from North'. There is much in it that is not authentic, merely fanciful and quasi-sentimental—I can see that now. But I seriously meant all of it at the time. It was the first work I did. And before I had finished it the technique thereof had advanced so much that I had to go back and write the first half again. So you may guess what it was to start with!

Well, I shall look forward to seeing you; and thanks very much for what in this district the élite call the 'invite'.

Sincerely yours,

E. A. BENNETT.

(3)

Visiting the Eden Phillpotts's at Torquay in 1899, he had returned to work "full of a desire to live in the country in a large house with plenty of servants, as he does, not working too hard, but writing when and how one likes, at good rates. It can only be done by means of fiction". And he added to his journal confession: "To write popular fiction is offensive to me, but it is far more agreeable than being tied daily to an office and editing a lady's paper; and perhaps it is less of a strain on the conscience. To edit a lady's paper, even a relatively advanced one, is to foster conventionality and hinder progress once a week." Moreover, to be happy, he avowed, he had to have a fair supply of money and writing fiction, he believed, would pay better than editing. "Also I have decided very seriously to aim at living in the country, to the entire abandonment of London."

Arnold Bennett to Miss May Beardmore:

Cosdonne
Torquay
30 Oct 99

MY DEAR MAY,—Your 21st birthday may have passed; I never could get any precise information as to the day; but do not imagine that I have forgotten it. Indeed, I lay awake thinking in the night what I could say to you of an improving nature. I asked Eden Phillpotts this morning whether he could give me any hints as to what to say to a woman of 21, and he offered me Marcus Aurelius. I said that wouldn't do. He said, 'Is she beautiful?' I said, 'Divinely.' 'Then', he said, 'begin by telling her so, and then follow your instincts.'

However, I find I haven't any instincts to follow. I wish you a long life, continuance of beauty, ever-increasing contentment, and and an energy which will enable you to go to bed every night with the feeling that you have exhausted yourself in the day's work. This is the best I can do for you. . . .

I am just going out now with Phillpotts to a village about 3 miles óff which is to be the scene of his next novel but one. I perceive more and more that the life of a successful novelist, though it is a strain, has immense advantages. The hours are short, for one thing. We write 'The Pagan' (which is to succeed 'Children of the Mist') only between 11 and 1 in the morning, and another 1 or $1\frac{1}{2}$ hours at odd things completes our day's work—except thinking. We have a large house, a charming wife, two children, simple tastes, and an ample supply of money. . . . I can see myself in this role with much satisfaction.

E. A. B.

He had begun whetting his appetite for the country by sharing a furnished cottage at Witley in Surrey called 'The Fowl House,' later 'Godspeace'. Madame Sarah Grand, author of *The Heavenly Twins*, a feminist novel that had startled the Victorians, was said to have lived there and Bennett described it as being "too picturesque for words and draughty as the neighbouring heath". Sturt lived only a few miles away, at Farnham, and the long friendship between him and Bennett was sealed by the opportunity of seeing each other more often: until then it had been kept alive by correspondence.

Sturt had one of those grindstone minds on which other minds are sharpened. Formerly a master at Farnham Grammar School, he had been called in to take charge of the family wheelwright business at Lower Bourne, a mile or so outside Farnham. Invoices, accounts and stocktaking vitiated his interest in the business without diminishing his sense of responsibility to a very old craft of the English countryside. He was a widely read and cultivated man whose work as a writer was admired by Conrad, one of the first to discern his quality as the author

[117]

of *Memoirs Of A Surrey Labourer*, *The Bettesworth Book*, and *The Wheelwright's Shop*. Arnold Bennett wrote after one of his cross-country visits to Sturt at Lower Bourne: "I had not been with him an hour before I was compelled to readjust my estimate of the depth of his immersion in literature. Writing occupies all his thoughts in a way I had never suspected. With the most perfect naturalness, he regards everything as 'material', and he assumed that I should do so too. A more literary temperament than his it would be difficult to conceive. He doesn't 'search' for stuff; his task probably is to cope with the masses of material which thrust themselves upon his attention. He sits down in his writing-chair and handles note-books and papers with an air of custom and familiarity which I have never seen in a writer before; it was like Sharpe at the piano."

During the Witley week-ends there was much coming and going by Chelsea friends and acquaintances, artists, writers, musicians, who had the air of "living the higher life", as Bennett put it, writing down his notes on them. Some were vegetarians, some teetotallers, others incorrigibly both.

... and all of us were pleased with Esther Wood (a writer on art), who has divorced her husband and who has an exquisite smile. But I said she was too earnest, and Sturt supported me. He said she yearned. Kennerley was angry and said she didn't yearn. I made no secret of my contempt for cranks and I called these people cranks. I admitted it was Philistine and I gloried in being a Philistine so far. I was glad that Sturt had the same feeling. Kennerley, of course, with his immensely wide sympathies, cursed us heartily for narrow-minded stupids. Nevertheless preserve me from all peculiar people, highly self-conscious people, vainly earnest people.

That night, he says in the journal, he dreamt that he wore sandals.

The decision about living in the country was taken for him by events outside his control. The drama of his father's terrible illness had begun to be unfolded to the family. Softening of the brain and no more than two years to live, was the medical verdict. Enoch Bennett was ordered to give up work, to leave Hanley and to seek the peace of the countryside. It was all that could be done for him. At once Arnold Bennett wrote out his resignation as editor of *Woman*. "I reached down a map of England, and said that I must live on a certain main-line at a certain minimum distance from London." He writes in *The Truth about an Author* as if the reshaping of his career was his only problem, as if he had himself put an end to his indecision. In fact he had been some months trying to make up his mind whether to have done with town life, and "its too multiform distractions".

The countryside he chose to live in was Bedfordshire, the house Trinity Hall Farm, Hockliffe, near Dunstable. "I ran over a list of our foremost writers: they nearly all lived in the country," and it is true that Hardy was at Dorchester, Meredith at Box Hill, James at Rye, Kipling at Rottingdean. "Monotony, solitude, are essential to the full activity of the artist," he wrote. "Just as a horse is seen best when coursing alone over a great plain, so the fierce and callous egotism of the artist comes to its perfection in a vast expanse of custom, leisure, and apparently vacuous reverie." He even thought himself "moved by some far-off mysterious atavism". His response to it made some of his London friends laugh. "You'll be back in a year," they said, and Rickards's caricatures of Arnold Bennett, the would-be squire, echo their mirthful scepticism still.

Trinity Hall Farm was a nondescript house, having nothing picturesque to commend it except its name and its setting of garden, orchard, and meadow; no character of period or appearance; the sort of house that perpetually looks rented, never owned. He had brought his father, mother, and sister Tertia down from Burslem to live there with him, and to the proprietorial contentments of being able to refer to "my house in the country" he added those of a pony and phaeton with a Dalmatian to run sagaciously between the wheels.

You invite an influential friend down for the week-end. You meet him at the station with a nice little grey mare in a phaeton, and an unimpeachable Dalmatian running behind. The turnout is nothing alone, but the pedigree printed in the pinkiness of that dog's chaps and in the exiguity of his tail, spotted to the last inch, would give tone to a coster's cart. You see that your influential friend wishes to comment, but as you gather up the reins you carefully talk about the weather and prices per thousand. . . . In a few hours Fleet Street becomes aware that young So-and-so, who lately buried himself in the country, is alive and busy. Your stock rises. You go up one. You extort respect. You are ticketed in the retentive brains of literary Shahs as a success. And you still have the dog left for another day.

Hales or no Hales, this is the authentic voice of the Card. One of the guests was Wilfred Whitten, editor of *T.P.'s Weekly*, whose well-known pen-name of John o' London was in due course transferred to a popular literary weekly which still flourishes. Recalling his visit, Whitten wrote in that journal: "My friend came in a dog cart to Dunstable station and drove me with supreme control of the reins and other knowingness to his home. The house might have been transported by magic from Hanley to a Bedfordshire knoll." Walking in a cornfield, Bennett told Whitten that he expected to earn five or six thousand pounds a year as a novelist. "I laughed to myself between the browning ears of wheat. But Bennett knew his powers and how to apply them. He built his career as methodically as a man builds a house."

He had returned to the novel which was to be *Anna of the Five Towns*, and while disposed to congratulate himself on having written two thousand five hundred words of it in a morning, he was disgusted because he lacked the power to work like Balzac, "who literally wore out four chairs, and died exhausted at fifty-two, despite a superb constitution. That is how I want to work—to pour it out in vast quantities, pell-mell, vast, immense, various. But I can't for the ridiculous reason that I get tired. . . . I think I have settled in my own mind that my work will never be better than third-rate, judged by the high standards, but I shall be cunning enough to make it impose on my contemporaries."

This was written to Sturt, who replied: "A good many times I have been grinning over the damnable arrogance which you own to in your last letter. Grinning at *it*, not at you. I know you mean it; yet all the time I can see in it only an attitude—a pose."

Whitten said that he never knew a man who so surely developed himself according to plan: "he swelled with the gummy persistence of a bud in spring." As his father's personality diminished, his own expanded. It was observed that he had adopted a more deliberate style of walking, what his friend Alcock, the chief Customs officer, called "Bennett's quarter-deck manner". Sobriety appeared in his neckwear and in his speech. A music-hall catchphrase of the day, "It's not so cold as it is, was it?" which he had inflicted on his friends long after it ceased to amuse most of them, particularly Gregory Hill who had to live with it, was heard no more, and he moderated his habit of declaiming on coming down to breakfast, "Full many a glorious morning have I seen, Flatter the mountain tops with sovereign eye."

But visitors to Trinity Hall Farm were likely to be startled by being required to catch plates which Bennett would take up from the meal table and send spinning towards them without warning.

H. G. Wells was one of the visitors. He went there to collaborate with Bennett in writing a play for the Haymarket Theatre. It was to be called *The Crime* and its chief character was to be a detective. They could not agree on the plot and at the end of three days abandoned the collaboration and the play. Arnold Bennett's mother and sister resented what both thought was Wells' patronising attitude to Bennett. They could not understand why Bennett put up with it. In one of his fits of impatience Wells threw a cushion at Bennett, who did not retaliate. As soon as Wells had left the house Bennett resumed his 'quarter-deck manner' and was himself again.

Wilfred Whitten saw Bennett at Hockliffe as a man "between two worlds, the one he had not quite left and the one he had not quite entered", a situation of opposing stresses with uncomfortable Procrustean implications for his future.

(4)

"The Pater finished his course in perfect quietness at 8.40 last night," Arnold Bennett wrote to William Kennerley, his future brother-in-law, on January 17, 1902. His father had dominated his impressionable years and cast his shadow well beyond them. Now that Enoch Bennett's personality was extinguished his fate rose up in its stead to oppress his son with powerful irrational forebodings.

The illness of Enoch Bennett is chronicled with relentless truth in *Clayhanger*. There were some who thought that it should not have been, that Arnold Bennett had exploited his father's sufferings for gainful ends. They had not the insight to understand that for Arnold Bennett this may have been a purgative process by which he sought to relieve his mind of a terrible burden of reminiscence. It could only have been out of his bedside experiences at this time that he was able to describe the climax of the disease which had reduced Darius Clayhanger from an intimidating presence to a writhing pullulation under the sheets: "his body seemed to have that vague appearance of general movement which a multitude of insects will give to a piece of decaying matter."

There is the painful episode in which his children watch his attempts at holding a sausage on his plate with his knife while cutting it with his fork:

'No, no, father!' said Maggie gently. 'Not like that!'

He looked up, puzzled, and then bent himself again to the plate. The whole of his faculties seemed to be absorbed in a great effort to resolve the complicated problem of the plate, the sausage, the knife and the fork.

'You've got your knife in the wrong hand,' said Edwin impatiently, as to a wilful child.

Darius stared at the knife and at the fork and he then sighed, and his sigh meant, 'This business is beyond me!' Then he endeavoured to substitute the knife for the fork, but he could not.

'See', said Edwin, leaning over. 'Like this!' He took the knife, but Darius would not loose it. 'No, leave go!' he ordered. 'Leave go! How can I show you if you don't leave go?'

Darius dropped both knife and fork with a clatter. Edwin put the knife into his right-hand, and the fork into his left; but in a moment they were wrong again.

Darius Clayhanger regresses into a stage still more terrible in which he swears at his family, and especially at his daughter, in language which horrifies them all. Not even Edwin, his son, has ever heard him swear before. "He heard him now . . . a brilliant and appalling revelation."

For Edwin, it was a whole series of fresh formulæ, brutal and shameless beyond his experience, full of images and similes of the most startling candour, and drawing its inspiration from the sickening bases of life. Darius had remembered with ease the vocabulary to which he was hourly accustomed when he began life as a man of seven. For more than fifty years he had carried within himself these vestiges of a barbarism which his children had never even conceived, and now he threw them out in all their crudity at his daughter.

Only a writer of intense sensitiveness and sympathies could have comprehended and reproduced in terms of literature the subtler cruelties of a fate that can rob a man of his dignity as Enoch Bennett was robbed of his. Enoch Bennett had been not quite sixty when what may have been the dark forces of his inheritance declared themselves. As Arnold Bennett approached the same period in his own life, he said grimly and as though not speaking for other ears: "I shan't stand for it!"

Dorothy Cheston Bennett recalled in her preface to the volume of his letters to her his allusions to this rarely voiced fear:

'I've always had an idea . . . you know, that *I* should. . .' But here my mental recording breaks off. Evidently he said 'that *I* should go the same way', or 'end in the same way', for certainly that was the sense. But I cannot hear his voice finish the thought, can only record my sense of tumult, of fear and revolt, and yet of inevitability. It was as if one had heard a sentence pronounced by a judge from some greater than human courts of law. . . During the last eight years I should think that Arnold referred perhaps four times to this subject. Yet when he spoke of it as long ago as the summer of 1923 I could tell by his voice that he was not giving utterance to a new thought.[1]

Enoch Bennett was buried in the Bedfordshire cemetery of Chalgrove. The memorial card was designed by his novelist son. " 'Enoch Bennett, born at Burslem, 6 May, 1843, died at Chalgrove, Bedfordshire, 16 January, 1902. 'In a little wrath I hid my face from thee for a moment; but with everlasting kindness will I have mercy on thee.' " Soon after the funeral his widow, asserting the independence of spirit which her eldest son said had hitherto been suppressed, announced that she would return to Burslem to live, alone. When shortly afterwards Tertia Bennett became engaged to William Kennerley, of the Board of Education, Arnold Bennett wrote:

8 April, 1902.

MY DEAR WILLIAM,—I could write an article about this, but not a letter. See? I experience a feeling of profound satisfaction and that is the end of it, in words. These upheaving affairs, of which the import-ance and beauty can only be slowly ingurgitated, leave me dumb for about a month, and then I begin to chirrup. And me only a spectator! Two people could scarcely be more at variance in temperament and ideals than you and me or Tertia and me. But the longer I live the less I think of temperament, ideals, intellect, and the more I think of one quality, which we all three possess and which I will name to you in due course.

Yours, E. A. B.

P.S.—I perceive that owing to this abduction and rapine I shall be under the necessity of starting life afresh, before the century is

[1] *Arnold Bennett: A Portrait Done at Home* (Cape, 1935).

[123]

much older. The mater will certainly return to her native heath. This aspect of the case may not have presented itself to you as vitally important, but to me it has a certain faint interest. I shall have about 5 times as much money as is good for me and no one to spend it on except your brother-in-law. However, don't mind me. Gather your roses.

He gave up Trinity Hall Farm a year after his father's death. He had used it in the intervening time only occasionally, going there for brief spells of work and to see his sister, who stayed on to keep house and to supervise the final removal. He himself was back in London, as his friends, Rickards and Alcock particularly, had said he would be. He had a room in a flat at 7 Halsey House, Red Lion Square, High Holborn, occupied by a friend of his at the Inland Revenue Department of the Treasury, Alexander Webster.

(5)

Anna of the Five Towns was published by Chatto & Windus in the early autumn of 1902. He had finished it with a flourish of satisfaction at a quarter to three one morning, after working on the last five thousand words continuously for seventeen hours. "I was very pleased with it; slept well for four hours, got up with a frightful headache, and cycled through Hemel Hempstead to St. Albans, lunched at the George, and home—forty-two miles." Meantime, *The Grand Babylon Hotel*, written as a serial, was successful also in book form despite its having been dismissed by *The Athenaeum* as "a mixture of rather fantastic comedy and slapdash melodrama". *The Spectator* found in it meritorious evidence of its author's capacity for better work.

When *Anna of the Five Towns* was published, the critics were baffled. Here, on the one hand, was a work of careful achievement, of fine texture, of deliberate art; there, on the other, was *The Grand Babylon Hotel*, reflecting a duality of performance that was like part of a juggling act. In his ability to work at widely disparate levels Arnold Bennett was exceptional among the major novelists. Henry James was prepared almost to immolate himself to achieve success in the theatre. "I should so much love to be popular," he told Alfred Sutro, the dramatist. "My works never go into a second edition." When this man from the Midlands showed how it could be done he was looked on as a literary bounder who wrote for money and not for the release that money might mean.

H. G. Wells to Arnold Bennett:

September 9, 1902.

'Anna' is very good indeed. Your style is not of course my style and there's not three consecutive sentences I should let stand if I had the rewriting of it, but that is partly individual difference. Partly it isn't. Partly it is that—blessed thought!—you are not yet artistically adult . . . on the whole, I should describe my impressions as being that of a photograph a little under-developed.

Arnold Bennett to H. G. Wells:

20 September, 1902.

MY DEAR H. G.—Knowing officially from you that for you 'no such thing as excellence exists', I will not conceal my satisfaction at your remarks about 'Anna'. I reckon no one in this isle knows more about the *craft* of fiction than you, except possibly me, and I am always struck by the shrewdness of your criticisms of novels from that point of view. But I think your notions about verbal style are fundamentally wrong, and nevertheless it just happens in this instance that what you say about my style is, I think, mainly correct. There *is* a "certain consciousness of good intentions" that has jolly well got to disappear. Also I am inclined to agree that I am not yet artistically adult (at thirty-five!)

I don't think the book falls off *much* after the death of old Price, and I think the emotional quality of the end is as good as any. As to the under-developed photograph, this is largely a matter of taste. But I trust you understand that the degree of development to which I have brought the photograph is what I think the proper degree. It is Turgenev's degree, and Flaubert's. It is *not* Balzac's. Anyhow it is the degree that comes natural to me.

Yours, E. A. B.

Arnold Bennett to George Sturt:

4 October, 1902.

. . . I have *not* studied the characters as though they were animals at the Zoo! When you say that I write about them not like 'the God who made them' but like a recording angel, I don't know what you mean, and I don't think you know yourself. But what astounds me most is your remark that I refuse to be emotional. The book is impassioned and emotional from beginning to end. Every character (except perhaps a passing figure like the coroner) is handled with intense sympathy. But you have not perceived the emotion . . . the whole thing, for some reason or other has gone right past you. You are looking for something which you will never get in my fiction, or in any first-rate modern fiction—the Dickens and Thackeray grossness. I 'let myself go' to the full but this does not mean that I shout and weep all over the place. . . .

Yours, E. A. B.

George Sturt to Arnold Bennett:

October 7, 1902.

If you had read between the lines with any discernment, you'd have been blushingly disowning my implied flattery instead of attacking me with a bludgeon. You have my full permission to go to the Devil.

Yours,
GEORGE STURT

Joseph Conrad to Arnold Bennett:

Pent Farm

6 Nov, 1902.

MY DEAR BENNETT,—I wonder what you think of me? Well, I have deserved some hard thoughts, but only in a certain measure. Obviously I might have sent a civil line to acknowledge the book [*Anna of the Five Towns*] but obviously too one does not like to send a civil line in acknowledgement of E. A. Bennett's book. The gift is on another footing of welcome.

. . . the reason was worry, the terrible worry of having to re-write a story (completed and then burnt by fatal accident), with the impossibility of concocting a reasonable sentence confronting me at every turn. It was like a nightmare. . . .

That the advance upon *A Man from the North* is great is undeniable. Just in what that advance consists it's not easy to say without losing one's way among mere superficialities—for there too the advance is very marked. The other, the deeper change, the essential progress, is felt right through but not so easy to hold up. The excellence (in its place) of the first par. of Chapter XII is easy to point out, or the mastery—the obvious mastery—of pp. 164, 165. My dear fellow, it is fine, very fine; I am thankful to see it written.

But there are other passages, other pages and the whole spirit of the book is informed by a less apparent excellence.

There is too the whole conception of the story, whence, of course, flows the characterisation. On this one could say much. I am afraid of falling into twaddle without the stimulus of your presence and your voice. I will only say that the conception seems to me too logical. It's a cryptic saying and does not make my criticism clear in the least —not even to myself.

But on that I end with a congratulatory and hearty handshake. It *is* good, my dear Bennett; and you *know* it is good: and I know that you shall do even better.

Kindest regards,
JOSEPH CONRAD.[1]

Having first gone to Burslem to see that his mother was comfortably settled there, Arnold Bennett left for Paris on March 15, 1903, to begin his career as a man of the world. The rice pudding era of his life was over. It was to be *crème caramel* from now on.

[1] G. Jean-Aubry: *Joseph Conrad, Life and Letters* (Heinemann 1927)

CHAPTER NINE

(1)

DURING his first weeks in Paris he wrote a despondent letter to his friend Raymond Needham in London. He was lonely. A passage in *Paris Nights* probably reproduces his feelings: "I was beaten down by the overwhelming sadness of one who for the time being has no definite arranged claim to any friendly attention in a huge city—crowded with preoccupied human beings." The crisis was resolved when a newspaper friend of his introduced him to a young woman of the theatre named Chichi, the 'C' of the journal, and no doubt in the Midland mind of Bennett it stood for the very spirit of *la vie de Bohème*. Chichi was often at his flat at 4 rue de Calais and it has been assumed on uncertified evidence that through her he was able to gratify his yearning for 'liaisons under pink lampshades' and what else it implied for him. There are unpublished journal entries about topics of their conversation from which it is clear that the young woman was wise in aspects of Parisian life on which he may be presumed to have been both imaginatively and practically ignorant. "Concerning sexual perversions, she gave me several of her experiences. They always wept afterwards. Yet she said to me: 'Mais tout est naturel.' The force of this observation struck me." It should be said that his abundant Paris note-taking gives no sign of abnormal sex interest. The lapsed Methodist was "eased from the strain of pretending that things were not what in fact they are", as he wrote after having "witnessed for the first time the spectacle of a fairly large mixed company talking freely about scabrous facts".

Soon he was engrossed in the Paris scene, though he was not able to shed entirely the mental attitudes of a stranger to it. He would have preferred to think as a Frenchman if not to act like one, but his processes of conscious identification were not to succeed as his deeper unconscious drives had already begun to do. A French portrait painter and writer, Jacques-Émile Blanche, saw him a little later "looking like a well-fed, wealthy business man, boasting, familiar, and coarse, showing off with exasperating patronage and posing as a French bohemian", which may have been exact observation but testifies also to the tenacious and deplorable intolerance of those born to ways of grace for those who are not. "Diaghileff was as antipathetic to me as ever," Bennett noted after going behind the scenes at the Russian Ballet in Paris in June, 1910.

At any rate, the Schwobs were finding him acceptable, Marcel Schwob, writer and bibliographer who wrote under the pen-name of Loyson-Bridet and did the French version of *Hamlet* for Sarah Bernhardt, and Margaret Moreno, his wife, a member of the Comédie Française; he was seeing a good deal of Calvocoressi, the music critic; he was embarking on his long friendship with Henri Davray, Paris journalist and translator; soon he would be the friend of Gide, Ravel and Larbaud, and would mount the heights of success with them. Schwob was a neurasthenic Frenchman whose eyes shone with strange light and who asked Bennett to believe that there was no day on which he did not rise with a sense of hopelessness, of his having no future (and so it proved). His social introductions were useful to Bennett, his critical gifts stimulating. Noting some comments of Schwob's, he added in the journal: "I always find French criticism of English work very instructive, disconcerting, and tonic." Schwob was an ardent admirer of Dickens, Bennett was not. Schwob did not admire Shaw. "He had been reading G. B. Shaw's plays, and broke out into invective against Shaw and all his works. He could see nothing in them at all. He said he could see what *we* saw and took for *esprit*, and what to *us* was *esprit*, but to the French mind it was nothing but foolishness." When they discussed Kipling, Schwob went on to remark: "An artist could not do as he liked with his imagination; it would not stand improper treatment, undue fatigue, etc., in youth; and that a man who wrote many short stories early in life was bound to decay prematurely. He said that he himself was going through this experience. He was in a very black and despondent mood when he said this." Speaking of the new Five Towns novel called *Leonora* which Bennett had begun to write not long after his arrival in Paris, Schwob said: "You have got hold of the greatest of all themes, the agony of the older generation in watching the rise of the younger."

It was the Paris that was still nervous about fires, following the disaster in the rue Jean Goujon when a hundred aristocratic dead were left in the flames started by the overturning of a cinematograph projector lamp. Chichi told Arnold Bennett that she and her colleagues of the theatre smoked cigarettes in the dressing-room though there was now a decree against it. "Everyone does it. But there is an official search of all dressing-rooms, etc., once a month by the firemen, and before that an attendant comes round and says to the artists: 'Kindly hide your matches, etc., as the pompiers will be here directly.' The extraordinary humour of this did not seem to occur to her. 'C'est bien Parisien, ça!' I said, and she cynically and bitterly agreed that it was. But she could not see the joke." He had himself been at the Theatre Française when the cry of 'Fire!' had gone through the audience. "The experience was of the highest interest to the professional student of human nature."

It was the Paris of the silk-blouse shops, of goat-milking in the streets, and of the new French-originated race of men called chauffeurs who wore wide gauntlet gloves, tight black leggings, and goggles over the peaks of their caps; the Paris of the cartoons of Caran d'Ache, of diminishing births and luxury funerals, and of the first gleams of the Anglo-French *rapprochement* which he believed would never mature into an alliance. "I have not the faintest hope of it," but he had a hope, he said, of a more than formal understanding, "if only we can drop our pharisaism and our habit of looking on the Moulin Rouge as a synonym for France." He saw Paris become a city of light as a compliment to Edward VII:

Even the churches wore tiaras of fire. Lighted gas (at something like seven francs a thousand of cubic feet) ran in quivering lines along the borders of all the massive edifices in which France administers education, justice, comedies, and music-dramas to the citizens of its metropolis. And as one travelled gradually from the east to the west by way of the principal boulevards, the blaze became prodigal, vast, overpowering. . . .

It was midnight. There was a rattle of horses' hoofs, and a detachment of cavalry with drawn swords trotted swiftly by. Then come carriages, and in one carriage—a long gracefully curved vehicle—I could just make out the familiar features of Edward VII. Cheers! Hat-waving! Cries of 'Edouard!' Then the breaking of the line of gendarmes, and a huge hum of excited conversation. It was all over in thirty seconds, but the symbol and the figure of the Majesty of England had passed by! Later still, I stood in front of the singularly mean entrance to that magnificent mansion, the British Embassy. In the profound shadow above the dazzling electrical devices I could faintly discern the moving folds of a large flag. It was

[130]

the Royal Standard. The suggestion of its presence there, imposing though scarcely seen, moved me strangely, and the emotion remains.

The journal was being filled with his carefully gathered impressions, written out with the serene legibility of hand which he had cultivated for the purpose. Occasionally there are declensions into an enfeebled scrawl, but the stream of notes flows on and on under the compulsion of his strictly disciplined attention. It is interrupted only when he is doing creative work: "it seems that I cannot do both." He went up to the Sacré Cœur on Sunday, October 4, 1903, for a panoramic view of the city.

I came out and surveyed Paris from the front. I could distinguish most of the landmarks—Notre Dame, Pantheon, Invalides, Gare d'Orleans, St. Sulpice, and the Louvre. . . . I could also see the Opera (that centre of Paris *qui s'amuse*) with its green roof (? copper). And it looked so small and square and ordinary. And I thought of the world-famed boulevards and resorts lying hidden round about there. And I thought: Is that all it is? For a moment it seemed impossible to me that, as the result of a series of complicated conventions merely, that collocation of stones, etc. (paving stones and building stones) could really be what it is—a synonym and symbol for all that is luxurious, frivolous, gay, vicious, and artistic. I thought: 'Really, Paris is not Paris after all; it is only a collocation of stones.' The idea, though obvious enough, was very striking for a minute or two.

He took his meals usually at the Duval in the rue de Clichy, a very long restaurant with walls lined by Empire mirrors reflecting clustered lights that hung from the high ceiling on stiff pendant rods. The picture-postcard he sent to his mother at 179 Waterloo Road, Burslem, on December 10, 1903, shows the spaciousness of the restaurant, "which is enormous," he wrote along the margin of the picture. "I always lunch at the same table. I have marked it with a cross," and the Duval beef-steaks with *sauté* potatoes, he mentioned, could not be matched in the native city of beefsteaks, London. The Duvals were to Paris what the Lyons' Corner Houses are to London. "You can divide the restaurants of Paris, roughly, into two classes, those where the customers eat to live, and those where the customers eat to enjoy themselves. The Duvals are the great type of the former. Everything is stern, business-like, sharp, and no extra food luxuries at all. In the second class there is always leisure and the waiters seem to be in a charming conspiracy to anticipate your wishes."

(2)

On the evening of November 18, 1903, he went to his Duval for dinner and found in the seat opposite his an abnormally stout middle-aged woman whose unattractive presence made him hesitate about sitting there. Seeing his doubt, 'his' waitress came forward and requested him to take his usual chair. He did so, thinking to himself: "With that *thing* opposite my dinner will be spoilt." As it happened, the woman seemed reluctant to sit at the table with him, more sensitive than perhaps he realised to his unexpressed hostility.

She went away, picking up all her belongings, to another part of the restaurant, breathing hard. Then she abandoned her second choice for a third one. My waitress was scornful and angry at this desertion, but laughing also. Soon all the waitresses were privately laughing at the goings-on of the fat woman, who was being served by the most beautiful waitress I have ever seen in any Duval. The fat woman was clearly a crochet, a 'maniaque', a woman who lived much alone. Her cloak (she displayed on taking it off a simply awful light puce flannel dress) and her parcels were continually the object of her attention and she was always arguing with her waitress. And the whole restaurant secretly made a butt of her. She was repulsive; no one could like her or sympathise with her. But I thought—she had been young and slim once. And I immediately thought of a long 10 or 15 thousand words short story, 'The History of Two Old Women.' I gave this woman a sister, fat as herself. And the first chapter would be in the restaurant (both sisters) something like tonight—and written rather cruelly. Then I would go back to the infancy of these two, and sketch it all. One should have lived ordinarily, married prosaically, and become a widow. The other should have become a whore and all that; 'guilty splendour.' Both are overtaken by fat. And they live together again in old age, not too rich, a nuisance to themselves and others. Neither has any imagination. For 'tone' I thought of "Ivan Ilyitch", and for technical arrangement I thought of that and also of 'Histoire d'une fille de ferme'. The two lives would have to intertwine. I saw the whole work quite clearly, and hope to do it. But I expect I shall have to do my humorous novel, 'A Great Man' first, not to mention other things.

Out of this small grotesque episode there was to come in time a great novel, *The Old Wives' Tale*, the beginnings of which he documented further in a preface written for an American edition of that work. There he speaks first of the two waitresses at the Duval who were centrally involved: "one a beautiful, pale young girl, to whom I never spoke, for she was employed far away from the table which I affected . . . the other, a stout, middle-aged, managing Breton woman, had sole command over my table and me, and gradually she began to assume such a maternal tone towards me that I saw I should be compelled to leave that restaurant. If I was absent for a couple of nights running she would reproach me sharply: 'What! You are unfaithful to me?' Once, when I complained about some French beans, she informed me that French beans were a subject which I did not understand. I then decided to be unfaithful to her, and I abandoned the restaurant."

The incident of the unattractive woman had occurred an evening or two before. He could understand his plain Breton waitress laughing as the fat woman moved angrily from table to table, dropping her parcels and suffering the discomforts of picking them up. It pained him to observe "a coarse grimace of giggling" on the pale and sensitive face of the beautiful younger waitress. Reflecting on this, he saw again how the fat old woman had once been young, like the beautiful waitress. "One ought to be able to make a heartrending novel out of the history of a woman such as she." He put the idea aside for a long time; "but it was never very distant from me."

And a few days later he reproaches himself in the journal for not having seen the truth about his possessive Duval waitress, that she, "apparently the image of shrewd content," was really a *névrose*, subject to irrational crises of temperament. "I ought to have known it from the day when, after a few days' absence from the restaurant, she greeted me bluntly with the question: 'Is she prettier than I am, then?' I only made sure of her nervous temperament yesterday, when she cried violently about some undisclosed thing at lunch."

(3)

His novel *Leonora*, the story of a woman who finds romance in middle age, was published by Chatto & Windus that autumn. *The*

Athenæum rumbled forth approval: "We find neither the smartness nor the gaiety of *The Grand Babylon Hotel* but a good deal that is better than either from the literary standpoint and much that is worth the serious consideration of any reader who claims to be a student of life. Mr. Bennett has the essence of the matter in him." H. G. Wells, to whom Bennett had sent an advance copy, "considered it no more than a creditable performance," this in a letter to Bennett. "The dreadful thing is the death of the husband. I don't see how you can forgive yourself that, and the subsequent petering out of the book. And, anyhow, you haven't wrung the guts of life though ever and again you get astonishingly near the illusion. One is impressed by the idea that the clever Bennett is going to be a fearful job for the artist Bennett to elude."

Arnold Bennett to H. G. Wells:

> 7 Halsey House
> Red Lion Square,
> London, W.C.

MY DEAR H. G.,   24 Aug., 1903.

Your letter robbed me of my afternoon's sleep today (I only got it this morning). I think your criticisms are usually tonic and wholesome for me. And you impress me fearfully sometimes—it may be your matter or your manner—I don't know which. I really do think you have a power of finding fault with fiction which I have not seen equalled. And yet I also feel that you are incapable of learning what I *know*, critically, of fiction. Your outlook is too narrow and you haven't read enough. You still cling to the Dickens-Thackeray standards, and judge by them. As when you say: 'How like Becky Sharp!' Would you say: 'How like Eugenie Grandet or Madame Bovary or Maisie?' The strongly marked character, the eccentric, the sharply-defined type, is the easiest thing in the world to do (you wouldn't believe how I despise my Meshach Myatt as a creation) in such a manner that the reader can recognise all his acts for *his*. But the less typical can not, and ought not, to be done in this way, for the reason that they are not so in life. It is in remarks like that that I think you give yourself away, and impair the 'sanction' of what else you say. Far more important, have you grasped the fact that what I aim at is the expression of general moods, whether of a person or a whole scene, a constant 'synthesising' of emotion, before the elucidation of minor points of character? We should never be able to agree

[134]

about the death of the husband. I take it you object to it because it is a sort of coincidence and because it solves (anyhow apparently) the difficulty of Leonora. I must talk to you some time about coincidences in fiction and in life. The fact that this death solves a difficulty is to me entirely beside the point. It is part of the inmost scheme of my book. I seem to think that the novelists who would object to it that it was too timely are too proud to take the genuine material of life as they find it. Or they are afraid to. Because life is simply crammed full of such timelinesses. . . .

I feel in spite of my judgment that most of what you say is half true, in the annoying manner of half truths. And I am much obliged to you for your candour (no one else will be so candid). I am conscious now of an intention to make you get down unconditionally on to your knees yet, in a future book. Of course, I see you are dealing with the thing at an extremely high level, and that is all right. I do honestly wish, quite apart from this book, that I could fill you with a sense of your artistic limitations. No one, except Turgenev, ever had more technical skill than you have. But your perception of beauty is deficient; at least it isn't sufficiently practised and developed. However, go on and prosper. 'My confidence is unabated,' says Sir T. Lipton today. So is mine.

'The Truth About An Author' may be literature. But it isn't imaginative literature, and so cannot enter into the competition.

Yours ever,
E. A. B.

4 rue de Calais

MY DEAR H. G., 8 Oct,1903

Many thanks for 'Mankind In The Making'. Like 'Anticipations', it is very wonderful and very uneven. Some of the things in it are so excellent and so persuasive that they make one promise oneself to forgive you all your sins, past, present, and to come. . . . Your remarks on literature as such betray your fundamental inability to grasp what art is, really. The literary sense *cannot* be quickened in the manner suggested at the bottom of page 372. If you could only see how you give the show away by such a remark as that about Plato on page 334! As a mere matter of opinion, my opinion is absolutely the reverse of yours that "every well-known living writer is or has been writing too much". Quite the contrary.

And in view of your terrific indictment of the English peoples for mauling the English language, I think the mere writing of a lot of the book falls short of even a respectable average. In 'Anticipations', the sentences were overloaded, and the words badly arranged, and often the meaning had to be disentangled. The same here, only more so. You have just got to face the fact that I was continually, except in the best passages, irritated by the bad technique of the writing. How do you defend this: 'It is one of the most amazing aspects of contemporary life, to converse with some smart . . . woman,' etc. (page 164)? There were sundry examples of bad grammar, scores of bad punctuation, hundreds of striking inelegance, and not a few of an obscurity that might easily have been avoided. You may say that these things are nothing, that you can't be bothered with them; in the spirit which asks me whether I can't see the humour of advising the literary aspirant to begin with spelling. But it won't do, my son. And I half believe you jolly well know it. I sit at your feet in many things, but when I open my mouth on the art and craft of your trade, it behoves you to listen. There is a blind spot in your eye; either that or you are wayward. Now reread page 1 of this present effusion.

Yours,

E. A. B.

Wells's disregard of the finer points of sentence construction and punctuation was a subject of Bennett's reproaches all through the years of what Wells called their "friendly rivalry". In 1904 Bennett told Wells that he had made a collection of his contributions to the "higher literary carelessness" which, if published, "would really show you up." When *The Outline of History* appeared in the early 1920s Bennett wrote appealing to Mrs. Wells to persuade Wells to take more trouble with his writing and also with the correction of his proofs. Wells had so slight an ear for words that he could write 'by us' and 'bias' in the same paragraph, as in the opening of *Tono-Bungay*.

Bennett had begun writing *Leonora* before he had found his first Paris flat, while staying at the Hôtel de Quai Voltaire. As he neared the end of the novel he experienced an unpleasant physical sensation mentioned on a number of later occasions in the journal: "I felt that the top of my head would blow off"; he could not bear to touch his head when this feeling was upon him and he spoke of it as among "the worst experiences" of his life. The symptom was an accompaniment of violent headaches, which often sent him to bed all day. "I was visited by an extremely severe and inexplicable headache which quite incapacitated me." He had violent liver attacks that were not invariably the penalty of imprudence.

Leonora was his retort to the convention which demanded a young and beautiful heroine in fiction. Leonora Stanway is the middle-aged mother of daughters who falls in love while remaining level-headed enough to judge the possible consequences of surrendering to her emotions. She is warm, vital, psychologically interesting; that is, as the chief character of the novel. None of the other characters is so sharply imagined, not even old Uncle Meshach and his sister, the Five Towns slave of a ruthless domesticity. The effects of age on women are observed as if in a preliminary trial of the imaginative force which makes time roll so sublimely over the lives of the two sisters in *The Old Wives' Tale*. Contemplating her daughter and son-in-law, just married, Leonora Stanway is made to feel sad—"sad, because Ethel could never again be that which she had been, and because she was so young, inexperienced, confiding, and beautiful, and would gradually grow old and lose the ineffable grace of her years and situation; and because they were both so innocent of the meaning of life. Leonora yearned for some magic to stay the destructive hand of time and keep them ever thus, young, naïve, trustful, and unspoilt."

November 20, 1903.—I worked till 10.30 last night on the fifth 'Windsor' story, but the following words from Whitten's review of 'Leonora' in 'T.P.'s Weekly', which I received by the last post, pleased and excited me so much that I had some difficulty in recommencing work in the evening: 'His claim as an artist is drawn from the source of all art—life itself. And from the standpoint of art it is significant that one naturally refers his book, not to the fleeting fashions of the circulating library, but to the great standards themselves—to Tolstoi, to Flaubert, to Thomas Hardy.'

Joseph Conrad to Arnold Bennett:

Pent Farm

19 Nov. 1903.

My dear Bennett,—You must think me a brute. I don't even attempt to palliate an inexcusable delay in thanking you for 'Leonora'. Still when I tell you that I am some four months behind with a wretched novel I am writing for Harpers you'll understand the state of my mind.

Yes. You *can* do things; you present them with a skill and in a language for which I wish here to thank you as distinctly as possible, and with all the respect due to such a remarkable talent.

Remains the question of conception; the only one in which discussion between you and me is possible. And here the first criticism that occurs is that there is not enough of Leonora herself. The pedestal is, as it were, too large for the statue. And that's about the only objection that can be made to the book as a *work*. With the sheer pleasure of reading it, that—say—defect does not interfere. It is only in thinking it over that the objection arises. And it is impossible to read 'Leonora' without afterwards thinking it all over—with great satisfaction, undoubtedly, and yet with some regret also.

You see I am frank with you; and I am frank because I have a great regard for your high ideals of workmanship, and for the ways of your thought. But one would need to talk it over with you to make one's meaning clear. Discussion alone could do that; for you must not imagine that I am trying to pick holes; I am too much fascinated by your expression, by the ease of your realisation, the force and the delicacy of your phrases. Whether you obtain them by hard toil or by an amazing inborn ability does not matter; these qualities are there. That you can also go to the bottom of your subject *Anna* proves sufficiently well; though even in that book, perhaps . . . ?

However, don't mind me. It is very possible that I am too romantic and don't seize quite your true intention.

Always yours sincerely,

JOSEPH CONRAD.[1]

As to the mischief of time, on his next birthday, May 27, 1904, Arnold Bennett wrote: "Today I am thirty-seven. I have lived longer than I shall live. My new series begins today in the *Windsor*. My name is not on the cover. Anthony Hope's stands there alone. And I am thirty-seven. Comment is needless." An amateur palmist, a friend named Young, presumed to be the publisher and bookseller who shared the cottage with him at Witley, had told him that he saw wealth for him, "but not a long existence."

(4)

Uneasy as he was about himself and his future, the publication of a new novel had improved his standing in the widening circle of Paris

[1] G. Jean-Aubry: *Joseph Conrad, Life and Letters* (Heinemann 1927)

acquaintance to which he was attracted. Davray thought fit to introduce him to the editor of the *Mercure de France* as "the hope of English fiction". He was going often to the Chat Blanc in the rue d'Odessa, where a group of writers and painters met regularly in a room set apart for them. It was there that Somerset Maugham first saw Bennett: "a thin man with dark hair smoothly done in a fashion that suggested the private soldier of the day." Maugham also recalled him as being more neatly and more conventionally dressed than the rest of the company. "He looked like the managing clerk in a city office," and was thought bumptious and common. "Our attitude," says Mr. Maugham, "was somewhat patronising," there being no reason to foresee a time when he would establish himself well beyond the range of any such pose. Life moved on for Mr. Maugham too. When, long after, they met again, he was struck by the contrast between the Bennett he had known in Paris and the transformed, public figure of the post-Armistice years. "His hair, very grey, was worn much longer and he had cultivated the amusing cock's comb that the caricaturists made famous. He had always been neat in his dress, disconcertingly even, but now he was grand. He wore frilled shirts in the evening and took an immense pride in his white waistcoats. . . . But it was not only in appearance that he was a very different man from the one I had known in Paris." This contemporary remembered Bennett's "small dark apartment". Everything was noticeably in its place; the apartment was overwhelmingly tidy, but not very comfortable by the Maugham standard. "It gave you the impression of a man who saw himself in a certain role, which he was playing carefully, but into the skin of which he had not quite got."

Bennett was observing Maugham not less closely. "He has a very calm, almost lethargic demeanour. He took two cups of tea with pleasure and absolutely refused a third; one knew instantly from his tone that nothing would induce him to take a third. He ate biscuits and *gaufrettes* very quickly, almost greedily one after another without a pause, and then suddenly stopped." The note concludes with the comment: "I liked him," a crystallising phrase which occurs frequently in the journal as his growing reputation extends his acquaintance beyond the boulevards. He writes it again and again: "I liked him," or her, after noting impressions of personalities newly arrived in his life, a gift of sympathy which he developed into a distinction of his character, until we find Somerset Maugham writing about him: "His kindness glowed like a halo about a saint."

[139]

Gerald Kelly, Sir Gerald Kelly, P.R.A., of later years, studying art in Paris at that time, remembers the *gauche* Bennett, the man from the Potteries who had brought with him a sense of social inferiority which he could not slough off. "I came to like him: it was odd to watch a man educating himself so visibly and so audibly" says Sir Gerald. He, Schwob, Bennett and Davray arranged to dine together soon after the publication of Bennett's novel, *A Great Man*, which followed *Leonora*. Davray was late, and Bennett was angry. His anger degenerated into a display of bad manners at the others' expense. Then Davray arrived, full of excuses, with which Bennett showed no patience until Davray said: "If you must know why I'm late, it's because I've been reading 'A Great Man'. It was all so amusing, I couldn't leave it." Sir Gerald Kelly describes the effect of this compliment: "Sticking his thumbs into the arm holes of his waistcoat, Bennett in his self-satisfaction leaned back in his chair so far that he began to slip and before he could recover himself he was under the table!"

Arnold Bennett's sister, Mrs. Vernon, will be reminded of the evening at Gatti's in the Strand, not long after he had written *Clayhanger*, when she and other members of the family had dinner with him in the long gallery restaurant. He had a habit, for which in earlier days he was often reprimanded by his father at home, of balancing his chair on two legs as he relaxed at table. Declaiming that evening with upraised hand, he suddenly disappeared, his chair skidding behind him along the floor.

Sir Gerald Kelly does not recall Bennett as a sympathetic personality of those Paris days. He and Bennett had met at the Schwobs' and it was Kelly who introduced Bennett to the *cenacle* at the Chat Blanc. Sir Gerald writes: "My recollection is that Maugham and Bennett heartily disliked each other at their first meeting, which I brought about. One evening Bennett had the nerve to correct Willie Maugham's French, which was usually extremely good. There was tension between them and I remember the general amusement at the look of rage in Willie's face. He and I always referred to Bennett as Enoch Arnold. Returning to London after a long absence in Burma and other places, I was met by Willie Maugham with the words: 'Wonderful things have happened. Enoch Arnold has written a masterpiece', adding that *The Old Wives' Tale* was "extraordinarily good.'"

Paris life exhausted him, but for him it was inexhaustible. He met again his former *Woman* contributor, Mrs. Roy Devereux, and her sister, Mrs. Laye, and drove out with them, privately proud to be seen in their company. "I crowded into the brougham with two large hats of the most excessive *chic*. They were both extremely pleased with their hats, which drew forth my high praise, products of the latest and greatest of all hat makers, a certain Georgette." Mrs. Devereux, talking about what he terms 'the only topic', pertinently observed: "Perhaps it is not love you desire, but only the experience."

Another of his Paris friends was Mrs. Richard le Gallienne, wife of the well-known poet of the '90s, who told him of the infelicities of the artistic temperament and of her resolve to have done with it, "her husband having discovered a love for America and the Americans." His habit of drunkenness was growing; her sister, Mrs. Welch, wife of the well-known comedian, had to come and stay with her for protection. "Mrs. le Gallienne has two journalistic jobs worth £200 a year and hopes to earn other money by art, etc." Mrs. le Gallienne added: "There is one thing I can say—he has never bored me."

Miss Berta Ruck, meeting Arnold Bennett at his Paris flat for tea with an American artist, Miss Thomasson, remembers him holding forth to that lady: "Women, my dear girl? I know women inside and outside. I know women as well as I know my own pocket." Miss Ruck, then a very young art student, could not understand how a man who to her was unprepossessing—"phenomenally ugly, he then seemed to me"—could talk in that fashion. She talked about him to Marie Belloc Lowndes, who assured her that "he had been loved—'yes, really *loved*'—by some of the most beautiful women."

> *May 26, 1904.*—I did no work yesterday. Miss Thomasson and Berta Ruck came for tea, and much enjoyed the *petits fours* and the Empire furniture. Berta Ruck, while agreeing with me that Bohemianism is hateful, sat down on the floor. She has a curious way of reciting stories that she has written. She seems to be able to recite a 3000 or 5000 word story almost word for word.

Miss Thomasson is remembered by Miss Ruck as "a small, slim, dark, effective woman, with large bright eyes and dark eyebrows in striking contrast to a tower of prematurely silver hair". She is the subject of a good many entries in Bennett's journal for 1904. "It is the faculty of living intensely that stimulates me in these American women. Yet they live intensely in such a small circle."

"Miss Thomasson came to dine with me. I talked to her nearly all the time about the relations of the sexes" (June 5). "Miss Thomasson came to paint a corner of my room for the Mater. I talked all the time, explaining at great length my ideas on women" (July 18). "Miss Thomasson dined with me at Sylvain's and we went to the Bois. I told her that M—— and I (she knows and likes him) had spent much of our time last night in telling each other stories of a kind that 'no decent woman' would listen to, and that no woman decent or indecent would really see the beauty of. She said she had known women who told such stories. 'They thought I didn't see the point of them, but I did, though I wasn't going to let *them* see that I saw it.' She had all the usual feminine ideas about stories. When I said that the difference between men and women in regard to stories was one of the profoundest and least explicable things in human nature, and that no one could quite explain it, and that it was a strange Fact, she seemed quite impressed. I pointed out to her what an advantage men had over women in being able to amuse themselves in this way and she replied that it was an advantage they were welcome to." They went to the Pavillon Royal in the Bois that summer's night and the journal contains a charming souvenir of the scene:

> Like all the other cafés it was crowded. The night gorgeous. Boats on the lake carrying crimson Chinese lanterns, all reflected in the still water. The trees had that unreal, theatrical appearance that trees do have under electric light. And within the circle of great trees the vast 'parterre' of *toilettes claires* and men's straw hats; and the red-jacketed musicians in the middle. The air 'laved' the hands and face like warm water. You knew it was a hot night by the direct feel and contact, of the air. Few things are more delicious than this. We must have driven many miles through the Paris streets—from Sylvain's to the Bois, thence to the Boul. Raspail, and thence, me alone, home. I got home at 12.30. I spent 24 francs and wondered if I had got enough for my money.

In a new attack on his speech problem, he summoned Godfrey from London and, as a result, was put off work by Godfrey's presence in the flat. There was a cryptic letter from Marriott in the post one morning: "Keep up your enthusiasm at all costs, for remember we expect great things of you," and Bennett made a journal note: "I don't know in the least why he should have said that." A night of eight hours' sleep was so much of an event in his life that he recorded it as such: "extraordinary for me." He went to a new café and was struck by the "distinguished flirtatiousness" of the *demoiselle du comptoir*, "a tall woman of forty with provocative eyes, and I should think bad health. I said to myself instantly that I would go to that place again."

(6)

He was coming to grips with the new novel, *A Great Man*: central character, Henry Knight, lawyer's clerk, lawyer's clerk turned purveyor of popular fiction. This was Bennett the man of business; there is a cousin Tom, an artist, who observes Henry's success with a jaundiced eye: this is Bennett the artist. All that needs to be said about this novel of Fulham and Paris was said thirty years ago by Harvey Darton: "It reads like a fictitious appendix to *The Truth about an Author*." There are comedy touches which foreshadow *The Card* and it was begun in a self-doubting phase:

December 8, 1903.—I succeeded far beyond my hopes in planning out 'A Great Man' yesterday, and in making a detailed sketch of the first chapter. I was, however, and I remain, extremely dissatisfied and discontented with my general condition. I suppose I shall always be more or less like this. I cannot think of any device or policy by which I could change my condition with any prospect of improvement. I want to be free and fettered at the same time.

What he calls "a fair specimen of one of my cogitating days" is given in the journal for December 13. It shows his working method before the evolution of the legend of his self-command as a writer who went to his desk every day with the resolute mind of a business executive:

After buying papers and tea yesterday, I lunched at the little creamery in the Place de la Trinité. Then I came home and read various papers and periodicals and 'Casanova', and fell asleep, sleeping uncomfortably. Then I tried seriously to find the ideas for Chapter 11 of new novel; I had been more or less asking for them all morning; no success. Then I went out for a walk, and felt tired even in starting. I walked through the St. Lazare quarter to the Madeleine and turned along the Grand Boulevard to the Grand Café.

I like the interior of this café. It is as much like the respectable ugliness of an English club as anything in Paris. I ordered a cup of chocolate because I felt empty.

I thought steadily for one hour over this chocolate and I seemed to leave the café with one or two germs of ideas. I walked home, cogitating. When I arrived, there was a telegram from Whitten requiring my weekly article two days earlier than usual. This upset my plans somewhat. I felt so tired—I had taken a chill—that I lay down under the eiderdown on the bed and went to sleep again, reading 'Casanova'.

When I awoke it was dark. I made tea and felt better. A leading notion for the chapter had now formed itself. I went to the Comédie Mondaine to book a seat for Brieux's 'Berceau' and then to the Duval to dine, where I read *Le Temps* all through. Then I bought a cigar and had coffee in the Place Clichy. I cogitated at the café for an hour, and then I had the whole chapter clearly outlined in my head.

This process of cogitation before putting pen to paper became the Bennett production formula, whether for a novel or a newspaper article. He invented for himself what he termed his 'thinking walk', in the course of which he would sort out his ideas, set them mentally in order, and return only to his desk when all was clear in his mind. In this process he developed a most rare facility, indicating a degree of 'lordship over the noddle' which could be held to justify the pontifying *Mental Efficiency*. It was not simply a matter of deciding what he wanted to say. It was a matter of mentally shaping the paragraphs and sentences in which he proposed to say it. He showed one of his friends from the Paris days, J. B. Atkins, his way of planning a novel. "He would divide his scheme into parts which he numbered, and divide each part into sections. He knew in advance what he would put into each part and each section," and Mr. Atkins asked himself whether the writer who forswears deviations from a plan may renounce the inspirations which often arrive when hand and brain are working in unison. "All I can say of Arnold's method is that it was in practice right for him. Evidently he had the exceptional power of making his thoughts obey his command, assemble themselves, and reach maturity before he put pen to paper. Other writers, also painters and sculptors, can only wonder."[1]

He went home to the Potteries to spend that Christmas with his mother. Seemingly with home thoughts in his mind, he concocted in an

[1] *Incidents and Reflections* by J. B. Atkins (Christophers, 1947).

idle moment a rhyme which he thought worth preserving in the margin of his journal note for the day:

> Mary had a little lamb;
> Its fleece was white as snow:
> She took it over to Longton—
> And look at the damn' thing now!

On his way through London he called on his literary agent, J. B. Pinker, at Effingham House, Arundel Street, Strand. Pinker had formerly worked on *Black and White* with Eden Phillpotts. When that paper closed down, he set up as a manager of authors' affairs. He had negotiated some small sales for Arnold Bennett, who by the end of the June half-year, 1903, owed him £47 10s. 11d., some of which had been incurred by monthly payments of £6 11s. to Sarah Ann Bennett at Burslem. After hesitating, Pinker now bound himself to pay Bennett £50 a month certain through 1904. Viewed as a business transaction, it was a compliment to both. Its formal confirmation launched a correspondence which lasted more than twenty years and dignifies a sometimes misunderstood profession. As Bennett's fame grows we find Pinker often adopting a markedly deferential tone in his letters, with Bennett remaining firmly judicial throughout but never forgetting his indebtedness to Pinker, who invested faith and money in him during those early years. For instance, at the June half-year, 1910, he owed Pinker £1,157 13s. 6d. Pinker was charging him five per cent and still believing in him.

Arriving in Burslem, "the great current topic," he found, was "vice". A parson, the Rev. Leonard Tyrwhitt, had laid about his flock from the pulpit and had caused a local outcry. "I wrote a letter to the *Sentinel* to pulverise 'the crusader', the Rev. Leonard Tyrwhitt." The letter was dated December 30, 1903:

SIR,—. . . When I landed at Newhaven a few days ago, the first printed thing that caught my eye was a newspaper placard: VICE IN THE POTTERIES. SHOCKING DETAILS. It was a London newspaper. Soon afterwards I learnt about the 'crusade' of the Honourable and Reverend Leonard Tyrwhitt. Upon this 'crusade' I should like, as a native of the district, to make a few remarks.

When I tried to buy the London newspaper which had placarded our 'vice' do you suppose that I could get it? Not a bit. It was sold out. It was sold out all over London. And the fact is that for days

[145]

past half England has been feasting upon the panorama of our alleged enormities. I am told that Mr. Tyrwhitt preached to a crowded congregation. Doubtless. . . .

. . . Mr. Tyrwhitt compares the illegitimate birthrate of the Potteries to that of the whole of England. What possible end could be attained by such a debating society trick? He ought to have known that the only fair comparison was with some similar industrial districts where the two sexes had to work together under similar conditions. Again, with a fine rhetorical flourish, he states that where drink slays its thousands, immorality slays its tens of thousands. Much licence may be allowed to a man in the frenzy of galloping his hobby horse, but he should contrive not to be absolutely silly.

It would be interesting to know whether any thinking man really believes at the bottom of his heart that human nature is worse in the Potteries than it is elsewhere. For my own part, I regard the theory that the Potteries is ultra-vicious as unworthy of discussion. I have lived in the Potteries, in London, in Paris, and in a pretty English village and I have found that the most profound of our physical instincts produced much the same result everywhere. (I know that in the pretty English village a *virgo intacta* aged 20 was looked on as a decided curiosity) . . .

Purification will have to begin where charity begins. What about the manufacturers and all the other pillars of society? What about the men of means who come back boasting from London and Paris? And what about those who attend chapel or church regularly every Sunday in our town, while carrying on an intrigue, idyllic but highly immoral, in another town? Mr. Tyrwhitt should have begun, if he was to begin, at the summit of the social structure.

179 Waterloo Road   ARNOLD BENNETT

He had previously noted in the journal the name of the man, a member of a well-known Burslem family, who "was taking his mother to chapel every Sunday morning while keeping a woman in Tunstall", citing it there as "an amusing instance of local manners". And he had noted, also, the statement of another well-known local man to him, that "on the banks the married women were the most preoccupied with sex and talked sex all day".

His *Sentinel* letter brought replies signed 'Ambassador of Christ', 'Staunch Potter,' 'A Potter's Wife,' 'Member of P.S.A. Brotherhood,

[146]

Hanley,' 'Neckender,' 'Country Girl,' and 'Queercuss'. A conspicuous advertiser in the same issue was H. K. Hales: 'Bechstein Pianos For Sale.' Hales wrote to say that while he had never seen any vice, though he had worked in all branches of the pottery trade, he supported Bennett wholeheartedly, presumably taking the opportunity of a little publicity which the prototype of Denry Machin could hardly be expected to resist.

December 30, 1903.—After the appearance of my letter on the 'Immoral Potteries' in the *Sentinel,* I went over with Dawson to the *Sentinel* office to see the editor, Barrett Green. We talked with him, then looked over the plant, with the up-to-dateness and completeness of which I was much pleased. Three 'Victory' presses and 8 linos. I watched one press printing 300 copies a minute of a six-page paper.

Beardmore's ball at the Park Road Board Schools. I sat out 9 dances with 9 partners, collected gossip, and scattered it again.

On his way back to Paris he looked in at the office of *T.P.'s Weekly,* where he heard from Whitten's assistant, Downey, of "the enormous amount of work T.P. O'Connor does, for one who is so idle". On the previous day 'T.P.' had sat for seven hours in the office, shivering, and doing only half-an-hour's work. "But in fact he can write eighty words a minute on the typewriter and can produce a 5,000 word article without a pause—that is, in about an hour. He writes without stops or spaces between words and his stuff is quite illegible to the printers and has to be specially transcribed. The bell of the typewriter seems to be ringing the whole time he is at the machine."

He had not been back in Paris long before 'T.P.' stopped his Novelist's Log-Book articles on the ground of economy. Bennett noted gloomily: "I don't suppose I shall get such a chance again." No doubt there was proffered consolation in the notice which Whitten inserted at the end of the final article in the series: "In taking leave of the author of the 'Savoir-Faire Papers' and the 'Novelist's Log-Book', I shall give many thousands of my readers pleasure by declaring the identity of the writer of these brilliant contributions. Mr. Arnold Bennett's name is well-known in the world of fiction, and my readers will do well to turn to his two admirable novels dealing with the life of the Potteries, 'Anna of the Five Towns' and 'Leonora'. . . . His next novel, about to be issued by Messrs. Chatto & Windus, is entitled 'A Great Man', and is purely humorous."

CHAPTER TEN

(1)

EARLY in 1904 he went to Mentone to collaborate with Eden Phillpotts in writing a play. No one believed more firmly than Bennett, man of imperious will and native sharp respect for the law of cause and effect, in opposing the rule of chance in personal life, yet the spectacle and the possibilities of the gaming tables at Monte Carlo seized his imagination and held it as if in a spell. "All the time I thought of gaming, gaming. The idea of gambling quite absorbed my thoughts; obsessed me." He won and lost in very small amounts and compensated by making Henry Knight, in the last chapters of *A Great Man*, break the bank. "If he had succeeded to the imperial throne of China, he would have felt much the same as he felt then." Sitting among the grand dukes in the casino and winning forty-five francs, "the art of literature seemed a very little thing," he wrote in *Paris Nights*.

Mrs. Alice Williamson of the well-known C. N. & A. M. Williamson serial-writing partnership, encouraged him in this erratic fancy. "She assured me that a number of people did make a regular income by gambling at the tables, and that the authorities allowed it because it was a good advertisement." Mrs. Williamson, writing what she remembered of their meetings at this time, chiefly recalled "his delightful smile", while wondering how it could be delightful, seeing that "he had a rush of teeth to the mouth".

In short, Monte Carlo menaced his thinking, disturbed him; but he got through a good deal of work. "In three weeks exactly, we have written, between us, (1) the play, (2) two short stories, (3) three articles, (4) a long chapter of my novel. This is what may be called the industry of genuine craftsmen. Nothing has been scamped except this journal, which doesn't count." As to the craftsmanship:

Eden and I were discussing the *Spectator* notice of 'My Devon Year' and its remarks on his style, and I formulated the theory that the faults (admitted) that the *Spectator* found in his style were due to the too-small proportion of verbs in his sentences compared to nouns and adjectives. On testing, I found that in the quoted passages there were 420 nouns and adjectives to every hundred verbs. In a famous passage towards the close of 'Hydriotaphia' [the full title of *Urn-Burial* by Sir Thomas Browne] I found there were only 183 nouns and adjectives to every hundred verbs. We both thought this line of inquiry might be pursued further with advantage.

They went on to a discussion of the poets, and Eden Phillpotts mentioned having met "an American woman who had aspired to be a poet and had submitted her verse to Longfellow in his old age, and called on him and received his advice. She was young then and very pretty. 'How can I thank you, Mr. Longfellow?' she cried earnestly. 'You can give me a kiss,' said Longfellow. She said to Eden: 'I was so taken aback and startled that I just kissed him and ran straight out of the house.' "

The picture-postcard flow to Burslem blazed out now in the vivid chemical blues and greens of the new colour processes. "This is Sir Thomas Hanbury's private postcard. It doesn't say much for his taste. But I am told his garden really is the finest of all gardens. You see his house. The town in the distance is Bordighera." At the battle of flowers: "I enjoyed pelting the women." An old gentleman met in the hotel, Sir John Rotton, K.C., spoke words of wisdom for the journal: "When one gets old one learns not to trouble one's head about things one can't influence."

A solitary morning walk along the coast road brought him to the frontier line and the reflections it inspired on the walk back to Mentone show us his mind at work on one of the unresolved problems of our human situation:

This was the division between the two greatest Latin countries; across this imaginary line had been waged the bloodless but disastrous tariff war of ten years ago. I was in France; a step and I was in Italy! And it was on account of similar imaginary, artificial, and unconvincing lines, one here, one there—they straggle over the whole earth's crust—that most wars, military, naval, and financial, take place.

Across the gorge was a high, brown tenement, and towards the tenement strutted an Italian soldier in the full, impossible panoply of war. He carried two rifles, a mile or so of braid, gilt enough to gild the dome of St. Paul's, and Heaven knows what contrivances besides. And he was smoking a cigarette out of a long holder. Two young

girls, aged perhaps six or eight, bounded out of the slatternly tenement, and began to chatter to him in a high infantile treble. The
formidable warrior smiled affectionately, and, bending down, offered
them a few paternal words; they were evidently spoiled little things.
Close by, a vendor of picture-postcards had set up shop on a stone
wall. Far below, the Mediterranean was stretched out like a blue
cloth without a crease in it, and a brig in full sail was crawling
across the offing. The sun shone brilliantly. Roses in perfect bloom
had escaped from gardens and hung free over hedges. Everything
was steeped in a tremendous and impressive calm—a calm at once
pastoral and marine, and the calm of the obdurate mountains that
no plough would ever conquer. And breaking against this mighty
calm was the high, thin chatter of the little girls, with their quick
and beautiful movements of childhood.

And as I watched the ragged little girls, and followed the brig
on the flat and peaceful sea, and sniffed the wonderful air, and was
impregnated by the spirit of the incomparable coast and the morning
hour, something overcame me, some new perception of the univer-
sality of humanity. (It was the little girls that did it.) And I thought
intensely how absurd, how artificial, how grotesque, how accidental,
how inessential, was all that rigmarole of boundaries and limits and
frontiers. It seemed to me incredible, then, that people could go to
war about such matters. The peace, the natural universal peace,
seemed so profound and so inherent in the secret essence of things,
that it could not be broken. And at the very moment, though I knew
it not, while the brig was slipping by, and the little girls were imposing
upon the good-nature of their terrible father, and the hawker was
arranging his trumpery pathetic postcards, they were killing each
other—Russian and Japanese were—in a row about 'spheres of
influence'. [1]

Refreshed, he returned to Paris with ideas assembling for the book
that was to be his masterpiece and title to an enduring reputation. A
newspaper account of a pretty Liverpool woman who was found dead
at 7 rue Breda after being robbed by a Spaniard stimulated the
imaginative processes. "It seemed to me that I might use up a lot of
the stuff in 'The History of Two Old Women', which it seems more
and more likely will be my next serious book."

It had not been a holiday so much as a change of climate and scene.

[1] *T. P.*'s *Weekly*, February 26, 1904.

And it induced the poetic mood of which there is little sign in his work as a whole but which is to be found in the journal where he describes emotions produced by his walks in the forest at Fontainebleau and by his excursions in the more distant countryside of France. As a result, we have his only known published poem (apart from the journal). It appeared in *T.P.'s Weekly*:

NIGHT ON THE RIVIERA

Out of the blind disorder and the plague
Of ravelled dreams that coil the pillow round,
Reluctantly I rise. Across a land
Spectral and unfamiliar, and vast
With mystic glimpses of infinity—
The plain that was and once again will be
My bedroom floor—I set a devious course,
All vision-harried, to the window there.

And lo!
Spectacular and cold,
Between the moonstruck sea-sward and the sky
Whose violet arches span the silver waste,
Flashes and burns the Mediterranean night,
Consuming in its frigid fire the sense
Of human, intimate things. And far below,
Gently the palms wave on the murmurous shore
In acquiescence. But not I will yield
To that pale dominance. Within my heart
The latent pantheism of endless time
Leaps proudly to self-consciousness and cries:
This peace is my peace and this kingdom mine!
Thus far (it says), O wandering spirit of the night!
Move largely o'er the earth, and whom thou canst
Intimidate! But at my balcony
Renounce . . . And then I gaze within the room,
Spectrally vast no more, but small and trite,
And habitable with foolish daily toys.
From out the fronded gloom that hides the beach
Up floats a sudden whistle, sharp and clear,

And the low call of shunters as they run
To couple and uncouple. And at the foot
Of the hotel's precipitous façade,
Four storeys underneath me, a sentinel
Watch-keeping while a hundred casements sleep,
The yellow porch-globe throws its modest ray
On marble steps and waits to die at dawn.

He wrote to his sister that he was going to "bring out a volume of poems", an unfulfilled intention. He very much wanted to write poetry and there was a period when he wrote or tried to write verse as a regular daily exercise. He said that for him it would be "a supreme satisfaction" to write poetry. But some unfathomed obstructive influence was at work and his poems refused to be poetry. Sadly he admitted to a friend: "It's no good—I can't do it," and his dismay was the more painful because he knew himself to be capable of genuine poetic feeling.

His return from the Riviera's exotic pleasures was marked by a change of taste in picture-postcards. Gravely he wrote to his mother in Burslem: "I now begin my series of artistic and topographical postcards to you. No more coloured prettinesses. And first you will have a series of 'old Paris' intermingled with classical works of art."

(2)

"It is a good thing I never write down here my moods and things," he says in the journal of this time, after noting a mysterious onslaught of depression. What personal history was behind the *soirée de réconciliation* of May 3, 1904? The journal mentions it and passes on to remark: "I must have lived more fully the last three days than for a very considerable time past. In fact, I have not suspected such possibilities in myself. Unfortunately, to work in such circumstances is impossible," suggesting a distracting range or depth of emotional experience. He had told the readers of *T.P.'s Weekly* how to look at life. There was a part of his mind, he said, which continually warned him against *preparing* to live instead of living. "Cultivate the intense consciousness of being alive. Revel in every manifestation of your being alive." Often when he had been miserable, or misjudged, he said, he resorted to the reminder: "This moment that you are living through now is a bit of life itself. Therefore live it thoroughly. Sad or joyous, it is really rather fine," sentiments which were to be bound up presently in the stiff dark blue covers of *The Human Machine, How to Live on 24 Hours a Day, Mental Efficiency,* and *Self and Self-Management.*

The disturbing interlude, whatever it was, upset his work on *Hugo,* the big-shop novel which drew its background inspiration from a bus-top view of Harrods' Stores in the course of being built. He had started it within a day or two of finishing *A Great Man* on March 13, his eighth novel "of one sort or another". And ideas for a new serious work were often superseding consideration of the lesser task. This last was to be as sensational as he could make it within artistic bounds.

March 25, 1904.—I spent a lot of yesterday afternoon in the Louvre picture-galleries trying to get into a frame of mind sufficiently large and expansive for the creation of the central idea for my sensational romance. The chief result was a bad nervous headache, which did not, however, prevent me from eating well. I went to bed at 10, and had the idea for the 'scene' of the book in the middle of the night.

Just now I am spending several days in the utmost tranquillity. I have gradually seen that my sensational yarn must be something remarkably out of the common, and that therefore I must take the greatest care over the conception. I found that ideas for it did not come easily. I did not, however, force them. Then I had the idea for the 'scene' of the book. Then I thought I would buy and read Gaboriau's 'Le Crime d'Orcival', of which I have heard so much, and see whether that would conduce to a 'flow' in me, as Balzac always does. It did, at once. . . . My sensational work does not and would not in the least resemble Gaboriau's, and yet Gaboriau has filled me with big, epic ideas for fundamental plot—exactly what I wanted. The central theme must be big, and it will be; all the rest is mere ingenuity, wit, and skill. I have not yet finished reading the Gaboriau book. I read it, and think nothing, not asking any notions to come; but they come, and I am obliged to note them down. The weather being extremely uncertain I have been unable to go out much, and so my existence has been quite extraordinarily placid. I go to bed one night, and then the next night. and there seems scarcely five minutes in between.

The headaches go on and on; his sleep is only intermittently good; he has liver attack after liver attack, each mysteriously beginning, each ending with a peculiar suddenness; he suffers otherwise obscurely, as he puts it, naming no symptom, no cause. After reading *Le Lys Rouge*, in which the *idées noires* of jealousy are described: "I had *idées noires* myself tonight. There are certainly times when the fact that existence is a choice of evils presents itself too clearly." Godfrey's speech ministrations served only to renew his disappointments in that matter.

He meets and talks with Aleister Crowley, "whose excellent poems I have read in a limited edition. He was wearing a heavily jewelled red waistcoat, and the largest ring I ever saw on human hand." They talked briefly of occult matters, and the journal notes of the encounter end: "I rather liked him." He is impressed by the dramatic beauty of Richard Strauss' new work, *Ein Heldenleben*, which produced hisses as well as applause at the end of its performance. "One more exhibition of the *bêtise* of an audience when confronted by something fresh, extravagant and powerful." He had written his impatience more forcibly in the journal a few days before: "The ideas of the average decently informed person are so warped, and out of perspective, and ignorant, and entirely perverse and wrong and crude, on nearly every mortal subject, that the task of discussing anything with him seriously and fully and to the end is simply appalling. This has struck me several times recently . . . and I have recoiled from a discussion. The state of that average person's mind can scarcely be contemplated by me, in certain moods," and although he never presumed to see himself in the popular educator role, it can be claimed for him that it was part of his subsequent great journalistic success.

Rickards arrived and upset him with his deteriorated manners, "concerning which I had to address him". Sir John Pollock, Bart., did not think much of Bennett's manners: "I found him clever, combative, low-minded, bumptious." The young Pollock, whom Bennett sympathetically and perhaps enviously describes at considerable length in the journal, had just become a Fellow of Trinity College, Cambridge, and had gone to Paris on a holiday with his friend Clive Bell, art critic to be. Both made a marked impression on Bennett, whose lower-middle-class mind had no resources such as fortune had placed at their command and who had to reach out and deliberately seek the intellectual affinities and satisfactions he required. "They neither of them thought, honestly, that they had anything to learn. They were tolerant, from their heights, towards the pathetic spectacle of humanity. Always Bell was the least priggish and convinced. But I liked them both."

A counterpoint to the self-assertiveness objected to by those who met him in the Paris years is supplied by a journal entry for November 23,

1905: "I am immensely flattered today by the receipt of an invitation from the 'Society of Moderns' to their fourth annual dinner at which my name was to be coupled with the toast of 'Modern Literature'. I declined it, because of the date. I don't expect the Society is much, but it seemed astounding to me that people should have thought sufficiently about me to send such an invitation."

Still trying to find the formula of words which would express the soul of Paris, still impelled to comprehend Paris in a phrase, he wrote his notes often at length in the journal, transferring them afterwards to the larger scope of *Paris Nights*, where they were worked up into the bold impressionistic chapters which Rickards illustrated with a brilliance that is seen at its best in his attempts at capturing the movement of dancers. "It seemed an uplifting and splendid thing to be there," Bennett said in one of his descriptive forays. "This was the city. This was what the race had accomplished, after eighteen Louises and nearly as many revolutions, and when all is said that can be said it remained a prodigious and comforting spectacle." He compared "the refined, neighbourly, and graceful cynical gestures of the race" to the "harsh and awkward timidity, the self-centred egotism and aristocratic hypocrisy of Piccadilly". He considered the Anglo-Saxon mind "hypocritical, pharisaical and intellectually dishonest. The Latin races are the intellectually honest ones". But it was impossible to strike a match in Paris "without being reminded that a contented and corrupt inefficiency was corroding this race like a disease". He reckoned Paris to be at its best in the evening, "when all the cafés are full of crowded languor." He watched the women, many pretty and well-dressed, in the Champs Élysées, "sitting patiently on chairs under the trees awaiting some masculine advance. I was astonished how distinguished some of them were." He saw them involved like everyone else in the battle of life and acquitting themselves as experts: "they inspire respect. It is—it is the dignity of labour."

It was an air of Verdi and not a phrase in words that finally epitomised for him the Paris he came to know and to be happy in—"about as near regular happiness as I am ever likely to get." Each afternoon and often in the evenings he heard a distant violin playing this air, never anything else, and constantly repeating it. "The sound was too faint to annoy me, but it was the most melancholy thing that I have ever heard. This phenomenon persisted for years, and I never discovered its origin, though I inquired again and again. Some interior, some existence of an infinite monotonous sadness, was just at hand, and

[155]

yet hidden away from me, inviolate. Whenever I hear that air now I am instantly in Paris, and as near being sentimental as ever I shall be. My ambition had long been to inhabit the rue d'Aumale—austere, silent, distinguished, icy, and beautiful—and by hazard I did ultimately obtain a flat there, and so left the rue de Calais. I tell you, I missed the undiscoverable and tragic violin of the rue de Calais. To this day the souvenir of it will invariably fold me in a delicious spleen. The secret life of cities is a matter for endless brooding." [1]

He was assimilating but not assimilated. At the theatre two actresses of the Comédie Française joined the Schwobs, whose guest he was in their *loge*. Madame Schwob kissed them affectionately and made much of them, all three voluble in reunion. "I'm going," Bennett said, rising abruptly. "I'm too English for this place." Invited to an evening party given by a French publisher, he offended the host by marching up to him, shooting his cuffs ostentatiously, and demanding to be told: "Do we speak French or English?"

(3)

A Great Man was published, and his first act, on untying the parcel containing the usual six complimentary copies from the publisher, was to read through most of the novel again. "On the whole, it amused me well enough. I was struck by the ease and virtuosity of the writing . . . and by the sound construction." Wells and Whitten thought it his best book. "And Phillpotts is enchanted with it." Sturt took particular pleasure in its dedication: *To my dear friend Frederick Marriott and to the imperishable memory of old times.* Wells wrote:

20 May, 1904.

. . . You don't know quite how well you can do this sort of thing and consequently you don't do it quite as well as you could—you hurry out of it at last. For all that, it's first rate and human and with something personal and distinctive that *Leonora* lacked. I'd congratulate most men I know on this book. As for congratulating you,—I don't know. I think you might have done it better.

The novel was an artistic success and a commercial failure. Its artistic success, he said, genuinely surprised him, contributing to the boulevard reputation which a little later on was given public acknow-

[1] *Things that have Interested Me.*

[156]

ledgment on his return to Paris from a visit to Scotland. Much of the humour of *A Great Man* has evaporated, but it is possible to see behind the management of the story signs of the mental efficiency of which very soon he was to proclaim the gospel. He was in business as a novelist and was bringing his mind under control to serve that end. Every page bears witness to the strictly practical address of his imagination to the task in hand. In the effective control of the imagination he saw not only the means to a higher level of personal efficiency but a pre-requisite of happiness as well as of success. "I can perceive that there are fields of thought of which it is advisable to keep closed the gates," he makes a character say in a later novel. Behind the deliberate marketing of his talents, with its extra tax on the will, there were already in action the mental training processes which he would presently advocate in the 'pocket philosophy' books. "Arnold Bennett tried in these novels to suit the public taste—to supply a market," says Harvey Darton. "To that end, he trained his mind, he learnt his trade, he formulated his ideals (or some of them) in very distinct words. He arrived at a gospel of mental and moral and practical efficiency which he had hitherto been following without writing it down."

Arnold Bennett to H. G. Wells:

18 April, 1905

MY DEAR H. G.,—Many thanks for the book. If it was a novel I could say something useful about it, but as it isn't I don't know that I can. The latter half of it is much more convincing and suggestive than the first half, and is also the better done, but all of it is better than 'Mankind in the Making'. The two things that strike me about the whole thing are the enormous difficulties you have had to face, and the continuous brainwork there is in it. It is a book that deserves to be called 'gallant'. Of course what interests me most and what will interest everyone most, is your development of the hierarchy idea. When I read your opening sentences about the Samurai I thought the notion was fanciful and impossible, but I was gradually convinced of its possibility. I see that some people are grumbling at you because such a caste could do a great deal of harm. But that is not the point. The point is whether such a caste will come into existence. It might. I think it would work first good and then harm, like most institutions. But anyhow you have handled it most fearfully well. It sticks in my mind. It is astonishing to me that a man of your imagination, so

[157]

untrammelled as it is, my poor boy, should be capable of the attitude towards the Hampstead middle class disclosed on p. 56. This is one of your class prejudices and you can't leave it alone. But you surely must see that what produces the Hampstead middle class will exist in no matter what Utopia. It is a relative matter. Relatively, the Hampstead middle class is a fine achievement of human progress; and relatively it is also the despicable thing you insist on rendering it. Your attitude to it is not that of a philosopher but that of a Chelsea painter who has not 'arrived' and sits drinking at the Six Bells while cursing all Philistines and plutocrats.

You are very good about women, I like all that. Personally, my ideas are more oriental, but still there are times when I am not oriental. What you say about the ugliness of modern women's dress is absolutely wrong. Indeed, your notions about material beauty are shockingly inferior to your other notions. You would like to laugh me out of being a Cultivated Person, but you never will, and as a Cultivated Person I say that your remarks on architecture, for example, are painful. And yet you *have* a glimmering, somewhere, even about architecture. It is most extraordinary how, immediately you come to the region of moral ideas, your language becomes distinguished. Your analysis of political parties in England fills me with awe. It is A1, and the indictment of Liberalism is excellent, though I *am* a Liberal, like yourself. There is something about the precocity of civilisation on p. 292 that also is worthy of you. But why should the Samurai have any religion? I hope you aren't going to defend that worn out platitude to the effect that religion is a necessity of man's nature. Because it isn't. Religion is done for— any sort of religion. Your notions of a religion for the Samurai startled me.

You understand my attitude towards this book is very humble. I could only authoritatively find fault with its grammar. It has much impressed me and some of its things stick brilliantly in my mind.

Yours, E. A. B.

(4)

A casual social interlude of this time was to be more significant for him than he knew. He dined with Mrs. Devereux, who was wearing "her finest 'Georgette' hat". They talked frankly. "I said it was singular that I had never got up a passion for her." Mrs. Devereux' reply to this was that she supposed it *was* singular, "because in some ways, I suppose, I must be the most attractive woman you have ever known in your life." A close friend of Arnold Bennett's remembers Bennett's pleasure in being seen with the lady, whose higher social status embellished her magnetism for him. "When she had told me all about herself ('I don't know why I should tell you these things', she said), I told her all about myself, and pretty well astonished her. She said she thought I had done very well for myself."

Mrs. Devereux having protested that she could not be seen at a café in the Bois with *one* man at night, they went back to her flat. "She said we should find Blanche and Mrs. Green in dressing-gowns, and we did. . . . Mrs. Green is a youngish American wife, with no trace of the accent; a rather fatigued face and manner of talking. She was wearing a superb rose-coloured gown and looked extremely luxurious, especially when she stooped to replace a highly ornamental slipper on her small foot. I talked to her for two hours about literature, art, women, and so on. She is a cosmopolitan, knows nothing really, but can converse very neatly."

Mrs. Green was the wife of an American oil man in charge of his company's European affairs. The Greens were Southerners of English descent and their family life in Paris has been sketched in *Memories of Happy Days* by Julian Green, their son, and in *With Much Love* by Anne Green, one of their four daughters. They had come to live in Paris in 1898, at a flat in the rue Rhumkorff, moving later to the rue de Passy. There Bennett was introduced to the family by Agnes Farley, a close friend of Mrs. Green. Agnes Farley, wife of an American dentist practising in the rue de la Paix, was co-translator with Violet Hunt of the memoirs of Casanova. Violet Hunt called her "the great *piocheur* in localities and scandals in old Paris and London", and said that if Mrs. Farley had lived to be old she would have been like Madame du Deffand. "I introduced her to Arnold Bennett, who at once appreciated her to the full. He used to show her his poems."

One of the young Green girls was red-headed and pretty, Eleanor, barely out of school and dreaming of a life of her own as a singer in opera. She had the secret charm of the young girl whose aspirations make her seem to be a dedicated being. Agnes Farley was interested in her future and introduced her to a number of celebrated contemporaries, among them Henry James. Mrs. Farley invited him to dinner and he cast a gloom over the meal by staring fixedly at Eleanor Green across the table and presently announcing in his important booming voice that she reminded him of 'one who had passed'. Miss Green (who became Mrs. Kenneth Joll) was much flattered by his attention and privately hoped, she says, that the lady who had passed had been an early love. As the evening wore on he cheered up and told Miss Green and her girl companion that they looked like the Botticelli portraits in the frescoes at the head of the stairs in the Louvre.

It was several months after Arnold Bennett's meeting with Mrs. Green that he was introduced to Eleanor, who received no very strong impression of him at the time. But Bennett begged Mrs. Farley to arrange another meeting. Unknown to herself, Eleanor Green had made a conquest.

At first she had no clear understanding of his position as a writing man; she says she was not specially curious about him. Learning of his growing fame, she had the idea that he looked as Dickens might have without the beard. "One day when we went to see him at his flat he was wearing a red waistcoat, and an old lady who was with us—she was probably Agnes Farley's grandmother—was reminded that on the one occasion on which she had met Dickens he was wearing a waistcoat just like it." Although her family and friends knew that Bennett was in love with her, Miss Green never fully realised it herself, nor did she understand that he was completely serious when he proposed to her in the forest at Fontainebleau. She liked him, considered him "nice enough", and always had a sympathetic regard for him, but she says that she never at any time thought of him in terms of the affections. He seemed to her always middle-aged and avuncular. For her his journal entry for June 15, 1906, had no importance: "At 5 p.m. on this day in the forest of Fontainebleau I became engaged to marry Eleanora," the name by which he chose to speak of her. Nor did she know that her lack of interest had caused him the mental suffering later attributed to it. He was thirty-nine, she eighteen. She tells of the days in Paris when she first knew him:

"Agnes and I frequently had tea with him at his flat. It was always China tea, the "delicate perfection" of which, according to him, I was incapable of appreciating. And after tea he would play Mozart sonatas, heartrending in their gaiety and innocence. He was charming and companionable and never dull. I like to think of the long summer afternoons we spent together, Agnes, Bennett and I. There was one day, a fine hot May afternoon, when we went to Versailles. How lovely it was just to be alive and young and to be 'noticed' by such interesting people! We had great argument over a lunch of beefsteak, potatoes,

ARNOLD BENNETT (RIGHT) IN GLASGOW WITH FREDERICK MARRIOTT

MISS ELEANOR GREEN (MRS. KENNETH JOLL)

cheese and fruit, and wishy-washy black coffee. Then we strolled to the Palace and sat on the terrace in the sunshine, Agnes and Bennett a little sleepy by then. He sat there with his hat tipped down over his nose, hiding what I always thought was his best feature, a nice thoughtful forehead. I went on talking, happily. Presently Bennett roused himself sufficiently to say in reply to a gratuitous piece of information from me: "One learns something, occasionally, even from the lowest of God's creatures." Agnes Farley often playfully referred to me, after that, as "the lowest of God's creatures".

On another day Miss Green appeared in a small and very fetching green hat, newly bought. She already had eighteen summer hats and says she did not really need a green straw toque trimmed with the wings of parrakeets. However, the main object was achieved; her appearance was a success and Arnold Bennett, among others, admired the new hat, which was posed lightly on one side of its wearer's red head with the hair pinned up to meet it, all round, with many short tortoiseshell pins made for the purpose. "I bought it yesterday—it's my nineteenth hat!" Miss Green told Bennett, proudly. He looked at it and said at once: "I shall write a story about it. I shall call it 'The Nineteenth Hat', and although Miss Green never knew it until recently, he carried out his intention the following year: his story, *The Nineteenth Hat* is in the collection published in 1907 under the title of *The Grim Smile of the Five Towns*. "She sniffed at most of the hats. But one of them, of green straw, with a large curving green wing on either side of the crown, and a few odd bits of fluffiness here and there, pleased her. It was Parisian." When, another day, Bennett saw Miss Green wearing a blue serge dress with a blue and yellow striped waistcoat, replica of the garment worn by French *valets de chambre*, he stared at her for some time and then said in a gasping voice that her appearance made "tears of joy come into a mere male's eyes".

Arnold Bennett to H. G. Wells:

June 29, '06

MY DEAR WELLS,—I meant to reply to your last letter, and then I waited for your return from U.S. and now I see the announcement of your articles in the 'Tribune', and I sit down at once to tell you and your wife that I am engaged to be married to a young woman of the name of Eleanora Green, a native of Savannah, Georgia, who has lived nearly all her life in Paris. Her age is 25. I can't tell you any more about her (except that she was destined for an operatic singer,

[161]

and I stepped in just in time to stop her debut) because I don't know any more.

Let us see what kind of a letter of congratulation a publicist and a professional penman can write under these circumstances.

Love to you both,

E. A. BENNETT

Arnold Bennett to H. G. Wells:

4 rue de Calais

(undated)

MY DEAR H. G.,—Your letter had an immense success with my girl. She has a passion for stern realism. I read her parts of it.

I am—I mean, we are—thinking of being married at a registry office in Folkestone, this being the handiest. If you are summering in Sandgate, I wonder if you will let us accomplish a formal residence at your house. It means 2 days at the beginning of the legal term of 16 days, and then another two days at the end—four days in all. Will this worry you? The marriage will not take place till October. Have no apprehension as to being worried in any way by the actual marriage. You will neither see nor hear anything of it. Eleanora will bring one friend over with her for a night and the other witness I will get in the registry office.

I see you are turning the Fabian Society inside out.

Yours ever,

E. A. B.

Arnold Bennett to his brother Frank:

4 Rue de Calais

9 July 1906

MY DEAR FRANK,—Your work on my novel is now over, I am thankful to say, and so is mine too—nearly. I never was so sick of anything before in my life. Had to read it aloud to the sex. So nice and cheerful to read aloud your most secret and unsentimental thoughts on the relations of the sexes, and particularly on divorce, to your betrothed during the first month of your engagement! No wonder the tragical parts drew tears, whether of sorrow or fury God knows.

I trust your summer is arranged. I'm damned if mine is.

Yours,

E. A. B.

[162]

P.S.—The first shock of the meeting of the two families occurred last week. Tertia conducted her share of it to perfection; though, except for their common hatred of sentimentality and their keen sense of humour, it would be difficult to find two women more violently different than Tertia and Eleanora. Tertia confirmed my opinion that the mater will probably without much difficulty be able to refrain from going into ecstasies over her youngest daughter-in-law. Still, as she is only marrying *me*, that doesn't gravely matter. I am genuinely enthusiastic about her family, and am prepared to marry it entire.

'Le romancier anglais' was projecting himself well ahead of events about which, it now appears, he had not consulted Miss Green, who knew nothing of these arrangements for the disposal of her future. Her family had protested because she continued to leave his numerous letters lying unopened about the house, and finally her mother, deploring what she insisted was a discourtesy, pressed a paper knife into her daughter's hand and made her slit open each envelope in a considerable pile even if she did not propose to read the contents. Miss Green says that she was never in love with him and, so far as she knew, had never given him cause to believe that his feelings for her were reciprocated beyond the terms of ordinary friendship. Six weeks after the journal entry recording his so-called engagement, he wrote again there: "*August 3, 1906.*—At 11 a.m. on this day, at Camiel, my engagement to Eleanora was broken off." He forgot to number the page, an omission almost unique in the thirty journal volumes.

Arnold Bennett to H. G. Wells:

> 4 rue de Calais
>
> (undated)
>
> MY DEAR H. G.,—I shall not come next Wednesday. My engagement exists no longer. Can't write to you about it now, but it's right bang off, anyhow.
>
> Yours ever,
> E. A. B.

Mrs. Joll, the former Miss Eleanor Green, has clear recollections of the final scene but thinks it unfair to Arnold Bennett's memory to recall them publicly in detail. It is sufficient to say that his speech difficulty appeared at its worst, that every aspirate deserted him in this extremity, and that he was reduced to uttering comically pathetic threats of social excommunication for Miss Green. "You'll lose the respect of the 'ole world—and Mr. and Mrs. Farley too." How deeply he was hurt can only be a subject for conjecture. He is thought to have expressed something of his bitterness in the poem called 'A Love Affair' which appears in the published journal volumes under the date August 2, 1907:

> Wit she had none to amuse,
> Knew not the trade of a wife,
> Heard not the voice of the muse. Now the muse
> Was his life.

A note of spitefulness appears in his novel *The Glimpse*, published in 1909, in which he describes a young American singer standing at the piano as applause greets the song she has just sung. "She dreamed, I knew, of more brilliant successes. But she would never have them. She lacked temperament. She was merely the accidental possessor of a small, agreeable, highly trained mezzo-soprano voice. On a stage, in a great hall, with an orchestra, she would be extinguished."

Miss Green never saw him again. In the early months of 1931 she was in Genoa. Waking from an afternoon sleep, she was overcome by a powerful impression of Arnold Bennett's presence. She had not been thinking of him. He had long since passed out of her life, though she was aware of his stature by then as a public figure. Composing on the wall in front of her was an image of him, "smiling in the way he did when he had made a joke at your expense." She did not know that he had been ill. The next day the papers brought news of his death.

A similar happening had occurred within his own knowledge. Dorothy Cheston Bennett later referred to it in her preface to his collected letters: "He told me a story of a person who presented himself to his mother and gave her warning that he had suddenly died in a distant place, a fact later substantiated."

(5)

Soon after he had published *A Great Man* and while he was writing *Hugo*, which did little to advance his fortunes though it achieved its purpose of enabling him to pay his bills, this mainly as a result of its serialisation in the weekly paper *Today*, he wrote to George Sturt at Farnham:

I do nothing but fiction now, and have arrived at the stage when I can make £20 a week at it, minimum. Five years ago I would have looked on this as the *ne plus ultra* of paradisiacal bliss, but I am no more content than ever I was. In fact, life is a devilish odd thing. I think I have learnt more about it during the last three years than ever I knew before. 1 have books planned that will keep me employed till the end of 1906. But if I am any happier than when I used to cycle down to Farnham or Witley after a week of rottenness in Fleet Street, I do not know it. My belief is that some people are born happy and others aren't. . . . I am in a position to state that constant honest artistic production does not produce in the producer any particularly ecstatic source of bliss. At best it is an anodyne. . . .

He had heard of a French speech therapist, M. Berquand, who might help him in mastering his old trouble. At their first consultation in Paris, Berquand told him he felt certain of success within a few weeks. Despite the assurance, Bennett left Berquand's consulting-room in a mood of doubt and depression, but with a promise to join him in Scotland some weeks later. "He has 'orders' from most European sovereigns," Bennett noted in the journal, a sidelight on royal heredity. He arranged to spend a day or two with Wells at Sandgate on his way to join Berquand in Aberdeen. He wanted Wells' advice on the wisdom of allowing certain of his sensational serials to appear in book form, for which Pinker had brought him several offers. "I couldn't think of anyone else whose opinion in a matter so involved between business and art I really cared twopence for." In the course of his stay at Sandgate he noted:

Wells was evidently very dissatisfied with his position. He talked seriously of gambling with six months of his time in order to try to do a couple of plays that would possibly bring in a fortune. He said he wanted £20,000 as a capital basis. . . .

Nearly all Wells's conversation would make good table talk and one has a notion that it ought not to be wasted; it is so full of ideas and of intelligent radicalism. It seems a pity it should not be gathered up. But after all there is a constant supply of it. You might as well be afraid of wasting the water from a brook. I read the proofs of 'The Food of the Gods' these last two days, and gave him my views on it. He was very keen and restless and nervous to hear them.

[165]

From Sandgate he went up to Scotland in the wake of M. Berquand, who had moved on from Aberdeen to Ardentinny. The course of treatment began at once. "It promises to be very absorbing. So, although there are plenty of astonishing things to note in this tiny village surrounded by lochs and hills, I do not expect to have both leisure and inclination to note them." He resumed the picture-postcard stream to his mother, sending several at a time and writing his news on all of them, one after the other in continuing instalments. "I have got into such a state that I often talk French when I mean to talk English. This is a fact. I can do with a little calm English society . . . Scotland is the land of churches and of quarrels about creeds . . . I am suffering from scones and cream. . . ."

Berquand told him that although his course ought to be regarded as a treatment, like a doctor's, his Scottish patients insisted that it should give way to their Sabbath. "In vain he argued that a doctor would not let a patient omit taking his medicine because it was Sunday. His pupils even insisted on having their usual Saturday afternoon; thus his course was interrupted three half days out of every fourteen."

While there he had a letter from his mother in Burslem, describing the course of an illness of hers. "Tuesday was my worst day . . . a dazed, stupefied sort of feeling, and my eyes were quite dim, and I had palpitations; *and I could quite comfortably have left you all and have done with it all for good.*" As soon as he could, he went to Burslem to see her, feeling all the time the pull of Paris. And having returned there: "I think I have never enjoyed the return to any place so much before. I could not keep my journal in England; there was no calm. And I was too busy with the Berquand treatment, which has yet to prove whether it will ultimately be a success." That hope was not realised. His visit to Scotland was a disappointment, but an unexpected consolation awaited him:

My absence has had the effect of showing me how well I am established in Paris. Wherever I go, in restaurants and shops, I am recognised and greeted with the warmest cordiality. In three places today I have been the subject of an ovation. You would not get the same treatment in London in any circumstances.

(6)

His visits to Fontainebleau with different friends, and particularly the latest, in which he saw the autumn forest looking "magnificently

[166]

tawny", fixed in him a wish to see more of that countryside of France and with Davray's help he found apartments at Les Sablons, in the house of an old couple named Lebert. "They exhale an atmosphere of a life's effort nearly accomplished. They may be narrow, but they have worked honestly and lived sanely. Imagine taking to a garden after thirty-one years of railway work in Paris!" Very soon he was persuading himself that he could easily renounce the life of Paris and become a countryman himself.

On his first week-end at Les Sablons he was bitten by a dog and nearly fainted at the sight of the blood on his hand. Granted that being bitten by a local dog might be as risky as drinking the local water, his nervousness caused the local doctor who was showing him round the district to refer to "le flegme anglais" as a legend. "I think you are very impressionable," said this companion of his, Dr. Vallée, of Moret, as he bound up the wound. Bennett had been told an unnerving story about hydrophobia, "which is still common in this department." A victim had been sent from Moret to the Pasteur Institute in Paris and cured, "but remained under the delusion that he was not cured and still thought he must bite people who got in his way." Bennett's courage, like that of many intellectual persons, was moral rather than physical. For once it seems that his stoic rule, 'Always behave as if nothing has happened, no matter what has happened,' had failed him. His friend J. B. Atkins, who spent several yachting holidays with him, says that he had small resources of physical courage in an emergency. Mr. Atkins stayed with him at Les Sablons, where they took long walks in the forest. Bennett did not approve experimental short cuts along paths which neither knew. He would insist that a French forest is not a safe place to walk in, that there were snares and bandits. No, he would say, it was idiotic to behave in the English way in a French forest; one should be as prudent as the French themselves. And so on, slashing with nervous energy at foliage and twigs with his stick as they walked.

Back in Paris, he gasped at "the electric splendour of the Automobile Exposition at the Grand Palais. It was astounding. Hundreds of motors waiting outside; the streets festooned with electric lamps. Inside, one immense crush of people and a perfect blaze of electric devices over the stands. Large band in the gallery that gave rise to the feeling of the joy of life", one of the few inexpert sentences to be found in the journal. "Unimaginably sensational," he scrawled to his mother across the face of a picture-postcard referring to motor-racing at Clermont-Ferraud. "Seventy miles an hour!" Electric light and motor-cars; the pulse of the tremendous new century was quickening. He spent an evening visiting "one of the new phonograph places", listening to recordings of Caruso, a chorus in a synagogue, and an *Ave Maria* of Palestrina. "The orchestral and violin pieces were merely grotesque. They gave no notion of real sound quality."

Chichi's name had vanished from the journal. That of a young woman named Jeanne succeeded it. He hints darkly at a "crucial interview" with her. Then the name of Cosette supplants Jeanne's; it occurs also in *A Great Man*. "Someone had told her that my portrait of her in *A Great Man* is cold and unsympathetic. I merely said: 'C'est un malin qui t' a dit ça!'" I don't think I ever met any woman with a prouder independence of spirit than that girl has."

The seeds of his masterpiece to come had been sown but they were not yet germinating with strength enough to divert his attention. He was drafting a new novel, *Sacred and Profane Love*, begun under the title of *Carlotta*, designed to make a third to *Anna of the Five Towns* and *Leonora*. It was to be a novel of female emotions, the narrator a Five Towns young woman who refuses to be ashamed of anything she honestly likes. She likes the idea of promiscuous love, and throws herself at the feet of a visiting famous pianist, Diaz. Bennett thought he was writing something exceptional in theme and treatment. It proved to a Ouida-esque travesty of a novel which one could almost be persuaded was written for a bet. "Will the British public stand it?" he asked Davray, his good friend. Davray did not think much of it, in spite of which discouragement Bennett went on with the story, incurring more headaches, more exhaustions, as if his reputation wholly depended on it. Georges Lafourcade read into *Sacred and Profane Love* a trial flight of the powers which Bennett was to bring to fulfilment in *The Old Wives' Tale*. There is no hint that he wrote it for money. His needs in that respect had been provided for by a sensational serial called *The City of Pleasure*, which by the expert management of his working day, he was able to produce at the same time. "To anyone who studies the plot closely," Lafourcade says, "it is obvious that the novel is merely a rough sketch of *The Old Wives' Tale*, which as we know was conceived years before Bennett made up his mind to compose it in its definite form."

Let it not be overlooked that in the lesser writing tasks which were his livelihood in those years he never shirked the claims of craftsmanship or tolerated a low standard of technical performance. Everything was carefully prepared and shaped and finished. There was no slap-dash and no contempt for the public that would read what he wrote. His writing was Corinthian in its precision and clarity even in the most blatantly fabricated of his novels. The wonder is that both kinds of production could have come from the same would-be immaculate brain.

Not that he felt impelled to apologise. "Life for me has many savours, which I relish keenly. Therefore many subjects interest me. I never write on a subject which does not interest me. . . . Nevertheless, journalists who are not novelists accuse me about once a week of potboiling. The argument is not stated very clearly; but it seems to amount to this: first, that a novelist who has written long realistic novels which have met with approval ought not, if he is a serious artist, to write anything but long realistic novels."

Wells read *Sacred and Profane Love* and wrote about it to Bennett:

25 Sep., 1905

. . . it *is* good and it *is* bad and it is most interesting and readable. . . . Your English though is much less clean and simple than it was—stresses in the epithets, and a surface of hard bright points. And I feel more than ever the difference between our minds. You are always taking surface values that I reject. Hotels are not luxurious, *trains-de-luxe* are full of coal grit, *chefs* and pianists are not marvellous persons, dramatic triumphs are silly uproars. But it isn't irony—you believe in these things. . . . For some unfathomable reason you don't penetrate. You are like George Moore. You have probably never been in love. I doubt if you ever weep. You have no passion for Justice. You prefer 'style' to beauty. You are not a poet, you are not a genius. But you are a dear delightful person and please let me know what time you come to England.

Yours,

H. G. W.

Arnold Bennett to H. G. Wells:

4 rue de Calais

MY DEAR WELLS,   30 Sept. 1905,

Amid the chorus ('A great book, a great book') which that glittering novel has naturally called forth from most of my friends, your letter, with its thin small handwriting, is like a grandma announcing that I have been having too much sugar in my tea and must be content with half a lump. My dear H. G., you move me to explain myself to you. I have not yet decided whether I am a genius, but I shall probably decide, with that astounding quality of self-criticism that I have, that I am not. I am probably too clever, and, what is more important, too infernally well-balanced. I am ready to agree with you that no such woman as Carlotta ever existed. No character in any novel is ever more than a hint at the real thing, and it is right it should be so. You can't honestly say that Mr. Lewisham ever existed. You know, we all know, that after all our satisfaction with Mr. Lewisham he never lived and couldn't have lived. He is an arrangement to suit the necessities of a convention; and here and there he bears a resemblance to a man. I choose Mr. Lewisham because he is one of the least unreal characters I can recall at the moment. All I could claim for Carlotta is that now and then she does what a real woman would do, and that her stiff lay-figure movements are sometimes really not so very stiff. Again, I must agree with you as to the style. But incidentally you must remember that this is not my style, but Carlotta's style, and that it cost me a Hades of a lot of trouble. I am inclined to think, however, that as regards style, the best book I ever wrote was 'A Man From The North'. The question of my style must really be looked into. I have never been in love. Sometimes the tears start to my eyes, but they never fall. These things are indubitable. I have no passion for justice. That also is profoundly true. I recognise that progress is inevitable and that it can only be achieved by a passion for justice. But I reckon I am above a passion for justice. Here we come to "the difference between our minds". I look down from a height on the show and contemplate a passion for justice much as I contemplate the other ingredients. Whereas you are simply a passion for justice incarnate. You are not an artist, except in so far as you disdainfully make use of art for your reforming ends; you are simply a reformer—with the classic qualities of the reformer. Hence your amazing judgments on Balzac, Milton, etc. Like all great reformers you are inhuman, and scornful of everything that doesn't interest you. Hence the complaint of the anti-Wellsites that in your 'scientific' novels there is no individual interest, that the characters don't exist individually. A not unjust complaint. The pity is that these persons cannot perceive the 'concerted' interest of your 'scientific' novels. You are not really interested in individual humanity. And when you write a non-'scientific' novel you always recur to a variation of the same type of hero, and you always will, because your curiosity about individualities won't lead you farther. You are concerned in big-crowd movements. Art, really, you hate. It means to you what 'arty' means to me. You live in a nice house, but you know perfectly well you wouldn't care what sort of house you lived in. When you say that a great pianist is not a marvellous person, you give the show away. For you he is not. The astounding human interest of a dramatic triumph is for you 'a silly uproar'. In these two instances you show clearly, as regards art and as regards life, where your interests stop. You won't have anything to do with 'surface values' at all. You don't merely put them in a minor place; you reject them. A couple of pages devoted to surface values will irritate you. You will never see it, but in rejecting 'surface values' you are wrong. As a fact they are just as important as other values. But reformers can't perceive this. They are capable of classifying chefs, pianists, and trains-de-luxe altogether and saying: 'Go to. I am a serious person'. You are, you know. The same spirit animates you as animated George Macdonald's grandmother, who objected to the violin as a profane instrument. And the mischief is that, though you will undoubtedly do a vast amount of good in the world, you will get worse and worse, more and more specialised, more and more scornful. All this is not an explanation of you; but an explanation of me. It 'connotes' the difference between our minds.

I purposed writing to you to offer Mrs. Wells and you the advantage of my presence for a night or so on my way to England, early in December. If this suits, I can then respectfully listen to your defence. I am much too vain to mind being called 'not a poet' and 'not a genius'. But to be called 'a dear delightful person' rouses my worst instincts. It makes me feel as if I was like Marriott Watson or Pett Ridge, and I ain't, not really.

Thine,

E. A. B.

Arnold Bennett's rejection of the role of "one fixed point in a changing world", as another Watson was called by Sherlock Holmes, fastens on to one's passing attention, reading this letter, because it proved to be the role by which he has been most gratefully and most explicitly remembered by his friends.

He took a long mid-year holiday of about two months in 1905, spent at Les Sablons and Paris, uncharacteristically idling. His word total fell heavily, to something under 200,000; "much less than usual."

It included the first 30,000 words of what he called his divorce novel, *Whom God Hath Joined*, a work in which we see more clearly than in any that had preceded it the qualities that were to make a success of *The Old Wives' Tale*. There has been critical agreement with Georges Lafourcade's view that "he came very near achieving absolute greatness in this novel", despite some drawbacks in its construction. Even so, it was not one of his more satisfying years: "genuine success seemed as usual to delay and postpone itself."

Arnold Bennett to H. G. Wells:

4, rue de Calais

9 Nov., 1905

MY DEAR H. G.,—The only real seizable fault that I can find in 'Kipps' is the engagement to Helen, which entirely failed to convince me. In fact it is useless to tell me that they ever were engaged. I do not believe it. If you had made of Helen a less real and lifelike figure than she is, then I might have been persuadable. But she is extremely well done, and so she gives you the lie in the matter of their engagement. Ann is more than well done, she is Very Fine, and the Ann scenes are the best in the book. After agreeing with myself that I read the thing all through with eagerness and joy, and after telling myself that I must not expect in your 'human interest' novels those aspects of life which you either can't see or disdain to see, I find myself asking what this book 'proves', and not getting any answer. As it is distinctly a fighting, 'tendancieux' book, I think I ought to have an answer. Why this immense animus against the 'nace' class of person, since we are all human together? Am I to understand that in your opinion as a purposeful observer of life the 'nace' class is more ridiculous, or less worthy of sympathy, or less the outcome of natural and inevitable causes, than any other class? I ask for information. I don't think your ferocious hostility to about five sixths of the characters in the book makes for righteousness of any kind and certainly not for artistic righteousness. Especially as you follow Kipps about on the stage with a rose-coloured limelight. What is the theory of this procedure? There is no doubt that you achieve the illusion of reality in spite of it, and not with its aid.

If you have set out to amuse and divert the B.P. you have richly succeeded in your aim. Ditto if you have tried to enlist their sympathies on behalf of the Kippses and the Anns. Ditto if you have

[172]

tried to give impartial portraits of the Sids, the Mastermans, and the Chitterlows. But if you have had any larger aim, any aim of showing how and why one class of persons generally is superior or inferior to another, then I don't reckon you have succeeded—at any rate, with thoughtful, judicious, and high-minded people like myself.

You said last year, you even faithfully promised, that you were going to write with more care. God-a-mercy! After the sentence on p. 409 beginning: 'Next to starting a haberdasher's shop,' I renounce the crusade. I respectfully give you up. Damn it, after all it doesn't matter how you write. But after your animadversions on the Head Master of Dulwich. . . .!

I have a sort of idea that my objections to 'Kipps' (except as to the enjoyment) are rather vague and 'theoretical'. But nevertheless I think they contain food for your thought. Such is my view. That there is 'a laugh on every page' is beside the point.

Yours ever,
E. A. B.

Although it was, he told his sister Tertia in a letter, a good fiction season, much better than for a long time past, he had got it into his head that his novel *Sacred and Profane Love* would not sell. "If it had any decent success, I could carry out my half-resolved design never to write any more sensational stuff. But there, I never have any real luck (Rickards)." He had felt a need for reforming the whole scheme of his existence, he wrote, and was privately annoyed when Madame Davray said the acute depression he had been complaining to her about was "merely indigestion".

A visitor of his at Fontainebleau at this time was the novelist Netta Syrett, who was taken to call on him by Ella D'Arcy, assistant editor of *The Yellow Book*, translator, and writer of short stories. Perceiving one truth about him and overlooking another, Miss Syrett says in some reminiscences: "It was the first time I had met Arnold Bennett, and truth compels me to say that neither then, nor when I again met him in Paris, did I find it easy to get on with him. I think men liked him better than women. I believe he was an excellent friend to men, and certainly very kind to young writers. Much later my youngest brother was grateful for the letters of criticism he took the trouble to write to him about his early literary efforts. But I always found him rather 'touchy' and aggressive in conversation. . . ." [1]

[1] *The Sheltering Tree* (Geoffrey Bles, 1939).

[173]

A long postscript note is written on the last page of the journal for that year:

I left Paris on December 8 and spent two nights with H. G. Wells. His principal news was that he had quarrelled with Pinker and was managing his own affairs. I then went to London and stayed there till Dec. 21st. On the 20th I dined with Violet Hunt at her club, the Victorian; she gave me bad champagne. Afterwards we went to the Alhambra and talked all the time. On the 21st I went down to Burslem and stopped with the Mater till Jan. 1st. Frank's baby was ill and so things were rather quiet. The last Sunday afternoon of the year I spent with Absalom Wood, going about Burslem and Tunstall seeing his architecture and his laying out of the Tunstall Park. I was very interested in it, and I had an important idea for a novel, or a series of novels, entitled 'The Town' or 'The Borough of Bursley', in which the development of the organism of the town under modern influences should be the chief theme. The conversion of town refuse (160 tons a week) into electric light at Bursley impressed me; it is one of those slightly sentimental, morally-spectacular aspects of municipal life that *do* impress. I mentioned this idea to several people and they have been impressed.

CHAPTER ELEVEN

(1)

"**I** HAVE now warned both the 'Mater and Tertia that I shall get married before I am forty," he noted on his thirty-seventh birthday; and it would be easy to make too much of it as a demonstration of his purposefulness. He reveals himself in *Things that have Interested Me*: "I used often to say to my friends, 'As soon as I am free enough I shall go and live in Paris.' I doubt if I had any genuine intention of going. But it was my habit to make such idle forecasts and boasts: seemingly they convinced everybody but me. . . . They have all been justified by events. Chance, of course, has aided. Thus, from about the age of twenty-five onwards I used to say: 'I shall marry at forty.' I had absolutely no ground of personal conviction for this prophecy. But, by a sheer accident, I did marry at forty. And everyone, impressed, went about remarking, 'He always does what he says he'll do! . . . Naturally, when I settled in Paris, all my friends said again, 'He always said he would do it, and he has done it.' My reputation as a man of his word was made indestructible. But to me the affair presents itself as chiefly accidental."

Eleven months after his discomfiture by Miss Eleanor Green he married Mlle. Marguerite Soulie, July 4, 1907. They had first met in January of that year, through Calvocoressi, the music critic. Mrs. Bennett has said that her husband consulted one of his closest Paris friends, Emile Martin of the Cercle de la rue Volnay, before finally deciding to marry her. "He was not sure of his own judgment about me." He told her that "his friend's opinion of me was high, that he valued his friend's opinion. . . ." Mlle. Soulie's social background is indicated in a journal entry made some time afterwards:

26 September, 1910—Auguste and Julia Soulie came yesterday for the day. Drive in the forest. It is in this sort of encounter that one feels the immense gulf between an artist and people who simply have no traffic with art at all. One can, however, find something in common in the discussion of relatives and in the contemplation of

[175]

nature. With Julie, who spent her youth in a baker's shop and is the widow of one artisan and the wife of another, sitting opposite me in the carriage, and smiling at jokes which she only half understood, but *did* half understand, and admiring trees and vistas and things, I had a most distinct feeling of sympathy and a perception of a faint charm that emanated from her.

Mrs. Bennett came from Nègrepelisse, near Montauban, where she returned after the separation to live out the years of her widowhood at the farmhouse known as the Château de Lolières. An aunt of hers had a Paris dressmaking establishment and Mrs. Bennett, as Marguerite Soulie, had seized the chance of going there to work from a somewhat distant countryside with its paucity of attractions for a young woman who dreamed of a career in the drama. In Paris she took elocution lessons and learned to recite the poems of Baudelaire and Verlaine with a spirit and feeling that brought her invitations to the 'evenings' which were as popular then in Paris as in London. She had some of the physical distinction of the tall *demoiselle du comptoir* who had compelled Arnold Bennett's attention some while before and whom he had felt he must see again. "It is easy enough to understand what attracted him to his future wife," says Georges Lafourcade: "as a man, her beauty and personality; as an artist, her talent; as a native of the Five Towns, her Parisian characteristics; as a practical man, her domestic assets."

Arnold Bennett to H. G. Wells:

3, rue d'Aumale
Paris

MY DEAR H. G.,   1st July, 1907

I had to come back to Paris by telegram, to arrange legal formalities for the accursed union. No end of trouble. However, I expect to be ruined artistically within a week from now, and all your warnings will have been in vain.

I am extremely glad that you class 'The Grim Smile Of The Five Towns' so high, though it shows a failure on your part to appreciate things like 'Leonora'. Still, I am very content.

Yours,
E. A. B.

The Marriotts had arranged to stay with him at Les Sablons. Hearing indirectly of the marriage, Frederick Marriott wrote suggesting

Photograph: H. C. Murcott

MRS. ARNOLD BENNETT

WRITING "THE OLD WIVES' TALE" AT FONTAINEBLEAU

that their visit should be put off for the time being, "in consequence of your new status." Bennett replied on a postcard; "Dear Frederick,—On the contrary, I shall need you all the more."

Arnold Bennett to his sister, Mrs. Kennerley:

Les Sablons,
près Moret, S. & M.

MY DEAR TERTIA,   29 July, 1907
    The only worm gnawing at the root of my mind is that this business of being married cannot possibly last as it is. It can last perfectly well on *my* footing; but it can't last on *her* footing. However, it is no use trying to explain to anybody facts about human nature which that body is not ripe for receiving. I am about a century older than my wife, though she is 32, and has been through pretty considerable things in the way of misfortune. Marriott put her age at 26 and Mrs. Marriott at 28. The fact is that she looked her age six months ago, but has steadily been getting younger during the last three months. So far as I can judge, the Marriotts are somewhat taken with her. He said to me in his solemn serious tone, with that peculiar look which he can't help wearing at such moments: 'Bennett, your wife is a beautiful woman.'
    . . . I am most frightfully busy. I do Italian every day. Also piano. And I keep my journal much better than I used to. I am writing my Five Towns play for the Stage Society. It only remains for me to do embroidery. . . . I have got hold of a whole new aspect of the Potteries which will result in prodigious books.
    Marguerite is continuing to learn poetry, and I am continuing to write it. I shall publish a book of poems next year, I think. I regret she will never be able to recite them. I get up at 6.30. I don't know how long it will last. But I know I can't keep awake at nights. I can only keep awake at 3 a.m. Marguerite sleeps like two logs—but not in *my* room. The one difficulty that I have in marriage is to refrain from looking after everything. I am so used to controlling every department of my household, from the washing to the dusting, that I continually forget that it is no longer necessary for me to worry about such things. . . . Marriage is just as exciting to me as your baby is to you, though I think I know perhaps more about women and living with women than you do about babies. However, I shall get my ideas clearer in about 2 years' time. At present I am reading

Goethe's *Conversations with Eckermann*. They are nearly as good as Sam Johnson, though in an entirely different vein. You ought to read *Wilhelm Meister*—again, if you have already read it. Your interest in Marguerite is not more acute than hers in you. If I had time and money I would come over to England for a week in September; but I have neither. I may say that Marguerite is staggered at my expensiveness. She is determined to cure it. Every now and then she drops a drop of water on the top of my head, always in the same spot. But as I desire nothing better than to be economical, provided I don't have to worry about it myself, she will certainly have her way. I shall be delighted and I may become rich. She has already settled to live on half my income. In fact, I believe she has already begun.

Love to all,

E. A. B.

He chronicled in detail the first dinner party they attended as man and wife. Describing the other guests, freely but also sympathetically, among them an Englishwoman, "my particular friend, and her English lover, pretending that there was nothing between them and that they were in Paris by chance," a Roman countess, a Second Empire baron and his simpleton wife, a once-famous Paris journalist who had been taken out to be shot in the Commune, a Greek spinster, "short of love," he considered his wife's appearance and deportment:

She had a cold, and a red nose, but it was smartly disguised by powder, and, besides, her dress fitted perfectly and she was satisfied with it. I kept my eye on her to see if she conducted herself exactly properly. Yes, I detected nothing, except that the *chroniqueur* and the Grecian talked too much across her and too much 'over her head'. Throughout the evening I watch my wife and never catch her in a *gaffe* or intellectual solecism.

After several hours the servants turn up again with drinks, silent, respectful, etc. Then at midnight we go. The patient servants stand outside waiting for us. They get our hats and cloaks. Very capable and nice human creatures.

'Good-night', says my wife to them as we depart. They are too well-trained to answer.

The story of their fourteen years together has been told by Mrs. Bennett in two books[1] which, if they add little to our comprehension of

[1] *Arnold Bennett* (Philpot, 1925), and *My Arnold Bennett* (Ivor Nicholson & Watson, 1931).

[178]

Arnold Bennett's character, have shown that not all the difficulties were of her making or avoidable by either. The chief impression they give is of an essential incompatibility. Bennett wrote in the journal:

May 18, 1908.—I am constantly, in my own mind, instinctively blaming M. because she is herself. And though, when I think of it, I reason with myself as to the absurdity of this, it still persists. I must be quite singularly sensitive, I suppose. As it is only when I am satisfied with her that I am at ease. But she can make me satisfied in a moment. And in that moment I am perfectly happy. It takes a long time to learn to get the best out of her and out of myself when we are in contact. But I imagine the general result is immensely superior to the average of such results. The differences between our temperaments and characters is simply tremendous. Reasonableness—the gift, the acquired habit, I should say, of always acting according to reason—and not yielding to instinct; this is what I am continually preaching to others and to myself. Only I don't preach it often enough to myself.

Miss Pauline Smith saw the first ominous signs of their fundamental disharmony and mentions them in her sensitive memorial study[1]: ". . . the sudden Latin tempests by which M., in unrestrained complaint of her 'so difficult English husband', was swept through argument and protest into a vehemence that gave no pause for reason were new and strange to me, and to my inexperienced ears made straight for disaster." Sir John Richmond remembers times when Arnold Bennett was "irritated beyond measure by Marguerite", and that he always "retained perfect self-command and was uniformly courteous and calm." H. G. Wells exhibits the married Bennett in *Experiment in Autobiography*: ". . . He set about marrying rather as he set about house hunting. For him it was as objective a business as everything else. Marriage wasn't by any means that organic life association at once accidental and inevitable, that growing intimacy, that it is for less lucidly constituted minds. . . . He experienced certain chagrins in the search for a wife, he was not able to carry it through with complete detachment, and when he came to the English home he had chosen at Thorpe-le-Soken, he brought with him a French wife who had previously been his close friend, a lady of charm and lucidity but with a

[1] *A.B.: A Minor Marginal Note* (Cape, 1933).

very marked personality which failed to accord in every particular with his realisation of what the wife of a successful London novelist should be."

"One day I shall look back to the evenings here, in the room where I work and sleep, with M. sewing or trying things on her mannequin . . . with regret as a perfect time." Thus Bennett in the journal for November 20, 1907. He was writing his greatest book, and that a project so long postponed or cogitated should have at last begun to fulfil itself may have been as much of a tribute to his wife's home-making instinct as to his own gift for self-organisation. The fact remains that he was at work on *The Old Wives' Tale* within five or six months of marrying and he had carried the idea and plan of it in his mind for as many years. Domestically fussy, like Dickens, he now had someone to do the fussing for him. He had referred to their honeymoon unromantically as "a period of industrious calm", this in a letter to his sister. Mrs. Bennett's role from the beginning was a difficult one. Alone among those around him she divined the nature of his tensions, the basic nervousness of the creative mind. Now he was in the toils of the most exacting task of his career and her good sense in ensuring that it took precedence over all else, even over the coffee-making about which he was so distractingly fussy, was her chief contribution to literature. If he had not written that novel the scale of his achievement as a writer would have been much reduced.

Ford Madox Ford was at their flat in 1909. "The leg of mutton—with the clove of garlic properly tucked into the knuckle—which Mrs. Bennett cooked for my benefit in that pretty little place near the Odeon is not more clear in my memory than poor Bennett's conversation. At first view he was queerly cockney in appearance with the cowlick at the back of his hair, his ready-made bow riding up over his collar and his protruding front teeth. But when he spoke he immediately—and again and again—gave me the impression that he was the wisest man not only that there ever was, but that there possibly could be. And his pronouncements about writing—at any rate in conversation—seemed to me of an astounding jauntiness. He disliked, it is true, the French from whom he had learned everything. But that seemed to be inevitable in the English intelligentsia of his generation. Nevertheless his *Old Wives' Tale* is one of the best artistic presentations of life in Paris that I have ever read." [1]

The statement that Arnold Bennett disliked the French was a too

[1] *Return to Yesterday* (Gollancz, 1931).

reckless interpretation of his attitude, which was rarely more than moderately critical. He certainly never retracted his admiration for the French contribution to the art of living in this world. "The French are indispensable, the most civilised people in Europe," he would say. "Through the centuries they have been the one reliable repository of Liberal thought." And so on. His friend 'Johnny' Atkins remembers his often holding forth in that strain during their evenings together in the cafés of Paris forty years ago.

(2)

The Old Wives' Tale is a great demonstration of controlled imagination. It is also a considerable technical performance. Arnold Bennett tells in the preface he wrote for one of the later editions that, having settled in his mind that it was to show the development of a young girl into a stout old lady, that it was to be the English equivalent of *Une Vie*, he went on to resolve that his book must 'go one better' than de Maupassant's tale and give the life-history of two women, not one. "Hence, *The Old Wives' Tale* has two heroines. Constance was the original; Sophia was created out of bravado, just to indicate that I declined to consider Guy de Maupassant as the last forerunner of the deluge." Incidentally, Bennett never bothered to correct his Five Towns pronunciation of that author's name; he went on calling it 'Mopesun'. Intimidated, he said, by the audacity of his scheme, "for several years I looked it squarely in the face at intervals, and then walked away to write novels of smaller scope, of which I produced five or six."

Having forced himself, in that autumn of 1907, to come to grips with it: "I calculated that it would be 200,000 words long (which it exactly proved to be), and I had a vague notion that no novel of such dimensions (except Richardson's) had ever been written before. So I counted the words in several Victorian novels, and discovered to my relief that the famous Victorian novels average 400,000 words apiece. I wrote the first part of the novel in six weeks."

A London visit interrupted his labours. "I tried to continue the book in a London hotel, but London was too distracting, and I put the thing away, and during January and February of 1908, I wrote *Buried Alive*, which was published immediately, and was received with majestic indifference by the English public, an indifference that has persisted. . . . I then returned to the Fontainebleau region and gave *The Old Wives' Tale* no rest till I finished it at the end of July, 1908."

J. B. Pinker to Arnold Bennett:

> Talbot House,
> Arundel Street,
> Strand, London, W.C.

MY DEAR BENNETT,   5th April, 1911.

I have just read your preface to the American edition of *The Old Wives' Tale*. You naturally do not mention there what I always recollect as a remarkable history of the novel, so far as my office was concerned. I remember your coming into the office one day, and telling me in your customary manner that you were going to write 'a great novel'. You told me the exact date on which you would begin it, and the exact date on which I should have the MS., and the length of the novel. In my experience it is remarkable for an author to begin a novel exactly on the day he fixes; it is still more remarkable for him to finish it on the day he fixes; but the astonishing thing was that the novel was a great novel, and that we both knew it would be.

> Sincerely yours,
> J. B. PINKER

(3)

The London visit was required by the production of a play he had made out of *Anna of the Five Towns*. As *Cupid and Common Sense* it had been accepted by the Stage Society and was produced by Frank Vernon at the Shaftesbury Theatre, London, on January 26, 1908, with Miss Sydney Fairbrother, Miss Mary Brough and Mr. J. Fisher White in the cast. "My aim in writing plays," Arnold Bennett said, "is strictly commercial. I want money in heaps and I want advertisement for my books." Rehearsals raised his spirits and just as readily cast them down again, and he spoke of this London interval as "a feverish and restless life". He took a curtain call at the dress rehearsal and not simply because the director of the Stage Society, Lee Matthews, wished it: "I wanted to." But the first-night ordeal frightened and exhausted him, despite an encouraging public reception. It was some time before he found the nerve to face such an occasion again. Mr. J. B. Atkins was called in to 'hold his hand' on more than one subsequent first-night of his. "He arranged for his wife to be in the theatre and to telephone her impressions during the intervals, while he and I dined at a restaurant somewhere near by. It was not at all easy, I found, to distract his attention. When his wife reported that "success seemed to be assured", he feared she was only trying to cheer him up. Why that note of expectation rather than of realisation? If the play had been going well, would she not have said . . . ? etc., etc." [1]

Social pleasures offset the stage worries. At a dinner given to Pinker he was put next to W. W. Jacobs, who struck a sonorous chord in Bennett's heart when he said: "It's disgusting, getting older. I hate having young men raise their hats to me out of respect for my superior age." Then Jacobs bent closer to him and spoke in his ear a limerick "composed to order" by E. V. Lucas, who was present. It made Bennett throw back his head in laughter:

> There was a young woman of Wantage
> Of whom the Town Clerk took advantage.
>   Said the Borough Surveyor
>   Of course you must pay her—
> You've altered the line of her frontage!

He lunched with the Shaws: "Mrs. Shaw, a very agreeable, sympathetic and earnest woman. She looked just like the mother of a large family. Shaw came in just as lunch was served. Naturally self-conscious and egotistic; but he evidently made a decent effort against this. Talked most of the time during lunch: has a marked accent, and a habit of rubbing his hands constantly while talking." A member of the Fabian Society had previously told Bennett "as a fact, that G. B. Shaw discussed with certain members of the Society as to whose 'duty' it was to marry the heiress".

Wells was delighted with the play; "impressed rather deeply, I thought." He took tea with Miss Lena Ashwell and felt that his impression of her being "a little embittered" might pass with greater intimacy: "she showed flashes of insight." At a musical evening at the Lee Matthews' he "met the beautiful eyes of Beryl de Selincourt", and at the Ilchester Mansions Hotel, 1, 2 and 3 Ilchester Gardens, Bayswater (telegraphic address: 'Mayonnaise, London'), he was depressed by the "numbers of idlers", and found it "almost disconcerting to think that all this vast idle class has 'to go' one day". He was uplifted by Mrs. Belloc Lowndes's news that "prices paid to novelists in London are still going up", and that Maurice Hewlett received £3,000 for one of his books in America. At his sister's, "a Swedish Miss Zetterberg recited

[1] *Incidents and Reflections.*

stories for children in foreign-English so well that I could scarcely keep from crying," which perhaps gave point to his following note: "We have certainly been living at a great pace; at least I have." Making up his accounts, he found that at the hotel he was living beyond his income by £2 a week. "This did not surprise me, but it disquieted me . . . I do not think we can live here on £50 a month inclusive of everything; but we shall certainly do February on less; for one thing, it is three days shorter."

His days had never been so full. Unmistakably, the pace of his life was quickening. He had become 'Jacob Tonson' of *The New Age*. A new play was building itself up in his mind. He had written *Buried Alive*. He was already at work on another novel, the Five Towns again: title, *Helen with the High Hand*. "Very proud of my extraordinary industry and efficiency at the present moment. Over 100,000 good words written in the first quarter of this year," 1908. He was practising every day, with an architect's pen, the art of beautiful handwriting commended to him as a hobby by his brother-in-law, William Kennerley. "At last I think I have got into a fairly 'formed' formal hand for 'fine writing' and for the writing of my next novel in particular." Marriott was enthusiastic: he believed that if Bennett could keep up his high standard his manuscript "would be unique in the world".

He took the chance while in London of going to the British Museum to look at the illuminated manuscripts. The manuscript of *The Old Wives' Tale*, which later Messrs. Ernest Benn, Ltd., reproduced and published, is in itself a work of art, the original now in American possession. Its completion called for an astonishing effort of will. Arnold Bennett told his wife more than once while writing it that he was sorry he had ever begun the task but that having begun it there must be no going back: he forced himself to finish what he had set out to do. And the journal and his letters to his sister from this time on were often given elaborate and loving ornament in the form of 'sprig'd' initial letters and decorative tailpieces, and now and again an heraldic flourish or a patterned border, giving the pages a most distinguished look.

Time's exactions did not escape his notice during this hectic London stay. Marriott, he observed, was "more deliberate, slower". A Swedish woman pianist, Tora Hwass, whom he had last met and admired at Semaphore House, Claygate, with his old friend Homan, the engineer, nearly ten years before, when he had been struck by "the child-like abandonment of her management of her skirt, her naturalness, her easy laughter", now impressed him by her "general ageing sadness". Wells he found more polite, "and more reasonable in argument and posture than ever before, but harder." Wells was still discontented about money matters, "while admitting that he was making £3,000 out of *War in the Air*."

Bennett was not yet in a position to talk in those lordly terms. Money discontents assailed him, too, as soon as he had got back to Fontainebleau and *The Old Wives' Tale*. His yearly earnings had fluctuated. In 1906 they were £712 8s. 10d.: in 1907, £303 12s. 4d.: in 1908, £532 12s. 4d.; and in 1909, £276 18s. 4d. During 1908 Pinker had advanced him more than £1,000, at five per cent, making payments for him to relatives and keeping up the premiums of a National Provident Institution insurance policy which Pinker held against his loans. Reflecting on his situation a day or two after returning from London, Arnold Bennett wrote: "I kept myself in hand very well until the moment arrived last night for me to receive a crucial letter from Pinker. It was handed to me in a dark street. I had some difficulty in not stopping to read it under a gas lamp. I read it at the station. All right. No mistake, the constant practice of M. Aurelius and Epictetus has had its gradual effect on me."

(4)

He had begun writing *The Old Wives' Tale* on October 8, 1907, at the Villa des Nefliers, rue Bernard Palissy, Avon-Fontainebleau, having left Les Sablons and the apartments of the Leberts, the solid French couple whose oddly casual memories of the Commune are used in the novel. "I felt less self-conscious than I usually do in beginning a novel. In order to find a clear three hours for it every morning I have had to make a time-table, getting out of bed earlier and lunching later." It was to have "a lofty nobility". He had attained that quality, he thought, in *Whom God Hath Joined*, which Wells considered the best of his works thus far. "In the next book I must increase the dose."

Within a few days he was writing in the journal: "I have now done 7,000 words of the first chapter . . . and am still very far from the end of it. Regarding it objectively, I do not see that it is very good, but from the pleasure I take in doing it, it must be." On October 21: "I seem to be rather uneasy as to its excellence." He finished 18,000 words in "two weeks, four days", and was troubled by increasingly misty eyesight, another of time's shoulder-taps. His writing average was over 2,000 words a day, a high rate for an important work, and this in spite of social claims and a determination not to forgo his piano-playing, his Italian lessons, his handwriting practice. He abandoned, instead, his intensive reading of the newspapers. His aim for the year was 365,000 words, and by the end of October he was able to say: "I have never done as much work before in the time." His grand total was 375,000 words: "this constitutes a record year."

April 5, 1908.—Habit of work is growing on me. I could get into the way of going to my desk as a man goes to whisky, or rather to chloral. Now that I have finished all my odd jobs and have nothing to do but 10,000 words of the novel a week and two articles a week, I feel quite lost, and at once begin to think without effort, of ideas for a new novel. My instinct is to multiply books and articles and plays. I constantly gloat over the number of words I have written in a given period.

"No mistake, my control over my brain steadily increases," and therein he believed to be the secret of his ability to produce the preparatory thought which enabled him to go to his desk with the confidence of the craftsman who has fully visualised the work he has to do. The effectiveness of it is demonstrated not only in the ordered presentation of his ideas but in the actual physical rendering of them on paper. To that the unblemished pages of the journal alone sufficiently testify.

Of the emotional ebb and flow which is the enemy of concentration Bennett was particularly scornful, calling it "clumsy living". He scorned it more in himself than in others. "The unnecessary friction. The constant slight inattention to my own rules. I could be a marvel to others and to myself if only I practised more sincerely. Half an hour in the morning in complete concentration on the living-through of the day, and I should work wonders! But this all-important concentration is continually interrupted. . . ."

Inspiration was coming to him from Annie Besant's book, *Thought Power*, which he hesitated to recommend because it could only be fully understood in the light of Theosophist teachings. "Yet I should probably be unjust if I did not recommend it, having regard to its immense influence on myself. It is the least unsatisfying manual of the brain that I have met with." Turning these ideas into weekly-paper articles, he was having "a success of popular interest" with them, and because of it was all the more disgusted by his failure to practise perfectly what he preached. He never rescinded his belief in what he did preach. As late as 1928, meeting W. J. Turner, poet and critic, in Hyde Park, he was reaffirming it. "Turner said that life could and did 'maim' a man. I replied: 'Very rarely.' I said that it was well to remember that nothing happened to a man outside his own head, and that therefore if the mind was under control, etc., etc. I left him suddenly, saying that though apparently idle, I was busy working," thinking out Act 3 of a play.

Incompetent thinking for him was the black mark of civilisation. "Multitudes of individuals never think consecutively, and few think consecutively for more than a few minutes at a time," he wrote near the end of his life. "The majority of us go through life from one end to the other without once properly exercising the most important and the most interesting of human faculties. It is very odd."

Arnold Bennett to his brother-in-law and sister (Mr. and Mrs. W. W. Kennerley):

Villa des Nefliers

MY DEAR PEOPLE,   5th August, 1908
    ... I have now written 15,000 words of the last part of the novel. I expect to finish on September 1st. I work from 6 a.m. to noon 5 days a week. Terrible, but I write 2,000 words a day. One day I give to my weekly article; one day to a complete holiday, and one day to arranging my ideas for the next 5 days' work. You will say that my week consists thus of 8 days. It does. Last week my Sunday was on Saturday. Next it will be on Sunday.

'Buried Alive' is selling only slowly, but regularly. Publishers disappointed. Say they are losing money. Much depressed. However, the directors conferred and said they would give me the same terms for the next book. Philanthropists! Tauchnitz has bought it. This cheered us. However, the outlook is dark, generally. I thank God our rent is only £36 a year.

Yours,
E. A. B.

The concentration needed to think out and produce *The Old Wives' Tale* owed nothing, then, to the frenzy, the passion, the abandon that have given the world some of its greatest works of imaginative genius. Arnold Bennett's was the practical, ruthless, loving concentration of the craftsman, not the self-losing delight of the artist. The artist is

inspired to create, the craftsman is impelled to make. *The Old Wives'*
Tale is a great feat, as a critic has said. It was architecturally planned, a
Parthenon of a book. The writing was set about in a formal, business-
like way, with its author getting up earlier, re-arranging his meal-times,
giving three hours to it each morning, and not rising from his desk
without having drafted the outlines of the succeeding day's work. More
than this, he was conforming to the highest traditions of craftsmanship
in keeping the tools of his trade in prime condition as he worked. The
mental gymnastics, the daily recourse to the Stoic philosophers, were
supplying him at this time with his bread-and-butter income, *T.P.'s*
Weekly being able to afford him as a contributor again. They were also
contributing to the disciplined thought that not only endowed *The Old*
Wives' Tale with a rare distinction among very long novels but helped
to make it the master work that it is: "the most striking imaginative
work of its period; in comprehensiveness, proportion and profundity of
impulse better than anything by Mr. Wells or Mr. Galsworthy."[1]

(5)

His articles on mental efficiency were successful, he believed, because
they were based on his personal experience: "it is the little franknesses
that count." What also counted was the tone of brisk dependable
confidence in which they were written, their assurance to the reader
that he could be the captain of his soul, etc. "For me, spiritual content
(I will not use the word 'happiness', which implies too much) springs
essentially from no mental or physical facts. It springs from the
spiritual fact that there is something higher in men than the mind, and
that that something can control the mind. Call that something the soul,
or what you will. My sense of security amid the collisions of existence
lies in the firm consciousness that just as my body is the servant of my
mind, so is my mind the servant of *me*. An unruly servant, but a servant
—and possibly getting less unruly every day! Often have I said to that
restive brain: 'Now, O mind, sole means of communication between the
divine *me* and all external phenomena, you are not a free agent; you are
a subordinate; you are nothing but a piece of machinery; and obey me
you *shall*. . . . This is extremely difficult, but it can be done, and it is
marvellously well worth doing." [2]

[1] Edwin Muir: *Scrutinies* (Wishart, 1928).
[2] *Mental Efficiency* (Hodder & Stoughton).

Come (we can imagine him saying), let us live more sensibly, more efficiently, more wisely. Let us make a profession of living: away with this amateurish muddling along! It insults the intelligence of man. This submission to the winds of circumstance, it is supine. This acceptance of the dictates of ill-formed predispositions, it is not civilised. This flabbiness of the will, it is ignoble; this indifference to the virtues of self-command, this loose tolerance of the ungirt loin, degrades the human spirit! "The Kingdom of Heaven is within you." Christ said it. Epictetus said it. Marcus Aurelius said it. Three great and good witnesses to an eternal truth, and, pray, who are you to disdain it? Now I, Arnold Bennett, say it. Why? Because I believe it, because I have tested its validity to my satisfaction and therefore, excuse me, to yours. . . .

He was writing out of the first decade of the century, our century. Maturity had come, and with it disillusionments, to the generation which had been the first to receive the benefits of the new enactments in education of forty years before. Just as the advance of industrialism had swelled the populations of towns and districts not able to house them, so had the challenge of the scientific spirit imposed stresses on minds not as yet tempered to withstand or absorb them. The massive change-over from illiteracy had brought bewilderments new in human experience. 'The strain of modern life' had become a cliché. 'Brain-fag' was another, and the advertisement columns of the newspapers and popular periodicals began to reflect the neurasthenia induced by the ruthless doubts of thinkers like Darwin, Spencer, Huxley, Clifford, Tyndall. These apostles of reason it was who, with the rhetorical support of Bradlaugh, Butler, Winwood Reade, Leslie Stephen, Clodd, FitzGerald, Swinburne and Hardy, paradoxically brought about the eclipse of reason by engendering the first symptoms of the modern malady of thinking with the nerves. The age of anxiety had come.

The sorties of these leaders of thought against the orthodoxies of faith and dogma, mounting to a sustained intellectual attack, originated far-felt mental tensions which pervaded every part of society, and only imagination can reach out and back to sound the despairs that followed. Hope was the hall-mark of the nineteenth-century temper, based on the optimistic deduction that science was about to reveal truths which would set men free and therefore make them happy. Some there were, like the forgotten poet Arthur Hugh Clough, who could hardly face the prospect of living on without the high consolations that had upheld them in former times, and some there were who did not face it. This was 'the strain of modern life', and Arnold Bennett, the woman's paper editor turned novelist, to whom the more nervous readers of popular literature were confiding their fears, was rendering it thus:

> Old beliefs have been shaken, and some of them have been overthrown utterly. And new truths have assumed the places and part of the authority of the old. And fresh truths are continually coming up over the horizon. The sum of human knowledge is still increasing at an enormous rate. And the resultant fact is that we don't know exactly where we are.

Life was to be had more abundantly by more people, and one of the effects was that more people, perturbed by its enormously quickened vitality, were running away from it. For this they were censured by Arnold Bennett as being guilty of "the supreme offence against life". He had hard words for those who feared the stress of the times and particularly for those who were complaining about the new competitive elements that had come into existence. "The stress of competition is only one symptom out of several . . . this generation happens to find itself in a transition age, and those who find themselves in a transition age are seldom comfortable."

Not that he was by any means being regarded as a solitary redeemer of lost confidence. The 'strain of modern life' called forth many consolers and counsellors. An American engineer, Horace Fletcher, preached that the way of regeneration lay in chewing the food with a thoroughness which in many instances must have put the victims right off their food. His gospel, expounded from Venice in a series of books, pamphlets, articles, and interviews, was endorsed by impressive references to the masticating prowess of Mr. Gladstone, and it had a wide vogue among the new dyspeptic class and the life-frightened. While in Vienna the new psychologists were sniffing like hounds at the tree of knowledge, Fletcher was percipient enough to see in advance that the 'inferiority' concept was a reality in human affairs and he invented his own word for it; fearthought. Likewise, the books of Annie Payson Call, *The Freedom of Life* and *Nerves and Common Sense*, and Ralph Waldo Trine's *In Tune with the Infinite*, were widely read and gratefully quoted in two continents. There was a 'power through repose' school and 'new thought' movements were propagating the view that it was bad mental hygiene to long for a return to the womb-like Victorian age with its firm principles and its sense of immutable security.

Christian Science, released by editors from the quarantine of quotation marks, was celebrating its hard-won recognition by restoring the confidence of architects in particular. And someone had persuaded large numbers of highly-strung people anxious about their future to believe that salvation was to be had from sipping hot water after meals, while a no-breakfast campaign was soon obliterated by the cereal-processing firms, whose advertising power was already strong enough to be decisive in such situations.

Arnold Bennett's sounded like the voice of experience and its high-pitched *timbre* carried authority to minds beset by the prolonged adolescence that is the most marked symptom of the twentieth century neurosis. They were not all hankering after the old invalidated assurances, the fallen altars of their youth, but the storm of life was rising about them and many were in distress. Studying the signs, and having undoubtedly read his Ruskin, Arnold Bennett declared: "We are entering now on a mighty change, on a world-movement, on a subversive, vitalising epoch, compared to which, in my opinion, the Renaissance and the Reformation are insignificant. . . . It is going to be the greatest storm that the ocean of life has ever witnessed. Nobody knows, not even the wisest, what will be the end of it—what craft will founder and what will ride it out." [1] For his early twentieth-century readers no doubt he stood out as a writer uniquely aware of his time, a sensitivity which he singularly failed to develop or to express in his later and more important work.

A self-appointed pilot of the storm, he was pontifical because as a journalist he knew the importance of being forceful as well as clear in his public utterances; possibly, too, because as a peculiarly afflicted stammerer he found mental relief in being able to proclaim himself unimpeded. He could not tell those who feared shipwreck where to steer to. "You say I am busying myself with the best method of getting there, and refusing to discuss where to go. Precisely. One man cannot tell another where the other man wants to go." But he could give them something to steer *with*: mind control. He had no doubt of its potential value in all the practical affairs of life. At the same time, he was for treating the subject not too seriously, dispensing his notions about it rather as a tonic for the invalidish temperaments of his readers with the knowing air of an elixir-of-life huckster holding up a bottle of coloured stuff at a wakes. "The correspondence which I have received shows that there is, among a vast mass of reflecting people in this country, a

[1] *T.P.'s Weekly*, 1909.

[191]

clear consciousness of being mentally less than efficient, and a strong (though ineffective) desire that such mental inefficiency should cease to be. . . . The Sandow of the brain has not yet loomed up over the horizon. On the other hand, there appears to be a general expectancy that I personally am going to play the role of the Sandow of the brain. Vain thought!" [1]

The tone of omniscience annoyed some people who failed to note that Arnold Bennett was urging his readers to school the brain, cultivate the will, discipline "the noddle", as he called it, while at the same time quoting with relish the dictum: "Do not accustom yourself to enchain your *volatility* with vows," adding with the parenthetical grin that is one of the engaging touches in the 'pocket philosophies': "The wisdom is Dr. Johnson's, but I flatter myself on the italics."

The 'philosophies', heralded in book form by dust-jacket adjectives that also prejudiced the more donnish reviewers, had a virtue which continues to withstand the verdigris of criticism, and that is their plain common sense. They were competent expositions of it. They summed up (and it is the one biographically important thing about them) habits of thought which were ruling Bennett's life at the time of his greatest mental achievement, the writing of *The Old Wives' Tale.* They are the textbooks of a teacher who was as keen to be taught as his pupils were to learn. He claimed no originality for them. Spencer, Mill, Pascal, La Bruyère, Emerson, perhaps even Smiles, perhaps Matthew Arnold with his life-long insistence on intellectual discipline, almost certainly William James, had supplied some of the stimulus for these essays in mental and moral control. They were an exercise and they were a testament.

We can decry the superficiality. It would not be unfair. We can object to the very nearly summary disregard of some of the deeper implications of psychology, which had not come of age as a science but which could hardly be ignored as a source of inferential ideas. It would be valid. We can smile at the chirpy extrovert style.

We cannot overlook the common sense. It would be perverse. If the volatile persuasiveness has evaporated, the astringent essence remains, potent enough to be taken as before. There is no normal individual whose mental lassitude it would not dispel, no society whose moral tone would not be improved. These "quite perfect lay sermons", a critic wrote, "contain the completest common sense, expressed with astonishing simplicity and directness, and based upon an unimpeachable

[1] *Mental Efficiency.*

[192]

honesty of outlook," and if behind the jaunty empiricism we seem to see the shadow of a dread, their relevance is not only of yesterday. They have a value for generations other than his own.

(6)

August 30, 1908.—Finished *The Old Wives' Tale* at 11.30 a.m. today. 200,000 words.

In the last weeks of writing it, "I simply did nothing but that book. Everything else gave way before it. It meant the utter defeat of all other plans." It had meant, too, mysterious physical disturbances, headaches, exhaustions, depressions, and worry about the future of his eyesight: "I know I run risks."

Having despatched the manuscript to Pinker in London, he set out on a recuperative cycling tour to Orleans and beyond. A head wind on the first day nearly thwarted his plans. "I had to *ménager mes forces*, or I might not have arrived." The unaccustomed physical effort was too much: "it is ageing." Putting his bicycle aboard a train, he heard reverberations of the 'life storm' about which he had been writing: "Travelled with a young sportsman, son of the proprietor of Hôtel de Bordeaux; very well bred. He said Frenchmen of property were very unsure of the future; placed their money abroad, largely in Holland. His father anxious to sell all his real property, as outlook so precarious owing to class hatred." His journal notes of the holiday are concluded with the entry neatly displayed in the centre of the final page:

Returned to Avon
3rd October, 1908
Exhausted

Meanwhile, Messrs. Chapman & Hall had accepted the novel, paying a royalty advance of £150. Bennett wrote to his sister and brother-in-law:

Villa des Nefliers

DEAR PEOPLE,   7th October, 1908
    Having rearranged my daily life once more, after this most strenuous holiday, I now in the appointed order sit down to write you a few lines. This district stands very well the ordeal of coming back to it after the Midi. I have walked out two mornings, at length, in search of ideas for my fine new play. I have found ideas with extra-

193]

ordinary certainty and ease. I must now be in my prime, I suppose. I shall never be any more efficient, but may hope to keep as I am for another nine years. I feel as if I could write a book or a play once a month. This play is to be entitled 'What The Public Wants'. And Harmsworth is the hero, and the press and the theatre the subjects. What *my* Harmsworth wants is not to be continually slighted by intellectual people. The play is the story of his disappointment in this desire. I shall call it 'a tragedy in five acts'. But it will be externally a farce. Among other people to be guyed in it is A. B. Walkley. I like him, but I owe him one, and in a coin more golden than his own I will pay. I tell you all this because 'What The Public Wants' promises to be a very gay lark.

I have corrected the proofs of 'The Old Wives' Tale'—678 pages. I am sure Tertia is wrong about those two chapters. I deliberately lowered the tension in the last part of the book, in obedience to a theory which objects to violent climaxes as a close; and now I have done it I don't know that I am quite satisfied. I know the public will consider the fourth part rather tame and flat, if not dull. And I am not sure whether I don't slightly share this view. This is amazing. Still, I must say it is a bit of honest work. And the effect as you finish the last page is pretty stiff—*when you begin to think things over*. It isn't in many books that you can see people growing old. I read 'Une Vie' again (than which I meant to try and go one better) and was most decidedly disappointed in it. Lacking in skill.

. . . My impression is that 'The New Age' will be sold soon, though they are trying to form a company. But it is too damnation clever to last long. I have the written certificate of the editor that commercially 'Jacob Tonson' is the most important contributor to the paper. But the question in my mind is: How long am I going to continue making them a present of £150 a year, at least? There is no virtue in me, because I only do it for the amusement of self and a few others. Young de Selincourt, having ascertained who J. T. was, wrote to me the other day in these terms: 'Damn you, Bennett, what hideous fun you must be having!' Rather cryptic.

It is now time that Tertia read 'La Chartreuse de Parme'. Balzac said there were only about 1200 people in Europe capable of appreciating it. Assuredly there is nothing in fiction more *distinguished*. . . .

Our loves,

E. A. B.

His 'Books and Persons' articles in *The New Age* were extending his critical repute during the time he was at work on the big novel, giving him a weight of authority that made itself known and felt beyond the paper's small circulation. So forcible an authority, indeed, that nearly twenty years afterwards the violent genius of Lord Beaverbrook saw the point of launching Arnold Bennett on a new 'Books and Persons' career in the London *Evening Standard*, with results that have passed into the history of London book-publishing and reviewing. "Bennett was the only man in my literary lifetime who could really make the fortune of a new book in a night," said Hugh Walpole enviously. His articles in *The New Age*, collected in book form,[1] bring before the reader of today a broad expansive view of the London literary landscape forty years ago over which his critical lightning is seen to flash with illuminating and sometimes deadly effect. Tumbled idols strew the scene. Reputations new and old are riven. "I have no hesitation in de-classing the whole professorial squad—Bradley, Herford, Dowden, Walter Raleigh, Elton, Saintsbury. The first business of any writer, and especially of any critical writer, is not to be mandarinic and tedious, and these lecturers have not yet learnt that first business." "Lord Rosebery . . . an ageing man, probably exacerbated by the consciousness of failure." "It is a solemn and terrifying thought that Mr. Garvin, who, by means of thoroughly bad prose persisted in during many years, has at last laid the Tory Party in ruins, should be so excellent a judge of literature." "I would give much to prevent Sir W. Robertson Nicoll from inflicting the intelligent when the solemn annual moment comes for him to make the reputation of a novelist."

The Bennett who contributed so successfully to *The New Age* is remembered by its one-time business manager, A. F. Palmer Phillips, who afterwards became a book publisher and then went into the motor industry, in which he has remained. "He arrived at the office in a broad check suit with a vivid yellow waistcoat, a bright tie with a large horseshoe pin stuck in it, and a grey bowler hat. It would have been easy to have mistaken him for a prosperous bookmaker." There was general agreement, Mr. Phillips says, that Bennett's weekly column was the best thing of its kind in the journalism of that period. He remembers being in the office with Orage, the editor, and Holbrook Jackson, who was also on the staff, when they were taunting Bennett about the "lack of sex" in his novels. "They were accusing him of dodging the issue. They wondered why. They told him they couldn't

[1] *Books and Persons* (Chatto & Windus, 1917).

[195]

understand why he avoided the subject. Bennett listened, saying nothing. It was fairly obvious that he had nothing to say."

As the publisher of two of the 'philosophy' books, Mr. Phillips, who was in business under the name of Frank Palmer, discovered what he calls "a beautiful little scheme" by which Bennett disavowed knowledge of the financial side of his work, dismissing it by saying always that he left everything to Pinker. Going to Pinker, "you were told, in confidence, that whereas he himself was perfectly ready to talk reasonable terms, his client had fixed the price and was not to be shifted from it."

(7)

On the day that *The Old Wives' Tale* was published in London Bennett was quite unable to hide the anxiety he felt. Mrs. Bennett says that he was putting on his necktie in front of the dressing mirror when he swung round and said to her: "This is the most important day of my life! I've done my best. I shall never be able to do anything better. It'll settle our future."

23 October, 1908.—Vaguely apprehensive about the fate of 'The Old Wives' Tale.' So much seems to depend on its success, and yet I have no real hope of its success. I see more and more clearly that the one wise thing to do is to work at what I want to do, to ignore competing activities, and to live on 'nothing'. To make popular success a condition of one's happiness is painfully silly. Yet the long list of other novelists' new novels, and the insignificant space occupied by my own in the advertisements—well, it disturbs me.

What was for him a major event of his career seemed to have been considered not much more than an incident, relatively, in the history of the well-known old publishing firm of Chapman & Hall who had published Dickens and had employed George Meredith as their principal reader for thirty years. "Nobody in the firm quite realised that we were attending at the birth of a masterpiece," wrote the late Arthur Waugh, for many years associated with the firm, in his *A Hundred Years of Publishing*. As the novel did not earn its advance, Messrs. Chapman & Hall, perhaps not so unreasonably as Bennett thought, allowed it to go out of print. At Pinker's suggestion, Messrs. Hodder & Stoughton took over its publication. Some good judges had by then

[196]

given their verdicts: "the best English novel of the past twenty-five years," said the great book panjandrum, Sir William Robertson Nicoll, writing in *The British Weekly* under his well-known pseudonym of Claudius Clear. H. W. Massingham, influential editor of *The Nation*, considered it to be "one of the really great novels of the last thirty years", and when on the strength of it he invited Bennett to write for his paper, Bennett said that he was flattered as he had never been flattered before. Wells sent him a postcard: "Ripping, enormous, various Balzac, Arnold has surpassed himself. No further question of *First Rank*. . . . We are satisfied with our Bennett. There are only two real contemporary swell novelists under fifty. He is one . . ." and followed it with a letter:

I think the book a quite pre-eminent novel, so that it at least doubles your size in my estimation. It is far too big, too fine, and too restrained to get at first anything like the recognition it is bound in the long run to bring you . . . I am certain it will secure you the respect of all the distinguished critics who are now consuming gripe-water and such like. It is all at such a high level that one does not know where to begin commending, but I think the high light for me is the bakehouse glimpse of Sam Povey. But the knowledge, the detail, the spirit! From first to last it *never* fails. . . . Go on, great man!

In return for the copy of *The Old Wives' Tale* Wells had sent Bennett a new book of his own, *First and Last Things*. This drew from Bennett a letter of some interest in view of his recent trafficking in the ideas of Mrs. Annie Besant:

Villa des Nefliers,

My dear H. G.,   23 Nov., 1908
. . . Those moments of 'worship'. Of all the points in your book, this has most stuck in my mind. I wish you had enlarged on it, and not got out of it by referring to 'poverty of language'. I should like to have known exactly what you did mean—*do* mean. I regard this as the most important thing in the book, and it is not really handled. I myself have never, at any rate for 25 years, had the slightest movement towards worship or anything resembling worship. That is why I want to know what people do feel in that line.

[197]

Against immortality and transmigration of souls: I think you are too summary here. Having regard to the enormous philosophic ingenuity of Buddhistic and similar dogma, I don't see how you can dismiss transmigration of souls as imaginings of 'a race of children'. The memory difficulty has certainly been smoothed away for me. Here is another immensely important matter which I think you deal with too brusquely. . . . Personally (again) I am at present a believer in the transmigration of souls, as the theory which presents fewer difficulties. But if you can indicate to me any full attempt to make it seem impossible, I shall be glad to read the same.

There is an implied reference to 'Platonic' love which gives the reader to think that you think that Plato brought into prominence the notion of friendship between men and women. I do not think this is so. My idea is that the phrase 'platonic love' has been quite changed in meaning and that Plato meant something quite different and even more spiritual.

For me, you scarcely justify your inclusion of 'metaphysics'. Nor do I consider that your metaphysics really *are* metaphysics. Metaphysics are inseparably connected with ontological speculation, the perfection of whose futility is unmatched by the futility of anything else in the universe. Whereas your remarks deal with *phenomena*. No, I will acquit you of metaphysics.

Yours ever,
E. A. B.

A letter from Frank Harris, who was editing *Vanity Fair*, brought with it a copy of his novel, *The Bomb*, which he hoped Jacob Tonson would notice. Addressing himself to 'Dear Mr. Tonson', Harris said that the novel was 'a sort of confession of faith', and that he was in need of "a little popularity". His hope was also for "a little profit in order that I may get out the ten or twelve books which I have in me still". He had received nothing as yet, he said, for what he had written, "not even enough to pay the cost of printing and paper."

Bennett's reply was highly complimentary. "You know as well as anyone what your work is, and you must be sure that anyone who can distinguish between literature and the other thing cannot fail to appreciate it very highly indeed." He suggested to Harris that it would be "a graceful act" if he ran down to Fontainebleau to see him when he was next in France. "There is no author in England whom I would more like to meet."

I myself live on literature, and as I spend over half my time in producing work that will only be remunerative 50 years hence (if then), the task of living on literature is somewhat arduous, particularly for a man of expensive taste! But I can do it here, and maintain 'the dignity of letters'.

He added his assumption that *Vanity Fair* had received a copy of *The Old Wives' Tale*. "It is extremely long. But I really should like to know what you think of it, and of its chances for 1958." Harris wrote his comments on the novel and acclaimed Bennett's reply as the best letter he had ever received, "a masterly epistle":

Villa des Nefliers,
Avon S/M.

MY DEAR HARRIS,   30th Nov, 1908
    I am not at the opposite pole to you. Because I am at both poles. I quite agree with your fundamental criticism of 'The Old Wives' Tale'. That is to say, I quite agree with it in certain moods. I am capable of regretting that Sophia developed as she did. My original intention was to make her a magnificent courtesan. But I altered this, after due thought. I conceive that what she did in fact become was just as interesting and as good as anything else. What *you* want in life and in art is the expensive—I mean the spiritually expensive. I want it too. But not much of it. (I did it in 'Sacred and Profane Love'). At bottom I regard your attitude as flavoured with a youthful sentimentality. At bottom I am proudly content with the Pentonville omnibus. Why not? If I cannot take a Pentonville omnibus and show it to be fine, then I am not a fully equipped artist. (And I *am*.) Ruskin of course was a sublime sentimentalist. There is nothing better in my book than the return of Constance from the railway station after seeing Cyril off to London. Pure Pentonville! Not even sexual passion in it! If anyone says that such material and such an event are not proper for the very greatest possible art, I say that they are. (I never could argue!) People may talk about ideal art, heroic art. But let an artist get away from the *average* truth into an ideal of his own, and whatever he creates I will say to him: 'But I can imagine something more grand than that. Why the devil did you stop *there*?' What you wanted, in reading 'The Old Wives' Tale', was another

[199]

book, but not a better one. To me the difference between one form of human life and another is insignificant. *It is all almost equally exciting.* That is my view. Some day I shall do another book in the vein of 'Sacred and Profane Love'. And then you will see. I shall be very much indebted to you if you will say in 'Vanity Fair' exactly what you think of the novel. Go for it with all your fervour. If the article is as good as your letter it will be very good. But shove the article in at once or it will be commercially useless. I can't send you a photo, as I haven't one. I detest photos of myself.

I made the mistake of reading your Shakspere play before your Shakspere criticism. So I had to read the play again. I cannot expertly criticise the critical book, because I don't know enough. To me, as a piece of constructive criticism, it seems not the best piece of work of the kind that I ever read, but rather the *only* piece. It is merely and simply amazing. What of Coleridge I have ever had the patience to read is not to be compared to it. More damned nonsense has been talked about Shakspere than on any subject on earth except metaphysics; and reading your book is like walking out of a lunatic asylum for Dowdens into an open field. What I should say of your portrait of Shakspere is, in a very modified form, what Hume said of Berkeley's philosophy: 'It admitted of no answer, but produced no conviction.' The epigram is as false as epigrams usually are. What I mean is that you have to fight against a popular conception of Shakspere which has been gradually growing up for over a century. To me, for example, your portrait was at first most disconcerting. I had an image of Shakspere as a successful, hustling, jolly playwright of immense artistic power, *but somewhat disdaining that power*, and keen on material needs; always thinking of an easy old age at Stratford. Of course I knew some of Hamlet was in him, but I thought it was quite lost for practical purposes in practical qualities. I thought there was a great deal of Falstaff in Shakspere (as there was in Balzac). You smash my image to atoms, but it keeps reconstructing itself again in spite of you—from mere habit. I shall have to get used to it. (I express myself ill, because I am off my own line.) For the general public your book is at least 30 years before its time. And in 30 years (or so) people will be beginning to admit that in the way of constructive criticism it marked an era. (I assume that it is not finished. If it *is* finished, I consider that it lacks at least a summing up. I think *I* could find a publisher for it.)

I thank God (except financially) that Tree never produced your play. What a hades of a mess the *cabotin* would have made of this character! My objections to the play are purely technical. . . .

Yours ever,
ARNOLD BENNETT

P.S.—I need not say that I am relying on you to write, *soon*, another of those 'dozen novels which you have in you'.—A.B.
P.S.2.—Sorry about the £500.—A.B.

Hotel Belvédère
Mont Pélerin
sur Vevey
Switzerland

MY DEAR HARRIS,   13 Dec, 1908
    . . . Every novelist (and dramatic poet) has his favourite characters which he draws over and over again. You know how often Wells has drawn his Kipps. *My* character is Critchlow in 'The Old Wives' Tale'. He keeps recurring (under different names, with slight changes) in my stuff. Yours is Shakspere! ! Have you noticed this? Joshua Christ, Mortimer, and Penry—they are all three the same man as the hero of your play—more or less, that is.

Your review of me is a most gorgeous affair, and gave great joy. But I don't know anybody else that could have successfully carried it off, at that pitch. What pleases me, of course, is that the article was bursting with the fact, between all its lines, that the writer of it was a man who knew what he was talking about. Nearly all the praise one gets is so infernally wrong and out of shape. As though the critic had arranged a nice little piece of praise and then dropped it in the street and let a motor-car run over it. Your choice of extracts did my heart good.

I have finished my play about the Yellow Press, and sent it to the Stage Society. It is entitled 'What The Public Wants'. It is a joyful thing, and would please you. If the Stage Society fight shy of it, it will be because they don't want to tilt at the most powerful interests in Fleet Street. But I think they don't care a damn for anybody and that they will perform it.

I am just going to write a long short story for the new 'English Review'. And then I shall do a shortish novel about the familiar theme of a man who is laid out for dead, but who comes back to life.

[201]

I don't know why I should have been saddled with this notion, but I seem to see something rather fine at the end of the tunnel.

I hope you will go on with the stories, and that we shall meet in March next. I want to have a whole series of yarns with you. I wish I had met you about 15 years ago.

Yours ever,

ARNOLD BENNETT

(8)

December 31, 1908.—I have never worked so hard as this year, and I have not earned less for several years. But I have done fewer silly things than usual.

He had written *Buried Alive*, most of *The Old Wives' Tale*, the Fleet Street play, *The Human Machine*, *Literary Taste*, *The Matador of the Five Towns*, several other short stories, and many articles: "total, 423,500 words."

He had gone to Vevey, taking with him thirty-five books to read. He began his notes there by recording that a Battersea woman staying in the hotel was antipathetic to him and had moved to another hotel on that account. Paris, civilisation's great finishing school, had not put its final gloss on the hard resistant surface of the man from the Midlands. The unfavourable impression he had made on the woman at the hotel supplies the opening paragraphs of Miss Pauline Smith's essentially sympathetic study of him: "Though *The Old Wives' Tale* had been published in the previous autumn, his fame as a writer had not yet reached our small English community, and he came among us as a rather disturbing element with his French wife, his high-pitched voice and difficult stammer, his riding-breeches and black silk bow, and that ruthless Midlands down-rightness. . . . At dinner on the night of their arrival the elegance of his wife, and the rather jaunty swagger with which, all through life, he sought to hide his own secret diffidence, caused much comment among his fellow guests. . . ." [1]

Where personality had failed, character triumphed. The down-rightness, which alarmed at its first impact, was to be the foundation stone of a friendship of which Arnold Bennett was the altogether painstaking, unselfish, and faithful architect. Miss Smith's invalidism doubtless moved the sympathies of one who himself never went long

[1] *A.B.: A Minor Marginal Note.*

unreminded of his own inherent liability to suffering. But he had discovered that she "wrote a little", and thereafter he showed the deepest unremitting concern that she should develop her powers in that direction. "I got Pauline Smith to talk about her novel, but I think I mentioned it first. Sheer magnanimity and obstinacy mingled," and, as Frank Swinnerton has said in reviewing Miss Smith's writing career, the "obstinate magnanimity triumphed". But for him her admired books, *The Little Karroo* and *The Beadle*, would hardly have been written and he took no less trouble in ensuring publication for them when they were. The account of their friendship of twenty years and more is a moving tribute to simple human loyalties. It shows Arnold Bennett's capacity for living up to the best that was in him.

Arnold Bennett to H. G. Wells:

> Grand Hotel Belvédère
> Mont-Pélerin-sur-Vevey

MY DEAR H. G.,   7 January, 1909

Many thanks. *Some* one has been doing some spade work for 'The Old Wives' Tale', so I put it down to you. I expected it to be an absolute frost, naturally, and it was at first. But after about a month it began to sell. It went into a modest second edition, and the last I hear is that it is still selling regularly. Anyhow, I have had some really pleasing reviews. Of course any article from you would have been butter on my bread.

> Yours ever,
> E. A. B.

Now chance and an American publisher come into the picture and, conjoining, ensure the fortunes of *The Old Wives' Tale*. Mr. George H. Doran, who had turned general publisher after a considerable experience of the religious book trade in Canada, had an arrangement by which Hodder & Stoughton of London sent him copies of new books brought out by their religious department. In the latest batch to reach him there had been a copy of *The Old Wives' Tale*, which may or may not have been included by accident. This copy was sent to Mrs. Doran, who had been ill and who had asked her husband to send her something to read in bed. By the evening of the same day she was telephoning to her husband's office the excitement of her discovery of *The Old Wives' Tale*: "a marvellous book." Doran told Bennett in a letter: "She insisted on my taking it up." Mrs. Doran's instinct for picking out book successes had been proved before. Nor had it failed this time. Arriving in New York on his American tour, Arnold Bennett made it his first duty to put personally into Mrs. Doran's hands a beautifully bound copy of the novel inscribed: *To Mrs. George Doran, the original cause of my second advent in America.*

It had been left to the book-lovers of America to discover England's George Meredith. They now discovered England's Arnold Bennett, spurred by the enthusiasm of a number of discerning experts in the book trade, among them Frederick G. Melcher, of the Charles E. Lauriat Company, of Boston. Mr. Melcher, reading the book, at once ordered and soon re-ordered supplies of *The Old Wives' Tale*, passing word of it to the firm's best customers. From Boston the news went forth to the critics and reviewers of New York and cities west, until a gathering sales momentum in the United States had an auspicious effect on the novel's reception in England.

It was Arnold Bennett who, in return, made the "first printed fuss", as he said, about Theodore Dreiser, as a result of which that writer's claim to attention was forced on his fellow countrymen. Years after that, Bennett rendered another service to American letters by being the first British critic to 'discover' William Faulkner well before all but a few discerning American readers had heard of him.

In terms of figures *The Old Wives' Tale* never was one of the great 'best-sellers'. Its success owed almost nothing to the normal advertising channels and almost everything to the verbal appreciation of persons of educated literary taste. Above all, it clinched the strange certitude of Arnold Bennett's letter to George Sturt ten years before: "I infallibly know that I shall make a name. . . ."

(9)

At that June half-year, 1910, he owed Pinker £1,157 13s. 6d. By December the amount had been reduced to £490 5s. 10d. A few months later Pinker was writing to him: "I have a balance to your credit of £195 18s. 8d. . . . I am delighted." As an investor in Bennett's capabilities at a time when probably no one else would have been found to back them, Pinker deserved some of the credit for his client's success. "I make careers," was his claim, and what he did for Bennett he did also for others. His office acted for some of the leading writers of the day and he conducted its business with the faintly inscrutable air of a lawyer, building up a considerable fortune for himself by bringing integrity and a keen judgment to his professional labours. Frank Swinnerton says that Pinker "did as much for his humblest client as for the most prosperous author on his books". In return for his ten per cent commission, he was practically valeting Bennett when fame and fortune came, insuring his yacht, paying the crew, finding him secretaries, making disbursements to relatives and friends, buying his theatre tickets and books and magazines, fixing up his hotel accommodations, dealing with passports and travel tickets, and seeing faithfully to this and that with a busy willingness that was a mark of respect for more than his client's earning power.

"As regards money, I do not think you need be in any anxiety," he wrote to Bennett on January 18, 1912. "I have in hand £1,244 10s.," and went on to detail further considerable sums due. His next statement showed receipts of over £6,000. The tide had turned for Arnold Bennett. It was now flooding in. "I am very glad that you are going to buy a motor-car," Pinker wrote. "I certainly think you owe yourself such a luxury." Bennett thought he now needed and could afford a private secretary and commissioned Pinker to find him one. Pinker sent along as one of his candidates a young man named Archie de Bear, son of the principal of Pitman's School, which gave secretarial and business training, in London. Young de Bear, who was well under twenty, had already been secretary to the Canadian statesman, Sir Wilfrid Laurier: when he left after temporary employment with Arnold Bennett he went on to become personal secretary to the fabulous armaments millionaire, Sir Basil Zaharoff, after that making a name for himself in the theatre. The Bennetts were staying then at 14 St. Simon's Road, Putney, which they rented furnished from their friends the Sharpes. Mr. de Bear remembers that there were rows between Arnold and Marguerite Bennett. The first piece of dictation he received from Bennett startled him. It was a long detailed description of a visit to the lavatory which he was told to type out and file for "possible future use" in a novel.

CHAPTER TWELVE

(1)

HEARING that a fourth edition of *The Old Wives' Tale* was likely to be called for, Bennett showed restrained pleasure. "I had not in the least hoped for this success. It alters the value of all my future books," the next of which was to be *The Card*, written in the Swiss hotel. "Yet I was depressed all the afternoon because I could not make a sketch. Another proof that public success is no guarantee whatever of happiness or content. I think that it makes no difference."

He confessed in the journal that he felt "tired more definitely and more consciously than I did four or five years ago", and put himself on a course of Sanatogen, reporting good results. He was addicted to patent medicine taking; oddly so for a man of sense. Lord Horder, who went with him on a holiday in Spain, was privately amused by the variety of pills and tonics and tablets which Bennett had in his luggage. Later on he was urging H. G. Wells to test for himself the merits of a widely advertised proprietary substance called Yadil which became the subject of sensational legal action. A woman visitor to Arnold Bennett's Essex house during the First World War was surprised by the quantities of nerve tonics he had accumulated there, apparently as reserve in case of need.

In Switzerland he managed his tiredness, with which was associated a phobia about spraining his ankle and lying unattended to die in the snow, so well that he was able to finish the 64,000 words of *The Card* in eight weeks. Judging it, he was no more than moderately well satisfied. "Stodgy, no real distinction of any sort, but well invented, and done up to the knocker, technically, right through." The task finished, he left for Paris the next day, and in less than a week afterwards was gathering in ideas for *The Glimpse*, the novel to be based on a dream in which he had stood by his own dead body and saw the pennies upon his eyes. Probably psychological points could be made out of his professional interest in death. Coffins are a conspicuous part of the furniture of several of his stories. *The Glimpse*, he said, was 'essentially autobiographical". It was announced in America as "a realistic novel of this world: a poetic interpretation of the next".

A rush visit to London in connection with his newspaper play, *What the Public Wants*, produced at the Aldwych Theatre, London, on May 2, 1909, left him "no time or inclination to keep journals", but he kept them. Lunches with H. G. Wells, Wilfred Whitten, Charles Hawtrey, E. V. Lucas, Frank Harris, J. B. Pinker; tea at the Savage Club; tea with A. R. Orage; music at the Sharpes'; dinner with the Omar Khayyam Club at Frascati's, where he braced himself to make a speech to "M.P.s, ambassadors, magistrates, academicians, publishers, poets, and scientists"; dinner at Ford Madox Hueffer's, there meeting Galsworthy for the first time. "Slight *gène* on my part on first encounter, seeing my recent articles on him. However, we did well together, and he asked me to dinner."

John Galsworthy to Arnold Bennett:

12 April, 1909

. . . I'm a very poor hand at discussing my own stuff. I daresay you're right. One does what one can. 'The Country House,' however, is a comedy and true comedy is always to a certain extent cruel. I imagine my cruelty (I believe as a *man* I'm not cruel) comes from my horror of intolerance (i.e., of barriers between man and man) which is so conspicuous in the lives and characters of so many English folk, especially of the upper classes. . . .

Max Beerbohm to Arnold Bennett:

9 May, 1909

. . . When I had finished 'The Old Wives' Tale' (having gone slow in the later parts of it, being so loth to have no more to read of it), I felt a real void in my life; and this void I instinctively tried to fill a little of by writing a letter to the man who had laid so large an æsthetic debt on me. I wrote the letter and meant to send it, but I said 'Why?' I am always saying 'Why?' That is the curse of the twentieth century (and Metropolitan and non-Bursley) nature. . . .

Bennett had temporarily forsaken Fontainebleau and was living in Paris again, at 59 rue de Grenelle. Back at his desk, complaining of "a nervous fatigue that is positively acute", and of "appalling migraine", he abandoned the journal for some months and concentrated on finishing *The Glimpse* and constructing a new play, *The Honeymoon*,

[207]

which was produced at the Royalty Theatre, London. American publishers and editors, prospecting for material with a thoroughness and enterprise that were new to this country, showed a lively interest in his work, equally impressed, Pinker said, by his ability to "deliver on time" and by the quality of the work he delivered. Doran was cabling for the rights in existing books of his and for options on others to come. Pinker to Bennett: "I quite agree with you that Doran is very acute, and the only doubt I have of him is as to whether he is not also a little flighty. He is certainly most attentive, and is honestly keen on your work, and it is impossible altogether to resist the effect of his diplomacy." And the thrustful, buccaneering figure of the American periodical scene, S. S. McClure, was buying the short stories of the Five Towns for the magazine named after himself. A lesser but, judging from the journal note about it, gratifying offer came from the publishing house of Nelson, who wished to include *Buried Alive* in their famous sevenpenny library of small red cloth-covered volumes which were bringing new pleasures to the reading masses. The failure of the novel in its original six-shilling edition had baffled him. "Extraordinary, how a really honest book won't die. I've noticed it again and again. I'm always noticing it. And I really had *not* given up hope for *Buried Alive*."

The Bennett market was indeed a rising one. *The London Magazine*, a Harmsworth publication in which the founder of the family success took a close personal interest at that time, wanted his short stories. Through Pinker, Bennett replied that *The London Magazine* would have to wait its turn. Pinker to Bennett: "I am glad to be able to be independent over it. It will do them good, as they were lacking in proper appreciation of Arnold Bennett." Others were having to revise their estimates of his powers: Sir Algernon Methuen, the publisher, for example. Pinker to Bennett: "I saw Methuen himself about *The Old Wives' Tale* and urged him to take it up," this after it had gone out of print with Chapman & Hall. "He said there was nothing to be made out of it, and he did not care to take it up." Messrs. Methuen published *The Card*, and when they accepted it Pinker wrote to Bennett: "Methuen is very pleased, I am not quite sure whether it is with you, himself, or me, over the business, but he told me one day that he thought you were probably the best writer I had. This is very amusing to me, because when I suggested you to Methuen he scorned the idea, and actually said he did not think you were ever going to be much good." To his next letter Pinker added the footnote: "I was lunching with W. J. Locke and Dion Clayton Calthrop, and both were talking with great enthusiasm of your work. Locke was specially loud in his praises, and said you were "a wonderful man". And outlining his strategy for dealing with the Americans, Pinker advised: "All you have to do now is play the part of the great prize."

Visiting the Aviation Exposition in Paris and being "startled by the completeness of the trade organisation of aviation, even to suits for aviators", he was tempted to write another 'fantasia' novel, "giving the sensations of flight. We first remarked the Farman aeroplane. Vast, and beautiful as a yacht. Same kind of beauty. Yet a new creation of form, a new 'style'." But his 'thinking' walks had lately had a more important objective, a realistic study, in the manner of *The Old Wives' Tale*, of a boy's growth to youth and manhood in the Five Towns.

Arnold Bennett to his brother-in-law and sister (Mr. and Mrs. Kennerley):

Villa des Néfliers

Peoples,   22 October 1909

No, I have received very few letters about the book [*The Glimpse*]. I am not convinced about the second part myself, but I am sure that the 1st and 3rd parts are as good as the best I can do. Some people who like the 2nd don't care for the 3rd; which unfortunately shows that they have not understood the 2nd. Also I am now supposed to be a Theosophist, a Hegelian and all sorts of things. The second part is simple Theosophy, nothing else, and taken bodily therefrom (with improvements); but I have now made Theosophy serve my turn and have done with it. I read Mrs. Besant three times, and made fresh notes every time, in order to do the second part; a fearful grind; and the Theosophical Society ought now to reprint my second part as one of their official publications; it is infinitely more graphic and coherent than any of their own tracts. I am glad you liked 'Bond Street'.[1] I did. Enough. What chiefly interests me now is the sales.

I shall positively appear in the Five Towns early in December, and remain there at least 2 weeks. I must have at least two weeks with Mr. Dawson. My next hero's father is the Pater plus Mr. Beardmore; a steam-printer. And the hero is a sort of Edward Harry Beardmore. This novel has to be begun on January 1st.

---

[1] Refers to a chapter in the novel consisting entirely of a description of that London street.

I have had dreadful *fights* with the Income Tax people, and am greatly joyed to find today that I have emerged with only £10 odd to pay. I wouldn't pay it; they couldn't make me—and I pay all French taxes; only if I came to live in England any time, there would be a hell of a row if I couldn't produce my papers in order.

Pauline Smith is beginning a novel, and has half an hour's remarks from me every night. My remarks are really rather good. Strange girl. She *can* write. But she won't talk.

'Ann Veronica' is not very good. You really ought to buy Kropotkin's 'Memoirs of a Revolutionist', the book of a great man.

Loves,

E. A. B.

Arnold Bennett to Frank Harris:

Villa des Nefliers

MY DEAR F. H.,   30 Octr., 1909.

Snobbishness. In Shakspere's time and much later an affection for courts and titles (combined with a corresponding antipathy to the common folk) was a perfectly proper affection and did not involve the disdain of intelligent people. The course of evolution has changed this. The word 'snob' distinctly includes the idea of vulgarity and pretentiousness, and I consider it to be inapplicable to Shakspere's case. Sycophancy is better, but even sycophancy is *much too strong*. Shakspere was of his time in this matter; that is all.

Pembroke. There are several sonnets which seem to me (as a layman) to exclude the idea of innocence with Pembroke. All I say is that you have not absolutely convinced me that I am wrong. The fact is you do not say much in support of your contention of innocence. You rather assume innocence because he sent Pembroke to Mary. Why should he not have had a liaison with Pembroke during the earliest stages of his naissant passion for Mary? If you say the idea is revolting, I say that I don't think it is. It wouldn't revolt me, and I think it would take a lot to revolt a man of Shakspere's intelligence. High intelligence is seldom revolted. I admit that I am an infant in the matter of homosexuality.

I hope you will speak with the greatest freedom in 'The New Age'. I also hope you won't sign your review of 'The Glimpse' in 'Vanity Fair'. But I am looking forward to it much.

I am too deep in my new play to be able to talk about it. It is a very light comedy of a honeymoon, and it all takes place between the wedding and the consummation of the marriage! Though a light comedy, I deem it to be true to life.

Gosse is no creative good. But I think he tries to be broadminded, honestly. I have heard him speak. That was enough.

You are carrying influenza to inartistic extremes. We sympathise with you. But get up.

Ever yours,

A. B.

(2)

November 19, 1909.—Yesterday I finished making a list of all social, political, and artistic events, which I thought possibly useful for my novel between 1872 and 1882. Tedious bore, for a trifling ultimate result in the book. But necessary. Today in the forest I practically arranged most of the construction of the first part of the novel. Still lacking a title for it. If I thought an ironic title would do, I would call it 'A Thoughtful Young Man'. But the public is so damned slow in the uptake. . . . In a week, I shall have nothing to do except collection of information on the spot for the novel.

In fulfilment of the last-named purpose, he shut up the Villa des Nefliers and crossed to Burslem, where at once he began taking in material for the novel that was to be published as *Clayhanger*, and for the third volume, too, of what he intended to be a trilogy but which in the result proved not to have been so expertly organised as that term must imply. While he was in the Potteries this time he took the opportunity of going on to Manchester to meet members of the staff of the *Manchester Guardian*—C. E. Montague, A. N. Monkhouse, James Bone, Haslam Mills, G. H. Mair, and "a man named Agate", among them. Montague, author of distinguished work apart from his journalism, "looked the typical provincial, though a Londoner born and bred; a rather tight, prim way of speaking". Bennett was wittily told in an aside during this office tour that "Montague is surrounded by a good deal of unrequited affection". Monkhouse he describes as "a large grave man, slow-speaking, with an extraordinary sedate and sincere charm". Mair was "evidently considered to be one of the stars of the future". Bennett subsequently became a close friend of Mair, a gifted and tragic young man of whom Herbert Sidebotham, another noted

[211]

Northern journalist, wrote that "he had an excellent vocabulary which unfortunately did not include the word 'no' ". The visit to the *Manchester Guardian* office was an enjoyable occasion for Bennett: "the fact is that *this* sort of thing is the real reward for having written a few decent books."

In later years, at the full tide of Bennett's success, Monkhouse sought contributions from him for the paper. Acknowledging the "very appreciative articles which I think I am right in attributing to you in the Manchester press . . . the sort of stuff I am grateful for", Bennett said: "Be it known unto you, my dear Monkhouse, that I have rather more journalistic work than I can do at the rate of 2s. a word. . . . The 'M.G.' offers me rather less than 2½d. a word, and it will not do."

Incontinently, for the author of *Mental Efficiency*: "My mind is in a whirl all the time. I have been here only five days, and yet Paris and Avon seem years off; I scarcely ever even think of these places and of my life there." A political manifesto writing job, pressed on him by some of his Burslem friends, did nothing to relax his fevered attention. "I was profoundly struck by all sorts of things," a morning on the bench of magistrates, the organisation of a local opera company, clog dancing, among them. As to the monumental new work for which he was gathering facts and information, "I had got into an extraordinary vein of 'second sight'. I perceived whole chapters." This state of heightened sensitivity, he had noted before, often coincided with the self-consciousness of exhaustion. Schwob, in Paris, had told him long ago that such a state of feeling favoured creative effort.

The sudden access of imaginative power by which he "perceived whole chapters" of the new work may have owed more than he admitted to *When I was a Child*, the recollections of a Tunstall potter named Shaw, who later became a Methodist minister: they had been published in 1903. He had not only read the book; he drew copiously from it for *Clayhanger* and especially for the descriptions of the frightful conditions suffered by Edwin Clayhanger's father as a boy at the workhouse at Chell, the "Bastille" of the novel. Certain it is that chapters 4 and 5 of *Clayhanger* could not have been written without the factual inspiration of that book.

Having ransacked the Potteries for what he wanted for *Clayhanger*, he planned to go down to Brighton, start work on the novel on January 1, 1910, and stay there until it was finished. London distractions, on the way down, put this programme back four days, a deviation from his settled arrangements which he took care to note.

He lunched with Mrs. Belloc Lowndes, "most of our talk about Wells's scandals and Barrie's scandals. Surprised to learn that the little Scotchman gave his wife £3,000 a year for dress." At Wells' he met, "and liked at once," Robert Ross, who had been Oscar Wilde's unremitting champion and friend. "I mean to cultivate Ross," and if Ross had kept a journal he would most likely have written the same about Bennett: as Hesketh Pearson states in his biography of Wilde, cultivating useful connections was part of Ross' personal policy. There, also, Bennett met William Archer, the dramatic critic who became more widely known as the author of the play *The Green Goddess*. "He bluntly asked me why I had said in print that he and Walkley," famous dramatic critic of *The Times*, "were the upas-trees of the modern drama. So I told him, less bluntly. I consider that he has no original ideas of his own."

December 28, 1909.—Yesterday morning I went over the Wesleyan Westminster building with Rickards. He is now gradually getting hold of me again as a great artist. . . . Huge tripod of derricks going up through reinforced concrete floors, and so on. Iron tufted bars for reinforced concrete. Pools of water. Going up and down ladders. Cement-y dirt and mud. Sticky feeling on hands afterwards. Vibration of talking in crypt-like basement. Sounds of people in street talking as if in building. Effect of grand staircases sketched out in stone and brick. The centre of the building was only a vast emptiness, with a long iron girder poised on either side—supporting, ultimately, the galleries. Blue light, distinctly blue, coming down into the basement through holes.

Only a few nights previously he had been upset by Rickards's "exasperated egotism". But Rickards's pride in the conception taking form and shape around them and the unchecked flow of the little man's delight in those aspects of it expressing his taste for baroque ornamentation seem to have fired Bennett's imagination, and we can believe that as he picked his way with Rickards that December day through the unfinished Wesleyan edifice he felt the "electric currents of renewed ambition", and that *Clayhanger* became a greater novel for it.

"This morning at 9.45 I began to write 'Clayhanger'," he noted on January 5, 1910. "I felt less nervous and self-conscious than usual in beginning a book. And never before have I made one-quarter as many preliminary notes and investigations." He had arrived at the Royal

York Hotel, Brighton, having made terms to suit his pocket with the celebrated host Harry Preston, who later recalled:

A serious young man with a slight moustache. . . . He liked the place, took a top room and arranged to make the hotel his home for some time. Writer friends of mine, hearing that he was there, impressed on me that one day he would be a great man. He was working to a definite plan, and would achieve what he set out to do—make his name as a novelist. . . . This was Mr. Arnold Bennett. He was writing *Clayhanger*. The 'Royal Sussex' of that novel is the Royal York; the housekeeper is Miss Beatrice Collings, my wife's sister; the page boy is Hardy, my valet. . . . Well, Arnold Bennett made his name and fortune, and came back. He wrote to say that he had heard that I had a new hotel, the Royal Albion, and would I reserve the best suite. He arrived with his wife, and stayed for three weeks, and his bill was so colossal that it could only have been achieved by the deliberate intent to do me a good turn.[1]

Writing *Clayhanger*, he worked himself to exhaustion once more and had finished the first part, 42,000 words (instead of the 40,000 he had precisely planned), in a little over a month. "I was nearly going mad." He had to be humoured by his wife and a friend of theirs, so intense was the strain he felt.

February 12, 1910.—Queer feeling in the head. Crossness, gloominess. Search for a cause, and no cause. No real desire to conquer it. Must be physical gloominess.

Slept an hour after lunch. I could have slept longer but I got up. I felt that *I had had a sleep.* Tea and a cigar. I meant to work then, but I saw that I was too tired. Head full. I lay down again and read, and slept $\frac{3}{4}$ hour. It was after this, when fatigue nearly conquered, as I lay on bed, that I began to have fine sensations. A perception that gloom was passing: what a fine thing life was; an intensified perception of myself as an existing organism. Still, a slight pressure in the head, at two points right and left near top. But a short enjoyment of these remains of fatigue, knowing that they would go. Largely a physical pleasure in the half-fatigued realisation of myself; a looking forward to the next activity; and a calm resting. This passed off after I got up, but not the memory of it.

[1] From *My Unwritten Diaries* by Sir Harry Preston (Hutchinson).

His eyesight was bothering him again: an oculist said that there was nothing for it but to wear glasses. This startled him; time at its insidious disintegrating work. Trying the glasses that had been prescribed for him, he re-read his much admired short story, *The Death of Simon Fuge*, and was "filled with enthusiasm for its author. But the mischief of being so pleased is that you are afraid you will never do anything as good, that your nadir is past". A much older affliction had returned to plague him: "neuralgia all these days." "Much beset with neuralgia." "But still, I stick it," as if proud of his capacity to do so. "Still averaging over 2,000 words a day of the novel."

There were restorative social compensations. Seymour Hicks arrived, deploring the imminence of his fortieth birthday and Bennett was "amused and pleased by his unavailing but well-meant efforts to appear natural and non-celebrated". Hicks took the opportunity of deploring, too, the capture by the peerage of some of the bright stars of the musical comedy firmament—"Sylvia Storey, become the Countess Poulett; Camille Clifford, the original Gibson girl, married to the heir of Lord Aberdare; a Miss Somebody-else who became Lady de Clifford." Hicks' "fine rich voice" was heard often in laughter as he told Bennett his stories of the stage, and Bennett noted that he "rolled about" when he laughed, as when he told him about a Jewish furniture family who had made great wealth and had been ennobled by King Edward VII, who liked the Jewish people: "The motto chosen by this family and submitted for approval was 'Value before Valour'." And Granville Barker arrived, with his wife, known to theatregoers as Miss Lillah McCarthy (now Lady Keeble).

February 19.—Granville Barker seems a simple man, half, I mean. We went out to see the high tide. We went on to the beach and stood out as far as we dared towards foam, then a wave overran. We both ran back, in ½-inch of water. G.B., who had an overcoat and shawl over his shoulders, fell down in his excitement. "Are you hurt?" I said. "No," he said. "*I did it on purpose. I couldn't get any further.*" Here is part of the man. Afterwards, having marked the place where a high wave had come to, he stood bending over anxiously like a boy to see if other waves ever came up to it. No general conversation. All art, and chiefly theatre. I should say deficient in humour. Very intelligent and nice. Neither of us says much of the other's plays.

No worldly conversation. I mean no polite insincere interest shown in personal things that come up. This is not from consciousness of strength, but from *'manque d'usage'*, I should say. Wife the same. She is a different woman when animated and fifty times better. . . . She tries to be interested in everything. Politics: 'what do you think of Winston's speech?' etc. The breaking up of the Poor Law. The Fabian Society. Literature. Art. A general yearning towards the *good* and the fine, perhaps; partly because it is correct and partly because it is good and fine. I ought to have begun to make notes on this woman earlier. She grows on you.

He finds a place in the journal for a story told by another visitor to the hotel, Sir William Treloar, sometime Lord Mayor of London: "Two Yorkshiremen were discussing the mayors of their respective towns. Said the first: 'Our mayor wears a bloody great chain.' Said the other: 'We let our old so-and-so go loose.' " He did not make a note of the episode in which his cavalier manners annoyed a lady visitor to the hotel: someone else who was there did so. They had been sitting together talking, while Bennett's wife carried on a lively broken English conversation with some people in a distant corner of the lounge. "Quaint, isn't she?" Bennett said, interrupting his companion when a burst of laughter came from the group as a result of something Mrs. Bennett had said. His companion agreed. She went on with her topic. Bennett was still inattentive. "She's droll, you know—droll," he said when the laughter came again. "A whimsical creature!" His companion, after a reproving pause, agreed that Marguerite Bennett was both droll and whimsical. Catching a caustic inflection, Bennett turned in his chair and seemed to be completely ready to give her his attention again, when the laughter was renewed. "You know, she's such a change from most of the women here," he announced, at which his companion rose and walked away, leaving him sitting alone.

He was assailed by misgivings about *Clayhanger*. "I was frightened by a lot of extraordinary praise of 'The Old Wives' Tale' that I have had. I was afraid 'Clayhanger' was miles inferior to it." His tiredness became so severe that he was overcome by nervousness when he went out for walks. Abruptly, he decided that it would be impossible to finish the novel in Brighton. The famous Brighton air had exhilarated him, he said, but like all tonics its effects wore off with too frequent doses. He called for his hotel bill, thanked Harry Preston for arranging the special terms for him, and returned impetuously to Paris.

June 23, 1910.—I have just (3 p.m.) finished 'Clayhanger' one week in advance of time. 160,800 words. For the last few days it has monopolised me. But quite contrary to my general practice towards the end of a novel, I have kept in magnificent health.

The novel was published that September. It received immediate and favourable attention from *The Times*, and other leading papers followed with varying degrees of appreciation which Bennett commented on in the journal, copying out extracts. "This time I will make notes on the newspaper criticisms of my novel." A review in the New York *Bookman*, giving biographical details of the author of *Clayhanger*, made his wife cry. "She had the delusion that she was reading my obituary." The *Manchester Guardian* review was a disappointment: "though good, it was not as good as I expected. I expected the eager sympathy of G. H. Mair & Co.!"

September 30, 1910.—I was put into a strange state yesterday by reading Methuen's advertisement in the 'Westminster Gazette'. My novel, having now been published a fortnight, had taken its place lower down on their list—was indeed only one of a very mixed lot of novels. E. V. Lucas's 'Mr. Ingleside', being their last published, was head of the list. They have just invented a new and striking dodge of indicating the number of editions printed of a work by putting a small elevated numeral after it (as if indicating a raised 'power'). Thus Lucas's 'Mr. Ingleside',[3] and it has only been out a week. No number after 'Clayhanger'. A '2' after many of the other novels. Yet I suppose anybody of any judgment would put 'Clayhanger' far higher than any other novel in the list. I began to see a comparative failure for 'Clayhanger' in England, and then also in America. Useless for one to argue that my contracts in England and America assure me a reasonable income for three years, whether the publishers lose or not! Useless for me to argue that it is absurd for me to *expect* even a good circulation for books like 'Clayhanger', which arouse enthusiasm in just a few beings! This in spite of the fact that I cannot make less than £1,500 next year, and may make £2,000 or over—and this by doing only the work that pleases me— my very best work. I was still gloomy this morning.

The Doran company had agreed to publish a number of his earlier books in the United States. This welcome news was offset by the slump in his play *Cupid and Common Sense*, based on *Anna of the Five Towns*. "A couple of years ago I said enthusiastically that if 'Cupid and Common Sense' was produced in Hanley it would play to £500 a week. Today I got the figures for the three performances in Hanley. Total £75 13s. 10d." A week later: " 'Cupid and Common Sense' was an absolute frost in Cardiff last week." He was much cast down, though his affairs were prospering as they had never prospered before. "Which shows how little content has to do with prosperity."

A three-column review of *Clayhanger* by Claudius Clear in *The British Weekly*, "which came out with my name and book flaring on its forehead," changed his mood. "Knowing this man's flair for what is going to succeed, and the influence of his praise, I was at once immensely bucked up, and have remained so."

John Galsworthy to Arnold Bennett:

23 Oct, 1910

. . . 'Clayhanger' is not so good as 'The Old Wives' Tale'; still it's amazing in its way. I enormously admire your zest and fertility. It's a wholly different conception of the novelist's art to my own, but it may be none the less right for all that, and it demands certain qualities that I have not got in anything like the same degree. . . .

In some notes he was making at the time Galsworthy wrote: "Reading 'Clayhanger': lacks selective power and temperamental poignancy. But what a demonstration of zest and industry"; and André Gide was writing in his journal that he could not get beyond page 125, "the book becoming less and less good as one gets into it." Bennett was working now on the play suggested by his novel called *Buried Alive*, writing *Paris Nights* for the *English Review*, and drafting *Hilda Lessways*, second of the Clayhanger books. "I think I can do something showing the point of view of the whole sex, against a mere background of masculinity. I had a sudden vision of it." *Clayhanger* had been published in America shortly after its appearance in London. "The two American reviews to which I looked forward with the most interest, 'Boston Evening Transcript' and 'Chicago Evening Post', are both absolutely satisfactory in their enthusiasm." *The Card* came out from Messrs. Methuen's: "reviews much too kind on the whole.

[218]

Dixon Scott's in the 'Manchester Guardian' one of the best I ever had, and no effusiveness either." Dixon Scott was a young Liverpool bank clerk whose astute critical intelligence, extinguished at Gallipoli, was mourned by Max Beerbohm in an essay which stands as introduction to Scott's collected writings, *Men Of Letters*.[1] Scott had written:

> *The Card* is genuine Bennett; it flings a happy light on the whole fascinating Bennett problem; and indeed the really fundamental thing to say about it, comparatively, is not that it ought to have *Clayhanger's* qualities, but that *Clayhanger* would be better if it had some of the qualities of *The Card*. . . .

Bennett acknowledged Harold Keates Hales of Burslem as his original for the character of the Card. The novel was published in the United States of America under the title of *Denry the Audacious*, which was the title Bennett first thought of using. The name 'Denry' was a contraction taken from the name given to Edward Harry Beardmore, a Potteries boy whose mother had wanted him christened Edward and his father Harry; they gave him both names and compromised yet further by calling him 'Darry'. This Beardmore supplied some of the characterisation of Edwin Clayhanger.

Another leading character in *The Card*, the Countess of Chell, was identified in the minds of local readers with the Duchess of Sutherland, who was often at the family seat at Trentham, near the Potteries, one of the great estates of England. Soon after *The Card* had appeared, Bennett was one of Maurice Baring's guests at a dinner party, with the Duchess, Anthony Hope, Austin Harrison, sometime editor of the *English Review*, and one or two others. Bennett had never met the Duchess and her name was wilfully mumbled when they were introduced by Anthony Hope, whose idea it was to place them together at table and watch events. After a little preliminary conversation, the Duchess faced Bennett with the question: "Why did you make fun of me in your book?" Bennett looked incredulously at her: the Duchess remembers his teeth sticking out of a nervous smile as the laughter of the others rose about him. She went on to make it clear that what she objected to about his representation of her was, above all, the insinuation that she was never punctual, whereas punctuality had always been as much a rule of her life as it was of his.

[1] Hodder and Stoughton (1916)

Arnold Bennett to the Duchess of Sutherland:

Villa des Nefliers
Avon-Fontainebleau

23 June, 1911

DEAR LADY,—I am now safely at home again and can collect my thoughts. The only thing that I did not explain to you amid the romanticism of North Street was the somewhat subtle fact that if there is resemblance between you and the young woman in 'The Card' it is simply because you are the sole representative of that particular class in the Five Towns. Obviously it would be absurd for an author with my material to omit from his work all the comedy that must inevitably spring from contact between the magnate class and the leaders of an industrial population. Obviously he cannot include that comedy without setting down the salient characteristics of each class, and obviously when one of the classes is represented by only one person, a certain amount of annoyance to that one person must result. I admit that it is a bit 'rough' on you. But then, as I told you, you are to consider yourself in the Five Towns not as a woman, but as an institution. This also is a bit rough on a beautiful woman. I may say, by the way, that if I had the advantage of meeting you before I wrote 'The Card', I should have insisted very much more on the Countess's beauty; indeed I should have tried to make some rather fine effect out of it (or I might have left the Countess out altogether; which would have been a pity!). Now I think you must admit that I am not the man to attempt the portrait of any person whatsoever in a novel, much less the portrait of one whom I had never seen. On the other hand, I willingly admit that certain characteristics of the Countess were suggested by public knowledge of you. But that is all. Considering that the whole book is written in a fiercely sarcastic vein, I think the Countess's portrait is a sympathetic one, don't you? Much more sympathetic than a caricature by Max Beerbohm! This is a clumsy letter, but I did not want to write you an article, and I hope you prefer it so. I hope too that you will be round here before the early days of August, as I have to spend August in London rehearsing a play, and then I am going to America.

Believe me, with a peculiar kind of glance that is at once admiring, apologetic and unrepentant,

Yours sincerely,
ARNOLD BENNETT

[220]

On August 1, 1911, he wrote the first words of the play which was to give him his greatest success in the theatre, *Milestones.* The idea was not his. It had come from Edward Knoblock, whose *Kismet* was a London theatre event of that year. They had been introduced by Frank Vernon, producer of Bennett's *Cupid and Common Sense*, a well known and well liked man of the West End stage. Vernon believed that Bennett would gain by Knoblock's great experience of writing for the stage. Bennett's idea was that they should write a drama about Don Juan, whose character, he insisted, had never been understood or truly interpreted. Knoblock held to the view that Mozart had reached the final expression of the Don Juan theme by setting it to music, a consideration which in no wise deterred Arnold Bennett from writing his version of Don Juan later on. In the end they agreed to collaborate in writing *Milestones,* the scheme for which Knoblock had been carrying around in his head for a good many years, mentally labelling it 'The Family'. The title *Milestones* occurred to Bennett while they were out driving in the Fontainebleau region. "I've got it—'The Milestones'," Bennett exclaimed, as their hired vehicle carried them along the highway. "Not *the*," said Knoblock. "Yes, *the*," said Bennett, who gave way on the point only when the play was finished. Knoblock said in his reminiscences[1] that the collaboration was harmonious. Bennett sometimes found Knoblock irritating. "If you don't stop apologising I don't go on," he snapped one day when Knoblock was too ingratiatingly polite. "We are working *together*." And a long journal entry for August 13 suggests other discontents:

Whenever he adds a phrase of his own it is heavy and uncolloquial, and has to be altered. Still, he knows the stage, and his help is valuable. Also the original idea of the play was his, and the skeleton his. But nineteen-twentieths of the actual imagination and invention of the detail is mine. The thing would have been tremendously inferior if I had allowed him to do the draft. In getting half the kudos and the money, he is doing well for himself. Nevertheless I do not in the least regret the collaboration. It will have occupied me less than a month.

His journal note on the opening night of the play, March 5, 1912, refers to " 'Milestones' by me and Knoblock. . . ." from which it

[1] *Round the Room* by Edward Knoblock (Chapman & Hall, 1939).

appears that his attitude as collaborator, if strictly proportioned, was basically begrudging. Anyhow, the play succeeded beyond expectations. He had the satisfaction of writing on December 1, 1914: "On Saturday ended the run of the first revival of 'Milestones'. For nearly three years I had had a performance, and frequently two, every night without intermission in the West End of London,"—'I', not 'we'. Another entry shows him enjoying a less public aspect of the triumph. He met Frederick Harrison, still in partnership with Cyril Maude at the Haymarket. They had turned down *Milestones*. "His cry was 'Peccavi!' I was wrong. We were all wrong. You alone were right. Etc., etc. Ingenuous snobbishness came out clearly." Harrison said that he would read another play of Bennett's fifty times before refusing it. "He no longer indicated that production at the Haymarket is the ultimate splendid goal of the playwright's ambition. Rather, that production of a play by the playwright was the ultimate splendid goal of the Haymarket's ambition."

Bennett's proprietary air seems ungracious; still, he had fairly earned the credit that came to him from the play's success. He had applied to the idea provided by Knoblock the values and perspectives of *The Old Wives' Tale*, with its parallel theme of time's dominance. The play's last moments, in which the grand-daughter, vibrantly young and contemporary, takes a flower from her dress and gives it to her grandfather, then quietly leaves the stage to the two old people sitting by the fireside, contain the essence of the Five Towns novels.

Knoblock's attitude was more generous. "I might possibly have written the play by myself after finishing the scenario. But it would never have turned out to be a play of the same mellowness, the same dignity, the same restraint. All these qualities *Milestones* owes to Bennett," who was delighted with the play's success, but whose "Five Town-ishness", Knoblock told Vernon, "won't let him say much." It allowed and doubtless prompted him to be honest in his appraisal of the play when it was successfully revived. "A fundamental fault is the monotony of the theme. The situation is very similar in each act. . . . But the thing is dramatic, full of minor varieties; something genuine about it, and it never flags."

(5)

The ascending enthusiasm of his American publisher—'I am proud to be your man of business over here'—had turned his thoughts to the visit to the United States, which, in the first place, Pinker—'always consider me at your service'—had proposed making on his behalf. But George Doran had urged on Bennett the importance of showing himself to his growing American public: "it is a duty that you owe yourself," and when presently Bennett committed the indiscretion, as Doran said that some Americans thought it, of writing approval of a new novel by Upton Sinclair, whose radicalism offended many American susceptibilities at that time, Doran felt that a personal visit was even more desirable in that it would help to allay uneasiness. "They look on you as novelist of the first degree, not as critic or journalist. It rather shocks some of them to find you writing in journals and sponsoring the work of others," and so on.

Requesting Pinker to look up possible sailing dates and ships, Bennett went off to the Potteries on another collecting trip, for the last part of *Hilda Lessways*. The visit yielded also a rich supply of by-product notes, some of which were subsequently given permanence in the *Things that have Interested Me* volumes. He went down the Sneyd coal mine, "a model pit . . . conditions appalling," and came to the surface in a mood of ironic comment. "Luxury was increasing everywhere. The masters had 'powerful and luxurious' motor-cars, and splendid residences in unspoilt rural surroundings. The miners had the latest appliances for saving their lives." He was among the massed spectators of a football match between Stoke Reserve and Leek United and the game was more important in the annals of literature than of sport, for out of it came a famous short story, *The Matador of the Five Towns*. "Curious fringe of hair under belly of mascot dog" is in the journal notes of the occasion, and he could make even that seem significant, his consciousness of the life around him was so acute. It was like the brilliant awareness of the invalid who lives on the edge of a precipice, but if a sense of precariousness was here involved one would have had to penetrate behind the proud Bennett *persona* to find it. He insisted:

Every scene, even the commonest, is wonderful, if only one can detach oneself, casting off all memory of use and custom, and behold it (as it were) for the first time, in its right, authentic colours, without making comparisons. The novelist should cherish and burnish this faculty of seeing crudely, simply, artlessly, ignorantly; of seeing like a baby or a lunatic, who lives each moment by itself and tarnishes the present by no remembrance of the past.

[223]

So he sees, precisely, the "tails of straw" trodden in the mud of the packing yards and on the pavements, the effects of varying winds on the prevailing Five Towns smoke, the "inward curve" of his mother's finger "as she finishes a phrase with a gesture", the "three distant pot-bank chimneys on Wolstanton slope" that are part of the view from his bedroom window at 179 Waterloo Road, where he is staying during his visit.

He was not perhaps a natural observer: he had deliberately taught himself to see. Walking in the streets across the Thames from Chelsea: "I passed sixty-eight seagulls sitting on the railings." His enormously industrious observation served the dual purpose of technical practice and mental discipline. One result, an increased facility in the power to grasp the salient characteristics of other people. He had caught John Burns at the National Liberal Club in the pose of egotism often noticed thirty years afterwards in the same place: "talking most of the time leaning back in a chair and looking round sharply if he thought any other person in the smoking-room was observing him." George Moore at a dinner party conversed "in his pseudo-effective strain, probably from nervousness". Gordon Selfridge, the much publicised Oxford Street big-store man, is recalled by his catchphrase: "Why on the green earth——!" And Mrs. Max Beerbohm, met for the first time, at the Café Royal:

She was of course preceded by the legend of extreme youth and beauty. Reddish hair, divided into two mops of unequal size, hanging loosely down in a shock on either side. Over this a black hat with a feather sticking out backwards from the left side. Very fair. Very thin. Very unassumingly dressed in black. Gloves ditto. Refined and rather worn features. About 35. Refined voice. Seriously interested in, and proud of, Max. Wondered whether his recent parodies of me and others were not *too* good for a creative artist to do. On the whole, a shade too serious, and fairly precious. Deferential. Constantly stopping, with a grave air, when we began a sentence simultaneously, and making way for me—and then going on. But agreeable, intelligent (perhaps too!) and with a fundamental decency. She thought London the most beautiful city in the world, etc. But she preferred to live among Italian peasants. Impossible that a woman presenting such an odd appearance could be balanced in the normal sense.

[224]

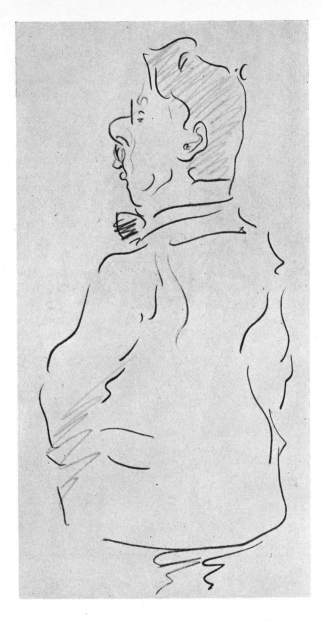

A CARICATURE OF ARNOLD BENNETT BY E. A. RICKARDS

By permission of Dr. H. V. Lancaster

CARICATURES BY RICKARDS

By permission of Dr. H. V. Lancaster

E. A. RICKARDS, SKETCHED BY
HIMSELF ON THE BACK OF A MENU

FREDERICK MARRIOTT
CARICATURED BY RICKARDS

From Burslem he went on to Glasgow, where we have eye-witness reports of him from his old friend Marriott, whom he had invited to join him for company, and from Mr. (now Sir) John Richmond of the well-known engineering firm of G. & J. Weir, Ltd. Marriott went with him to the first night of *The Great Adventure*, done by a local repertory company. It was well received and there were shouts for the author. Bennett was so unnerved that he crouched in a corner of his box and then pulled Marriott by the coat-tails to stand in front of him so that there could be no possible chance of his being seen. Nor would he move until the audience had finally gone. On Sir John Richmond he made the slightly aggressive impression he so often did on meeting a new acquaintance. Sir John remembers thinking him too assertively the dandy—"the large fob, the grey bowler hat." Sir John entertained him at the Arts Club, where there is a long tradition of hospitality to visitors known and unknown, and the occasion led on to a lasting friendship. Bennett took the opportunity of that first meeting to advance the claims of certain young artists and induced his host, and through him other business leaders, to buy works by needy young painters, some of whose names have since become well known. Sir John Richmond and Arnold Bennett were later associated with Sir Nigel Playfair at the Lyric Theatre, Hammersmith, and in the Vedrenne management at the Little Theatre, Adelphi, London, and Sir John's testimony to Bennett is of an undimmed regard for his self-command, his integrity, and his unfailing observance of the duties of friendship.

On the day that Arnold Bennett wrote the last words of *Milestones*, he had made a decision to return to England to live. His position as a novelist established, he could at last enjoy the fulfilment of a dream he had had from the days of his summer holidays with the family at Llandudno, that of owning a yacht. East Coast of England sailing was his ideal; some of his happiest days had been spent with his old friends the Atkins's in their yacht. Mrs. Atkins suggested he should find a country house in Essex, giving him access to a harbour: she knew of a house that might suit at him Thorpe-le-Soken, a few miles inland from the sea at Frinton. It was a Queen Anne house of much charm and with a name that Bennett repeated caressingly when he heard it—"Comarques." Rickards went with him to inspect it, reported favourably on its structural state, and recommended him to buy it. When his friend Atkins told him he knew where there was a good Dutch-built yacht for sale, Bennett lived through some of the best moments of his life. These large indulgences, a house with a hundred acres, a yacht, the reward of years of stern self-exactions, gave him very great pleasure. They also increased the self-exactions. John Galsworthy wrote congratulating him on having "made a fortune" and hoped that it would be "a warning to you not to make another".

Meanwhile, Pinker had arranged the visit to America. Bennett sailed in the *Lusitania* on October 7, 1911.

CHAPTER THIRTEEN

(1)

HIS American publisher recorded that during the period of Arnold Bennett's visit to the United States, six weeks, the two of them "were not separated for more than a few hours at a time". Bennett's collaborator, Knoblock, who had crossed to New York in the *Lusitania* with him, was a little scornful about this in a letter written to his friend Vernon in London: "Bennett I haven't seen but three times here. He is being fed to death. Besides, his publisher clings to him jealously and so B. hasn't really seen the best Americans, as Doran (the publisher) is a good sort but about what a publisher might be in London—or even a little less important. However, B. is having a very good time and that's the main thing." Knoblock may have been feeling a little peeved. Arnold Bennett, the man of the hour, had been taken under the Doran wing before the *Lusitania* had docked, the publisher having astutely got aboard a revenue cutter with some newspaper friends who had gone out to meet the ship. Bennett noted it admiringly in the journal as "Doran's great exploit". He noted also that "a big swell in the Customs" had specially marked his baggage in return for promised autographed copies of two of his books. Setting foot in New York was "a profound and delicious thrill", a sensation which, as he entered the grand canyons of its streets, was enlarged into what he described as "an enfevered phantasmagoria".

The publicity which followed, spontaneous and organised, was extraordinary for a writing man to receive. His name flashed in and out of the headlines like signs marking his progress through the country. He was interviewed almost at once by the bearers of great names in American journalism—Irvin Cobb, R. H. Davis, Dorothy Dix, Franklin P. Adams. He was lavishly photographed, quoted and misquoted; in Chicago, sorrowfully apologised to by members of its Press Club for the way he had been treated in a Hearst paper interview, Cobb remarking to him that "if American interviewers had achieved the excellence of American oysters, American journalism would be better than it is". This aphorism Bennett used as his own in the book he wrote about his trip. Cobb did a pen-sketch of him for the *American Magazine*: "a smallish, slightly wearied-looking man, with a small impediment in his speech, a large leather-backed notebook in either side coat pocket, a Turkish cigarette in his fingers, and in his head the brightest, quickest brown eyes you ever saw—an eye that is interested in everything that has happened or is happening or is going to happen."

"One continuous triumph" was Mr. Doran's verdict. "Within a week contracts were concluded for the serial rights of three unwritten novels at from 20,000 to 25,000 dollars, and yet immediately after the publication of *The Old Wives' Tale*, I had not been able to sell the rights of one of his important books, with the complete manuscript in hand, for 4,000 dollars. No other author from Europe had had such a reception since the visit of Charles Dickens," who up till then had queered the pitch for British authors visiting America. There were banquets, lunches, literary club soirées, and autograph-hunting queues that trailed out of the bookshops into the streets. "Complete counter given to my works at Jordan Marsh's, largest booksellers in Boston." At one shop a man came forward four times with copies of *The Old Wives' Tale* for its author to sign. Amused, Bennett inquired his name and on hearing it wrote: "To my old friend John J. Roberts——"

In Chicago he was mobbed by women excited by publicity which held him up to be an author "who really understands the female heart". Observing that American men "admire one another enormously: they call one another by their Christian names, fondly", and sustain "wonderful friendships in business", he debated with himself the "singular position of the American woman", seeing her as tragically victimised by a fate which diverts the American man's affections to his career and reduces his love-making to "animal nonchalance".

"Too unwell to make any notes," he was writing after a very few days of American hospitality, but the notebook's only hint of it is in an extravagant decline from his standard of neat legibility. On the contrary, he seems to have been in an ungallant haste to note the effects of time on the American woman in her various challenging identities:

Lunch at Aldine Club given by John S. Phillips, editor of the 'American Magazine'. Miss Marbury, Miss Anna Morgan, Miss Ida Tarbell. These 3 women all extremely interesting, all different, yet intimate, putting arms round necks and calling each other by Xtian names, coming together on a purely personal basis, just like men.

[228]

Elizabeth Marbury. Age 55–60. A very business-like woman. Fat. Human. Kindly. Shrewd. Very shrewd and downright in her remarks.

Anna Morgan. Beautiful but waning. Age 35–37. Handsome, complexion going. Apparently doing nothing, but interested in everything. Art, for instance (and art dealing) and reform. Knew France and Germany well. Spoke firmly and *efficiently*. Showed her beautiful new enamel cigarette case, with her monogram worked regularly into all the crossing lines of it. A peculiar accent. Evidently an energetic woman with no outlet. Again, efficient. Good judge of human qualities and wide in interests.

Ida M. Tarbell. The most wistful and inviting of these 3 spinsters. 52 or 53. A very nice kind face, of a woman aged by hard work and by various sympathies and by human experiences. A sort of appealing face, and yet firm and wise. When asked to go down to Washington with Anna and Bessie, she said: 'I've only just come back. I haven't been at my desk for four or five days.' Just like a man.

Whether or not he was meeting the right people by his play collaborator's definition, he was exposed to the impact of an astonishing array of new and vivid personalities. Playwrights, bankers, musicians, theatre producers, architects, musical comedy stars, Trust presidents, university professors, artists, authors, impresarios, editors lined up to meet this man from the Five Towns whose books many of them had not read but whose prominence as a visiting celebrity was beyond anything they had known and to meet whom flattered their vanity even more than it did his. At Chicago, Mrs. Judson, the wife of the President of the University, held a reception for him. "She looked after me grandly. Told girls not to talk till I had had tea. Then stood in corner of drawing-room and procession of faculty and wives filed past me and I joked with each."

Dining with his friends the Herzogs at their New York home near Central Park—"good and bad books; ditto etchings"—he was warned by the hostess at the beginning of dinner: "This party is awfully dull and gloomy because everybody is afraid of losing anything that you have to say." Afterwards in the drawing-room, to quote the journal: "All the women in front of me most of the evening. . . . This evening was one of the rewards of being at once a literary lion and seriously considered as a first-class author. The frank admiration of the men was just as agreeable and more impressive than that of the women." He told his dinner

[229]

neighbour of that evening, Mrs. Hellman, that he had never been in love until he was thirty-nine.

Mrs. Paul M. Herzog to Arnold Bennett:

New York

November 15, 1911

. . . How thankful I am that your personality, which dominated ours so strongly the other evening, has been quite powerless with all these miles between! I have wondered since Saturday night if the person who drew out at will a generally reticent myself was Arnold Bennett as such, or Mr. Arnold Bennett, novelist, connoisseur and exploiter of women. Was it this person or the Personage to whom I responded . . . ?

Arnold Bennett to Mrs. Herzog:

20 November, 1911

. . . It was the person and not the personage to whom you were talking. It was the person and not the personage to whom you promised some very interesting written particulars; the which promise you have broken, and the which I beseech you to repair at once. How on earth do you expect this person to write true novels about women unless he can depend upon the friendly and frank collaboration of a woman now and then who isn't afraid of examining herself honestly? It was not nice of you to burn your communication. *I* would have burned it, a la rigueur! It was nice of you to write to me, but not nice of you to omit the enclosure so positively promised.

It is the person and not the personage who writes my novels. The personage appears only on very formal occasions.

I had a most agreeable and inspiring even at your house. Please give my very kindest regards to Mrs. Hellman, and to your husband, and believe me, expectant,

Yours sincerely,

ARNOLD BENNETT.

When two Chicago doctors told him they regularly prescribed his 'pocket philosophies' to their patients, and one of them added that his life had been entirely changed by reading *The Human Machine*, he seems to have had a sudden vision of America as a Wedgwood Institute expanded to continental magnitude, a land of people dedicated to self-improvement, to whom he might not unreasonably expect to sell a succession of books like *How to Live on 24 Hours a Day*. But it was always *The Old Wives' Tale* and *Clayhanger* that they brought him to autograph.

It was adulation all the way, from New York to Washington, from Washington to Chicago, on to Indianapolis, and thence to Boston and Philadelphia and New York again. And exhaustion lay in wait for him there. "Pretty nearly dead." "Exhausted, utterly." Some of the nervous wear and tear was the result of train travel. Like Charles Dickens (and the likenesses in their lives are oddly close in certain particulars), Arnold Bennett had suffered the psychological rather than the physical shock of a railway accident, Bennett in France two or three years previously; and the hurtling American trains with their "very bad brake applications" made him continually apprehensive. He was attentive as always to the amenities they offered, but still more so to every untoward sound and jolt, which increased the tensions of the tour. "Always afraid of collision," he noted on the journey from Washington to New York.

The fact remained that somehow in New York his exhaustions did not exhaust him. Like many visiting Englishmen whose native inhibitions are apt to lose force from the moment of setting foot on American soil, he discovered reserves of energy which he did not know he had, and he could go on with the merry-go-round past the point at which, before, he would have been plunging into the depths of depression. That was to come. "Tell your Mr. Bennett he stinks!" Doran heard an irate voice say as he picked up his office telephone on a morning when the headlines about Bennett were thicker than ever. Even so, Bennett's own words for it, "indescribably triumphant," were by no means excessive.

The pressures he was subjected to are shown in the journal not only by his continuous and often agitated narration of events but by the Stendhalian technique he had abruptly adopted—verbless sentences, the stripping away of needless words. Stendhal could help him to keep abreast of the rolling waves of experience, where the method of the brothers de Goncourt, with its introspections and ceaseless febrile snatching at the "momentary reality", could not. Bennett's American notes, severely abridged for the published *Journal* volumes, are sharply pertinent reporting and make better reading than the articles into which he expanded them for magazine and book publication later. H. L. Mencken said that *Your United States* marked "the decline of the author's vogue among us", a high-flying dictum that had to be hauled down after the publication of *Riceyman Steps* and the later *Imperial Palace*. ". . . Bennett had been to the United States; the newspapers had hailed him in their sideshow way; the women's clubs had pawed over him; he had, no doubt, come home a good deal richer. What he essayed to do was to write a volume on the Republic that should be at once colorably accurate and discreetly agreeable. The enterprise was quite beyond him. The book not only failed to please Americans; it offended them in a thousand subtle ways," none of which was cited by this famous critic, who found himself patronised by Bennett in the published *Journal*: "This fellow is getting better. He has a general basis of common sense and really writes very well for a journalist."

(2)

Soon, after the sumptuous, unsparing entertainment and the whirling pace of celebrity existence: "Longing for Paris—not London—where human nature is faced and people not imbued with Puritanic ideas," hardly complimentary to his American hosts and friends, the Edgar Selwyns, the Messmore Kendalls, the Crosby Gaiges, the Herzogs, not to say the Dorans who had shepherded him so attentively on his way. In Chicago, after the great goings-on, the craning of the bookshop assistants over their counters "to see me and get my autograph", the reception at the university, the meetings with Thomas Nelson Page, Floyd Dell, Hamlin Garland, and Herbert Kaufman, and the sightseeing to which prominent citizens gave generously of their time and powers of description: "General impression of shallowness left after seeing all these people, as if one had come to the end of them at once."

The best host he had so far met, he noted, was Charles L. Hutchinson, Chicago banker and benefactor of art and education: "His idea of hospitality and how to look after a sought-after visitor, and how to leave him alone, is unequalled by anybody else's in the U.S.A. Still, a general impression of commonness": the judgment of the connoisseur from the Five Towns is given a paragraph to itself on its journal page. He discovered in Chicago "a curious wistful quality in their constantly expressed aspiration after 'The City Beautiful' ". He liked a city to have a soul, he said, and scrawled in lead pencil across his page of Chicago notes: "Smell of stockyards."

Indianapolis, where he was dined by an admirer, Booth Tarkington —"rather round-shouldered and ripe"—was a town "full of old silver".

[232]

Malaria, he noted, had been conquered: "quinine no longer staple article of diet." Still subjected to "variegated murders and hold-ups", Indianapolis was beginning to rise to its dignities as a State capital:

> Even now rather daring to buy a picture. Formerly you could spend money only on a house, because that was solid and could be sold. And of course you had to have wallpaper and stoves. For example, old man who knew the swamp and now worth 8–10 million dollars, always refused to have horses, now has cheap auto. And so gradually to Art Institute with loan collections and ripping aquarelles by Winslow Homer.

While there he paid a call of respect on another famous local personality, "Indiana's most-loved citizen," the poet James Whitcomb Riley, whose poems of the West had a very great popularity throughout the United States.

> Fine old man, recovering from paralysis. Red face, yellow teeth, right hand affected, sitting in corner in easy chair. Fire. Mid-Victorian feel. An old friend near him. Talk about a picture of a literary town. Riley has infectious laugh. Told funny tales of his tragic adventures on lecturing tours. Enquired about Lucas. "Tell me about Lucas." Then talked about my books, with wet eyes. "I didn't mean to talk about them, to talk 'shop', but I couldn't help it." Women talking in another room.

Washington for him was "a plantation of public edifices amid a rather unkempt undergrowth of streets".

> Pennsylvania Avenue the great street. Cheapness of its buildings (old private houses turned into business) as the thoroughfare approaches the Capitol. The White House very nice architecture. Rather small. Distinguished. Dome too big for substructure. The wings rather fine.
> Saw Washington Monument. Phallic. Appalling. A national catastrophe—only equalled by Albert Memorial.
> Lunch at Shoreham Hotel. Very great oyster stew, with cream and butter. Very great mushrooms on a sort of mushed brown toast.

What made Boston for him different from the other United States cities he went to was that "it is finished; I mean complete. Of the other cities, while admitting their achievement, one could say, and their own citizens invariably do so, 'They will be. . . .' Boston is".

Mean station. New smell of taxis, probably benzine: good fun could be made about recognising a place from its taxi smell. Touraine Hotel. Reporter of 'Globe' waiting there for me. Fire engines passing up street. Bells. Theatreland at door. Across 'Boston Common' to State Capitol. Dome illuminated. Then to high-class residential quarter, Mount Vernon and Chestnut Street. Delightful *light* Georgian with addition of shutters; fanlights, bow windows. Louisberg Square. Old brick pavement. Old cobblestones. A few studios. Dignified. Reflections of distant lights in water. Then back along Charles Street. Electric light signs very suddenly. First we saw was the 'Bijou Dream'. Perhaps a bar.

Later: Narrow noisy curly streets; business character of England. So much so that nothing struck me as queer or curious the whole morning—except the size of everything. Jordan Marsh's probably bigger than Harrods'.

Philadelphia he found "startlingly unlike its European reputation. Throughout my too-brief sojourn in it I did not cease to marvel at its liveliness. I heard more picturesque and pyrotechnic wit at one luncheon at Philadelphia than at any two repasts outside it", a tribute to his hosts for the occasion, George Horace Lorimer, editor of *The Saturday Evening Post*, Sam Blyth, and Irvin Cobb: "racy tales and slang. Politics and murder." His amiabilities towards Philadelphia, expressed to the reporters, were rebuffed in a local evening newspaper which headed an editorial about him, 'Offensive Flattery.'

In Philadelphia he received an invitation to view the famous Widener art collection. He may never have known that it was the outcome of a carefully laid plot by an American *dilettante* who could think of no other way of being seen with the lion of the hour. Bennett had a letter from him mentioning that Widener would be gratified to meet him. At the same time Widener had a letter informing him of Bennett's wish to see his pictures. Receiving this intimation, Widener asked the writer of both letters to bring Bennett along. He did so and it appears from the journal that Bennett was equally interested in the conversation of a lady whom he met during the visit. "She told me a lot of her story coming up to hotel in auto. Asked if I believed in an ardent friendship between man and woman. I said no. She said thirty was a

[234]

great turning point and asked whether there oughtn't to be ~ ~ne 'trial institution' to take the place of marriage. Evidently greatly bored."

For him New York was the paramount American ci.y. Returning there after his various outward excursions, which took in visits to Harvard and Yale, he never ceased to marvel at the life that swarmed around him. "You must not expect me to talk," he had said to a friend on arriving there for the first time, he was so overwhelmed. He had never thought of such lithic adventurousness, such abounding vitality. Looking upon it, breathlessly, he was aware of "a poignant sympathy with those people and those mysterious generations who had been gradually and yet so rapidly putting together, girder by girder and tradition by tradition, all unseen by me until then, this illustrious, proud organism, with its nobility and its baseness, its rectitude and its mournful errors, its colossal sense of life". This was Wordsworth's "emotion recollected in tranquillity", no doubt; the American notebook of Arnold Bennett shows him very seldom pausing for reflection and the mood of *The Old Wives' Tale* is only occasionally allowed to come between him and the myriad teeming impressions it records, though when he sees young New Yorkers coming out of college he visualises them resentfully as "these invaders of *our* time, *our* earth".

"This is my sort of place," he made Denry Machin say of New York in *The Regent*, sequel to *The Card*. "I liked New York irrevocably," Bennett wrote in *Your United States*, the city above all of bold imaginative thinking, efficiency, luxury, gadgets, and overriding self-confidence. The romance of it as the handiwork of men struck him full in the senses, sending him reeling paralytically to his notebook again and again, the scarcely controlled scrawl of many of the pages being unrecognisably his, but rather that of a temporarily dissociated personality. "Metropolitan Insurance Company offices. Filing apparatus. *Millions* of documents; but organisation broke down over size of girls' hats— wouldn't go into lockers provided." In the Bronx, rents, sizes of rooms, refrigerators, stuffiness, vermin exterminators, "swagger pillow-cases" in a doctor's apartment: "all this business of *creation* of homes from drilling into rock, so *interesting*."

Messmore Kendall's lunch. Judge Gary, United Steel Trust president, on my right. Slow to talk. Rather dull. But very wise and upright. Said he was making 75,000 dollars a year as a lawyer when he chucked law. Referring to power of press and excellence of 'New York Times', he said editors had asked him to go and see them and

[235]

the editorial board had cross-examined him. Said he was glad to go and had nothing to conceal. Advanced and good honest views on women's suffrage.

Kendall on my left, and then Dan Guggenheim, short, merry man. I liked him very much. Very frank. I said his name was known everywhere. He said, 'Not like yours.' He was U.S. envoy to coronation of George V. U.S.A. used to pay 150,000 dollars a year for his advice on mining, etc.

Later, Cosgrave called. Talked very interestingly. Then on presidents of Trusts. Judge Gary, whom I said had seemed to me, positively, an honest man. He denied. Still, he admitted Gary was honester and had the sense of right and wrong to a greater extent than any of his rivals. But he had done all the usual bad things that Trust presidents have done. I must admit that I had seen in Gary a peculiar *cruel* and ruthless quality.

Sitting in the restaurant at Delmonico's at a table next to 'Diamond Jim' Brady, he jotted down: "Stout, coarse fellow, about fifty-five. Said to have 1,000,000 dollars' worth of jewels at bank: emeralds, rubies, etc., unsurpassed. In shirt front, two *enormous* pearls." He was dined at the Dutch Treat Club by a hundred of its members. "Wallace Irwin gave a good skit on 'How To Live On 48 Hours A Day'." Bennett acknowledged the compliment by saying that he would thank him in print. His visit to Columbia University reduced him to scrawling the words 'vastness' and "incoherence' in capital letters across the notebook pages: "Saw Thorndike, head of English department, grey-haired, young-looking jolly man. . . . Appalling stained glass" in the chapel and, after walking many corridors and in and out of faculty rooms, "came away pretty nearly dead." At the studio of Pirie Macdonald, "photographer of men," incidents, atmosphere, even inflections noted. Macdonald, from behind his camera: "Not *at* my eyes. *Into* my eyes. That's it. Just a little more challenge. A *little* more. That's it. Don't wink." And after that: "Put your back against the chair. Get your back right against it, like an Englishman," raw material later transferred from the notebook to the New York chapter of *The Regent*. "At dusk the effect of the massed skyscrapers illuminated from within, as seen from any high building up town, is prodigiously beautiful. Alongside the beauty, ugliness, in which was the poetry of it. . . . Each storey of a skyscraper means a life sacrificed. Twenty storeys—twenty men snuffed out. A building of some sixty

[236]

storeys is now going up—sixty corpses, sixty funerals, sixty domestic hearths slowly to be rearranged, and the registrars alone know how many widows, orphans, and other loose by-products!" Taking a morning walk:

This was election day. I saw the sinister but genial fellows bearing openly the insignia of Tammany. Don't, please, think that Tammany is a disease that happens to have attacked N.Y. It is as much an expression of N.Y. character as the barber's (remember my shave this morning at Waldorf), the pavements, the fineness, the interest in education, etc., etc.

(3)

He had written on October 24: "It is only seventeen days since I left London and it feels more like seventeen weeks." Now he was on board the *Lusitania* again, the voyager homeward turning. He had given a successful farewell lunch: "Everybody said it was a great lunch, the best lunch in America," written notes and sent *au revoir* flowers to the ladies, been interviewed and photographed all over again, and had then gone to his stateroom and slumped from mental reaction. "I wondered what the hell was the matter with life."

Arnold Bennett to Mrs. Hilda Hellman:

On Board The
Cunard RMS 'Lusitania'

DEAR MRS. HELLMAN,

It is appropriate for me to write this on Thanksgiving Day. Why are people so good-natured? Why are you so good-natured? . . . I hope you are by this time well into 'Les Liaisons Dangereuses'. And if you do not deeply admire 'La Chartreuse de Parme', please remember that the fault *is* yours. I have now sundry good reasons for coming back to New York, and not the least of them is to see you and George Sidney again. My kind regards to him. My best thanks and best wishes to you. And may you not lose that *nuance* of maliciousness!

Yours sincerely,
ARNOLD BENNETT

In the American notebook he had scarcely mentioned his insomnia. It now returned, giving him one good night's sleep in six. The journey to America had been a more drastic deviation from the settled patterns of his existence than he might have admitted. Now he was moving again into the penumbra of old dark forces of suggestion and discord that would revive familiar symptoms—the insomnia, the neuralgia, the unaccountable depressions.

As the house at Thorpe-le-Soken was still in Rickards's hands, he went to Cannes and began at once to write his American articles for *Harper's Magazine* and to make a start on the sequel to *The Card*, the serial rights in which had been sold in advance for £2,000 to *The American Magazine*. The editor, John S. Phillips, was an admirer of Bennett's work and had given out the opinion that literary craftsmanship in the United States would be improved if every author who respected his profession would read *The Truth about an Author*. While at Cannes Bennett was attacked by an illness afterwards thought to have been undiagnosed typhoid. He was, he said, "quite ill." It left him recurrently enfeebled for many months. He had lived in France long enough to be afraid of typhoid, a fear which he fatally spurned, as if by a predestined act, when later his faltering, exhausted spirit could no longer support what he had called in *Clayhanger* "the exquisite burden of life".

Arnold Bennett to Mrs. Herzog:

Grand Hotel Californie
Cannes

14–4–12

. . . Impossible for me to divine what are the mysterious passages in 'The Old Wives' Tale' that puzzled you! I will however admit that no English novelist ever suggested more unspeakable things, and got away without being understood, than me in that book. I was inspired to make the attempt by Wells' assurance to me once that one could say what one liked even in an English novel if one was ingenious enough. By the way, Wells' new novel, 'Marriage', of which I have just read the proofs, contains more intimate conveyances of the *atmosphere* of married life than anybody has ever achieved before. I am rather annoyed, as I am about to try to get the same intimacy in my Clayhanger-Hilda book, entitled 'These Twain'. These coincidences are distressing.

. . . I am getting more and more determined to write a book of verse. Please remember me to the other Hilda.

Yours sincerely,
ARNOLD BENNETT

[238]

CHAPTER FOURTEEN

(1)

"A YEAR of worldly success and intestinal failure," was his summing up of 1912. Concerning the stomach malady, "I shall ever be feeble in that quarter," as his friend Dr. Farrar had warned him many years before. He had been "covered with second cousins to boils", unable for five weeks to wear a collar. One has the impression that his physical organism was at last in revolt against the intemperate demands he was making on himself: *The Regent*, for example, 78,200 words in two months, three days. Critical judgments apart, it was high-pressure writing and he did not deviate by so much as a comma from his standard of good workmanship.

As to the worldly success, this was his £16,000 year. By far the larger part of his earnings came from *Milestones*, though he had laughed guardedly when Lee Matthews of the Stage Society had telegraphed: "Unparalleled success." Pinker was bringing him greater advances from publishers of books and greater payments from the magazines, and, satisfying though all this was, it meant that he was involved in commitments that mortgaged his peace of mind and therefore his health as well as his talents, for the mental load he had to carry was heavy and increasing.

At Cannes, where he wrote *The Regent*, he received a visit from a friend of his Paris days, André Gide, who noted in his 1889–1912 diary: "Cannes. Found Valery Larbaud and Arnold Bennett, the latter installed at the Hotel Californie. Earns around a thousand francs a day; he is paid at the rate of a shilling a word." In fact it was an unsettled, seriously interrupted working year for Bennett and but for the play his receipts would have been heavily down, though in seven months he wrote over 200,000 words for publication. But he was moving about more than usual: Cannes, Paris, London, Brighton, and back to Paris, while Rickards, who seemed to have been taking his time, supervised the alterations and additions to "Comarques".

Arnold Bennett to Mrs. Herzog:

14 St. Simon's Avenue
Putney, S.W.

4 December, 1912

DEAR MRS. HERZOG,—. . . I have not written before because I couldn't. Many stars have to sing together in unison before I can sit down to write a letter which I am not bound by the code to write. Can you imagine—you can—what the daily correspondence of a notorious author is? I do not delay answering when I can dictate the answer. But many answers I cannot dictate. . . . When I cannot dictate the answer, I usually let it go unwritten for ages, without a pang, and deliberately without imaginatively putting myself in the position of the correspondent unanswered. Moreover, I have been reading Meredith's letters—undoubtedly one of the masterpieces of English literature—especially the first vol. When I contemplate the sheer brains that he frequently puts into his letters I marvel, but have on desire to imitate. I have merely a desire to write no letters whatever. When my letters are collected and published—and nothing that I can do will stop that happening—my posterity will certainly be disappointed and feel itself aggrieved. And I shall and do feel a malicious delight in its 'deception'. Posterity wants too much, and will pay nothing for it.

My health is restored, I believe. Anyhow, I am in full work—not upon Edwin and Hilda, but on a novel for 'Harper's', which will bear no resemblance whatever to anything by Gilbert Parker or Mrs. Humph W. The writing of it will be interrupted by our removal into the country. We now possess an early Queen Anne house near the Essex coast, and in February are going to remove ourselves there definitely for everlasting; our deaths will one day cause a sensation in the village we shall dominate, and the English villagers and landed gentry will wonder, as they stroll through the deserted house, why the madman had 3 bathrooms in a home so small; they will not know that it was solely due to a visit to the U.S.A.

We shall spend Christmas in Paris, where art and conversation are understood. Still, I amuse myself in London. It is the biggest place yet.

Yours sincerely,
ARNOLD BENNETT

[240]

MARGUERITE BENNETT (MRS. ARNOLD BENNETT) WITH HER
FRENCH RELATIVES AND RICHARD BENNETT

ARNOLD BENNETT AT CANNES WITH HIS LITERARY AGENT,
J. B. PINKER (LEFT)

AT CANNES IN 1912

He moved in to "Comarques" on February 25, 1913, and the next morning the lapsed correspondence with Sturt was resumed:

DEAR ARNOLD,—I am glad to have your address: who knows but I might want to write to you some day? For the moment I only want to wish you good luck in the new house, and to you and yours in it. If you can find peace in it, and health too, for finishing up the story of the Clayhanger couple, there are quite a lot of people who will be glad you have gone there. My only quarrel with it is that it's too far away—isn't it?—for you to motor over and see me for an afternoon.

But no matter. You are still, as ever, Arnold Bennett; and I am, as ever,

Your friend,

G. STURT

His health deterioration was marked. The insomnia was worse. He was experiencing "mysterious and disconcerting" symptoms, undefined, and recording "bad nights", "couched all day," "extreme fatigue," "dreadful headaches," "rings round eyes," "colics," "vomitings," "work constantly interrupted by liver attacks".

June 19, 1913.—Exhausted by work, and by an excess of physical exercise (taken to cure liver). I took a *froid sur la digestion* on Monday night. Yesterday I wrote 1,900 words between 10.15 and 1 o'clock. Enormous. Went to bed immediately after dinner, feeling cold on shoulders and *ventre*; had a hot-water bottle, which so stimulated me that I had no desire for sleep until 3 o'clock, when it was light again. I had 3 hours sleep at most. Nevertheless, I feel fairly fit this morning. This is a fair sample of 'how I go on'.

The metabolism of the artist is more precariously balanced than that of most types of individual; the brain of the artist is at war with the stomach of the artist, a dichotomy which may indeed make victims of all intellectual men. Flexing his power of will, Bennett went manfully on with the novel he was writing, *The Price of Love*, trying to elevate his imagination for it by reading *War and Peace*, a prescription which failed, for he had a feeling, he said, that what he was doing was not good enough. Years afterwards he wrote to Pinker saying he considered *The Price of Love* to be among his best works.

His play, *The Great Adventure*, had opened successfully at the

Kingsway Theatre, to run for 673 London performances alone. He wrote to his friend F. S. A. Lowndes, who was on the staff of *The Times* and was the husband of Mrs. Belloc Lowndes:

> Lucas went into the pit, and he said he heard a man say: 'This play is full of sly digs. I never saw a play with so many sly digs in it.' Hence Lucas has christened 'Comarques' 'The Sly Diggings'. . . . Anyhow, the play is a most striking success.
>
> We are enchanted with our house, but not yet reconciled to the clime; it is too *strong* in April and May and upsets my liver. However, I am taking measures. We are now settled and I am trying to work, but the yacht is a great enemy of industry.
>
> Wells on agents is a chump. I have often told him so. He is down on agents *because* he knows he has made a chump of himself and dropped a lot of money by trying to manage his affairs himself.
>
> 'The New Statesman' is pretty bad, eh?
>
> Ever yours,
A. B.

The authority on mental health and efficiency could relax only physically. Every new experience, no matter how insignificant, presented itself as possible 'material' and was seized indiscriminately for storage in the volumes which his old craftsman friend, Bagguley of Newcastle-under-Lyme, was binding with admiring care. Twelve hundred words describing tension between his wife, Marguerite, and Rickards, whom "she had twitted because he had offered her flowers in what to her was the wrong way: 'les Anglais ne savent pas,' etc. Infinitely precious scene here for fiction—uninventable." Five hundred words about the Feast of the Antiente Corporation of Hanley which he attended: "It appears Alderman G—— is a moneylender and has certain members of the Council in his hands." A hundred words on the nose of Sir Alfred Mond, seen at the Reform Club. Two hundred words about Harrods' barber's shop; six hundred words about the barber's shop at Frinton: "Parted my hair on wrong side and badly. Shoved his sleeve in my eye. Didn't show me back of my head. Doubtful towels." Fifty words about the young son of a friend being shown round an art exhibition and exclaiming before a nude figure: "What a place to put a fig leaf!" Two hundred and fifty words about the first performance in England of *Der Rosenkavalier* at Covent Garden: "an explosive shout when Thomas Beecham came to bow." Two hundred words on Henry

James, in Pinker's office: "An old man, waning, but with the persistent youthfulness that all old bachelors have." Seven hundred words about one of Ellen Terry's husbands. A thousand words about "the fascinating talk" heard at the Adelphi Terrace flat of the Glasgow engineering brothers Weir. Four hundred and thirty words on seeing *Bunty Pulls the Strings* at the Haymarket Theatre. Three hundred-odd on a reception given by the novelist Mrs. C. N. Williamson at the Savoy: "Mrs. Williamson hasting about from guest to guest, carrying a bunch of pink roses."

(2)

A supreme tragedy of the sea had shocked the world: "Yesterday the Edgar Selwyns came to lunch. Only their anxiety to hear the rest of my comic novel [*The Regent*] prevented them from going home on the *Titanic*." Members of Parliament in London were glancing nervously over their shoulders in fear of suffragettes. Returning from hearing Sir Edward Grey, the Foreign Secretary, speak in the House of Commons, Arnold Bennett noted his opinion that "there has been a change in the fibre of Grey's character due to the shock of his wife's sudden death some years ago", and an influential political friend had assured him that "Grey's hatred and fear of Germany amounted to a mania". The Kaiser had inspected Krupp's; the organisation of a British Expeditionary Force for possible Continental emergencies had been completed by Lord Haldane; Winston Churchill at the Admiralty was frowning over German naval plans; residents of the Thames estuary district swore they had heard a Zeppelin cruising high overhead on a foggy night. Ben Tillett, the dockers' demagogue, had shouted to a mass of cloth-capped men on Tower Hill: "Oh, God, strike Lord Devonport dead!", the object of his apocalyptic wish being the chairman of the Port of London Authority. A by-election in the Potteries, caused by the death of a Labour leader, Enoch Edwards, saw Labour displaced there and sent to the bottom of the poll.

Coal strike began last Friday. Said Mrs. Frankau [well-known as the novelist 'Frank Danby'], who came for tea: 'I'm feudal. I'd batten them down. I'd make them work. They *should* work. I'd force them down.' . . . Coming up to hotel in omnibus, an oldish, sea-captain-ish sort of man said to a youngish red-haired woman, that miners had refused the terms of the Minimum Wages Bill. "But of course they refuse everything," she said scornfully. It is very funny that all the English inhabitants of grand hotels should be furious because miners insist on a minimum of 5s. a day for men, and 2s. a day for boys.

His physical ailments and an absence of the heroic mood delayed the writing of the third Clayhanger novel, *These Twain*, and there were grumblings from America, where it was due for serialisation. Pinker had to write to John Macrae, *Harper's* editor: "Until Mr. Bennett fell ill there was neither in his mind nor mine the least idea of departing from the agreed programme. . . . I am sure you are as convinced of Mr. Bennett's good faith as I am." Pinker was having to face Bennett's lofty refusals of some of the offers he was bringing him. *The Illustrated London News* editor, he told Bennett, was not satisfied with G. K. Chesterton's widely-read 'Notebook' articles in that distinguished weekly. "Chesterton's political activities are a drawback to him," he and his brother Cecil having become prominent in the Marconi shares sensation in which Lloyd George and Rufus Isaacs, later Lord Reading, were implicated. "You are just the man for them." Hinting at prestige, Pinker mentioned the price, which Bennett promptly refused. Lord Northcliffe sent the editor of the London *Evening News* to ask Bennett to write an article on the future of newspapers. "He would personally see that you went through the building and were shown everything," at a handsome price, £150 for two columns. Again a 'no' from Bennett. Perhaps it was prudence, perhaps it was pride. Pinker wrote:

Of the writers I have known intimately, the three greatest (I am not now thinking of you or H.G.) have always in my experience felt and frankly discussed a desire to meet the public taste, and to win popularity, and all the best men of my acquaintance have been keenly anxious that their work should be made to produce as much money as possible.

Finishing his reading of *War and Peace*, Bennett noted: "Terrific book. I wanted to write one of the same dimensions, and the final thrills of it *did* inspire me to a good basic scheme for the foundations of the third 'Clayhanger'." And a few days after this: "The third 'Clayhanger' must be quite different from 'Clayhanger' and 'Hilda'. I think I am now beginning to be anxious to write the 3rd 'Clayhanger', but there is a play, also two stories, to come in front of it." And a world war.

On an evening in June, 1914, he supped at the Connaught Rooms in London with the Granville Barkers, after seeing the 500th performance of *The Great Adventure* at the Kingsway Theatre across the street. Asquith, the Prime Minister, arrived uninvited. "When I bet Ainley a quid that the play would not be running on September 1st," Bennett wrote in the journal that night, "Asquith took the stakes. He was in great spirits, not at all 'drunk' but lively. He drank a little, but more mineral water than champagne." Asquith saw *Milestones*. "Being not at all pro-Bennett," he had written to a woman friend, "I was surprised at the excellence of the dialogue."

Seeing Dreadnoughts during one of his voyages in the *Velsa* later that summer, Bennett wrote: "Desolating things—so ugly and so futile. Gloomy sight." Memories of dusty regiments marching down the summer roads of France came back to him as rumours of menace flashed across Europe; of a regiment of artillery at Montigny, "pervading the little town with the number '32' "; of a doctor friend of his at Fontainebleau appearing "in a goodish pair of white ducks and new gloves" for his two-months' military service; of the young men of Les Sablons receiving their *feuilles de route* and marching through the village to the gander-call of a crazily blown bugle.

2nd August, 1914.—Velsa. Dover. No movement yesterday except that we went out to look at the weather by the w. entrance and returned by the e. entrance. Choppy sea, rather rough, sw. wind. I worked. Then went on to Esplanade. Esplanade rather good. Curved. Characteristic bay-windowish South Coast boarding-house architecture. Beach well filled with coloured throngs. Orchestra. Dignified young conductor, who saluted in response to applause. From the beach you get a good idea of the great size of this harbour. The outer mole seems miles off. Many warships close to beach. Sewage of hundreds of men and refuse, oil, etc. of all these boats, interesting for bathers. Also when wind southerly the beach is crossed with smoke from many funnels. Still, good. I got an evening paper. Usual distortion of news. No real news. All day thought of war was pre-eminent in mind, despite common sense against it. Every phenomenon observed was brought into relation to it. Soldiers and sailors on government part of moles, looking at booms, etc. A royal train came on to P. of Wales pier at 3 p.m. Who was on it I don't know. Ropes, crowds, police. Even if one saw a soldier with a woman one said: 'It can't be war, or he wouldn't be gallivanting.' Or: 'It must be war—he's taking leave of her.' Same instinctive absurd irrationalities with everything. Every uncomprehended sound related itself at once to war.

Calais (same day). Health officers. We began to talk of war. We agreed as to rightness of France and wrongness of Germany. They were convinced that Germany wanted a war. I assumed that England would join in. I said the result would be a certainty. The elder said he hoped I should prove right. I said I had no doubt. He said that if Germans defeated it would be a magnificent memory for England and France. Discussing German character, I stated my objections. The elder said: 'Still, some of them are good. Others, from the North, one sees that they have bad dispositions.' Elder said he would be called up tomorrow. Pilots called up. Douaniers called up. I found I had given them a rather false impression of all my ideas. To begin with, I was not certain that England would join in, or that, if she did, it would be a wise thing to do. But an instinct led me to take the line I did. These men were by no means Chauvinists. I went ashore, and saw the notices of general mobilisation.

3rd August, 1914.—Brightlingsea. Left Calais 5.30 a.m. Arrived here 4.30. SW wind, favourable tides. Saluted Fr. submarines outside Calais. Were questioned by British t.b. near South Edinburgh Channel. Customs inspector told me Germany had declared war on Russia and was invading Luxembourg.

(3)

Frank Swinnerton, who by then had come to know Arnold Bennett fairly well, after an inauspicious first meeting described in his auto-biography[1], said: "The war, much overwork, and—as I think—a profound disillusion with what he might have called the power of decency in human affairs, all had their influence upon the abnormally sensitive nature which lay behind his apparently unshaken front; and these things were destroying his strength."

In short, Bennett's was the eternal tragedy of the good mind doomed to share the life and the fate of the not-so-good minds which make wars possible. He had written in the journal a few months before:

[1] *Swinnerton: An Autobiography* (Hutchinson, 1937).

Walking last night for exercise along the Station Road (6.30 p.m.) I saw the light of Clacton (not the lights—the light) and of Frinton, over the brows; a reflection in the sky. . . . Idea of a desolate coast (relatively) with the human settlements rather precariously here and there upon it. Darkness everywhere and just those lights on the clouds from below. Sense of the adventure of living on the earth at all; and of the essential similarity of all human existences. Idiocy of loathing or scorning a different kind of existence from your own; e.g. my attitude towards the primness of Frinton and its golf club.

This perception of the "similarity of all human existences", which Donne had memorably expressed, was related to his feelings about war and the responsibility of men as individuals rather than as communities. He believed, he said, that war was the evil which civilisation was most concerned to drive from its midst. "But no nation whose citizens do not foster in themselves, in the conduct of their private affairs, the ideals of justice and goodwill can possibly hope to work effectively for the abolition of war," and the same was to be said, he insisted, of the class war. "To practice individual injustice and ill-will is to make inevitable the triumphs of national and international injustice and ill-will. Righteousness begins at home. If it has not begun at home, it cannot prosper in the chancelleries, or in the conference-rooms of capital and labour." As for war emotions, a subject of much of his note-taking during the autumn fervours of 1914, he had not abated views which he had written out for his private relief fourteen years before. The news of Ladysmith had been given at one of the musical evenings at the Marriotts', when "Sharpe led a great demonstration of flag-waving, cheering, and singing of *Rule, Britannia*":

It was distinctly an exhibition of insularity. I must say that I have been quite unable to join with any sincerity in the frantic and hysterical outburst of patriotic enthusiasm of the last few days. Such praise of ourselves as a nation, such gorgeous self-satisfaction and boastfulness are to me painful.

Professionally, the war had an instantly adverse effect on his affairs. Serial publication of his novel suspended in the *Daily News*, "ostensibly on account of paper famine." Book publication of the same postponed indefinitely; other work in hand "probably ditto". A heavy fall in the receipts from *The Great Adventure*. Asked to forgo his royalties on a

Milestones tour. Reflecting that less successful writers would be worse hit, he dictated instructions to Pinker to give money from funds in hand to any who might need help, and at the same time he told Miss Winifred Nerney, who had recently become his secretary, to look into needy cases in the village of Thorpe-le-Soken.

When Frank Swinnerton went there for a week-end visit, he found Bennett a suffering man. "I am delighted to see you. I have been . . . extremely *gloomy*," and from his tone Swinnerton felt "that something was seriously wrong". Discussing the effect of war on Bennett as artist, a present-day critic has said: "It is fascinating, though futile, to speculate on what he might have done had there been no war of 1914–18 or had he not been caught up in it." He was forty-seven and far from vigorously fit, but there could hardly have been any question of his not being caught up in it, even if we rely only on his testament to human liberty published in *The Saturday Evening Post* and in book form on both sides of the Atlantic: "We do not care for the conception of war as an instrument for regulating human affairs, and we will not have it. We don't want to argue about it. We want to fight about it. And we are fighting about it."

His personal contribution consisted of placing his common sense at the disposal of the Allied cause and of the home authorities. He set out his views in the journal two days after England had declared war on Germany.

I think the belligerency of England is a mistake—for England. Yet if I had had to choose, I believe my instinct would have forced me to make war.

Sir Edward Grey's astounding mistake, in his big speech, was the assertion that the making of war would not much increase our suffering. It will enormously increase it. The hope for us is in the honesty and efficiency of our administration. The fear for France springs from the fact that the majority of French politicians are notoriously rascals, out for plunder. The corruption of the Russian administration is probably even worse. The seriousness of the average French private will atone for a lot, but it will not—for instance—create boots for him.

The war is a mistake on our part, but other things leading to it were a mistake, and, these things approved or condoned, the war must be admitted to be inevitable. Judged by any current standard Sir E. Grey is a man of high common sense. He has not yet grasped

[248]

ON BOARD THE "VELSA" AT BRIGHTLINGSEA

THE "VELSA", BENNETT'S FIRST YACHT

By permission of Miss Winifred Nerney

"MARIE MARGUERITE" DRESSED FOR A BIRTHDAY

the movement of social revolution; but then very few people have. And you cannot properly or fairly try to govern a country on a plane of common sense *too* high above its own general plane.

Having jettisoned his serial story, *The Price of Love,* the editor of the London *Daily News*, A. G. Gardiner, who afterwards became one of his intimates of the Reform Club, invited Bennett to resume relations with the paper as a regular contributor of articles on topics of the day, and they were a feature of the paper for the next two years. Bennett's opinions were given a hearing round the Cabinet table at 10 Downing Street, and he was flattered when the Liberal Chief Whip, enthusiastic about his outline of a policy for the Liberal Party, announced that he would show it to Asquith, the Prime Minister. "Majestic and impressive phrase," he wrote in the journal. "Show it to Asquith!" He joined a number of committees, military and civil, and was very soon summoned to London by the Chancellor of the Duchy of Lancaster, the Right Honourable C. F. G. Masterman, "for consultation as to the war." The day after their talk he sat with Hardy, Barrie, Hall Caine, Chesterton, Wells, Zangwill, Gilbert Murray, and one or two others on what was described as a conference of "eminent authors" to discuss war propaganda. "Thomas Hardy was all right. Barrie introduced himself to me. Scotch accent; sardonic canniness. Zangwill talked too much. . . . I had such a headache I had to dine alone."

Later in the autumn he was appointed military representative on the Thorpe Divisional Emergency Committee formed to deal with preparations against a German invasion. In deference to this new responsibility, or perhaps as a gesture to the all-pervading masculinity of the times, he mounted a horse one morning to visit his sector of the coast, impervious to the grins of villagers whom he saluted with a wave of his borrowed riding whip as he cantered off on his imposing errand.

Arnold Bennett to George H. Doran:

> Comarques
> Thorpe-le-Soken
>
> 10th September, 1914
>
> . . . Between you and me, there are two English authors who have displayed common sense in this crisis. One is H. G. Wells. When she started out, Germany had no idea what she was arousing in England. I hadn't myself. You know that I am not a Kiplingian

patriot, but rather the reverse; nevertheless, I have the greatest confidence in the handling of affairs here and in the general spirit of the nation I have been really surprised. We have scarcely begun yet. And with the Navy 'in being', there is no reason why we should unduly worry. For myself, I would give every cent and acre I possess, and start again with nothing, in order to secure the overthrow of a handful of men at Berlin. . . .

If we are beaten—and everything is possible—then you had better begin to build ships and train armies; you will urgently need them.

Yours,
A. B.

Arnold Bennett to Mrs. Herzog:

Comarques

15 September, 1914

. . . As no good purpose can be served by letting the imagination loose, it is best to keep it in control. If you were here you would probably say that I was very callous and matter-of-fact. My wife's nerves have now largely recovered. I have lived, the sole man, in this house with four women (not counting servants) for six weeks, and I have squashed about 1,000 alarms and false rumours every day. For this labour of love I have been well cursed; but the effect up to date is admirable on the household mind.

(4)

That November his mother died. Her sister, his 'Auntie' Bourne, the formidable original of Mrs. Hamps of the Five Towns novels, who had given him his first paint-box as a child and thereby supplied no one knows what impetus to his career of self-expression, had predeceased her by a year. Time was removing his familiar seniors and investing him with seniority in their place, and the war, with its agonising emphasis on youth, went on confirming his promotion. Observing yet more of its effects on himself, he noted "the pleasures of doing a thing in the same way, at the same time, every day and savouring it." Sitting by his mother's bed, the tide of consciousness ebbing in the middle of sentences as she spoke and flowing again in sudden accessions of lucidity, it seemed to him strange "that this should necessarily be the end of a life, that a life couldn't always end more easily". Her final condition was distressing, "though less so than the Pater's," and he took some of the details of it for the death of Mrs. Maldon in *The Price of Love*: "her skinny veined right hand" emerging from under the bedclothes, "the loud stertorous sound of her drawing the final breaths of life."

At his mother's funeral at Burslem he gave his arm to his ancient, stumbling Uncle Longson, observing as they walked to the cemetery chapel "the vault of John Ford, with records of his young wives ('The flower fadeth', etc.). This could be exaggerated into a fine story". As Balzac had said to a bereaved friend on leaving a graveside: "Getting back to serious things, who will marry Eugenie Grandet?" Bennett was controlling his feelings just as he had controlled them at his mother's death-bed by observing every detail of every article in the room and every nuance of every sound that came from outside it. "On medicine table, siphon, saucer, spoon, large soap-dish, brass flower-bowl (empty). The gas (very bad burner) screened by a contraption of Family Bible, some wooden thing, and a newspaper. It wasn't level. She had it altered. She said it annoyed her terribly. Gas stove burning. Temp. barely sixty. Damp chill, penetrating my legs. The clock had a very light delicate striking sound. Trams and buses did not disturb her, though sometimes they made talking difficult."

It was a formula for checking imaginative indulgence. It was essential to nervous well-being, to mental efficiency, not to let the imagination engage itself beyond its competence. Death was the imagination's greatest incitement to unprofitable and positively harmful mental exercise. As for grief: "It is a form of indulgence and it ought to be bridled more than it is. The human heart is so large that mere remembrance should not be allowed to tyrannise over every part of it." Pre-war sentiments, these: his thought for the feelings of others would hardly have permitted him to write so bluntly when grief was shadowing so many homes, though we can believe that they governed his own feelings as he hurried back to London as soon as his mother's funeral was over. He made some notes in the train: "Sham brass handles on the coffin. Horrible lettering."

Arnold Bennett to Mrs. Herzog:

Comarques

6 Nov 1914

. . . I can't spoil the simplicity of my novel by letting Edwin and Hilda procreate. They have young George, and he's quite enough for my purposes.

At present I am devoting 1½ days a week to the prevention of conscription, and the proper treatment of soldiers' dependants, in this country. It is no sinecure. I have made a lot of people extremely angry, but they never argue with me. I wish they would—in print. They only suggest that a shoemaker ought to stick to his last. The British Army is really very fine. I am honestly convinced that size for size it is unequalled on the Continent. This does me good. There may be a few Zeppelins over us one of these days, but the affair will have no importance whatever except that it will aid recruiting.

At this moment Belgian wounded, convalescent, are strolling in our garden. Talk about 5-Towns' nonchalance. It is nothing to Belgian. These chaps convince me that I am emotional, mercurial, light-headed. Their cheerful calm is an absolutely staggering phenomenon. . . .

Always yours sincerely,

ARNOLD BENNETT

(5)

Up to 1916 *Clayhanger*, published 1910, had sold 37,000 copies; *Hilda Lessways*, published 1911, 34,000; *The Card*, published 1911, 53,000; *The Regent*, published 1913, 30,000; *The Price of Love*, published 1914, 33,000; and *These Twain*, published 1916, 34,000. In authorship reputations are often in excess of earning power. These figures for Arnold Bennett's books were good, but they were not good enough for an author who owned a country house and a yacht, both expensive to maintain, and who had to pay for them entirely by his own mental labours. Having written and published *These Twain*, in which he had resumed his role of regional novelist, Arnold Bennett let his creative gift go into abeyance for something like seven years, for the reason that it could not support him in the manner to which he was by now accustomed. He had to find £2,500 that year for income-tax. He had the money but hated parting with it. Moreover, life in the country cut him off from the sources of inspiration to which he most readily responded—the anonymous life of towns. "Comarques" was all right for week-ends with his wife and friends: E. V. Lucas, Mrs. Belloc Lowndes, the Atkins', Miss Pauline Smith, Rickards, Frank Swinnerton, Doran from New York, and Ravel from Paris, whose music he had written about so ecstatically in *The Glimpse*. But, creatively, it was a bad investment, and so it was in the market sense, for property values

on the East Coast had fallen heavily. In fact he was landed with it and
with the rising costs of keeping it going, and the only solution of the
problem was more and more journalism, an increasingly intense
preoccupation with the topical and timely, with "Some Thoughts On
War Saving", "More About The Air Situation," "The Next Campaign,"
"The Desire To Make Terms," with anything that editors wanted,
always subject to his wanting to write it.

The heart of the German soldier is in the war, and that heart is
governed by two motives—the motive of self-defence against Russia
and the motive of overbearing self-aggrandisement. 'Prussian
militarism' may annoy many Germans, but it pleases more than it
annoys, and there can be few Germans who are not flattered by it.

The Germans are a great nation; they have admirable qualities,
but they have defects also, and among their defects is a clumsy
arrogance. It is a racial defect, and to try to limit it to the military
autocracy is absurd.

The *Daily News* was good for a thousand a year, Lord Northcliffe
and his brother had started a Sunday picture paper for which they
desired him to write at £100 an article, and Pinker was getting him
magazine commissions from America at better rates of payment still.
He would have liked to extend and consolidate the reputation which he
had gained for himself by writing *The Old Wives' Tale* and *Clayhanger*.
But as a conscious artist, who would never be swept by a turbulent
imagination into the production of best-selling masterpieces, he was
obliged to write what would procure for him the means of keeping up
the style of life he preferred and, indeed, now could hardly abandon
even if he wished to do so. He was not the kind of employer, for
instance, who would think nothing of summarily changing the direction
of other people's lives in order to readjust his own.

Miss Pauline Smith gives in *A.B.: A Minor Marginal Note* her
remembrance of life at "Comarques" in the war years, when "the peace
of the old house and its garden, and of the little village beyond its gates,
had fled with the peace of the world". Officers were quartered on the
Bennetts. Mrs. Bennett threw herself with French vivacity into
organising entertainments for the troops. She became exceedingly spy-
conscious, herself aware of the scrutiny of the villagers, suspicious of
all foreigners, friend or foe. The tennis lawn had to stand harder wear
than ever before: there were garden flower shows, bazaars, and drawing-
room concerts and dances in aid of this and that. Miss Smith says:

In this changing world in which for M. as for many others a sense of proportion was becoming more and more difficult to maintain, A., not yet called to the Ministry of Information, remains in my memories of him almost obstinately his ordinary, everyday, well-balanced self. Upheld by his blunt Five Towns grit and sincerity against both the assaults of war and its feverish social activities, he makes, against the background of those first three years of upheaval, a sturdy yet somewhat withdrawn and solitary figure, doggedly pursuing his own set course in the midst of those whom the call to arms had brought so strangely as guests to his house. Through all the alarms and gaieties which swept M. off her feet he stuck calmly to his regular routine of work, to his appointed hours of repose. . . . His interest in every phase of the life around him, and in the men and women, young and old, who played a part in it, was the interest of a detached observer, almost of an outsider, with a notebook. Yet behind this detachment lay the quick sympathy and understanding, the rare patience and tolerance which came increasingly to be, throughout the years, his gifts to those around him.

Bennett was putting on weight and not only physically. One of his older journalistic friends, seeing him sometimes in the London of 1916–17, observed that his rigid carriage had become more marked and that he had developed a trick of staring in half-humorous appraisal at newcomers to his expanding circle of acquaintance before responding to their greetings. "Hullo, I say!" was a familiar form of greeting with him and a new acquaintance, a Ministry of Information official, took it amiss. "Hullo, I never say," he retorted tartly. The late Sir Eric Maclagan, who from the war years became one of Bennett's admiring friends, said that "when occasion warranted it Arnold could carry himself like a pro-consul". The manner could be intimidating, perhaps the more so because he himself had no idea of it. " 'A.B.' was the antithesis of the superior person": the statement came from one who knew him well, the late Sir Desmond MacCarthy.

Arnold Bennett to Hugh Walpole:

Comarques
Thorpe-le-Soken

1st April, 1915

MY DEAR HUGH,—. . . The drink question is now agitating us. I have suggested that total prohibition should begin first in the Cabinet, the

[254]

Reform Club, and the National Liberal Club! I met three Cabinet Ministers at dinner on Tuesday and this scheme seemed to please them. I doubt if they will adopt it. Personally I should be in favour of prohibition as a national act of self-discipline.

Everybody high up seems to be perfectly confident about the war, and I have myself laid bets to the sum of £25 that hostilities cease by the end of July. . . .

Our affections to you,

Ever yours, A. B.

(6)

He went to France and, touring the battleline, was showered by earth from shelling, his self-esteem possibly invigorated as a middle-aged man rendered immune from the hazards of military service. "So you've come to watch other people do things," a general said to him on being introduced, a greeting which Bennett considered "impudent". The book that followed, *Over There*, was a work of effortless dexterity, a job of good reporting by an urbane and highly selective observer. Not a book that mattered and the dust of another war has settled thickly upon it. He met the Commander-in-Chief of the British Expeditionary Force and noted chiefly that "his finger-nails are full of character". He was photographed with Marshal Joffre of the French armies, and the photograph shows the turn-up of Bennett's right trouser-leg caught in the tab of his boot, an oddity of his appearance recorded in other photographs at other times and of which he was comically oblivious. Once again one seems to hear a gnomish cackle off-stage.

He returned from the Front in no mind to write. Marguerite Bennett says that his nerves "went all wrong", that he had been much affected by the sights of war. "He stayed in bed for days and days" after his return and would not discuss what he had seen. "The officers billeted with us were anxious to hear his impressions but he refused to talk," telling them to read his articles as they appeared. Extra thick carpets were laid on top of those already covering the servants' bed-rooms so that he should not be disturbed by footsteps overhead. It made little difference. He would get up in the middle of the night and stalk into his wife's room, vowing vengeance on "those girls upstairs: they must be stopped". His wife had the shock of finding a loaded revolver in the drawer of his bedside table. She sent for the doctor.

"All nerves. Take no notice", but she persuaded a friend to unload the revolver.

Nor would he relax his attention to the smallest details of house-keeping. He developed a habit of leaving notes of criticism about the house for his wife to find, thus: "When the red bedroom is not occupied the windows of its bathroom, etc., must be shut and blinds drawn. It was not done on Sunday night." A note left on the kitchen-table cryptically reminded her: "Cost of fowls 1st Dec. to 28th Feb. three months £6 13s. 6d. Thirteen weeks . . . 10s. per week." Other subjects dealt with in this oblique and doubtless irritating fashion were noises made by ducks, vegetables in and out of season at the time of writing, wages of gardeners, the dilatoriness of a maid, the necessity of saving table scraps, and household economies generally.

Arnold Bennett to Mrs. Herzog:

Comarques

17 Oct 1915

. . . Since I wrote to you I have had 2 days' holiday. I drove over to the Wells', about 42 miles from here, on a Saturday morning and returned on the Monday morning. I seem to have played games—including hockey and Badminton—all the time. Wells is not a good games-player, but he is fully aware of their value and of the value of exercise, and whenever there is a lull in the intellectual movement of social relations he turns on a game. His energy is astounding. This 2 days' holiday—my only time off since August, 1914—did me much good.

I shall continue to be in a state of surprise that New York women of leisure and wealth and 'Allied' sympathies don't cure their distress about the war by some form of regular organised activity.

Our kindest regards
to you both,
Yours sincerely,
ARNOLD BENNETT

Arnold Bennett to Mrs. Marsden (formerly Miss May Beardmore):

Comarques
Thorpe-le-Soken

24 Oct 1915

MY DEAR MAY,—. . . I have looked at the casualty lists for months now solely for that name. Mixed up with your desolation there must be some rather fine thoughts and sensations. It is a terrible event, but it is also magnificent. I expect you often feel as if everything had broken loose. However, you will now know what sort of stuff you are made of. . . .

In any way in which I can possibly be of the least assistance to you, whether material or otherwise, I am absolutely and completely at your service, not only now but always, without fail. The same for Joan.

Yours,
ARNOLD

His war journalism took him constantly to London and the train journey there and back in a day was tedious and tiring. There was only one thing that he could do about it, stay more often in London. It meant hotels, clubs, restaurants, dining out, theatres, and getting to know and being known by more and more people. He was emulating no one in becoming a man about town, nor was it a role that he consciously sought. It was thrust on him in the flux of events and by his own irrefutable competence as a journalist, resulting in some of the best article-writing of the war years. He wrote to Mrs. Belloc Lowndes on October 13, 1915, that he had heard indirectly—"we authors are never told"—that his *Daily News* articles "have had an excellent effect on the circulation of the said newspaper". Pinker several times passed on to him the congratulations of fellow authors and at intervals out of Farnham in Surrey there would come a letter from Sturt, quietly praising him for some pronouncement that had impressed him by its common sense. The wheelwright had the craftsman's mistrust of enthusiasm; his compliments were not lightly given.

The Bourne,

MY DEAR ARNOLD,   16 Feb, 1916

Let me say 'Thank you' for your 'Daily News' articles. They are almost always a comfort. It seems to me, though, that you condescend, when you rebuke Mr. Shaw . . . his opinions are of too small importance to be attended to in these times. The man is a Pedant: one who makes up his mind what opinions to hold, and then holds them, by rule. He isn't worth your notice.

I am tickled though to learn (from your article) that he has got a new form of 'intelligence'—with a special spelling of his own, and that he wants it to prevail over our old-fashioned English common sense—Asquith's brand. This priggishness of the superior person is really funny.

You should have heard my brother Frank about it last week. Talking, he was, of people who are 'ignorant' *because* they are educated—*because* they have been to the universities. On that account, he urged, they fail to understand practical life, and become doctrinaires. Frank usually keeps cool; but now and then sizzles up, and then it is inspiriting to hear him. I forget the occasion. But he was urging me to write an essay against intellectual pride.

Indeed, the absence of intellectuality is the central English quality, I begin to think: the one saving grace; the source of our queer humour; of our obstinacy and quarrelsomeness in politics; and of the immovable and unreasonable good temper of the men who are fighting. To the best of my belief, Shaw, being of an alien race indeed, never understood it and is negligible for that reason. For the English outlook and understanding work at a deeper level than his 'intellect' can ever fathom; get nearer to realities. . . .

I often wish that I could see you; and, as that doesn't come off, I take pleasure in repeating that you are doing good work for democracy and for England. It is certain, and I am immensely glad of it, that a good deal of England's best sanity is getting itself very well expressed in your articles concerning the war.

Ever your

GEORGE STURT

The Lord Chancellor of the day, likewise congratulating him, added other words that made music in Bennett's ear—"the best praise of 'The O.W.T.' I ever had *viva voce.*"

Arnold Bennett to Mrs. Herzog:

25 March 1916

. . . I was *most particularly obliged* for your letter and your efforts on behalf of the Wounded Allies Relief Committee, and the cheque. You say these efforts will continue, and I hope they will. It is my business to keep the W. A. R. C. in funds and the difficulty of doing so increases each week. In fact personal appeals to the British public are now almost useless. I have obtained over £5,000 out of the U.S.A. public, but if I could find the way I ought surely to be able to get a great deal more than that!

[258]

For myself, I am like a vast number of other people here in that my own work has been practically stopped by the war, and I don't see much hope for it until the war is over. I have absolutely to write a play, however. The war has turned me into a political writer, and I have somehow created a new notoriety for myself in this department of my Wanamaker store. But immediately after the war I shall close it down.

He went to Scotland that summer, for his first real holiday since the war began. He stayed at Blanefield, Kirkoswald, Ayrshire, which continues to be the home of his friends the Richmonds. From Edinburgh on his way south again he sent a picture-postcard to Mrs. (now Lady) Richmond: "We are leaving Edinburgh tomorrow morning for York, and are rather pleased with the place. The people, however, are badly dressed and the shops and cafés dirty, while the town is so very well kept. D. K. has sent me a second telegram, thus conceived: 'Am leaving for my holiday broken-hearted.' To this I have maintained a masterly silence." 'D. K.' was Doris Keane, the actress, who had had one of the great stage successes of the war in *Romance*. She was anxious to see a new play which Bennett had written.

Arnold Bennett to H. G. Wells:

Comarques
Thorpe-le-Soken

My dear Herbert,   8th July, 1916

I like the book [*Mr. Britling Sees It Through*] very much. It is extremely original and sympathetic, and the scenes that ought to be the best are the best. In fact it is an impressive work. Also as a tract it is jolly fine. It would have been finer if old Brit had made the slightest attempt imaginatively to understand the difficulties of the British Government, or what it *did* do. If he had given to this business a quarter of the skill and force which he gives to understanding what it failed to do, he would have been liker God. Also his notions about the 'steely resolution' of the French nation are a bit *Morning Post-ish*. I say this because I know it would anger him. There is much more steely resolution in England than in France. The spirit of Paris has not been good. The spirit of the Midi has been rotten. This I know of my own knowledge. What has saved France is nothing but the accident of first-rate generalship. If the Battle of the Marne had been lost there wouldn't have been a semblance of steely resolution in France. Even after the Marne every military set-back has been instantly followed by civil crisis. Much more might be said on these points, but old Brit should not be harried.

Thine,

A. B.

At this time he was frequently in the company of Wells, Shaw, and the Webbs. "Apropos of Squire's poem in the 'New Statesman', the Webbs were both very funny. Mrs. Webb especially. She said, 'Poetry means nothing to me. It confuses me. I always want to translate it back into prose'." Sidney Webb, "more than ever like a Jew, but a decent one," told him that his wife could not sleep when there was bad war news, and that "he had to exaggerate his usual tranquil optimism in order to keep the household together", to which Bennett added the comment: "It was one of the rare human touches I have noticed in the said household." The Webbs had prevailed on him to join the board of the *New Statesman*. "Due to their fascinations," he had written free articles for the paper when it had no money to pay for them. Shaw also was on the board. "Shaw had no conception of public opinion at all," Bennett wrote after one of the board meetings at which Shaw had urged a campaign in favour of Haldane as Prime Minister. They had walked away talking together and Bennett added to his note: "The fundamental decency and kindliness of Shaw was evident throughout." Wells, who "slanged the Webbs as usual", complained that he had had his day. "My boom is over," he said to Bennett. "I'm yesterday." Meanwhile, Bennett noted, "the Royal Academy continues to provide grandiose evidence that the flight of time is an illusion."

Arnold Bennett to Mrs. Herzog:

4 Dec 1916

. . . I have learnt more about what are called 'ordinary people' during the war than ever I knew before. By 'ordinary' I simply mean people with the sense of art practically undeveloped, people without any subtlety, who don't understand what you are talking about unless you translate for them. As an experience, it was interesting, but really very trying sometimes. For me, part of the war.

I now have a second home in my yacht club in London, and am seeing more of my old sets. And I have been 3 times to the opera!

[260]

And I have read Dreiser's 'The Financier'. This book, despite its dreadful slovenliness in details of phrase, is an extremely remarkable affair indeed. It gave me intense pleasure. This is praise. I wish I knew Dreiser intimately. Wells's new novel is very fine. I doubt if mine (a quarter written up to date) is. We are supposed to be very gloomy just now in England, but it will pass. We have about cleaned up the Zepps, I think. One superb specimen of them lies naked a few miles from here.

At one of the lunches at the house of the Chancellor of the Exchequer, the Right Honourable Reginald McKenna, Bennett sat next to the dapper, combative 'Jacky' Fisher, who told him: "I was the only one who objected to the Dardanelles Expedition. Kitchener was in favour of it. He's dead. Won't say anything about him. He got the Order of the Garter. I got the Order of the Boot," a joke which possibly Bennett did not know that the deposed First Sea Lord was barking out rather too often by then. He gave Bennett his favourite quotation, duly committed to the journal: "Not heaven itself upon the past has power. What has been has been and I have had my hour." Bennett's journal entry continues:

Pamela McKenna had asked me to arrange for her to meet Wells. The first lunch I arranged she could not attend, as she had to lunch at home. I arranged another, and she wrote to me that she really ought to be lunching at home that day, but she would like to see me for a moment, if possible, as she didn't care to write what she wanted to say. I called yesterday morning for a moment. She was nervous, and turned away to a table as she told me that Reginald didn't want her to meet Wells, had indeed told her that she 'couldn't' meet Wells. . . . However, I behaved very well. She handed over a book which Birrell had given me in exchange for 'The Golden Remains of the Ever-Memorable John Hale', which he bought from me about 24 years ago when I was doing a few experiments in book-selling—and never paid for.

George Moore and Walter (later Richard) Sickert were his guests, and he decided that Sickert was "more normal" than Moore, who said "several entirely foolish things. Moore is naïvely and harmlessly vain, and very agreeable". Talking with Wells at his rooms in St.

James's Court, Westminster: "I noticed that he had photographs of three of his lady-loves on the mantelpiece as well as of Mrs. H. G."

Arnold Bennett to Hugh Walpole:

> Royal Thames Yacht Club,
> 80, Piccadilly, W.

> 1st May, 1917

MY DEAR HUGHIE,—I finished my damned novel yesterday, and now I take up your two letters. The novel is entitled 'The Roll Call', 114,000 words. I am glad you are alive. I heard of your desire to bathe in a dock or harbour, but you might have removed your eyeglasses before plunging. Touching Russia, on behalf of the 'New Statesman' I desire you most particularly to write us an article. . . . We want something *absolutely true* and first-hand. You will perform a real service in attending to this at once.

I went to the Russian exhibition yesterday, not for pleasure, but to put the sacred autograph in books, and to answer questions by Lady Muriel Paget and other toffs about how to make these enterprises hum. I liked Lady Muriel P. much. Never met her before. I could get on with her. The Russian theatre in the basement of the Grafton Galleries is most excellent. To see a play with ideas in it was like having a bath. It made me want to sit down and write more plays at once.

The chief factor in English life at the present moment is the weather, which is suddenly lovely. There will doubtless be a great mess over submarines, but the weather seems likely to continue grand. I am sick of work and am working for 3 Government departments. I meant to take a holiday this week, being completely exhausted. I came up to my beautiful Club yesterday and it is a solemn fact that I hadn't been here ten minutes before I had undertaken to write an article for 'The Strand Magazine' in three days. A bit thick. Then I ran off to lunch with the Sidney Webbs, who live in a house entirely constructed of blue bricks, a marvel of ingenuity— recalling the labours of beavers and coral insects. I get on very well with the Webbs (my co-directors) but they do not understand (what I call) life. Squire is an A1 chap. But he is a vegetarian and he doesn't understand life either. And either he or his wife doesn't understand shirts. I am 50 on the 27th current, and, considering that, I am very well. Marguerite is now what she calls 'toppole'. She has the gilded nephew in town for 3 days before returning him to school. This raw 5-Towns boy is a wit. He will have a brutal sardonic wit in the nature of his benevolent uncle's. Now don't forget about the 'New Statesman'. . . .

Thine ever,

A. B.

During these war years Bennett lent his name and energy to a number of charitable causes connected with the war. He was primarily responsible for organising the very successful concert given at the Haymarket Theatre for the Wounded Allies Relief Committee, a memorable occasion on which "rows and rows of celebrities", he said, were to be seen in the stalls. "I had no particular trouble but I will never organise another." He wrote to Hugh Walpole: "The only thing the matter with me is that I am worked to death with war charities and so on, and they are *not my line*." The well-known, almost historic, box-office chief of the Haymarket Theatre, W. H. Leverton, recalled in writing his association with Bennett at the time of the grand concert there for which Bennett was responsible. "He was inspiring in his helpfulness to others and generous in the extreme." With the help of his New York friends, the Paul M. Herzogs and George Doran, he succeeded in collecting a further thirty thousand dollars from American sympathisers with the W.A.R.C.

Arnold Bennett to Mrs. Herzog:

(Undated)

. . . I am now exceedingly busy and exceedingly worried. This kind of situation always seems to suit me. I am worried about the 'New Statesman', of which I am a director. The editor has been called up for military service. Awful rot. The War Office is adamant. We can exert influence, but not enough to get him off! In the U.S. we could have done it. His departure means extra work for me, and also a constant effort on my part to keep the policy of the paper straight. Further, I am very worried about my brother, a lawyer, whom the war and other things have spectacularly ruined. Still, I don't seem to mind.

Have you read Frank Harris's privately published 'Life and Confessions of Oscar Wilde'? It is a strange and powerful book, written by a man who is a curious mixture of impulses noble and ignoble.

[263]

In July, 1917, he was in London on *New Statesman* and other business and went to dine with Barrie at his flat in Robert Street, Adelphi. Thomas Hardy was there. Bennett noted:

Barrie has an ugly little manservant, and the finest view of London I ever saw. Mrs. Hardy was a very nice woman, with a vibrating attractive voice. Hardy was very lively; talked like anything. Apropos of Tchekoff, he started a theory that some of Tchekoff's tales were not justifiable because they told nothing unusual. He said a tale must be unusual and the people interesting. Of course he soon got involved in the meshes of applications and instances; but he kept his head and showed elasticity and common sense, and came out on the whole well. He has all his faculties unimpaired. Quite modest and without the slightest pose.

Later in the evening Barrie brought along both Shaw and the Wellses by 'phone. Barrie was consistently very quiet, but told a few A1 stories. At dusk we viewed the view and the searchlights. Hardy, standing outside one of the windows, had to put a handkerchief on his head. I sneezed. Soon after Shaw and the Wellses came Hardy seemed to curl up. He had travelled to town that day and was evidently fatigued. He became quite silent. I then departed and told Barrie that Hardy ought to go to bed. He agreed. The spectacle of Wells and G.B.S. talking firmly and strongly about the war, in their comparative youth, in front of this aged, fatigued, and silent man—incomparably their superior as a creative artist—was very striking.

Bennett was present at a spiritualistic séance in the company of W. B. Yeats, Roger Fry, and Mr. (later Lord) Jowitt and Mrs. Jowitt. The medium, named Peters, handled objects brought by each person.

He succeeded, with my toothpick, in getting me to the Potteries, and into the office of the 'Staffordshire Knot' or 'Sentinel', and described a man that might be either Goold or the Editor of 'The Sentinel', and said that, known or unknown to me, this man had greatly influenced me. He insisted on the name 'Zola'. 'Zola.' He said there was a message to tell me I hadn't done my best work. I am morally sure he hadn't the least idea who I was.

He was a guest at a war-time Lord Mayor's Banquet at the Guildhall: "Funny to see Asquith followed by wife and daughter. The name of

Venizelos aroused easily the most cheering. Asquith was best. Diction uneven, but phrasing absolutely perfect throughout. He was grim but not boastful." In a letter written then to Professor Bodkin asking for information about certain aspects of Irish affairs, Bennett said: "I have no first-rate interest in politics. I have a first-rate interest in the arts."

Arnold Bennett to Mrs. Herzog:

10 November 1917

. . . I hate amateurishness more and more, even in water-colours. I am not an amateur by temperament. I am more and more mixed up in politics, which I do not like; but there is no escape. I solace myself with the notebooks of Samuel Butler.

December 15, 1917.—Dined with Benchers of Gray's Inn in hall, to meet Lloyd George and heads of Air Service. F. E. Smith in chair. A very 'short' ordinary dinner, plenty of wine. I think Lord Halsbury [aged 92] made the greatest impression by his forceful way of saying that a man who made a bargain and didn't keep it was 'a dirty scoundrel'. Ll.G. spoke for over an hour, too long, and said all sorts of platitudes for public consumption. His 'set' effects were failures. But he had some great similes. Winston Churchill, after the principal speech, made an amiable tour of the tables. He wore all his military medals dangling on the lapel of his dress coat. (I suppose this is all right, but I had never seen it before except on the dress coat of the hall porter of the club.)

Amid these spectacular pleasures, his ascending progress into the more prominent artistic, social and political circles of his time, he still indulged a lowly habit of his free-lance days in Chelsea. "I curiously enjoyed going to an A.B.C. for hot milk and a sandwich," and later as tenant of the £800-a-year house in Cadogan Square he would often slip out for a twopenny cup of tea at the Express Dairy Company's shop in the King's Road, Chelsea. "I always enjoy this place; it is rather romantic for me."

His views on mental training were being privately sought by the head of the Pelman Institute, which was doing brisk business with the young officer classes concerned to improve their chances of promotion at a time when their chances of survival to be promoted were daily being diminished by the bloody battles of the Somme and elsewhere on the Western Front. Worried fellow writers were seeking his influence in procuring them immunity from war service, some with valid reason. "I arranged to get Robert Ross protected from military service." Ross was now a Trustee of the National Gallery. "Whenever he talks about the war his whole face changes. Speaking of air raid damage, I asked him: Is it worth seeing? He said with an air of triumph, ingenuously giving away his perverse joy in the German success which should teach these English a thing or two: 'It *is*.' And later: 'They have done it!' with the same curious and secret triumph." Ross had been strongly pro-German before the war, an admirer of the German cult of masculinity. Bennett liked him; "the most *indirectly* creative man I have ever known," he told Siegfried Sassoon.

20 December, 1917.—Walpole and H. G. Wells and I lunched together at the Reform. Hugh said he had decided to go into the Army if he was passed A1. I objected to his going into the Army. He said he must. He could for the present do no more good in Petrograd. So long as he was useful in Petrograd, *where there was danger* (my italics), he didn't mind not being in the Army. . . . It seemed to me that his leading motive was to prove to the world that he had been in danger, that is to say, he was not afraid of danger.

A piece of information given to him at this time about a matter far remote from the war produced in him a feeling of satisfaction which he thought worth recording. "George Whale," of the Reform Club, "told me of the discovery that Wordsworth had had an illegitimate child (girl) while living in France. This news somehow delighted me."

Arnold Bennett to Gregory Hill:

> Comarques
> Thorpe-le-Soken

MY DEAR GREGORY,   7. 2. 18.

I am delighted to hear from you and that you are well, even if not comfortable! I well understand what you mean when you talk of the discomforts felt by anyone who has been used to an ordered existence. They must be exceedingly trying, and you have all my sympathies. But for my age, I should probably be in the same boat, which boat I should most strongly object to. . . .

I think that the war is drawing to a close, and I should be rather surprised if it didn't end this year. The food situation here is grave.

In Germany and Austria it is appalling. It would be sufficient for us if Austria caved in. If Austria did, Germany would have to.

The United States have now 400,000 men in France and the number is increasing all the time. Up to the present, however, the U.S.A. have not displayed much talent for turning men into a coherent fighting machine. They are not concerted, and they admit this. So far, they are inferior to us in this respect. I see a good many people of all sorts who are in a position to know the facts and who talk freely to me. Russian news is scarce, and much of it is censored. . . . An intimate friend of mine, Hugh Walpole, has been at Petrograd on behalf of the Foreign Office during most of the war. He has the most astounding stories to tell of robbery and violence and so on.

My wife and I are all right. I have just finished a book, but it doesn't leave me much freer, as I am always worried with articles and oddments of this tedious war. Our best wishes.

Yours,
ARNOLD BENNETT

Announcing his purchase at Christie's of a Brabazon water-colour for twenty guineas in a letter to Professor Thomas Bodkin, Bennett went on to say: "I am now on the Imperial War Memorial Committee, and as the other members are Charles Masterman and Rothermere I'm the only one with a first-class interest in the subject. The object of the Committee is to procure a complete record of the whole blooming war in paint, ink and sculpture. I have succeeded in turning down *all* Royal Academy painters, except Clausen. Some feat, believe me! Yes, I have turned down the inevitable Brangwyn."

There was an evening when the Galsworthys dined with him in London:

As I was very larkish and indiscreet, the evening went well, and Galsworthy had to laugh again and again. Ada's hair is a nice dark brown and she is immensely improved. I liked her.

Air-raid warning at about 10 p.m. We went down into the basement, which is well-heated, and stayed till 12.30 a.m., Marguerite and the cook knitting. I noticed that John was just as chivalrous to the cook as to any of the other women. He even gave her a chocolate.

His manuscript of *Helen with the High Hand* was sold at Christie's on behalf of the Red Cross for £27. "Galsworthy's ms of 'The Free-lands' sold for £26. Some satisfaction in this." At the 'War Fair' held at the Caledonian Market: "Great success. I sold books at M's stall. Demand for Kipling, Chesterton, Conrad, and me."

In January, 1918, the Labour triumvirate, Henderson, MacDonald, and Webb, issued a War Aims statement under the title, *Labour and the New Social Order*. Bennett made it the subject of a warmly commendatory review: "A publication of first-rate interest and first-rate social importance, which everyone can afford to buy, which everyone ought to read and which everyone of average intelligence could read with pleasure." That same month he noted in the journal that Robert Ross had reported to him that Bonar Law had said, apropos the British Museum: "I wouldn't mind if the whole damned show was burnt to the ground." Sturt wrote to him in a distressingly palsied hand on a subject that has not ceased to be important in human affairs:

Verbum (from me; to you) *Sapienti*. It's borne in on me that an artist, like you, might be doing greater things for the League of Nations. Make it visible to the public as a lovely and delectable thing—a reality already in the spirit, to be worked for. The *feeling* for it is even now growing. Those who like it don't yet see what it is they like. Can't you help them to see?

To my mind, the League should be an outward and visible sign of an inward spiritual grace (*vide* Church catechism). If it is only an intellectual dodge there is no life in it. But it's more than a dodge. It's *alive*. It exists as a mutual understanding, a mutual desire for friendly and helpful behaviour and for democratic freedom.

The volunteering of the first armies proved it to be alive, here and in Australia and Canada, etc. Then a proof of it came from America. But still even the volunteers don't perceive what moved 'em. And people like Lloyd George, Carson, Milner, the Kaiser, etc., etc., never have perceived and have done their best to stifle the life in it.

It's possible Pres. Wilson has seen it. I doubt if Grey has. There's the great inter-personal thing, drawing people together, yet, for want of knowing what it is, they permit themselves to sneer at the proposed outward sign of it—the League of Nations.

I can't get at it; am more paralysed in tongue even than in fingers, or I wd try dictating. But I shd love to see you have a try. It wants an artist to show how comely the feeling is: afterwards lawyers and statesmen may come in, for the less vital job of formulating a working

[268]

scheme. Let the artist get to work first. I suggest that you are the artist.

But for the disabilities mentioned above I shd have proposed that you come and see me. But I am still n.b.g. Patience is indicated, the doctors say. Strength is gradually coming back though, and the world seldom fails to be interesting. How are you? I hope you are going strong. More power to you.

Yours, as ever,

GEORGE STURT

Arnold Bennett was no longer "the novelist", though he went on writing novels: five during the war years. He had become "the publicist", and if he had now reached the heights of unqualified recognition dominated in popular journalism by Horatio Bottomley, it was as a man of quality and not as a cheapjack of the pen and the placard that he was taking his place in the new society being thrown up by the war.

Arnold Bennett to Hugh Walpole:

Comarques

Thorpe-le-Soken

4. 4. 18

MY DEAR HUGHIE,—. . . I feel really relieved that you admire the book [*The Pretty Lady*]. One can't judge, oneself, under about 2 years. It is possible that you are right about Concepcion. I must do her again, that's all. It is a rare Shaksperean scheme to draw the same character again and again till you get it. Most of the reviews of the *P.L.* so far are specially footling. Astonishing, the number of critics who daren't *mention* that the chief character is a whore!

I must now close as I am much enfeebled.

Thine with thanksgivings,

A. B.

Arnold Bennett to F. S. A. Lowndes:

Comarques

Thorpe-le-Soken

MY DEAR LOWNDES,   6. 4. 18.

I am sorry you have returned to P. H. Square [Printing House Square, London, the address of *The Times* newspaper], which is really G. H. Q. I am scathing some of this lot in *my* new play.

[269]

I am much too deeply plunged in work. The play, aforesaid! Sitting on one of Beaverbrook's chief committees, which means a hades of a lot of cerebration, as the whole of the work is done by Charlie Masterman and me! And more and more journalism. I have just beaten all journalistic records. 'Lloyds Weekly News' have contracted to pay me £100 a week for a weekly 1500-word article. I offered to bet Pinker he wouldn't get £100 a week. He wouldn't bet, but he said if he didn't get it he wouldn't agree to me taking the contract at all. Other people can say what they like, but I say: Give me Pinker.

Our kindest regards to you all,
Ever yours,
A. B.

(7)

"The whole thing a vast make-believe, with an audience of which a large part was obviously quite unintelligent and content with the usual hollow rot." Dickens, so impatient of Parliament, could hardly have been more impatient than Bennett, writing after visiting the House of Commons with Spender, editor of the *Westminster Gazette*, and Gardiner, editor of the *Daily News*. It was the spring of 1918. Lloyd George was introducing the Man Power Bill, raising the conscription age to fifty. Listening to him, Bennett appears to have been visited by the old unaccountable revulsion: "Unpleasant Nonconformist voice. Very cheap oratorical effects—like Lyceum melodrama. No applause as he sat down." In the matter of the age limit, he was himself a few weeks on the right side of 51; not that he would have been a likely subject for recruitment. But desperation was in the air. "The sternest and most critical hour of the war," said *The Times*.

A week later Bennett went to see Lord Beaverbrook, the Minister of Information. "He asked me to accept the directorship of British Propaganda in France. He said that no one could know French psychology better than I do—this conclusion he drew from reading 'The Pretty Lady'!" He took up his duties at the Ministry, which was occupying an hotel in Norfolk Street, Strand, on May 9, 1918: "On the whole, the first day was rather a lark." Various people on the Ministry staff, he was noting a couple of days later, kept coming into his room "on various excuses, but just to look at me".

[270]

May 15, 1918.—Yesterday I had the greatest compliment I have ever received as a journalist. Spender asked me whether if he was ill or really had to take a holiday, I would write some of the 'Westminster Gazette' leading articles.

To balance this, I heard from Cassells' that the Catholic Federation of the Archdiocese of Westminster was seriously moving against 'The Pretty Lady'. So I wrote to F. E. Smith with a view at any rate to stopping any police prosecution.

Passages in *The Pretty Lady*, which had for its heroine a French cocotte in war-time London, had drawn a threatening letter from W. P. Mara, honorary lay secretary of the Catholic Federation: "Several remedies can be employed by my Committee. Before using any of them I am writing to you in the hope that you will take adequate action in the matter." The novel, he claimed, contained references that offended Catholics. Bennett wrote to Messrs. Cassell & Company:

It is surely unnecessary for me to point out, first, that in so far as the book deals with Catholicism it does so exclusively from the point of view of an ignorant and superstitious courtesan anxious to justify her own conduct to herself, and, second, that all the details given as to the legends of the Virgin Mary can be found, with hundreds of others, in devout Catholic literature.

Seeing that the objection of the Catholic Federation is a purely religious objection, I am afraid that no purpose would be served by arguing it further. Does the Catholic Federation wish us to suppress the book, or to suppress certain parts of it, because in their opinion it offends Catholic susceptibilities? If so, I can only reply, with respect and regret, that such a course is absolutely out of the question, and that I personally should oppose it by every means in my power. The book is a serious and considered work; it has received the very highest praise from many periodicals and critics of the highest reputation, and I shall most assuredly stand by it.

I greatly regret that Roman Catholics should find offence in 'The Pretty Lady', and the more so as I have greater sympathy with their religion than with any other.

Arnold Bennett to George Doran:

80 Piccadilly,
London, W.1.

May 13th, 1918

MY DEAR DORAN,

I suppose you are about to publish, or have just published, 'The Pretty Lady.' Here, a few of the lower class papers have gone for it rather heavily as being pornographic and unsuitable for war-time, etc., etc. The higher class papers, however, with the exception of 'The Star', have treated it very well indeed, and I expect that next week it will have reached a scale of 20,000 copies at least.

Some of the good reviews have said that it is decadent and cynical, and that it gives an entirely ruthless picture of heartless people in London. This is not so, and I particularly want you to note that the war has a good effect on the three principal characters, namely, Christine, Concepcion and G. J., all of whom do what they can. The book is emphatically not cynical. Nor does it portray heartless people, and I should like this to be insisted upon.

I have just taken charge of British Propaganda for France, so that I have rather more than I can do.

Affectionate regards to all of you,

Yours,

ARNOLD BENNETT

Arnold Bennett to Gregory Hill:

Comarques

30. 6. 18

I was glad to have your letter. I scarcely have any time nowadays to write private letters. I have been appointed Director of British Propaganda for France, and it is some job. I am Lord God (from London) over a bureau in Paris and over I don't know how many provincial committees in the said France. I only come home on Saturday evenings and I leave by the 8.20 train on Monday mornings. I thought my cup was full, and just now, lo! I am having a play produced! It is a satire on the Government (of which I am now the servant—unpaid), and will create some row—that is certain. I will have a copy of my new novel sent to you. It is supposed to be highly daring and obscene; and prosecutions have been threatened. (It isn't really obscene.) We have had 2 gardeners killed in the war, and now the head gardener (aged 45) is being called up. As the whole place rests on him, and he is thoroughly capable and trustworthy, I don't know what will happen.

Everybody I have seen from the Front speaks in the *very highest* terms of the American soldiers. So the prospects are good. But Paris is very much shaken up.

As a member of the Writers' Group, started in the Reform Club to give expression to Liberal views on the war and still more on the peace to follow, and of the not less exclusive Other Club with its small membership elected primarily on social qualifications, Arnold Bennett's circle of acquaintance and friendship was significantly widened. The Writers' Group had in it J. A. Spender, Sir George Paish, Lowes Dickinson, A. G. Gardiner, Gilbert Murray, J. A. Hobson, Hartley Withers, Graham Wallas, Leonard Hobhouse, a considerable concentration of intellectual force, and it was able to command the attention, and the presence, of eminent political leaders of the time—Smuts, Asquith, Grey, among them. "I made the acquaintance of Smuts," Bennett wrote. "He has a peculiar accent (foreign) and puts his hand on your knee constantly while talking to you. A man of principles and a fine man; but I doubt if he is the great man some of us thought. I think rather less of Smuts' fundamental brain-power than I did before."

The Writers' Group entertained Asquith at the Reform and there was a very good dinner and plenty of various wines. Twelve people. Asquith looked very well. He came in a smoking jacket and a good soft silk shirt, but his overcoat and soft hat were ridiculous. Only Spender of the hosts was in evening dress. Asquith ate and drank and laughed well. He has a good 'contained' laugh at implications. He showed no signs of decay. He was surrounded by first-class men, some very first-class, but easily held his place as chief man.

The Other Club had been started by F. E. Smith, later Lord Birkenhead, and some of his friends, one of them Winston Churchill, as a strictly private, almost secret, rival of Grillon's, for a long time London's most exclusive dining club. The Other Club held its dinners at the Savoy Hotel and Arnold Bennett was elected without his knowledge. "Thus will my relations with the Reform Club-detested Beaverbrook be tightened! Gardiner is already alarmed." At the first dinner he attended: "I sat next to F. E. Smith, who is a lively companion, inclined to recount his achievements, but interesting and informed.

Duke of Marlborough in the chair. Lutyens amiably played the amusing fool."

The dining-and-wining was not always so sumptuous as the companionship and talk. The napery and silvery gleamed as of old; for the rest, food shortages were increasing. "It was strange not be able to get butter at the Carlton. Sugar in tiny gummed packets." For the 'Comarques' week-ends he had instituted a no-bread-at-table rule; if a guest wanted bread he had to get up and go to the sideboard for it: "Wells gave me this tip." Austerity was manifesting itself in other ways. Calling on Lord Beaverbrook, who was ill in bed at the Hyde Park Hotel, he noted: "B——'s pyjamas second-rate."

Arnold Bennett to Mrs. Herzog:

Comarques

7 September, 1918

DEAR FRIEND,—I have been intending for about three months to thank you for what you did about Ben Nicholson. That young man's mother died rather suddenly not long since. She had Spanish influenza and did not recover from it. She smoked a cigarette and went away. She was a good painter, and a good friend of mine and of many other people—chiefly of her husband's. I have been too busy and important to write. Also ill, as a result. Having lived on the edge of a collapse for 3 weeks, I am now going on a holiday. In my Ministry I have led a bureaucratic life and acquired the most marvellous material for a book. I don't reckon I have done anything but establish order. Nevertheless, I hear that I am about to be promoted to a still higher grade of autocratic departmentalism. The fact is, my Minister adores me.

I may inform you that 'The Roll Call' is a much better book than 'The Pretty Lady'. The latter is too brilliant. No really first-class book is ever glittering. With regard to verse, I am going to acquire and run a quarterly started by one Frank Rutter, 'Art & Letters'. He cannot keep it up. You have an American poet, T. S. Eliot. I was so struck by his work that I made his acquaintance. He came to see me, and I was well content.

I should like to see some of the women's war-work done in New York and Chicago. There is a vast amount of genuine work done in England, but the female artistic snobs are terrible here. I mean to be still more sarcastic about them later on. They are at every function. I was at the first night of the Russian ballet. They were all there; I knew they would be; headed by Lady Cunard. Yet I believe they believe they are seriously helping the war along. I doubt if any of them do any surgical dressing.

I was rather startled by the reception given to certain articles of mine that (without my knowledge or consent) were cabled over to the 'N. Y. Times'. Comment by me would be inept. I thought of writing to Lane Allen to reason with him about his inelegant protest and to tell him that in England we have nothing to learn from any part of the earth about the business of sticking-to-it. But I refrained.

Yours sincerely, .
ARNOLD BENNETT

(8)

4 October, 1918.—. . . I found myself appointed at the M. of I. to the post of Director of Propaganda (vice Sir R. Jones), together with general supervision and co-ordination of all departments of the Ministry, i.e. Deputy Minister. This is the most marvellous, disconcerting, and romantic thing that ever happened to me. At any rate, whatever happens, I, an artist, shall have had the experience. It would be enormous fun except for the responsibility—and the 3 a.m. worryings.

Looking more ministerial than the Minister, he was intensely absorbed in what he now had to do and more troubled by it than he showed, as he sat grandly at his desk initialling minutes, drafting directives, reading and writing reports. None the less, he made himself keep up his private correspondence with old friends and found time to embark on the long exchange of weekly letters with the young nephew, "easily the most Bennetty Bennett that I have struck," whom he had adopted and was having educated at Oundle. Describing his duties as jauntily as he could, he told the young Richard: "The organisation is vast. I am the head of it." To his friend Squire, then literary editor of the *New Statesman*, he wrote: "You will understand that the work is terrific. I mind that less than I mind the responsibility. Of course, I am not cut out for the job by nature at all. I can only keep my head. It is my fatal gift for inspiring confidence and never saying anything that lands me in these messes."

He believed that he had "set in motion a great thing" in arranging that the King should be present at a service in Westminster Abbey commemorating the war sacrifices of France: "a great thing to my credit." It did not prove to be so. "I was misled. I took things for granted, made mistakes on them, and the whole affair had to be cancelled. Religion was at the bottom of the trouble."

When Lord Beaverbrook announced that he was resigning as Minister, Arnold Bennett was alarmed by the thought of being fully and finally responsible and, battling with his speech infirmity, said that he too must resign. Dissuaded from this nervous reaction, and confirmed by the Government in his new estate, he went to see Lord Beaverbrook.

He was in bed, bandaged, depressed, having been told by the doctor in the morning that he had septic poisoning. When Lady B. and Needham had left the room, he began to smoke and to talk intimately, and said: 'You know, Arnold, my life has been all crises. I was worth five millions when I was twenty-seven. And now this is a new crisis, and it's the worst.' However, he cheered up. Bonar Law came in and was very courteous and cautious to me. He said his sister had been a very great and constant admirer of mine, but since 'The Pretty Lady' she had done with me.

To help him with propaganda in France Bennett appointed a brilliant linguist of the Five Towns, W. S. Hawley, who spoke every European language, including Russian. Hawley was an admirer of Bennett's character as well as of his work. "You know, 'A.B.' is a *good* chap," he told a Potteries bank manager, T. B. Roberts. "When the French were belittling our war effort, he set about them, good and proper. He sent to us in Paris a great number, thousands, of small booklets setting out British war achievements, letting the facts speak. The French confiscated the lot: they wouldn't face having the truth known. We told 'A.B.' He immediately got in touch with Lloyd George. Lloyd George gave way to the French and 'A.B.' never forgave him. If the armistice had not been imminent, he would have resigned."

The Armistice became the prime possibility and topic almost overnight. One of Bennett's ministerial projects, worked out with the Foreign Office, was to procure ideas about peace terms from leading writers whose views had weight. Ford Madox Ford was one of the authors consulted. His never thoroughly reliable temper, probably exacerbated by the embarrassments of his German ancestry, soon showed signs of introducing heat into the discussion. Bennett reached for the telephone and, asking for Sir William Tyrrell (later Lord Tyrrell, British Ambassador in Paris) at the Foreign Office, handed Ford the receiver when Tyrrell came through. And it was Tyrrell who had to stand the explosive violence that Ford could no longer restrain, Bennett sitting blandly at his desk with the half-smile that always indicated his appreciation of his own cleverness.

Arnold Bennett to Gregory Hill:

Ministry of Information
Norfolk Street
Strand, London, WC.

MY DEAR GREGORY,   7.11.18
I don't think your commission business has the slightest importance now. The war will almost certainly be over within a week. You needn't trouble about Germany not accepting the Armistice terms. If she doesn't accept instantly (but I feel sure she will) she will accept even worse terms after a short time. So many people seem incapable of believing that Germany can be humiliated at this point. But why not? When you are beaten you are beaten. She will lick the dust (and the boots) . . . I am now the head of this Ministry and have command over Generals, Colonels, Majors, M.P.s, Bank directors, Railway directors, millionaires, baronets, peers, and I don't know what. It is a highly responsible position but a great lark—especially giving orders to generals, as you will appreciate. In spite of the greatness of the lark my own idea is to chuck it, and get back to my own work.

Best wishes for your recovery and for your return speedily to civil life. And I do hope bank clerks will form a Union and get decent treatment for themselves at last.

Yours,
ARNOLD BENNETT

CHAPTER FIFTEEN

(1)

IN less than a week after Armistice Day, Arnold Bennett's brief and hectic period of service at the Ministry of Information was summarily terminated. "The behaviour of the Cabinet to me was scandalous. But they treated many others scandalously, so I was not surprised. The only notice I got was a roneo'd copy of the War Cabinet minute. I was never consulted in any way." He blamed John Buchan: "He had undeniably gone behind my back. Pure chicane." Bennett had given his war services free and he was careful to make a note of the fact that he had paid more than £10,000 in income tax during the war years, which may have had rather less relevancy than he seems to have supposed. His mood quickly veered away from the rejoicings of the hour: "Inexpressible melancholy of London." And the neuralgia comes back violently: "So acute I had to burn my face with eau de Cologne: great state of exasperation and fatigue."

These reactions strike a discordant note in the prevailing atmosphere of relief, which he nowhere hints that he shares. Describing his experiences on the great day itself, when he was sucked into the swirling human vortex of Piccadilly, he shows no sign of identifying himself with the popular emotion, but chooses to give utterance instead to thoughts of lonely soldiers in the crowd: "No one to talk to. But fear of death lifted from them."

In spite of the weight of his responsibilities, the 3 a.m. worryings, he had enjoyed his first and only experience of the corporate life and especially the authority with which it had invested him. It had been exhilarating, this overlordship of a Department of State which commanded the allegiance of personages of spectacular military and political position. "Considering that he"—C. F. G. Masterman—"had been a Cabinet Minister early in the war, and that I, politically a nobody, was now his superior, he behaved excellently in an extremely trying situation. So did I."

War Cabinet peremptoriness at such an overwhelming moment in history can hardly have been a matter for intense personal intolerance.

Some of Arnold Bennett's friends had the idea that his play, *The Title*, had done him harm in Government circles, that sly representations had been made about it to influential persons. The play had been put on that summer at the Royalty Theatre, London, its theme the brokerage market in titles, its moral that where Governments are concerned honours are not invariably honourable. Information given him by Spender had supplied the gist of the play, which had two hundred and eighty-five performances in London and was not successful in the provinces and a failure in New York, where its production probably surprised its author as much as it did the critics.

Whether or not his friends' suspicions were warranted, he was sounded at the end of 1918 about his willingness to accept the honour of knighthood in the new Order of the British Empire instituted by King George V. His reply was that he did not wish to be rewarded for any war work he had done but that he would be found not unappreciative of some recognition of his services to literature, and one of his closest associates at that time believed that he had hopes of the Order of Merit. But his place in literature had not attained the monolithic dignity of Hardy's, for example, and the pre-eminent civil distinction was not for him. When the suggestion of a knighthood was renewed a little later, he retorted: "Give it to Harry Lauder!" The rest was silence.

Arnold Bennett to Miss Lillah McCarthy (Lady Keeble):

                                        Yacht Marie Marguerite

MY SWEET LILLAH,   13 July, 1922
    At first I thought I would like to write to Freddie [Sir Frederick Keeble] and congratulate him on his title, and then I thought I wouldn't, and then I thought I would, and so on. You see: I wrote 'The Title'. Awkward position. But it does me good to see a *decent* title for once. After all, it isn't he who ought to be congratulated but the order of knights bachelor. So I'm damned if I will congratulate him.

                                        Ever yours,
                                                A. B.

    Shortly after the war had ended, he was in correspondence with the College of Arms about the possibility of a grant of arms to him. An old friend, an artist, Percy Jowitt, made an armorial design which included crossed pens, with the motto 'Strive For Perfection'. The correspondence, which was conducted on the official side by Norroy King of Arms, appears to have come to a close with an estimate of the preliminary fees, £76.

Offsetting his resentments against the War Cabinet of 1918, Bennett had profited more by his experience of the Civil Service, permanent and otherwise, than he admitted. He could hardly have written his much talked-of political novel *Lord Raingo* without it and particularly without the opportunities it gave him of being able to call on Lord Beaverbrook's guidance. The journal contains detailed notes for the novel supplied by Beaverbrook, who also gave him a scheme for another novel based on the closing years of his, Lord Beaverbrook's, father, a Nonconformist minister. "Max's description of his father's last years was absolutely brilliant, showing how his own great worldly success had brought about an almost startling change in the old man's ideas and tastes. Its possibilities excited me," and so did those of an account which Lord Beaverbrook gave him of collusion between the parties to a divorce case: "he gave me material for a fine, grim, ruthless novel on the subject."

Arnold Bennett to Hugh Walpole:

> 12b George Street,
> Hanover Square,
> W. 1.
>
> 12. 12. 19

MY DEAR HUGHIE,—. . . I don't know what you think of plutocratic society in N.Y. I couldn't stick it. I have just been to Cambridge to stay with W. H. R. Rivers, ethnologist and psycho-analyst. This fellow is one of *the* most interesting. And, your bent being what it is, he would certainly interest you. You will have to meet him.

The war picture show at the Royal Academy is opening today. This show would have been a reactionary mass of R. A. and A. R. A. work but for Beaverbrook having the wit to leave the commissioning of pictures for the Ministry of Information to Masterman and me. (Ours are the only names that haven't been mentioned in connection with it.) It is a truly great show and is having a terrific press. I have been ill and am well. Marguerite is very well. She is just now flaunting over London a fur cloak whose existence in her wardrobe

Picture Post

ARNOLD BENNETT IN 1918

WITH MISS LILLAH McCARTHY (LADY KEEBLE)

is due to the cardinal fact that I must either earn money or spend it. At present I am not earning it. George Moore's 'Avowals' is highly agreeable.

Our love,
A. B.

(2)

His letters to and from Pinker were much concerned in those post-war years with the theatre and the success he hoped to repeat there and never did. He had received a lot of money from *Milestones* and *The Great Adventure*, more than from all the novels and the other plays put together; disquieting thought. The handsome three-figure royalty cheques arriving promptly week after week over several years as the reward for the labours of only a month or two made the exhaustions of novel-writing, for instance, seem quite out of proportion and article-writing insignificant, creating dissatisfactions which in future would intensify the exhaustions. Like many of his generation he felt older by more than the four years of war and there was no assurance of financial security, or of rest from labour, ahead of him. Another resounding play success would bring at any rate relief from the strain of continuous mental concoction, the tiring constant application of his nervous force to the working out of subjects, themes, and plots, in order to provide for his heavy running costs. Sturt wrote to him, "with fingers benumbed by paralysis," that he had read 'a par' in a newspaper to the effect that "you had been twice called on to the stage as author, etc. This may have been a bit of an ordeal for you; yet I should like to believe it also points to that capture of the West End theatre world you have resolved on. . . ."

He took out of a drawer the *Don Juan* play he had written before the war. Matheson Lang liked it but they could not come to an under-standing about finance and scenic design. He had contracted to write four plays for four different managements: the lure of the big weekly cheques was drawing him into a new series of future commitments which would prey mercilessly on his energies and assist in inducing the weary-Titan look which the bus-top posters advertised so lavishly to London's not particularly sympathetic millions. His attitude to the dramatist's art was almost casual, contrasting with his highest artistic canon as a novelist: "I would sooner write two plays than a novel; the technique is crude; the emotional strain lower." When a play of his

[281]

was in production he saw to it that the players should have no doubt about what he expected of them. His play *Judith* was produced at Eastbourne in April, 1919. He wrote to Miss Lillah McCarthy, who was playing the leading role: "I hate to praise star-actresses. They get too much praise as a rule, especially when they are beautiful. I must, however, say that your performance wholly, entirely, completely, and rather more than completely, fulfils my expectations. It is a very great and very finished performance. Don't go and tinker with it. Let this be clearly understood henceforward between us."

He tried again and again to recapture box-office approbation, but there was relatively little response and sometimes almost none. He wrote *Don Juan*, *Judith*—"by Arnold Bennett, of all people," said the eminent *decor* artist, Charles Ricketts, while Bennett himself was noting that "the news that Hardy was enthusiastic about *Judith* gave me more satisfaction than anything that has happened to me for a long time"—*Sacred and Profane Love* (which had some success in the U.S.A.), *The Love Match*, *Body and Soul*, *The Bright Island*, *London Life*, *Mr. Prohack*, and financially it represented a great outpouring of largely unproductive effort. He was unusually frank, for an artist, in acknowledging his failures and not less frank in ascribing the responsibility for failure to himself. Along with the disappointments came the distractions of dealing with what he wrote down as "the unsatisfactory temperaments of the theatre", impresarios whose simple affirmatory 'yes' had many shades of meaning (much about this in the Pinker-Bennett correspondence), actors and actresses whose fatuous unreliability made him squirm with dismay. Behind the impeccably clear and business-like tone of his letters of inquiry and reply we seem to hear now and then a groan torn from the man of probity who feels that it is his fate to have to traffic with insincerity, equivocation, and worse. "You promised to let me have your decision on the play not later than Thursday last. I do not complain at your being unable to decide. I do complain at your discourtesy in not letting me know that you had not decided. A postcard would have sufficed to relieve me of the conviction, to which I must now adhere, that you have no use for ordinary good manners." Again, when another promise has not been kept: "I am always being treated like this by people of the theatre. I really don't know why," and to Pinker, of a certain well-known stage manager: "He is a rogue, but an engaging rogue, by which I do not mean that you should let him crawl out from under our bargain. But give him a chance to state his case." Or: "He's a very decent chap. I like him.

[282]

I suggest we don't worry the life out of him for the present, whatever we may decide to do later." And writing of the ways of theatre people to Frank Swinnerton, he declares that "they are all children".

Arnold Bennett to Hugh Walpole:

> 12b George Street
> Hanover Square, W. 1.
>
> 23. 3. 20

MY SWEET HUGHIE,—You must be very strong to withstand all your journeyings, lecturings, and laudations. It is about time you came back among your frank friends who ill-treat and despitefully use you. Your judgment on U.S.A., although damnably true, is not the whole truth, and is in my opinion rather severe. But, by heaven, I know how you feel. This flat is now furnished and quite the resort of the beau monde. After enormous idleness I am working again. A fantastic play. In the year 1919 I managed to collect 2 theatrical failures. But I am somewhat compensated by the apparent success of 'Sacred and Profane Love' in the U.S.A., that benighted country. The receipts so far immensely surpass those of any other play that I ever had anything to do with. But I made a fatal error with the film rights. I sold them for £1,500, just half what I could have got. . . .

Son, I have got an idea for a novel (which I shall write in 1921) that bangs any idea I've had for many years. Believe me! I'm dying to write it. But no. It shall ripen.

In the critical world the Swinnerton camp is gradually triumphing over the Squire camp. Swinnerton and ilk flourish exceedingly. Squire is very depressed and dull. I am having great larks with Massingham and Murry in 'The Nation'. Massingham is spending Easter with us at Comarques. Marguerite is off to France just before Easter. This woman with whom I live is now placidly sewing by my side. A touching Sunday night picture of the life literary. She says you must marry a young widow. Do—with money. It would be the greatest fun.

> Benedicite.
> Ever yours,
> A. B.

He would like Belasco of New York to do one of the plays. Pinker: "I should warn you that it is a case of Belasco first and last and all the time and of the author having to look out for himself." Bennett likes the idea of John Barrymore doing his *Don Juan*, "but there is the accent problem." Pinker: "Yes, and the temperament problem too." Barrymore said he would do the play. A producer was found; all was arranged. Bennett's hopes were reasonably high. At the very last moment Barrymore would not sign and went off to do something quite different in the theatre, leaving lamentations to be exchanged between Pinker and Bennett and Doran, who had roused Barrymore's interest in the first place.

Doris Keane buys an option on a play which he writes specially for her but does not take it up and pays the forfeit. Lord Lathom, the amateur London manager, does the same. Pinker collected option money from Dennis Eadie, Norman McKinnel, Marie Tempest, Arthur Bourchier, Basil Dean, a satisfaction with an insipid flavour.

Comarques

My dear Pinker,   August 30, 1920

I have had Gilbert Miller here for the week-end. As a matter of fact, I invited him in order to find out more about how things stand in the West End, and also to become more intimate with him for my own purposes. . . . I certainly think him a man to know. He appears to me to be more cultivated and to have more initiative and a better conception of business than any other manager. But of course he has a very clear notion of his own importance.

Yours sincerely,
Arnold Bennett

Stratagems of this kind were to have no marked effect on his theatre fortunes, to which Shaw had attempted to apply the corrective of his experience and insight when Arnold Bennett's play *The Bright Island* was produced by the Stage Society in 1925: "the worst Press any play of mine ever had," Bennett said. Shaw had read the play before seeing it on the stage and he had written to Bennett warning him that "humanity cannot stand one hundred and fifty minutes' unrelieved scoffing, no matter how witty it is. There must be refuges for the affection, the admiration, the detestation of the audience; or else you must fill the gaps with refuges for its concupiscence and ferocity, as the Restoration playwrights did, or enchant it with all the art of the opera

[284]

and the ballet. . . ." After the coldly received first production at the Aldwych Theatre, Shaw wrote to Bennett again:

. . . There are gleams and strivings in that play which seem to indicate destiny. But like all inveterate novelists you will not take the theatre seriously enough. And you will study the wrong models. You have nothing to learn from Scribe & Co., and everything to learn from Beethoven. A play should go like a symphony; its themes should be introduced emphatically at the beginning and then hit on the head again and again until they are red hot, the pace and intensity increasing to the end with every possible device of unexpected modulations and changes, and sudden pianissimos, as in the Prieslied and the finale of Mozart's Figaro. You never think of this, you depend on your confounded invention, and keep ladling in primitive matter right up to the end without ever working it up, so that the last fifteen minutes of your play are exactly like the first, and there is no reason why they should be the last rather than the first, or why you should not, like George Moore, go on like that for ever. A play must have a destination, even if it be to the bottom of an abyss, in which case the further it falls the faster it goes. Here endeth the first lesson.

There were the film companies, responding with ruthless indiscrimination to the post-war demand for entertainment: what were the chances, Arnold Bennett asked Pinker, of doing business with them? Pinker mentioned that he might be going to America "to explore the film outlook there". Bennett replied that it was a good idea and inquired in what may not have been an opportunistic postscript: "When do you expect to leave?" He disclosed, a trifle pompously, that he had been having "private talks" with Lasky, of Famous Players, "a rather dull, ignorant, and clever man", and hoped that Pinker would be able to bring them to a successful conclusion. He appears to have liked keeping something up his sleeve in his dealings with Pinker; it supplied the necessary stiffening to a relationship that must not be allowed to become flabby. For the time being there was no special interest in his works as film material, though Lasky told him that he would "undoubtedly do original work for the screen". Meanwhile, his old friend Eden Phillpotts was having a very great success in the theatre with *The Farmer's Wife*.

Discussing his play *Sacred and Profane Love*, Bennett wrote to Frank Swinnerton that "999 good plays out of 1000 are 'episodic'.

They cannot be anything else—unless they are practically in one scene like 'The Trojan Women' ". Most people continued to insist, he said, that his plays were not plays, but something else. "My aim is and always has been to widen the meaning of the word 'dramatic'. That is to say, I was determined to prove that the interest of an audience can be held by the presentation of material generally held to be undramatic." To his friend Frederick Lowndes of *The Times* he wrote: "I doubt whether I ever said to you: 'Any fool can write a play.' What I probably did say was: 'Any fool can write a first act'."

The nearest he came to the kind of success he now most coveted was when he stood in the wings of the Lyric, Hammersmith, and watched the first-night triumph of *The Beggars' Opera*, which ran at that theatre for three and a half years. There was a small personal satisfaction in it for him. As chairman of the board of the theatre, for which he had found the capital from some of his rich friends, he had successfully carried his colleagues in his belief that there was a new public for the piece, 'the book' of which he rearranged in two days. The nightly scenes of enthusiasm were managerially most uplifting, and proof, too, of the chairman's infallible judgment. But what the chairman knew in his heart was that there could be no pleasure for him in the theatre comparable to that of producing, by his own imaginative competence, the sudden marvellous hush of expectation that had come so thrillingly at the end of each interval in *Milestones*. And he was never to do that again.

Arnold Bennett to Hugh Walpole:

> 12b George Street,
> Hanover Square, W.
>
> 25. 3. 22.

MY DEAR HUGHIE,—. . . I have been passing through vast tribulations. My play 'The Love Match' is the greatest failure that ever was. The first-night audience received the last 2 acts in silence; the whole of the press without exception was frankly hostile, and the public is sedulously staying away. The loss being about £100 a night, the piece will be withdrawn at once. My previous record for shortness of run was 36 nights. This comes of writing modern, otherwise new-fangled plays consisting of realism delicately enveloped in wit. (The tragedy of course is that I am unteachable.) But I bet that one day that play will be revived. My previous record failure, 'What The Public Wants,' is about to be revived in New York—and with *éclat*.

[286]

Wells is back, and in the greatest form, and is occupying himself with Ireland. Messrs. Cassell have officially informed me that they are enthusiastic about my new novel, 'Lilian', but wish me to modify two sentences in it for serial use. The sentences are: (*a*) 'I am going to have a baby' and (2) 'I am seven months gone'.

It is a great world!

Thine,

A. B.

(3)

He had fancifully projected himself into the world of material splendour ever since as a Five Towns youth he had dawdled in the streets of Burslem on Saturday afternoons as the cheers of distant football crowds came over the roof-tops with the diminished week-end smoke. Now he had arrived in the world of his dreams and was spectacularly identified. with it, while never being wholly of it. "The spirit cannot soar until the millstones are lifted", says the armaments maker in *Major Barbara*, the millstones being obstacles that only money can remove. But money, as Shaw omits to tell us in the play, makes its own millstones and Arnold Bennett was feeling their weight. He was too wise, always, to live beyond his income and—unlike Balzac, whose extravagances fascinated him and from whom he had copied the conceits of gold fobs and a gold toothpick—he never did so; but to avoid that folly, he had to commit another, that of working beyond his means, of taxing his physical and mental capacity to the utmost and beyond. "$3\frac{1}{4}$hrs. last night. Exhausted". "Half dead with fatigue and nerve strain". "Great state of exhaustion". "No creative energy left. Insomnia worse": the journal of the post-war years is the casebook of a man who, having reached public eminence by his own powers, was straining them to their last limits in order to retain his hold on success and, above all, to make it finally assured.

The storm of life, of which he had reported the distant thunders two decades before, had threatened his future by severing him from his roots as a novelist and bringing about a recession of interest in his work from the consequences of which he could rescue himself only by superhuman and self-destructive efforts. Critical opinion had conceded the persistence of some of his higher virtues as a writer in the third Clayhanger book, *These Twain* (1916); almost none in the five novels which came after. Some of these novels sold well enough—*The Pretty Lady* passed the 50,000 mark—and serialisations in American magazines brought good results in cash; but it was becoming increasingly obvious to their author that the reviewing coteries were embodying hostile new-generation attitudes to him, as to his contemporaries, and were dismissing his later works as much inferior to those by which he had made his reputation. And an important voice had spoken out of America in the tone of a prophet of declining prestige and sales. "He is not completely forgotten, but it must be plain that Wells now stands above him in the popular estimation", was a Mencken pronunciamento of 1920.

Surveying that decade in his career, the years 1911 to 1921, *The Times* observed that while it had seen a marked waning of popular esteem for his work, it saw also his rise as a figure of the public scene. "If the war interrupted his development as a novelist, it certainly aided, through the contacts brought about by his propaganda work, his social progress."

Arnold Bennett's chin, taking the new critical blows, was fitting more rigidly back into his collar wings as he stepped gravely forth on his morning 'thinking walks' in London, in the course of which he was still liable to be pursued by long-haired youths on bicycles demanding his autograph or engaged in annoyingly intrusive conversations by strangers who recognised him from the cartoons. The 'thinking walk' had become, it seemed, a necessity of his existence and rarely a day passed, wet or fine, when he was in London in which he did not perform the dual exercise it represented. The habit of applied cerebration enabled him to keep his head above a rising sea of troubles until, finally exhausted, he lost his vaunted control of circumstances and the waves closed over him.

Arnold Bennett to Hugh Walpole:

> 12b George Street,
> Hanover Square, W. 1.
>
> 23. 1. 20.

MY DEAR HUGHIE,—There is no particular talk in this house except the slump in theatres and the general and increasing badness of 'The London Mercury'. I find the L.M. very dull and pompous. We dined at Osbert Sitwell's last night. Very good dinner and the most fantastic and hazardous service. Sickert was there. He is, I regret to say, becoming rather mannered, but his imitations of his old and

'COMARQUES', THORPE-LE-SOKEN, ESSEX

BENNETT IN THE COUNTRY, CARICATURED BY A FRIEND

intimate friend George Moore are still priceless. Wyndham Lewis was also there—in grey flannel. He left early—piqued, as some said, by remarks of Sickert. I am told that my comments on things and people in general had been outrageous. Nobody minded.

Osbert took us off later to Ottoline Morrell's. She has rented a house in Vale Avenue for six weeks. Many persons there, Middleton Murry, Gertler, Mrs. Aldous Huxley, the unavoidable Iris Tree (whom I cannot stick), etc. Ottoline looks younger. She is paler. Her hair is still more like a mop. She was very sweet and kind; but what a bore! It was like Osbert's effrontery to insist on taking us. He marched into Ottoline's at the head of his squad with much quiet and noble pride. . . .

Thine,

A. B.

(4)

He was living now in George Street, Hanover Square, London, a stone's throw from Bond Street, so that he was where a leading journalist required to be, near the most fertile sources of inspiration and information. In consequence he was seeing less of the country, while being glad enough to go there when the London pressures had tired him out. During the last months of the war he and his wife had lived separately in London, she in her own flat at 53 Oxford Street, he at the Royal Thames Yacht Club in Piccadilly. This was an affair of purely domestic convenience and they moved in together at the George Street maisonnette, 12b. But there were discords which were becoming penetrating enough to be a subject of comment and speculation by the Bennetts' friends. Marguerite Bennett was often alone and, what could be worse, left to apologise to others for her husband's absences. Mr. Ernest Thesiger has told in some reminiscences of his stage career how at a party given by one of London's better known hostesses he saw a woman guest "wearing a large crimson jockey cap adorned with marabout". He was told she was Arnold Bennett's wife and when he was introduced to her and felt free to ask her about the remarkable hat, she explained: "I wore it so that everyone in the room should say, 'Who on earth is that woman in the hat?' and they would be told, 'That's Mrs. Arnold Bennett'. 'You see,' she said, 'no one seems to know that there *is* a Mrs. Arnold Bennett'." [1]

[1] *Practically True* by Ernest Thesiger (Heinemann, 1927).

Arnold Bennett to Hugh Walpole:

12b George Street
Hanover Square, W. 1.

27. 10. 21.

MY DEAREST HUGHIE,—I have seen an envelope addressed in what I took to be your handwriting and to my wife. She is not here, and it has been sent on to her. I am only writing to you to guard against the risk of your having possibly invited her at the same time as myself. The very gravest trouble has arisen between her and me. She is not here, and she will not be here if I can possibly help it. I positively and solemnly desire you to say nothing about this affair, nor to hint at it even in the vaguest way, to anybody whatever at present. And I know that I can rely upon your perfect muteness.

My affections,

Thine, A. B.

The truth may have been that Bennett found domesticity tedious in contrast with the high-voltage friendships he was enjoying and forming, the glittering circle of new acquaintance of which he was often a centre of admiration, the brilliant night life, the dancing, the unending dinner parties, the gay talk, the persisting party mood and spirit of the early 1920s in London's West End. His sense of responsibility being at all times adult, this can hardly be the final explanation of his situation *vis-à-vis* his wife. Grievances of some magnitude had come between them. During a lunch at the Reform Club he had scribbled a note on the back of the menu and handed it in silence to his friend Raymond Needham, sitting opposite. It announced that he was leaving his wife and gave his reason for doing so.

Arnold Bennett to his sister, Mrs. Kennerley:

12b George Street
Hanover Square, W.

MY DEAR TERTIA,   23 Oct., 1921.

A great calamity has occurred in this household. I am obliged to arrange for a separation from Marguerite. . . . She has several times suggested a separation . . . and at last I was obliged to take advice, both legal and from friends. . . . Various persons have tried to make her see reason. No success. Even her own people have each written to her to protest and to warn her of the consequences. . . .

[290]

I am most acutely distressed by the fact that Marguerite is behaving with tragic idiocy and that nobody can stop her. Otherwise, if I thought she would be happier, I should be only too pleased at the change, though of course nothing can end my responsibility for her material welfare. (In this latter view my friends scarcely agree with me). I think I must come down tomorrow night after dinner.

Yours,

A.B.

The evidence of his letters and journal notes is that, above all, he was determined to be fair in the resultant transactions, as part of which, he told his sister, he bequeathed to his wife "3/4 of my goods and un-fettered use of £2000 a year." Thus, in another letter to his sister he takes care to cite other people's refutations of views he had expressed about his wife's conduct. "I am telling you this in justice to M., and because previously I had told you only my side of the case". And he adds: "I perceive that this change is an enormous relief to me," referring to the change in his domestic circumstances. Writing to his sister, Mrs. Kennerley, in 1929 he said that his wife had some time before "begged me to take her back, admitting that she was in the wrong". Mrs. Belloc Lowndes, who had known them both for a long time, ventured the role of mediator. Bennett thanked her and hoped in writing that she would continue her friendship for his wife as for himself. There was nothing anyone could do but be reasonable. It had been a slowly gathering crisis of infelicities.

A crisis that may in the last analysis have been implicit in Arnold Bennett's own emotional history.

(5)

The neuralgia struck him more frequently without its warning signal, a sudden fearsome stab, often under the right eye or at the temples, and spreading in a slow pervasive agony over one side of his face, trans-fixing his expression of the moment and giving him the witless look of a carnival mask. "Terrible neuralgia. Thousands of interesting things to note these last 12 days, but all drowned in neuralgia and no work of any kind done". And still more frequently: "Horrible neuralgia" and "great neuralgia". As a consequence, the days succeeding the attacks saw him indenting ever more deeply on his reserves of strength in order to catch up with work in arrears. The neuralgia was no longer amenable to his more-meat remedy and, having written somewhere that the man who is his own doctor has a fool for his patient, he was experimenting with the new drugs which the war-activated laboratories were producing for the relief of a generation whose nerve force, heavily drawn on by the four years' struggle, was being yet further depleted by the excesses that followed. The Billie Carleton drug sensation implicated the community if it did not indict the nation. In Arnold Bennett's case the drugs, though varied and numerous, were used as soporifics and pain-killers and in no habit-forming sense or for any morbid purpose. His maladies were an older institution in his life than the 'twentieth-century blues'.

The insomnia ravages were now becoming more serious. He was making cups of tea for himself through most nights, his only true sleep often being an hour's neurasthenic oblivion when the rest of the world was getting up. Mrs. Somerset Maugham "knew of some tablets". Sir Nigel Playfair suggested soda-water drinking. Sir Harry Preston proposed taking him to a masseuse and, another time, to a gymnasium where he could "discover the sleep-inducing virtues of a really heavy sweat". Sir Eric Maclagan wondered "if coffee was the enemy". An unnamed and possibly perspicacious Reform Club member advised him "to lay off dancing". Lord Castlerosse invited him to the ancestral estates at Killarney, "where he said there would be nothing to keep me awake". Another friend persuaded him to embark on a long course of electrical treatments which at first raised his hopes considerably, only to dash them in the end. "I am now preoccupied all the time with the insomnia question," he wrote, November 26, 1928.

The doctors, taking their soundings and assuring him with brisk professional *bonhomie* that he was a fit man for his years, could find no organic disease or deterioration, which leaves us with the psychosomatic inferences already drawn, the invasion of the physical domain by inimical energies generated elsewhere. The frontiers of the conflict that had dynamically worked for his undoing were being extended. "I have been out for idea-collecting walks and in each case returned with a headache due to physical fatigue . . . proof of a thoroughly rotten condition," and the journal is not the confessional of a hypochondriac. "Health," he observed there in his last years, "is a very strange thing," so strange that he received "a most satisfying medical report" on himself and two days afterwards was recording the onset of "very heavy rheumatism".

He kept his distresses to himself. Proud of the triumph of his will "over pain and pessimism," he made no bid for sympathy in his letters to friends, making one of his rare references to his physical vulnerability in writing to Mrs. H. G. Wells, who had been taken suddenly ill:

DEAR LADY JANE,   8. 12. 20.

The whole Jane world (extensive, orbicular) has been shaken to its depths by this affair of yours. Happily it now has reason to recover, and is recovering, and I am once more getting the limelight. Before your unhappy appearance in the pathological theatre I was attracting a certain amount of attention by means of pyorrhea, high frequency electrical treatment, microbic injections, dentists, specialists, etc. But you wiped me off the map in one day. However, I think I can beat you in permanence of sickliness and I am doubly glad of it.

I saw H. G. last night. Dr. Shufflebotham, who was there, predicted he would have to stay at home today, and lo! it is so. He is immensely proud of the fact that he can make out cheques and pay bills without your help. In fact the entire club is much bored by his interminable recitals of feats in the cheque and payment line. You will have a horrible skein to unravel when you return to management.

We went to Edith Sitwell's reception last night. Crowds of poets, many of whom sat on the floor. Still not tedious. The St. John Ervines were my standby. At least, *she* was. We are just beginning to know them.

This last week you have doubtless felt within you a peculiar but enheartening *in*fluence. You didn't know it, but it was the *aff*luence of my blessing.

Yours ever,

A. B.

(6)

The separation from his wife having been legally accomplished, he put 'Comarques' up for sale: "a weight off my mind," He seems to have been in the grip of an urge to rearrange his existence, perhaps no more than the common symptom of middle age, perhaps because he felt there was danger in continuing to flout the fastidiousness imposed on him by his propitiatory drives. He had rid himself of the domestic issue, though it was to produce alarms and anxieties for him from time to time in the future. He was reviewing his responsibility for the nephew whom he had adopted: "I am greatly preoccupied with the Richard question. Though still damnably 5-Towny, he is all right. But to manage him

[293]

without a home base is rather on the difficult side," and he wondered whether the adoption had been wise.

The desire "to get things straight", expressing itself in the small obsessional regularities of habit such as always folding a newspaper carefully after reading it and insisting on his extra-long fountain pen being placed in strict alignment with the blotter on his desk, as well as in the larger demands of his hag-ridden conscience, was blocked by what he conceived to be the professional necessity of knowing 'everybody' and of being known. It meant more inward conflict, more psychic peril. The journal pages of the last year of the war and of the years that followed contain numerous 'names' that had not figured there before. He was 'in the swim' and the tide would carry him on to destruction. Mr. Maugham said that social success ruined Arnold Bennett by cutting him off from the original and only sources of his inspiration: "He never knew anything intimately but the life of the Five Towns . . . and it was only when he dealt with them that his work had character. When success brought him into the society of literary people, rich men and smart women, and he sought to deal with them, what he wrote was worthless." [1]

That cannot be passed as quite fair comment. It ignores some highly regarded examples of the art of the short story. It ignores *Imperial Palace*, which is not a worthless novel, if it is not a great one. The war had lessened Arnold Bennett's reputation as a novelist and enhanced his reputation as a journalist. He had found that he could not be creative in war-time, just as had many other artists the world over; also that country life did not supply the imaginative incentives without which he could not do his best work. As a conscious artist, he required the stimulus of great achievement in the arts, as we have seen, and in these latter years he had recourse to it with the pathetic eagerness of an addict turning to the drug that has been denied him. "To the Courtauld-Sargent concert. Lots of friends there. Concertos of Beethoven, Mozart, and Brahms. All terrific. All sublimely played by Arthur Schnabel . . . my creative mood has been considerably exalted and improved." At other concerts he experienced "unique sensations", "ideas much uplifted", "a desire to rewrite whole chapters". He was drawn often to Westminster Cathedral for the secular purpose of "meditating creatively" and some of the chapters of *Imperial Palace* were thought out there. The Elgin Marbles at the British Museum were another source of refreshment and renewal. At the Victoria and Albert Museum,

[1] *The Summing Up.*

[294]

"sat among the Constable sketches, where I got one or two notions." Hearing a gramophone record of *The Twilight of the Gods*, "I had a mood for really lifting up the love scene between Harriet and Luke in 'The Vanguard'." After seeing the Blake drawings at the Tate Gallery: "What terrific stuff. These in their largeness and simplifications are quite as good on inspection as any for the novelist who is trying to move on a high plane." At the National Gallery, "I looked for twenty minutes at the 'Coronation of the Virgin' by Orcagna, and the ditto by Gaddi. Also 'The Immaculate Conception' by Cuvelli. All these pictures are more interesting to me than the Ansidei Madonna of Raphael. They lifted up the plane of my thought of my play." He said that he received "an immense lift" from an exhibition of sculpture in Bond Street, and after seeing an exhibition of paintings at Burlington House he was aware of "fine new impulses" to finish work in hand. It was as if he regarded the Pierian spring as a British spa, a utilitarian view which the Muses may have resented: he drank deeply at it while writing his last novel, *Dream of Destiny*, which they did not allow him to finish.

Trapped in a web of complicated circumstances from which there may have been no escape except into illness, he assumed the bland impregnable air of a favourite of fortune. With gladiatorial disdain, he refused to show his hurts while being forced by public attention to acknowledge that he suffered them, that his marriage had broken down, that a novel had been ill-received, that a play had failed. His income had fallen in the last war year and remained at about £8,000 for the next two or three years, when it rose sharply again to the £20,000 mark. But his expenses were no less and taxation was more, so much more that he considered the feasibility of forming a holding company in Guernsey to take over his literary properties, which Pinker valued "at from eighteen to twenty thousand pounds". Writing to a friend who he hoped would agree to join the board of this enterprise, Bennett said that it would "help to cripple the wastefulness of the British Government to the extent of the bulk of my income tax and super-tax." He was giving money away freely and not in every instance to friends. He gave away large amounts over the years, to individuals rather than to causes. He was not well insured. His investment experience was one of profit and loss, with the depression of 1929–31 putting him heavily "in the red", so far as that class of transaction was concerned. Everyone thought him a rich man, whereas for several years his capital was represented by the Essex property, which he sold at a loss, and his yacht, which he had bought, he said, "just to show these rich chaps that a writer can make money too."

Webster, his Treasury friend of the early London days, died with shattering suddenness and a link with Bennett's past was snapped. Only a few weeks afterwards Rickards died, and a still greater tumult of quickened memories and sentiments had to be brought under control. Bennett had commented tartly in the journal on what he had thought to be Rickards's laggard response to the call of duty in the war. Now he felt that it was Rickards's war service that had killed him. "Glimpses, through Rickards, into a vast world of sickness and tragedy —a whole word, complete in itself, and looking on angrily and resentfully and longingly at our world." He was deeply moved by one of his several visits to Rickards in hospital, during which time he had been trying to manage the patient's tangled finances: "a dreadful nuisance to me for fifteen months past." He had asked Rickards if there was anything he wanted. The dying man, gazing up at him with burning eyes, had cried to him out of the torturing fever of tubercular meningitis: "Yes, I want the world!"

Only a little time before he had had to write a letter which caused him considerable private pain, marking the close of a friendship which had given him much pleasure over the previous eight or nine years.

Arnold Bennett to Paul M. Herzog:

8. 3. 19

MY DEAR HERZOG,—What am I to say to you? And what are the feelings of your young son? Professional users of words have a special duty of decency to say little on these occasions. I am very sorry. The news was a great shock to me. You and your boy have all my sympathies. I should like to hear something from you, if you feel inclined to write. It was touching of her to remember that I wear a fob, and I am glad to have the memento.

Always yours sincerely,
ARNOLD BENNETT

Then Pinker died with tragic unexpectedness during a business visit to New York, succumbing to pneumonia after an attack of influenza. Shortly before sailing he had made a sentimental gesture when Bennett had inquired about the rights in *The Truth about an Author*. "I own the copyright and if you would accept it from me as token of affection I should be very pleased." Arnold Bennett in reply: ". . . the monetary

[296]

value of this gift is not negligible, but as you will guess there is something in the affair which I appreciate infinitely more than the monetary value."

With remarkably few lapses in twenty years they had written letters to each other almost every day in a succession of transactions, large and small. Though Wells objected to the intervention of literary agents as "an irritating poisonous flow of business activity", theirs was a correspondence distinguished by integrity and great civility. More than once Pinker was impelled by admiration for Bennett's practical good sense to thank him for helping to make difficult negotiations less difficult. "It is so rare to find an author willing to back one's efforts as you have always done." Constrained to break through the basic formality of their long relationship, Pinker occasionally ventured to begin a letter: "My dear Arnol'," apparently recalling a speech habit of Marguerite Bennett's when addressing her husband, and to sign himself "Yours ever". It never worked: Bennett persisted in "My dear Pinker" and "Yours sincerely" to the end.

The summary dissolution of their association had more than emotional significance for Bennett. Running low in ready funds, he had arranged with Pinker, just before the latter sailed to New York, to borrow £1,000 on the old terms against money due from the United States. "It does not matter now," he wrote disarmingly to Eric Pinker, who had taken charge of the agency on his father's death. "It was not really important"; but he could not keep up the pose of self-sufficiency more than a few weeks, when he wrote again: "It seems to me that there is a considerable sum owing to me for articles from *The Strand Magazine* and the *Cosmopolitan*. I should like some pretty soon. Otherwise I cannot carry on for long."

Time's attrition was at work on another of his friendships. "I can scarcely move across the room now," Sturt wrote to tell him. "Can't wash or dress myself and an hour's chatter reduces me to mumbling. But I giggle a good deal; keep cheerful; and enjoy life intensely."

(7)

Following *These Twain*, the last of his Five Towns books, published in 1916, he had written *The Lion's Share*, *The Pretty Lady*, *The Roll Call*, *Lilian* and *Mr. Prohack*, a series of rent-paying novels which increased his fame and diminished his reputation: critical opinion was frequently disrespectful, though the 'dreary-in-extreme' verdict of a

[297]

later critic[1] is something less than just. He himself thought well of *The Pretty Lady*, and hidden away among the technical details of the yachting diary which he was contriving to keep in addition to the journal of his everyday life there is his opinion of *The Roll Call*, the novel in which he said he had brought the Five Towns to London.

27 September, 1921.—Off the Maplins. I finished reading 'The Roll Call'. I could find less fault with this book than with any of mine that I have re-read. In fact I thought highly of it. It certainly seemed to me to be the most accomplished. And the race-course chapter and all the second part impressed me as being genuinely the goods. As for the writing—well, of course, it is nothing like equal to George Moore's, but I don't see any other novelists now doing anything so consistently sound. Reading this book gave me plenty of inspiration for beginning my next one. I only hope I shall think as well of 'Mr. Prohack' when I re-read him in a few years' time. You get a better view of your own work after a considerable interval for two reasons. First, you only see what is actually on the paper and therefore don't rate it too high by imagining that what was in your head is on the paper—reading into it all sorts of things that really aren't there. Second, your appreciation of what actually *is* there is not spoiled by comparing it with what you had intended the book to be. You have forgotten your intentions and hopes, and the actual achievement unaffected by odious comparisons is in front of you. Whatever it ought to have been and was intended to be, 'The Roll Call' is a pretty fair thing as it stands.

In the early post-war years he was constantly afloat through several yachting seasons and he wrote the novel, *Lilian*, entirely at sea in *Amaryllis*, the yacht of his friend Herbert Sullivan, nephew of Sir Arthur Sullivan of the great Savoy partnership. In his own *Marie Marguerite* he had a specially fitted desk at which he was able to write in bad weather. "*August 4, 1923. The Downs.*—We rolled like the devil. Seventeen ships sheltering. Gale from the west. I did 1700 words," at which his friend, A. E. W. Mason, himself a keen and experienced yachtsman, greatly marvelled. Arnold Bennett's yachting engrossed him to a point at which he could say that he enjoyed every minute, "even when lying sleepless at night."

Reading his yachting diaries, mostly written at sea and perpetuating,

[1] Walter Allen: *Arnold Bennett* ("The English Novelists").

remarkably, the handwriting virtuosity he had patiently evolved, it is clear that there was little mental or social rest for him in this supreme hobby and recreation to which he had long and eagerly aspired. When the ship was dressed for a commemorative occasion, the owner communed with himself at his desk on the subject of yachting as a pastime:

Brightlingsea.—I was thinking about the sociological side of dressing the ship. This job took the captain and the mate, two highly skilled men, one and a half hours. I don't see how it could be justified economically. It can't. But all important yachting would be similarly unjustifiable. Yet what a real calamity it would be if these magnificent objects called yachts were put out of action! It would be a retrogression of civilisation. Still, I often ask why I allow myself to keep eight men, and very good men, solely to extend my personality and serve my pleasure.

Yachting brought him respite, not remedies. At sea off Ryde with Sir Chartres Biron, "the destroyer of Bottomley", as Bennett liked to call that well-known Bow Street magistrate: "These eight days have been severely disfigured for me by a continuous and generally acute neuralgia, night and day. I am taking Phosferine for it": at its climax the attack becomes "simply fantastic". Off Ostend: "Too much insomnia to write even brief notes in a journal. The worst insomnia I have had for a number of years." He now slept seldom more than $4\frac{1}{2}$–5 hours a night and wrote that "during the hours awake in bed I am too lacking in energy to read or consecutively to think". His yachting diary shows that at a time when he was least fitted to do so he was seriously overtaxing his imagination, with disturbing consequences:

Southend.—Considerable melancholy owing to my too vivid conception of a minor character for my next novel [*Lilian*], a jealous and melancholy woman who longs ardently and ingenuously for 'the peace of the grave', thinking of lying there quiet, everlastingly quiet, years of unconsciousness; goes to sleep with a sigh of eager anticipation and wakes up with a sigh of satisfaction that she has had unconsciousness. The vividness of my realisation of the woman's feelings almost made me think that I was going off my head.

Imprudence of that sort was highly uncharacteristic of the Bennett who advocated mind control. And the admired common sense—one wonders about it, reading that he entertained as lavishly in the yacht as in Cadogan Square: at Dieppe, Sir William Orpen; at Torquay, Mrs. Patrick Campbell; at Deauville, Lord Beaverbrook "and party"; at Fowey, 'Q', whom he found "somewhat callous and indifferent, but having humour".

Torquay. July 4, 1923.—Mrs. Patrick Campbell came for lunch and stayed till 4.30. She made a sensational entrance both into the lunch and into the ship—the *cabotine's* entrance. But she gave a magnificent conversational display. In fact it was dazzling. Only she is incapable of listening. She gave me the impression of a tremendous personality, a considerable genius, and a woman without scruple when she really wants anything. She told a good story about Duse, not blaming Duse but her manager. Duse asked Mrs. Pat to lend her her scenery for some play that both had done. Mrs. Pat said it was a great honour and did so. She then asked for a box for the *première*, and an account for 4 guineas was sent with the ticket. She paid. In the first interval a page boy came into the box with a large box of flowers. She asked who they were from and the page boy said: "Please throw them on to the stage after the second act." She said to me: "I thought this was going rather far. I lent the scenery for nothing. I paid for my box. And then they wanted me to throw flowers at her!"

He needed relaxation more than most men and at least at sea he could have had it; but the grandeur of yacht ownership, it seems, of being able to afford a crew of eight, of the opportunity of showing that a writer could make money enough to support such a luxury, over-rode this urgent necessity of his existence. In every harbour there was someone to call or to be called on; often troops of theatre friends from London would be waiting on the jetties and the yacht would be gay with the popping of champagne corks and the voices of attractive women. Miss Lillah McCarthy [Lady Keeble] remembers that the peace of the last minutes of a beautiful dusk at Cowes was shattered for her by his sudden Midland harshness. She and Bennett were leaning in silence over the rail of *Marie Marguerite*. A rowing-boat was heard approaching. As it drew near, Miss McCarthy recognised an acquaintance of Bennett's who was an old friend of hers. The rower, resting on dripping oars, called out: "Good evening!" Deliberately, pointedly, impassively, Bennett called back: "Good night!" Silence; then the oars

[300]

dipped again and the boat receded into the evening. "How *could* you?" Miss McCarthy asked Bennett. His excuse was: "I—I couldn't help it. He's too interesting to invite on board on a night like this." Contrasting with the brusqueness, we find him during the same cruise instructing Pinker to 'make it easy' in the matter of fees for an East End working men's club that wished to perform one of his plays and to release from payment of royalties a manager who was having a thin time at the West Pier, Brighton.

Out of the social side of his yachting activities came an idea which in its ultimate development restored his prestige as a novelist and brought him a kind of appreciation and acclaim that for over a decade had been missing from his life; a reminder, sudden and surprising, that the creator of *The Old Wives' Tale* and *Clayhanger* was not exhausted of his powers or lost to literature. On June 29, 1924, he wrote in the yachting diary: "Southampton Water. I went ashore and bought two books at James' (original shop of 'Riceyman Steps'). The place was much tidier; but Mrs. James said, as she always does: 'We're in a bit of a mess here just now'." Discovering the shop in 1921 with some of his yachting guests, he had seen it at once as the setting for a short story: "a short story about two old misers." Going there again in 1922, he noted: "I had the idea that my projected short story about two misers would make a fine novel; and within about an hour I had decided to make it a novel, and was much excited." In 1930, his last year, he revisited Clerkenwell and his *Riceyman Steps* scenes, recalling in an *Evening Standard* article that at Plum Pudding Steps—his old passion for rice pudding seems to have been an associated idea in his concoction of the new name for them—there "was performed a feat of transport surpassing anything ever done in that line in the U.S.A.—the moving of an entire bookseller's shop with all its books and dust from a South Coast port to the foot of the Steps".

Arnold Bennett to Frank Swinnerton:

19–2–23

MY DEAR HENRY, [1]

No, I cannot agree with your estimate of your powers. There are here and there scenes in your novels of first-rate power, scenes which remain in the mind for years. Proof enough of what you *can* do when circumstances are favourable. What is wanted is staying

[1] Mr. Swinnerton was given this name by some officers billeted at "Comarques" during the war.

quality, and my belief is that this depends largely on health (physical and moral). I wrote a fatherly letter to Hughie [Hugh Walpole] and told him the error of his ways and also that I didn't like 'The Cathedral' well enough even to say anything about it to him at all. He replied that he was *delighted* with my letter, and he evidently was! All he desires is for people to be really interested in him. And he wrote me a most intimate *confession*. Unfortunately he douole and treble marked the damn' thing private, so I can't say anything about it. He swears that I alone, etc., etc. I don't know how true this is. But it was a most taking letter. I have now written 80,000 words of my novel. I think another 10,000 ought to finish it nearly. I had the happy idea of reading the McLauchlin trial, one of the most captivating of the Hodge series, and found it full of small useful 'sordid' details of daily life in a small house. . . . A1 stuff. I have a sort of idea that my novel is not so bad. But it is infernally monotonous. I have written on Proust, and written the preface to 'Don Juan de Marana', and corrected all proofs of 'How To Make The Best Of Life', and given 2 dinner parties and am about to give 3 more, and talked to George Moore, and nursed Mrs. Loraine's baby, and improved my health and sleep astonishingly by means of exercises, and got a shade thinner, and paid my income tax, and arranged for the next season's yachting, and engaged a rather pretty house-parlourmaid; and there was something else awfully interesting; but I can't recall now what it is. . . . Look here, I've exchanged books with W. B. Maxwell, and read 'Spinster of this Parish'. The opening of it is a masterly exposition of narrative—the sort of thing Hughie would like to do and can't. . . . I hope your novel is going ahead and, if I may say so, that you aren't forcing it.

Yours,

A. B.

CHAPTER SIXTEEN

(1)

FOR Arnold Bennett the early 1920s were a renaissance period which every middle-aged man dreams of and few experience. His creative phase was thought to be well behind him, ranking him as a rarity of the brief Edwardian years, an important novelist. A generation had grown up which hardly knew him as an artist. Most people regarded him as a foremost journalist who was shrewd about cash and wealthy because of it. They would have been surprised if they could have looked over his shoulder as he sat writing in his extra-journal on April 16, 1926:

> I dined alone at home last night. It does not suit me. I couldn't find anything to do after dinner and the dinner would have been ruined if I had not talked obstetrics with Fred. I couldn't read, and couldn't play the piano and couldn't go out. I could only be bored and think about the insecurity of my financial situation.

It was his reaction from his first experience of fatherhood: his daughter had been born three days before (a secret which was not going to be as well kept as Wordsworth's). In his fifty-fifth year he had fallen in love with a young woman in her twenties and his pleasure in her response sounded emotional chords with childishly suggestive echoes, as, for instance, when he signed himself to her, 'Little' and 'Little Mr. Dot', and drew hearts over his letters with the secret throb of the schoolboy who is awed and thrilled by the sensations of private love. In the journal of the first year or so of their friendship he refers to 'D.C.' as if with a fearful joy. In his middle age he was experiencing for the first time, also, romantic feelings which come to most men in their twenties if not before.

Such emotional cosiness was certainly not adult. It was of the adolescent order of feeling which caused him to give his young women characters 'precious' names like Annunciata and Laurencine and Concepcion, and insist on calling Miss Green 'Eleanora' though her name was Eleanor, the feeling he had of the sex being remote, mysterious, unattainable. Now Miss Dorothy Cheston had come into his life with her strong and vivid personality, her mental athleticism, her good looks, her style and dash, giving him a companionship which, as Miss Pauline Smith says, "never ceased to interest and surprise him." And Dorothy for him had to be pronounced 'Dorothea'.

The story of their life together had been told by Miss Cheston Bennett, as he wished her to be known, in the long autobiographical preface she wrote for the collection of his letters to her. For some time after their first meeting, in 1922, their developing intimacy was confided only to a few friends. Bennett's first journal mention of Miss Cheston was in December, 1923, almost a year later. His references to her there for the next two or three years are often oddly impersonal; at times almost begrudging. "*August 4, 1924.*—D. Cheston said: 'Autumn has come, summer is over,' with a sigh. Difficult to find a more characteristic expression of the naturally pessimistic, self-pitying temperament." He rarely in those years gave her full name; it was nearly always 'D. Cheston', when the names of other people are given in full in the same entry. What, if anything, this meant psychologically may have been quite trivial: it suggests adolescence again, though to be set against it there is the fact that he was addressing Miss Cheston affectionately in his letters. Following out their relationship from his side in the journal and in his letters to relatives and friends, and to Miss Cheston herself, one is left believing that while she was the means of releasing some of the subjective power which he had so long and so rigidly held in check, he preserved his critical balance and his capacity for assessing his situation with often disconcerting frankness; in short, that he was largely enslaved on his own terms. "I have my feelings on the curb," he told her. The subjective power, perhaps, had been too long and too rigidly held in check; and he may have believed what Coleridge said, that while "the man's desire is for the woman, the woman's desire is rarely other than for the desire of the man". He wrote in the extra-journal of 1926–30:

A youngish woman may say, and believe, that an oldish man is astonishingly young for his age; but underneath that doubtless quite genuine feeling is the deeper and stronger feeling that he is incapable of seriously interesting her. I doubt if this is equally true of a young woman as distinguished from a merely youngish woman. A young woman might be deceived.

[304]

HIS "RATHER NOBLE THING IN HOUSES", 75 CADOGAN SQUARE, LONDON, S.W.

By permission of Mr. D. Macdonald Hastings

AN IMPROMPTU SKETCH OF ARNOLD BENNETT MADE AT THE LONDON PRESS CLUB BY
JOSEPH SIMPSON, R.I.

The publicly significant part of their relationship is that not long after they had met Bennett began work on the novel which was to reclaim him from the disregard of readers and critics, *Riceyman Steps*. Artistically, he had achieved little since *Clayhanger*, twin pillar of his reputation as a novelist. His French biographer noted the effect of the new influence that had come into his life:

> . . . it seems that some such revival of the spiritual or emotional faculties in him was just what was wanted to save his art from that gradual hardening and exhaustion with which it was seriously threatened. The plain fact is that in the years 1922–26 he wrote *Riceyman Steps, Elsie and the Child, Lord Raingo, Accident*, each of which possesses high literary merit, though in a varying degree. And in each precisely the most felicitous effects are due to this vein of half-repressed sympathy and disguised compassion which, to tell the truth, was not quite absent from his earlier works, such as *The Pretty Lady*, but now reasserted itself in a purer and, as it were, more classical manner. [1]

Riceyman Steps was received with unanimous high praise. It reaffirmed Bennett's lost distinction as a creator of character, and character creating, he now insisted, was the mainspring of the best fiction, "character creating and nothing else." The critics were forced to acknowledge that he had accomplished a great new feat of craftsmanship, demonstrating a creative resurgence of which they had deemed him no longer capable. Their capitulation was rounded off for him when he received a leading literary award, the Tait Black Novel prize, a kind of satisfaction that had not come his way before. "The first prize for a book I have ever had." He was delighted.

H. G. Wells to Arnold Bennett:

1 November, 1923

. . . I have to join the chorus. 'Riceyman Steps' is a great book. I hate to go back on an old friend, but I think it is as good as or better than *The Old Wives' Tale*.

[1] *Arnold Bennett: A Study* by Georges Lafourcade (Muller, 1939).

Arnold Bennett to Frank Swinnerton:

75, Cadogan Square
S. W. 1.

21–12–23.

. . . I gave a dinner last night to Sinclair Lewis and his wife. You know, I like both of them. I don't say they are great shakes, or in the least educated, or much de-cruded. But I like them both. They live near here—Elm Park Road. Sinclair said to me: 'How is it I can talk to you and I can't talk to Wells?' I said: 'Because he is too self-conscious.' Amazing, how they like 'The Cathedral' [by Hugh Walpole]. I wasn't going to stand for that. However, they all like 'Riceyman Steps'. In fact the reception of this book is staggering me. And it's all on account of Elsie. What a way of appreciating a book: good God! Same thing in a different way: the Aga Khan told me some weeks ago that the best of all my books was 'Lilian'. Lilian was doubtless his ideal. Indeed he had a Lilian with him; it was at Ciro's.

Desmond MacCarthy has at last got a supplementary job. Well paid. He was here last night, and absolutely radiant. That chap must have been damned hard up. I met Theodore Powys at Dorothy Cheston's the other afternoon. Believe me, a damned strange fellow. On the strength of his unbalanced interestingness I bought 'Black Bryony' and I began to read it today. It promises. I also bought the other Powys's 'Ebony and Ivory' and thought nought of it. I hope you'll meet John Cowper Powys, as I want a sound opinion of him. Dorothy, who knows him and his sister passing well, speaks very highly of him. I know another brother, an architect, who is *not* interesting, but just nice and decent, like me.

In case of fatigue, rest *at all costs*. You don't want to fall ill in the Middle West. It would be dreadful for you. Such is my most solemn advice. I think often of you sniggering in secret at the earnestness of George and others. I hope too you'll see Tarkington, and tell him I love him. I want to know what old Chrissie Morley is like.

Comps of season,

Yours, A. B.

Joseph Conrad to Arnold Bennett:

Oswalds,

2 Jan, 1924

MY DEAR BENNETT.—I am wholly delighted with your R. S. [*Riceyman Steps*]. You will give me credit for not having missed any special gems, but it is the whole achievement as I went from page to page that secured my admiration.

As I closed the book at 7 in the morning after the shortest sleepless night of my experience, a thought passed through my head that I knew pretty well my 'Bennett militant' and that, not to be too complimentary, he was a pretty good hand at it; but that there I had 'Bennett triumphant' without any doubt whatever. A memorable night.

Don't imagine that this is the morbid receptivity of an invalid. In fact I have been captious and 'grincheux' for days, as is always the case when I am not well. *Entre-nous* I feel as if I were fighting my Verdun battle with my old enemy. It isn't that the symptoms are unusually severe, but it goes on and on. . . . I begin to wonder whether I have sufficient reserves. But I am not hopeless. Only I feel unfit to talk to you about the book as it deserves and as I would like to talk of it. There is no doubt that there is something quintessential about it.

Always with my real affection,

JOSEPH CONRAD[1]

P.S. Did I thank you for your letter about 'The Rover'? It was the greatest comfort.

Arnold Bennett to Frank Swinnerton:

75, Cadogan Square,

S. W. 1.

22–1–24

. . . I have just received with thanksgiving your letter from Cleveland, O. You must be very strong to stand what you are going through, especially by yourself. But of course you have Intellectual Resources, which I never have when travelling alone. However, the gaffes which you hear must lighten the burden of life considerably. It is good about 'Felix' [*Young Felix*, a new novel by Mr. Swinnerton].

[1] G. Jean-Aubry: *Joseph Conrad, Life and Letters* (Heinemann 1927)

I think Doran said he should try for 40 thou. It was either 40 or 50. I bet you it goes over 30. George also said of 'Riceyman' that he would eat every copy he didn't sell up to 60,000. This boast was called forth by Flower's boast that he would sell 40,000. If 40 in England, then at least 60 in U.S.A., you see. Flower had actually sold 31,000 a fortnight ago. So he ought to reach 40, despite railway strikes. If anybody thinks that I am not as pleased and self-satisfied as an infant with the sales of R.S., let him or her be undeceived. It is a solemnizing thought that I have never had what I call a sale. (I don't mean cheap editions.) George said the other day that *The Old Wives' Tale* had just passed 60,000 in U.S.A. This in about 15 years. Hence, if I have made money by my pen, it is the fruit of the fact that I produce as much as H.G.W. and 3 times as much as most other people.

George was in the greatest form while here; but noticeably excitable and even a bit hysterical on the subject of Hughie. He even said he meant to quarrel with Hughie (but he won't). Hughie told me that George was ill at the Savoy. I saw George in the evening, very lively. 'Hullo,' I said, 'I thought you were ill. I'm glad it's over.' 'Ill? Who told you I was ill?' He was simply furious against Hughie. . . . Said Hughie called on him at 9 a.m., in itself inexcusable, and found him dispensing castor oil and then goes about the town saying he is ill. Can't a man take a dose of castor oil? But George has been very witty this visit. He is improving each visit. The women, including all mine, adore him. He gave a farewell dinner, Savoy: me, Harriet Cohen and Dorothy Cheston. These creatures were in especially good form, and got on to the subject of Christ. 'You can't get anything like this in New York, Arnold.'

. . . Tommy Wells has had the singular idea of asking me to review the whole field of English literature from Chaucer, for 'Harper's'. But I don't think I shall do it, partly because I don't want to write and partly because he doesn't want to pay.

Yours, A. B.

Conrad's opinion of *Riceyman Steps* Bennett thought "rather a masterpiece". This lofty praise, all the praise the novel brought him, was a shoulder-bracing experience of a kind that had been denied him for some years. His friends complimented him on "the youthfulness and extraordinary healthiness" of his appearance, he wrote; he was aglow with success once more and life was good, though Lobb of St. James' Street had not succeeded with the new boots they had made for him: he had gone on wearing boots long after the fashionable world had taken to shoes, and his plantigrade walk, from which the more superficial observers inferred pomposity, had now become oddly like that of a man being forced unwillingly along. Here, again, he was the victim of the malice of fate. He was not a pompous man but was made to carry himself like one by a tendency to ankle-swelling which exaggerated his gait in the last years, a weakness which not even the best of the bespoke boot makers could master.

However, 'the King's tailors' had finally corrected the faults in the new white evening waistcoat for which he had insisted on having no less than eleven fittings, in the course of which he was seen progressing along Piccadilly with the garment over his arm. Sulka of Bond Street had made him "some truly astonishing soft shirts" that were the envy of his friends and had caught the eye of the Prince of Wales (the Duke of Windsor). He was living in the lordly surroundings of Cadogan Square. And Thomas Hardy "had not been so interested in a novel for years. We were so sorry", Mrs. Hardy sent word to say, "when we came to the last page. My husband was absolutely absorbed by it."

He lunched with James and Muirhead Bone at Simpson's in Cheapside, where an elderly man took the role of chairman and said grace. Not knowing it to be the custom of that old City eating-place or possibly not hearing, Bennett went on talking until he was rebuked in front of the company. "He was thoroughly put out. He did not recover himself for some time," James Bone remembers. It was another custom of the house that those signing the visitors' book should name the person they would most like to bring with them on their next visit. Bennett had written 'Princess Bibesco'.

Arnold Bennett to Frank Swinnerton:

> 75, Cadogan Square,
> S. W. 1.
>
> 12–2–24

. . . Thank God for something sensible said to me at last about 'Riceyman'. I am sick of the praise of Elsie. It is an acid test (forgive the cliché) of critics. Jack Squire has fallen into it. As if the sympathetic quality of Elsie had anything whatever to do with the quality of the book. . . .

Desmond MacCarthy. He has much taste (except for the stage) and he is one of the best talkers I ever heard or squashed.

George Doran. All publishers are about as much alike as all authors are alike. George is getting far too sentimental, and comes nearer in this respect to being like Hughie than he suspects.

I am negotiating direct with 'The Strand' for some reminiscences. I am also just finishing a 20,000 word story about the adored Elsie.

At the Lyric we have recently been rehearsing 'The Way of the World'. I never comprehended the plot, and still don't. I announced publicly that it was bound to be a complete frost, the plot being silly and the dialogue far too subtle for any public. I convinced everyone in the theatre that we were in for a perfect frost.

Well, it has made a perfect furore. The cars of the highbrows throng our slum. The booking far exceeds that for 'The Beggars' Opera'. (Of course it won't last, but it now is terrific.) Edith Evans in it is the finest comic show I ever saw on any stage in this wide world. The gallery nightly 'eats it'. You should have seen all the highbrows together on the first night: Clive Bell, St. John Hutchinson and Co., Duff Cooper, Lytton Strachey, the Viola Trees, the Goossenses—all side by side. By the way, I have been getting much more intimate with Viola lately. She is a most charming creature, and I love her—after Dorothy, Harriet, Marjorie, and Pauline.

I have been all over the working parts of the Savoy Hotel and was much impressed. I helped Sybil Thorndike (a decent creature) to judge the costumes at the Hassan Ball and was interfered with by the other judges, Lady Terrington and G. Frankau. I hope you will continue to conquer. I am well, except ill-sleeping.

Yours, A. B.

(2)

A sequel to Bennett's war-time official service had been his friendship with Lord Beaverbrook, the pocket Rhodes from Canada and a forceful figure in the inner politics of the time. Arriving in London only a few years before as a rich self-made young man, he was looked down on from the more rarefied altitudes of English society as if he embodied the sacrilege of a Cromwellian trooper quartered in a holy place. His fantastic trespass had gained him an influence which Bennett envied and admired. For Arnold Bennett he seems to have been 'the Card' raised to the nth power, economically all-conquering, socially masterful, temperamentally intimidating, an ennobled gnome whose ear-to-ear grin proclaimed good-nature and disguised harshness. Lord Beaverbrook's name is written often in the journal pages of the 'twenties, estimony to an intimacy which Bennett relished and on which this great friend of his set the seal of a sincere and moving tribute when the time of farewell came: "He evoked so strong a feeling of affection in me that I sometimes doubted whether I could judge his work impartially. He was a supremely honest man." With Arnold Bennett's regard for Lord Beaverbrook there went a deep admiring affection for Lady Beaverbrook, one of the most beautiful and lovable women who ever came to these shores from her Canadian homeland. "I would rather be under her roof than anywhere else," he said once when the doctors had ordered him to rest, and her death in 1927 was a tragedy with emotional overtones for him which, most unusually, he made no effort to conceal: "I could not speak."

Arnold Bennett to George Doran:

27th September, 1924

MY DEAR GEORGE,—Beaverbrook rang me up last night and said: 'Arnold, I want to tell you. The 'Daily Express' has been offered a biography of you written by Mrs. Arnold Bennett. It was offered through Curtis Brown. It is 15,000 words long. I have read a lot of it and I think it is pretty good. It contains nothing offensive or indiscreet so far as I have read, and my editor says he would not object to having anything said of himself during his lifetime that is said in this biography about you. I should like to buy it for serial publication in the 'Express', but of course I shall not do so if you have any objection.'

I reflected upon the matter, and then told Max that so far as I was concerned he could do as he liked, and I therefore assume that he will buy it.

My reason was as follows: Marguerite is bound to get the thing published somewhere, and I should prefer it to be in the hands of someone who will take care to cut out anything which might be offensive.

Of course I should never be surprised at anything that was done in that quarter, but I must say it seems to me rather outrageous that Marguerite should write and sell this little book without consulting my wishes in any way. Probably it has never even occurred to her that I should find anything objectionable in a biography by my wife being published during my lifetime. Comparatively few members of the public are aware that she and I are separated, and those of the majority who possess any decent feeling will certainly consider that both she and I are guilty of a grave offence against good taste. However, things are what they are and it cannot be helped.

The book is certain to be offered in America, and I shall therefore be obliged to you if you will make it known *viva voce* that the book has been written without my knowledge and consent and that I very strongly object to it, but have no power to stop its publication.

Ever yours,
A. B.

The Beaverbrook place and power never failed to impress Bennett, who was not less susceptible to the fascination of his friend's excessive mental vitality, dooming him to a ready boredom with lesser men and to bouts of loneliness which Bennett's own brisk acquisitiveness of mind did a good deal to mitigate: "Beaverbrook told me he has not been bored for nearly three months." Possibly it was his insight into this peculiar fate that inspired his protective attitude when Lord Beaverbrook's personality and reputation were assailed by Bennett's intellectual acquaintances. One of the more famous among them, finding himself placed next to Beaverbrook at lunch, complained afterwards to Bennett that to expect him to enjoy himself in the circumstances was going "rather beyond the limit". Bennett was strict and uncompromising in reasserting the warmth of his feelings for Lord Beaverbrook. "You are too narrow," he retorted, fixing the critic with a disciplinary eye. When, another time, a well-known public personage asserted that Beaverbrook was "a genius but not a great man", Bennett, who had remained completely silent while the argument was going on round his table, wound it up with feeling: "Look here, I say, he is . . . *all right*," and the complementary thought obtrudes that Bennett was a great man but not a genius.

Not that his admiration for this formidable friend of his reduced him to critical sterility. He stated his distaste for what seemed to him to be Beaverbrook's contempt for the private mind which Bennett cherished and thought was the natural right of everyone to cultivate: "One *must* have one's private mind." Writing of Lord Beaverbrook in *Memoirs of a Polyglot*, William Gerhardi says that Arnold Bennett was the only man he had known who had "so to speak, shaken him by the collar". When Bennett kept Beaverbrook waiting for eight minutes, a famous physician who was with him looked at his watch and expressed surprise that Bennett should risk his impatience. Bennett was indulging a private revenge. Lord Beaverbrook had kept him waiting eight

LADY BEAVERBROOK FROM THE PAINTING BY G. M. LAMBERT

GEORGE STURT ('GEORGE BOURNE')

minutes at their last meeting. And while he professed alarm at Beaver-brook's often embarrassingly intimate knowledge of other people's business, he was glad to draw on it for the new novel he had written, *Lord Raingo*. When Winston Churchill spoke "very flatteringly" to Bennett about the novel and especially about the accuracy of his description of Cabinet meetings and surroundings—"you must have been a fly on the wall"—he was also complimenting Lord Beaverbrook, who had supplied many particulars which Bennett had written down in his notebooks.

(3)

Arnold Bennett to his sister, Mrs. Kennerley:

75, Cadogan Square,
S. W. 1.

DEAR TERTIA,   14. 7. 25.

I had something to tell you and I didn't mean to write it. But as I can't come down before Saturday, when probably you won't be alone, I must write you. I was summoned home a fortnight ago by the news of the probability that Dorothy Cheston would become a mother. . . . I found her excited and delighted. One or two of her friends also. The 2 or 3 of my friends whom I have told are equally delighted. As the event won't be till April, she will play for the present, under doctor's orders. By the way, I have had nothing whatever to do with putting her into the play. She knew Playfair before me. In fact I knew her through him, as he cast her for the lead in 'Body and Soul' at Liverpool, where I sat next her at supper. . . . She is daughter of Chester Cheston, the architect (dead), and sister of Cheston the painter. Her mother is a rich woman of 70 who lives in hotels. When I speak of my age, her reply is that her father was just over my age when she was born. She is as tall as I am, and a hefty wench. I see all the drawbacks of this matter, but am getting rather excited and pleased too. Socially there will be little difficulty as my friends have greatly taken to her and generally ask us together. Sissie [another sister] met her several times and likes her very much. Georges Bion tells me that in his opinion Marguerite will never agree to a divorce; but this remains to be seen. The Phillpotts are enchanted. I think I won't tell you any more now.

Yours,
A. B

[313]

He wrote to Wells in the tone of a struggling amateur reporting to the highest authority: "I perceive that I shall have a new and violent interest in life," but Wells was not impressed by the spectacle of a profoundly inhibited man pretending to defy the inhibitions of society. Bennett set himself to observe and record the temperamental phenomena of gestation and the journal shows him preoccupied by his approaching new state and beset, too, by his insomnia, which he was now regularly logging: nightly sleep average for 1926, 4½ hours. Marie Tempest told him: "Before my son was born I drank a pint of champagne at lunch and another at dinner every day." She, like so many of his friends, "behaved splendidly over this business." He wrote to his brother:

> 75 Cadogan Square
>
> 13. 4. 26
>
> MY DEAR FRANK—Official. Failing to get a divorce from Marguerite I am now in unofficial conjugal relations with one Dorothy Bennett (her own name): a daughter was born of this union at 7.50 a.m. this day, and all is going on well. You can never foresee what your morning's post will contain.
>
> Yours,
>
> A. B.
>
> Dorothy is recognised by all friends as my wife.

He took flowers to the nursing home with a young man's ardour and, kept waiting, noted the dog-eared journals on the table, the state of the carpet, the manners of the nurses. One nurse had been at the birth of a first child to the Duke and Duchess of York, later Their Majesties. "The Duchess said she was so pleased it was a girl because if it had been a boy and her husband ever succeeded to the Throne, to which he stands second in the line of succession, he would be the King's boy and she would never have any control over him." He had written to Dorothy Cheston Bennett from the yacht:

> . . . What disturbs me is the extreme difficulty of the father, who will be in his 60th year, doing his duty by the child. When that child is ten I shall be seventy. I daresay I shall be in great vigour; but I shall be seventy. The economic aspect also troubles me. You see, the bulk of my possessions, under our separation deed, goes to my wife, and nothing can alter this. Of course I shall take every means

to put as much as possible of my possessions into other hands as opportunity offers. I shall have to work harder, but I doubt whether that will cause me much discomfort. We shall have to be more careful, in fact much more. The whole balance of life will be altered. . . . These things having been said, I must also tell you that I have a curious feeling of elation, of response to a challenge from destiny.

His elation flickered in the draughty atmosphere of social dis-approval, which he vainly thought he had dispelled with the co-operation of his friends. Mrs. Somerset Maugham; the indefatigable Lady Colefax; Mr. and Mrs. (now Sir Alan and Lady) Herbert; Countess Russell ('Elizabeth'); the pianist, Miss Harriet Cohen; the actress, Miss Jeanne de Casalis: he named these and others as having brought their good-nature as well as their good sense to bear on his problem and said that he was much helped by their sympathetic understanding.

But the problem continued to rise up and vex him. Especially, it created servant difficulties: below stairs, the Bennett moral standard was distantly regarded; malicious tongues put it about that this was "a house of sin"; the child's nurses were waylaid by mischief-makers in the street.

November 26, 1926.—More trouble with the nurse over Virginia's illegitimacy. 'It's all over the Park.' Nurse said anything known to one or two nurses in the Park was soon known to all of them. Of course the previous nurse had told the great tidings. The present nurse said: 'At first I couldn't understand why they looked at me in such a queer way. I thought my petticoat must be coming down.' She said she had heard remarks in the Park: 'That's the baby.' And that somebody outside Peter Jones's said in passing: 'That's the Bennett baby,' though whether illegitimacy was implied I don't know. I presume half the nurse world is a world of its own. Nurse told both her sisters and her mother and father. She said: 'Mother and father are good living people and they go to church.' The present arrangement is that her parents shall come and see me. Strange—but not strange—that while all our friends accept the situation without a murmur, indeed with a sort of eagerness, the servant class does not seem to be able to accept it. Dorothy stands the *contretemps* very well.

The crucial interview was conducted not by the nurse's parents but by her uncle, a coachman. After talking with Bennett, he agreed that his niece might reasonably stay on but thought she ought to consult her sisters. "I offered him a cigarette, which he took but would not smoke. " 'No, sir, I've been a servant all my life.' Still," Bennett added to his note of it, "he was a perfect gentleman. I loved him." Bennett's sensitiveness as an employer of menial persons was sincere enough. It was often remarked and is still remembered by some of those who served him domestically that he habitually showed no less courtesy in his dealings with them than to the guests who came to his table. Some of the most elaborate journal entries were prompted by their personal histories and discontents.

28 Aug, 1926.—Look at their health. Annie, the upper house-maid, is gastrically very wrong. Edith, the second housemaid is anæmic and recently had an attack of boils. Fred is gastrically wrong and constantly has indigestion. Emily is apparently quite healthy now for the reason that since she gave up being cook and became nurse to Virginia she leads a more healthy life. I don't know about the cook's health: she has been here only about a fortnight. And be it noted that our servants are supposed to be well-treated! That is the funny thing. I am told that they are 'spoiled' and so on. I know that I am always trying to make others imaginatively realise that their life is really not a very joyous one. It most positively is not a very healthy one, or in the least a free one. Then there is always the tyranny of the bell, with its sharp summons (as described in 'Ricey-man Steps'). I laughed this morning when I received from McWhirter, the editor of the 'Sunday Pictorial', a suggestion that I should write an article: 'Why Do We Not Keep Servants?' I shall certainly write it. I feel sure that in another 20 years the present condition of servants will be regarded as having been barbaric, just as now we regard the conditions of servants 30 or 40 years ago as having been barbaric. I think we shall move more quickly in the next 25 years.

Despite his tolerant insight, the servant question constantly plagued him during the Cadogan Square years and the journal bears witness to painful scenes that were distracting him from his work and requiring of him obviously the limit in patience and restraint. Domestic disturb-ance on this scale was a new experience for him who had so long preached and practised the ordered life. "I awoke acutely nervous" typifies the stress he was put to. "Too ill—just had to exist," and: "Blankest day in my memory—no desire for anything." After giving details of one more domestic crisis: "A strange manner of life and rather trying. But it is not a bore, anyhow." *Lord Raingo* was written amid a series of recurring emotional tempests which again and again sent him in exhaustion to bed.

The price of belated happiness was high, the challenge of destiny at sixty too exacting. Adjusting his measured style and habits to the tempo of a young and eager vitality brought tensions of a kind that were quite new to him. Dorothy Cheston Bennett saw him as essentially 'a sad man', a definition of himself which he sought to rebut but which touched the truth. "There were things which he suffered that he showed to no man, not even his greatest intimate," she says in her introduction to his published letters. Powerful irrational suggestion hung like a sinister cloud over the horizon as the author of the famous 'pocket philosophies' approached his sixtieth year.

(4)

This was not one of the great public affairs of the heart, and the biographer, picking his way through the remnants of the once intricate maze of Arnold Bennett's friendship and acquaintance, is confronted by the fact that the private loyalties were riven by controversy and prejudice which long survived him. Dorothy Cheston Bennett's theatrical ambitions and ventures were held by some to have burdened him to breaking point, though there is no evidence of it in what he himself wrote on the subject. Others saw peril for him in her social activities which distended his own already enormous acquaintance. Her appearance in his life meant a diversion of emphasis in his relations with members of the Bennett family, some of whom resented it. The pains and the penalties were not only on his side. Dorothy Cheston Bennett, enamoured of the proximity of fame, eager, inexperienced, had not only to endure the stares of prejudice. Her abounding energy of mind was called on to function at what for her were unaccustomed heights of success and prominence and it would have connoted exceptional good luck rather than genius if she had not sometimes faltered. For instance, he exposed her to the unfair handicap of ignorance about his true financial condition; all she ever heard from him on that matter was stated in the jauntiest of cautionary terms, as if intrinsically he was infallibly secure, which not unnaturally she assumed him to be. Her role of hostess, for which she had received no benefit of rehearsal, brought her under the scrutiny of celebrated intellects, not less of an ordeal because he thought her admirably equal to it. And

[317]

again, where the age disparity is so great as here, the weight of comment and criticism invariably falls more heavily on the woman, who may be credited with every virtue except sincerity: "Of course, she can't possibly be in love with him!" The difficulties of their unlegalised partnership did not always evoke the imaginative sympathy which would have helped to minimise them. Even by some of their closer friends often little regard was given to Dorothy Cheston Bennett's inexperience: "I was capable of great unrealism in domestic matters. I was psychologically immature." She agrees that there was truth in judgments that she added to his burdens. "But the criticism does not touch the vital truth and happenings going on at other planes of our relationship. Taken quite by itself, such a judgment is as true as any judgment of appearances and surface facts. Always there is a side not seen and therefore beyond judgment by those unaware of it." The costly theatre ventures, for example: they were not seen as attempts to secure for herself an economic self-sufficiency which in principle he would hardly have discouraged. And in many places in the journal of his last years he speaks of the stimulus of her mental companionship, in which they attained their closest intimacy. "You and I deeply understand one another," he wrote in their last year together.

(5)

"You can't have a baby and a yacht too," he decided, and gave up the yacht. His future was troubling him. "Eric Pinker gave me absolutely no good news about myself and my market." There were income-tax arrears, disputed through his accountants, but the pressure was being put on. He was caught up in a style of living from which only a revolutionary change could release him, a change which, as he saw it, would involve an admission of defeat. And how could he, who had known conspicuous success, face that?

He finished *Lord Raingo* in Rome. "130,200 words. Intense fatigue after a three-hour night." The night after: "Six hours. What relief! I saw the whole world differently," and sat down in his bedroom at the Hotel de Russie to start a new novel, *The Vanguard*, though he was there supposedly in search of rest and change. When at Pisa the translator of Proust, C. K. Scott Moncrieff, called to offer his friendly services as guide, Bennett described the day they had together as 'a holiday', and set himself to write 2,200 words of the new novel the next day, atoning for the lapse.

Arnold Bennett to Frank Swinnerton:

Rome,

4. 2. 26.

. . . I finished 'Lord Raingo' on 26th at 5.30 p.m. The 'Saturday Evening Post' will buy it if they like the last part; but I know they won't like the last part. £3–4,000 gone to pot through my damnable artistic integrity. (But I know it pays in the end: that's why I keep it up.) I now have new material for 40,000 novels. But nothing for that mystery novel which I determined to write. I found myself in a headline of the 'Continental Daily Mail'. Then trouble began. Journalists. Photographers. One woman wrote to me: 'I have met Mr. Locke through the good offices of Mr. James Milne. Cannot I meet you, so that you may tell me just how you work? Can you not give me a half-hour on some golden afternoon at an hour to suit you?' Pretty good. But I have met one very sound female: Miss Baskerville, Rome correspondent of the 'New York World'. She is the stuff.

I have nothing to do except 6 short stories, 4 articles, and the mystery novel. What I say is: There is no place like Rome. 13 years since I was here last and I'm only just beginning to see what Rome is. I must admit Dorothy has a passion for archæology. She froths in the Forum. On Saturday last she climbed from the roof to the cupola of St. Peter's. It's about 200 feet. . . .

Yours, A. B.

P.S. My youngest brother (50) is apparently dying of consumption.

The sudden improvement in his sleeping was all too temporary. Soon he was writing: "Can't sleep, can't read," and the neuralgia raged again in one of the longest assaults he had known. "This was one of the worst neuralgia days I have ever had and that is saying something. Completely laid low," and he goes on to record over several days the effects of the attack as it rises to its crescendo of "dizzying pain". Seeking rest, he went to Amberley in Sussex and, the morning after his arrival, notes "the worst bout of insomnia I have had for a long time. But my work goes on much the same", astonishingly. He was driven to try a new drug, Dial, "which upset my head, and I prefer Tommy Horder's sedative." When he had said that "health is a very strange thing" he was probably not generalising. His unpublished journal notes from now on tell the tale of a physical organism tried to the limit. Yet at the height of what seems to have been an unusually acute series of bodily stresses he could write that he felt better than for some time and reported to his masseur that Hornibrook's exercises, combined with diet, had reduced his weight and enabled him to "work more satis-factorily than for many years". It seems that what for him was well-being would have been considerably below par for the average of men.

Arnold Bennett to George Doran:

5th August, 1926

... You do not seem to be altogether optimistic about the American sales of 'Lord Raingo'. We can only pray to God and hope for the best. I am never surprised when my books do not sell and always surprised when they do sell.

As regards another novel, how many novels of mine do you want? I have just finished another one. It is in the vein of "The Grand Babylon Hotel' and 'Hugo'.

I can tell you about 'Lord Raingo', that politically and medically it is impervious to criticism. The political part was carefully vetted by Beaverbrook, and the medical part was carefully vetted by my own doctor. And I will tell you another thing—unimportant perhaps, but interesting. The mutiny of German regiments at Brussels really did occur, as I have described it. But Lloyd George would not believe a word of it, and so no use was made of it.

Lord Birkenhead, in a *Daily Mail* interview, attacked novelists who introduce real persons, living or dead, into their fiction and charged Wells and Bennett with committing that offence. Bennett's Lord Raingo, he told the interviewer, was widely understood to have been modelled on a member of the Coalition Government of the war. "In fact, the work was vulgarly advertised on this basis." What right, Birkenhead demanded, had Bennett, "whose public services, as apart from his literary merits, are unlikely to be celebrated in song and story," to use a real statesman for fiction purposes?

When Bennett wrote a letter in reply, the newspaper asked him for an article. "I crossed out the Sir and Yours truly, and called it an article and charged £60 for it." He denied that Raingo had existed in the person of any known statesman. As regards the statesman Lord Birkenhead was thinking of, "I may say that I never had the slightest acquaintance with him." Lord Birkenhead was "a bit cross", he said, and his emotion led him to use certain vituperative clichés. "The

[320]

Photograph: Sasha

DOROTHY CHESTON BENNETT

By permission of Mr. Frank Wells

ARNOLD BENNETT PHOTOGRAPHED
BY H. G. WELLS EARLY IN THEIR
FRIENDSHIP

By permission of Miss Dorothy Cheston Bennett

VIRGINIA MARY, HIS DAUGHTER

By permission of Mrs. John Galsworthy

JOHN GALSWORTHY, WITH MRS. GALSWORTHY, HUGH WALPOLE AND ARNOLD BENNETT
AT BURY, SUSSEX

vituperation one can excuse and enjoy; but the clichés will afflict the lettered." A thrust calculated to tell, for Birkenhead was making authorship a large part of the business of his retirement.

Bennett was invited by the National Magazine Company to become supervising editor of the *Pall Mall Magazine* at £5,000 a year, "the work not to exceed six days a month." The negotiations, conducted on the magazine side by Ivor Nicholson, who afterwards became a well-known book publisher, broke down for lack of assurance that Bennett would be "absolute boss of the contents of the magazine". Another business proposal made to him had to be reported at once to Frank Swinnerton, as "one of the funniest things you ever heard in your life": he had been asked to "take supreme control" of a new advertising agency about to be launched in London. "High remuneration from the start and no capital required from me," adding: "This is serious. At first I thought it wasn't."

Lord Raingo was serialised in the London *Evening Standard*. "The booming of this novel has been terrific," *vide* the journal. Club talk in the West End held that the principal character in the novel was based on Lord Rhondda, the Food Controller of the war years. Arnold Bennett denied the imputation: the journal contains several pages of notes supplied by his Reform Club friends about the late Minister's career as business man and politician. Raingo is 'the Card' again. elevated to the national plane, a figure of power and importance in a crisis of history and endowed with the several kinds of success which his creator had dreamed of for himself.

The Saturday Evening Post of America declined serial use of the story, as Bennett had jauntily feared it would. He learnt also from the Pinker office that three of his new plays had been declined by forty-six managements in England and the United States.

On February 5, 1927, he read in the *Continental Daily Mail* that Sturt had died, news which "produced no effect of sadness on me at all. George had been ill and half-paralysed for many years", and they had not met for sixteen years. Reading all the letters he had received from his old friend as a preparation for writing an introduction to a posthumous book of his: "These letters are extremely good, and many of them ought to be printed in full. They made me feel sad, somehow; because I saw in them a reflection in commentary of the history of all my literary life—over thirty years." Falling into the subjective mood, he made some notes about himself:

I rarely worry in a practical way about happiness or unhappiness. I just enjoy it or stick it. I seldom ask myself what gives me most happiness or unhappiness. I never worry about a future life, and very rarely think about it for a moment. Although I have slowly acquired a scientific habit of thought, I have only applied it to the not-me part of the universe, scarcely ever to the Me. I have been an instinct more than anything else. . . . I began to write novels because my friends said I could. The same for plays. But I always had a feeling for journalism, which feeling is as strong as ever it was. I don't analyse or realise the characteristics of my novels. They seem sometimes to me to be so simple and obvious that I wonder anybody can feel any interest in them at all.

(6)

"I have no doubt that they are easily the highest paid book articles in the world. I get £300 a month for them from the *Evening Standard*, and the length runs from 800 to 1,000 words." Giving this information to Eric Pinker, Bennett wrote: "A number of newspaper syndicates in the U.S. are inquiring for rights. I think it might be worth your while to go into them with expedition."

'Books and Persons' in the *Evening Standard* brought him a large new province of readers and a new sphere of influence; also the envy of certain of his fellow novelists, particularly of Hugh Walpole, who had written letters in his sumptuously looped handwriting beseeching various newspaper editors to employ him in a similar role. The *Evening Standard* circulation, though chiefly metropolitan and though it included the clubs of Pall Mall and St. James's, where books are rarely one of the conversational gambits, gave him a prestige far exceeding that of any other writer on books in our time.

There has been a line of notable book reviewers, as of notable dramatic critics. The number of dramatic critics, eminent and not, who have been able to influence the box-office returns has always been small. Likewise, book reviewers have not often immediately affected a publisher's profits or an author's royalties. This is not to state a discrediting thing. The function of the critic is centred in standards and his influence may be imperceptible and remote in time rather than spontaneous. Arnold Bennett was almost unique in his power to produce a prompt effect. A column of praise from him could fill the hearts of publishers and booksellers with great expectations. He sent up the British sales of *The Bridge of San Luis Rey* to best-seller limits, admitting afterwards that he had over-praised it. He raised the fortunes of the author of *Jew Süss* to a height not predicated by other critics' views of that work. An article by him on a book about a system of physical exercising for the corpulent sent a queue of middle-aged men and women to the publishers' premises the next morning.

"The man in charge of one shop, Henderson's, said that when he saw my notice of *Vivandière*, by Phoebe Fenwick Gaye, he at once ordered over a hundred copies. I have heard this kind of story several times before, if not many times."

Seated magisterially above the jealousies and the little feuds inherent in all professional activities based on self-expression, loftily ignoring the operations of the mutual admiration groups in literature, splendidly susceptible to the claims of youthful promise, acutely responsive to the necessity that books should be sold as well as written, Bennett achieved a weight of influence matching at last the air of profound assurance with which he had so long carried himself. "To be fine for a few minutes is not enough," he tells Virginia Woolf. He pokes fun at *The Waste Land*: "I once asked T. S. Eliot whether the notes to his renowned poem were a skit on such notes or meant to be taken seriously. He said they were meant to be taken seriously. I bowed the head." A new work by Miss Rebecca West is "infested from end to end by irresponsible silliness". March 14, 1928: "Just as I was leaving lunch [at the Savoy], in a hurry, Lawrence of the Medici Society asked me if I could say something helpful about a new book on painting. I temporised. The next minute Doran asked me whether I would say something helpful about Michael Arlen's new book. I said that a contributor to the *Evening Standard* had no friends."

Lord Beaverbrook telephoned to ask him to review a novel by Lady Eleanor Smith, daughter of their old friend, Lord Birkenhead, [F. E. Smith], on the day of its publication instead of waiting for the 'Books and Persons' article day, which was every Thursday. Bennett snapped down in the journal: "I refused." He noted that on one day, "Philip Gibbs, John Henderson, secretary of the National Liberal Club, and Arthur Waugh of Chapman & Hall, all wrote asking me to take notice of books by their sons." He was not unsympathetic; he understood this natural bias and often responded to it, but with the reservation that he was possibly being a little less than fair to writers not having the same facility of access to his attention.

Surprisingly soon he was complaining in the journal that the articles were "becoming rather a nuisance. . . . When an author, perfectly unknown to me, calls with a book . . . when editors and publishers are continually sending books to me personally, in the hope . . ." and when some publishers misquoted his opinions in their advertisements, he wondered whether to be the world's best-paid book reviewer was worth it, after all. "Every morning I answer a mail full of letters from people wanting me to review their books or the books of their relatives and friends. I wonder who next I shall find demanding help from me." He told Professor Bodkin that he ignored "perhaps twenty-nine out of thirty books that come to me. When the pile becomes monstrous I often disregard it and write about something not in it at all. Freedom and enough money to buy a cigar are the only important things." And in another letter to the same friend: "Books come into this house in stacks and most of them I don't look at. Don't because can't."

Arnold Bennett to Frank Swinnerton:

> 75, Cadogan Square,
> S. W. 1.
>
> 10th November, 1927
>
> . . . Hughie [Hugh Walpole] was here yesterday. He is going to have all his teeth out on Wednesday, and my first night is on Wednesday. He said: 'Arnold, you think of me on Wednesday morning and I will think of you on Wednesday evening. Just give me a thought. Just let us give each other a thought.'
>
> Thine,
> A. B.

CHAPTER SEVENTEEN

(1)

IN the last years his name stood boldly out of its context of journalism and publicity in the capital letters of fame. He was novelist, dramatist, critic, moralist, and something more than the sum of them. At the heart of his character was the 'central righteousness' which inspired Aldous Huxley to write of him memorially as "a supremely decent man" and led A. G. Gardiner, long the editor of the London *Daily News* and admired essayist, to say of him that he was "one of those rare men to whom you would go, not when you had a mere grievance against fate, for he hates weakness, but when the pillars of your firmament were falling. And you would not go in vain". When the former Liberal Cabinet Minister, C. F. G. Masterman, was dying he counselled his wife: "If you're really in a hole, go to 'A.B.' He's the one."

Seldom a day without its appeal for help from some friend of past or present or from soliciting strangers. "I answered a mail full of requests from people who want my help. Every day I am expected to subscribe to funds for starving geniuses." Continually, too, came requests for permission to perform one or the other of his plays without fee. Passing on one such request to the Pinker office: "My heart is like butter," he wrote. "Tell them they must pay the normal fee but that I will give a subscription to their club, though I know nothing about it. If I must be charitable, I may as well get some credit for it." His agents referred to him a query from the Newton Abbot Repertory Company regarding their use of *Milestones* without permission: "They say they merely had a private reading by their members. But they think of producing it next year and would like to know if you would accept a percentage of takings, instead of the usual fee. They say that Galsworthy, Shaw and Barrie all do." Bennett, in reply: "The financial policy of Galsworthy and Barrie does not interest me, but that of Shaw does. You might tell them that I will accept the same terms as Shaw. Not that I approve the system. I don't."

Deserted wives brought him their problems, economic and emotional. One went on her knees in his drawing-room. "She begged me to lend her the cash to start in business; a teashop or something of that sort." A. E. W. Mason poured out to him a secret grief: " 'I haven't told anyone else. I was utterly devoted to that girl. She's sentenced to death. She can't last to the end of the year. She has brains and looks—and in three months she'll be on the dust heap.' Then he cried, sitting at table and turning to me. He really did cry, and sob, and his voice broke." T. S. Eliot and Humbert Wolfe called to discuss the future of the *New Criterion* magazine. "Their real object was to find out whether I would find capital. I showed little interest. The *New Criterion* is a dull production and always will be." Mrs. W. J. Locke, widow of one of the most prosperous of novelists, consulted him "about William's divine charity and gross incompetence in business. She said she had no one competent to advise her. . . . I spent one and a half hours in studying his infinitely foolish contracts and in writing to her about them". Lord Rothermere, brother of the late Lord Northcliffe and chief proprietor of the *Daily Mail* and its associated newspapers, "invited himself to lunch with me alone" at Cadogan Square. "He answered all my questions with perfect frankness," an unburdening about which Bennett made the note: "I couldn't understand why he wanted to talk to me and I still don't understand. I liked him." Lady Lavery, "very full of Ireland," requested his advice about an Irish friend of both of them who she believed would make a suitable High Commissioner in London. "I told her he probably wouldn't consider it at the salary—£1,500. She said she might get it doubled."

Charles Laughton called for "advice on intimate matters". Beverley Nichols "wished to refresh his memory of my face". Lance Sieveking "switched from B.B.C. affairs to his own literary problems", to which, Sieveking says, Bennett "gave grave and attentive consideration". Robert Nichols, poet, wearing his opal ring, "was waiting downstairs, full of himself. I was dying to sleep, but I had to listen to him. He had got in through a window." An old friend of his early days, confined in an inebriates' home, "implores my help in getting him out." Someone called with a scheme for a Co-operative Authors' Publishing Company, "in which idea I soon pointed out a few snags."

A man named W—— called, without an appointment, to see me. Editor, he said, of an undergraduate magazine. I refused. He insisted. I then said I would see him in 15 minutes. I did. A pale young man, well-dressed, Oxford. He is running a new illustrated monthly, rather on the lines of the *Bystander*, which I detest. I saw the first number (1/–). I could see no point in it. However, he was young, and just starting a new monthly for the young, and he asked me for an article gratis, and somehow, like a fool, I couldn't refuse him. I talked to him for 50 minutes.

The young invariably evoked his deliberately cultivated put-yourself-in-his-place gift of imagination and were rarely sent empty away. The brothers Sitwell have been generous in their remembrance of his encouragement to them as young writers of the '20s. To them Bennett became "Uncle Arnold". They arranged an art exhibition. He undertook to give it a send-off by writing the preface to the catalogue. Sir Osbert Sitwell has told about it in *Left Hand, Right Hand*: ". . . accused so often of avarice and stinginess, this writer, the most highly paid of his epoch and the continual victim of overwork, had accepted to write the preface without payment of any kind, solely in order to help two young writers in whom he believed, and whom he knew to be undergoing a difficult time financially. But, in truth, there was always something big and generous about him."

Noel Coward stood in the same nephew-ish relationship. "Don't leave me," he begged Bennett at a public banquet. "I feel on the very edge of hysteria among all these important people." Henry Williamson, dining at Cadogan Square and talking about "his intimate affairs", remembers Bennett's "wisdom and goodness". Stephen Potter met Bennett at the A. P. Herberts' at Hammersmith.

He heard I was doing a book on D. H. Lawrence and must have known from my talk that it was going to be a pretty brash, hero-worshipping affair, though certainly sincere. It does not now seem to me that this is the kind of book I would in his place have encouraged in a young man; but he *was* encouraging and told me helpful things about Lawrence. He asked to see the publisher's contract for the book, read it with great care, and made measured suggestions about this particular document and about contracts in general. My chief impression of him was that he combined great natural dignity and a careful style of conversation, always saying exactly what he meant, with a touch as light as a feather. I was very greatly struck by his unobtrusive and deliberate kindness to an aspiring writer who had no name whatever.

[327]

At the same time he thought it "a lark and a desirable thing" to give the young "a flick now and then". No one, he claimed in the *Evening Standard*, had done more for the young than he. "We are becoming great friends," he said, mentioning Noel Coward in a letter to his rightful nephew, Richard Bennett. "It is remarkable how I consort well with persons young enough to be my grandchildren."

(2)

His tufted forelock had become a true *panache*: "it took men's eyes," wrote Gerald Gould in the London *Observer*. You could pick him out by it at once in the crowded *foyer* at a fashionable first-night. It was conspicuous in the throng at the Royal Academy private view. "There's Arnold Bennett——!" Or, as an artist whom he did not know very well shouted to him across the pavement of Sloane Street one morning: "Why, if it isn't the big-pot from the Potteries!" Apparently the obvious joke had not reached Bennett's ears before. He was amused and "laffed like anything", he said.

If this acquaintance had followed him on that morning's 'thinking walk', he would have crossed the river at Battersea Bridge and turned right along the Albert Embankment to Lambeth. This had become his route more often now in these last years. It took him past the old Doulton works (*circa* 1873). Pots were still being made there then and there are streets of houses to the rear that cannot have failed to remind him of what he had escaped from long ago, the dingy repetitive homes of an artisan society which he had known so well and had so faithfully described. Vauxhall Walk, Lilac Place, Bolwell Street, Granby Buildings, Salamanca Street: the names are more colourful than Burslem's, but the grime of their bricks was the by-product of the same great upheaving industrial change. Sometimes he would walk into the still more grimy hinterland dominated by Lotts Road Power Station, where the housewives were beset by precisely the same worry as those of Dalehall, how to keep the curtains clean. "The smoke grit is a great problem here."

More frequently now, too, he was admitting inferior results from his 'thinking walks' or, as he occasionally called them, his 'reflection outings'. Successful or not in that way, he almost never failed to add more words to the journal as soon as he was indoors again. He meets an old friend who is full of pleasure in his son's games prowess at school. Bennett is unimpressed by the prowess. What strikes him as the worthwhile part of the recital is that it disclosed "ghastly stories of public school hygiene. Six towels among thirty boys and six or eight bath-tubs often liberally coated with mud as the boys come in from footer. Towels black, floors black," and it all goes down under the compulsion which he admitted to himself in the extra-journal of 1926, a constant concern with the number of words he could write in a year: "it would annoy me to let my average fall below 1,000 a day."

Almost it seems that some morbidity was at work in him: this increasing preoccupation with the not-significant was a veering away from the artistic canon and still more from the common sense on which no small part of his reputation rested. But the perversity in existence which can prevent the best-intentioned of human beings from keeping their bargains, which can cheat us of the opportunity to live up to the best than is in us, had forced Arnold Bennett into circumstances in which his almost renowned common sense was often of little avail.

"Everything has gone wrong, my girl," he said to Dorothy Cheston Bennett out of the woe of his last illness. It was as if he realised, recessionally, that his common sense was now of no avail. Or was it that he saw, what one seems to see with sharp clarity at this distance, that recent actions of his had been most uncharacteristically imprudent? The new flat in Chiltern Court, in particular: he had taken it with a precipitancy that might have had pathological significance, so alien was it to his accepted habits of mind and judgment.

That impulsiveness had not governed his most inexplicable imprudence, his failure to provide security for his old age, carries one on to the speculation that Arnold Bennett's deepest drive was towards the grand surcease which lies beyond the sanctions of insurance policies, annuities and funds. The energy behind his prodigious and sometimes memorable labours was self-destructive. For him there could be no old age.

(3)

"Career as a dramatist closing!" he wrote on June 18, 1928. "I really doubt whether I will do another," the play he was then at work on being *The Return Journey*, which he called his 'Faust' play. Hardly anyone was taking him seriously as a dramatist any longer. Success in the theatre had deserted him. His play for the Theatre Royal, Drury Lane, called *London Life* and written with Knoblock, had been a serious failure for the theatre, as for him and the producer, Basil Dean. One of the directors of the theatre, Bennett said, had been so sure that

[329]

the play would fail that he had resigned in protest against the board's decision to produce it. Bennett wrote to his sister from Le Touquet, where he was photographed wearing his boots on the sands as he played with his daughter Virginia:

. . . I have had to go over to London to comfort Gerald du Maurier. Like all theatrical persons, he does his correspondence by telegram. His wires usually begin: 'Great Arnold, help, help, help.' He rehearses till the end of this week, then takes three weeks' holiday; then about two weeks more of rehearsal. Production supposed to be 30th August (but I doubt it). His production of the play is due to sheer accident. I was walking down Regent Street about ten weeks ago, and an arm was put on my shoulder, and a voice said: 'Arnold, you'll get killed if you moon along like that.' Gerald! I said: 'I shall not. I know exactly what I'm doing. I'm thinking out a play.' He said: 'It's mine!' Of course I said he couldn't possibly have it. This always sharpens their appetite. He wouldn't leave me alone. He sent Viola Tree to wheedle me. He offered to buy the play in the dark. I refused. At last I said he could read it when it was finished; but he must say yes or no in two days. He did, and bought the play instantly. He will be very good in it. He knows he has produced only one good play in fifteen years: 'Dear Brutus.' And he is now getting alarmed for his prestige; wants to produce something by a good author. He is very nice to work with; but very *nevrosé*, if witty. I must say they all adore me, and are frightened of me.

This is by no means all. I wrote a film for British International Pictures, with which B.I.P. is *enchanted*. It also is being done. Dupont is the producer. He enchants *me*. German-French. He really is an artist. He did 'Vaudeville' and 'Moulin Rouge'. Having taken delivery of the last film, 'Piccadilly', B.I.P. at once asked for another one. Of course I said: 'Out of the question.' And of course I graciously agreed in the end. This has to be delivered in the autumn, too. Add to this that I have eleven short stories ordered but unwritten, six special articles ditto, one article a month for the 'Pictorial' and one a week for the 'Evening Standard', and you will understand that my brain still has to function at intervals.

Love,

A. B.

P.S. My only important job is a long, dull, novel about the entire organisation and total entity of a big hotel (Savoy).

The postscript reference was to *Imperial Palace*, the background of which he later publicly announced was *not* the Savoy Hotel, London. But before committing himself to that immense if not finally impressive task he had two other novels to write, *Accident*, in which he contained the story he had to tell within the time and space limits of a train journey from London to the Riviera, and *The Strange Vanguard*, yet one more 'fantasia', attempting to blend cosmopolitanism in Italy with Five Towns character and producing an unsatisfying and somewhat insipid result. *Accident* ran as a serial in the London *Daily Express*: price, £2,250. It drew on his memories of a railway smash in France described in *Books and Persons* and *Things that have Interested Me* and in a letter to Mrs. H. G. Wells immediately after its occurrence in 1911. Its smooth competence does not suggested the tired writer: at work on it, he complained of "evil nights", "acute exhaustion," "enormous enfeeblement," and there were days when he was too low to work on it at all. "Great rumpus over servants. Nurse had packed up her things and was going. Her uncle was waiting outside for her. Great scene between the four of us in the dining-room, both Dorothy and Nurse crying. Yes, great scenes. As this servant rumpus develops more the less I understand it. It has happily comic aspects, but in the meantime it is the damnedest nuisance." He wrote to his sister:

. . . Would you like to have Virginia for a fortnight from the 17th? I only mention it because you seem to have a certain partiality for the child. The reason is that Dorothy has been, and is, terribly racked with jaw abscess trouble. The thing culminated in an operation, with doctors and dentists in league. On the day before the operation the temporary cook walked out. On the day after, Annie gave notice. And on the day after that the second housemaid said she must go, and the kitchen maid wanted to go, but isn't going. A new cook came in yesterday; but she mightn't stay. Nurse must have a holiday. Annie has always acted as nurse in her absence, but that can't be now. The ever excellent Annie is in a high state of nerves and will shortly depart. She told me today that we had both been very kind to her, and she was very grateful and devoted, and so on; but that she *must* go. . . . Well, well! And I'm supposed to be writing a novel!

And still he worked on, at the novel, at films, articles, reviews, at the heavy correspondence every morning, his "chores", the thorns in the cushion of success, which Thackeray had found so onerous too, and at finishing the play for du Maurier. It was produced at the St. James's Theatre, where Bennett, sitting in the back row of the dress circle, heard "a self-complacent gent directly in front of me" say to his companion: "To think of one of our leading actors doing this kind of drivel!" On the other hand: "G.B.S. and H.G.W. both think well of it," he reported to Professor Bodkin in a letter.

Bennett's work secret was that he would allow no mood to come between him and his desk. "Writing has no business to be an affair of moods," he told the then editor of the *Sunday Pictorial*, W. A. McWhirter. He contended in that editor's hearing that if a writer had thought out efficiently what he proposed to write, the temperament question should not arise. Mr. McWhirter was seeing much of Bennett in the middle '20s. Recalling their meetings, he says:

> It is not easy to estimate him truly. Some of his characteristics appeared to me to be entirely contradictory. My view of Arnold was that he always essentially remained the man from the Midlands who thought he had mastered his youthful awe of London and all that it implied but who in fact had never finally done so. Luxury dazzled him to the last, yet he never lost his great understanding of and sympathy with 'ordinary people'.

"The only writer I have encountered whose work needed no subbing," meaning sub-editing, said another of the editors who bought many of Bennett's articles and stories. "Except for the catchline"— a temporary heading put on when sending copy to the printer—"I could always send Bennett's stuff to the printer exactly as he sent it to us," a compliment which Bennett would have wished to share with Winifred Nerney, his secretary. He was scrupulous about length: an article must contain the number of words contracted for as nearly as possible. One of his *Daily Express* articles, commissioned for interment with others by famous writers in the foundations of the new office building in Fleet Street which has housed that newspaper since 1932, exceeded the stipulated length by nine words. In fun, the literary editor of the day pointed out the discrepancy to Bennett on the proof. Bennett deleted nine words. "I shall be glad of them for my next article." To the same editor he made the point: "Few of your writers understand that an article should have a shape, a curve, that it should be constructed. I must inform you that mine always conform to that requirement. I go to the greatest trouble to ensure that they do."

The *Sunday Chronicle* offered him £350 for an article on the Potteries. "I said no. It would be to invite all sorts of trouble. Also it would mean going there, and that I have no wish to do."

(4)

He was not rebounding so buoyantly from the fatigues that were endemic in his life and probably an inescapable part of his physical inheritance. Perhaps aware of it, he had resumed the Hornibrook system of exercising. Combining it with diet, he reduced his weight by a stone and a half and had to have his clothes altered to fit his changed figure. He had heard of the Hornibrook system from a friend who had learnt the exercises direct from their originator, F. A. Hornibrook. Bennett practised them at secondhand. Discovering its virtues, he became an enthusiast for the system and recommended it to everyone who remarked his changed appearance. He was startled when a friend at the Reform Club, George Sampson, said that he did not like the change: "he repeated that he did not like it at all." Taken back, Bennett was relieved when Gardiner showed "obvious interest". He told Gardiner "all about Hornibrook". He told the Duke of Marlborough about it at lunch and passed on the good word, also, to a fellow guest at the Duke's table, Sir William Berry (now Lord Camrose), "whom I am getting to know better and to like even more." Two old friends, met in Lower Regent Street, "commented at once on my new appearance of physical fitness. I recommended Hornibrook."

January 19, 1928.—We dined at Cynthia Noble's, Kent House. I expected a small dinner, but there were 20 covers. I sat next to Mrs. Saxton Noble and liked her. Later in the evening, she asked me to give her a demonstration of the Hornibrook exercises. We could not find an empty room, so we took a retired corridor in this vast house. I lay down and did the exercises. She lay down and imitated me. She must have been very beautiful—still is, in fact.

Another of his preachments at this time was that "the secret of health and equanimity" is to be in bed before midnight and the earlier the better. He told this to the supposedly Anglophobe William Randolph Hearst, "a very agreeable man of about fifty-eight, with a striking nose, urbane, smiles easily and listens well. He seemed to me to have a lot of character. I liked him. He didn't agree about the early bedtime, saying that as a morning newspaper man, 5 a.m. had been his time for bed for very many years."

His social activities at this period, catalogued in the journal, might be read as having casebook significance, symptoms of change in his personality. At a time when his metabolic rate was infallibly slowing down, he was quickening his living pace, dining late, dancing late, sitting up late at the Kitcat, the Gargoyle and the Cave of Harmony, where Elsa Lanchester and Harold Scott held their revels. "Great jollification at the Garrick. Pat Hastings in a terrific rag. Home at 12.30, when neuralgia began." A remembered midnight session was at Lord Beaverbrook's London house, with Dean Inge, Winston Churchill, Reginald McKenna, and Dr. Archibald Fleming, the Scots divine of St. Columba's, Pont Street. "It was rather a lark to see him and Inge quaffing champagne like anything at that hour." "Extremely exhausted after late nights," is an entry for October, 1928. "G. B. S. and wife, Lili d'Alvarez and Drummond Wolff for lunch. I was *hors de combat*, but I had to keep up."

That year he made £22,000, every penny by his own exertions, as unremitting on his holidays and week-end visits as at his desk in Cadogan Square. He had to keep up and it was killing him.

He went to the memorial service at St. Martin-in-the-Fields for Leslie Faber, a distinguished actor and Garrick Club friend of his, in August, 1929. "A desolating affair, because through unwise living and overwork towards the end he had lost all reserve power. If he hadn't been a fool he might have been alive."

(5)

Journal, *September 25, 1929.*—Today I began a long novel. At 3.30 p.m. The hour has an interest—but only for me. I have not written a long novel for years. As a man with a secret tendency towards idleness I prefer to write a short novel. It is easier. Not easier to *do*, but less of a strain on the creative faculty. What generally spoils long novels is the untimely supervening creative fatigue. This happened to 'The Heart of Midlothian'. It is a calamity which the author has very little power to prevent. Heaven in its wisdom decided to give you a certain amount of strength. You cannot, increase it. Towards the end of the race, if you are tired you are tired, and there you are! Nobody can pour a quart out of a pint pot.

No work on earth is more trying than creative writing. As you write the first words you are self-conscious. When you finish the first page of manuscript you think: 'I have so-many hundred more pages to write. Every one of them has to be written, and every one of them must be good. Every one of them must be the best. No letting down.'

I reckon that this novel will fill 900 pages of manuscript. How do I reckon? I don't reckon. I just know. Experience has taught me pre-knowledge. When I began 'The Old Wives' Tale', I announced to the domestic hearth: 'This novel will be 200,000 words long, divided into four equal parts.' Well, it was. The new novel will be 150,000 words long[1] and probably not divided into parts. I think I have now grown out of dividing novels into parts. Today such a division strikes me as being a bit pompous. I know the main plot, but by no means all the incidents thereof, though I have a few titbits of episodes which I shall not omit. The episode of the gloves, for instance, which I found in and appropriated from the Journal of the brothers de Goncourt. I know the three chief characters, but by no means all the ins-and-outs of them. They won't alter—I would never allow any character of mine to get the whip-hand of me—but I shall fill them out. I know the 'feel' of the novel. That won't alter, either. And I have the whole of the material for the novel; and it is indexed, in a notebook. I would sooner lose fifty pages of the manuscript than that notebook. If I did lose it, I think I should be capable of abandoning the novel for ever. And yet I leave the notebook lying about.

I have been fighting for years against the instinct to write this particular novel. About thirty years ago I was taken to the Savoy Hotel for tea, came out, went home, and wrote 'The Grand Babylon Hotel' in three weeks of evening work. 'The Grand Babylon Hotel' was a mere lark. The big hotel de luxe is a very serious organisation; it is in my opinion a unique subject for a serious novel; it is stuffed with human nature of extremely various kinds. The subject is characteristic of the age; it is as modern as the morning's milk; it is tremendous, and worthy of tremendous handling. I dare say it's beyond me. But nobody else has caught hold of it, and if I am not audacious I'm nothing. Today I wrote three pages. 897 left to do! The thought is terrifying.

And when I have finished it and corrected the manuscript and corrected the typescript and corrected the slip-proofs and corrected the page-proofs, and it is published, half the assessors and appraisers

[1] It was 243,000 words long.

in Britain and America will say: 'Why doesn't he give us another 'Old Wives' Tale'? I have written between seventy and eighty books. But also I have written only four: 'The Old Wives' Tale,' 'The Card,' 'Clayhanger' and 'Riceyman Steps.' All the others are made a reproach to me because they are neither 'The Old Wives' Tale', nor 'The Card', nor 'Clayhanger', nor 'Riceyman Steps'. And 'Riceyman Steps' would have been made a reproach too, if the servant Elsie had not happened to be a very 'sympathetic' character. Elsie saved 'Riceyman Steps' from being called sordid and morbid and all sorts of bad adjectives. As if the 'niceness' of a character had anything to do with the quality of the novel in which it appears!

(6)

The novel, *Imperial Palace*—title taken from the hotel of that name at Annecy—was a size of task which he had not attempted since *The Old Wives' Tale*, exactly twenty years before. It represented a still more imperious effort of will, for he was very tired and pathetically less susceptible to the refreshments of rest and change which from now on he was increasingly forced to seek. The preparatory work for the novel was in itself a considerable task of organisation. With the full co-operation of the Savoy Hotel directors, headed by George Reeves-Smith, Bennett explored every department, making innumerable notes as he went and sometimes returning home half-dropping with fatigue. He had long since made it known to the reading public that he was fascinated by the life which flows through a great hotel and especially by the magic, as he saw it, which keeps the establishment running so smoothly. Indeed, it had been held against him, sometimes irrelevantly, as an unworthy obsession; most critics of his work had taken exception to it, among them Desmond MacCarthy, admirer and friend: "To me the 'luxury hotel' is awful. I prefer lodgings." Bennett said once that he had wanted to be the manager of a grand hotel. He made George Cannon declaim about the splendours of the hotel future to Hilda Lessways. In *Paris Nights* he worked himself up to fervent appreciation of the spectacle of a great hotel rising out of a snowy Swiss landscape: "The apparition was impressive, poetic, almost overbearing. It was of a piece with the mountains. It was indubitably and movingly beautiful," and so on. In his last summer Bennett had as his guests for lunch at the Garrick Club Sir Newman Flower, the publisher, and his son Desmond, who recalls:

ARNOLD BENNETT (LEFT) WITH SIR EDWIN LUTYENS IS SHOWN OVER THE 'DAILY MAIL' OFFICES BY THE HON. ESMOND HARMSWORTH (NOW LORD ROTHERMERE)

HOTEL CONCHA · MIRAMAR

JUAN JAUREGUI

FUENTERRABIA

(MARINA)

29 - 4 24

Dear Miss Nerney

[shorthand text]

INSTRUCTIONS TO HIS SECRETARY

My father mentioned that he and I were going to Munich, and it turned out that Arnold was going to be there at the same time. My father asked him what hotel he would be staying at and he replied, making subtle use of his stammer, of which he was such a master: "I can't remember the name, but look for the biggest and most expensive—I'll be there." And he was.

In 1924 he had made more notes after a visit of inspection to the Savoy, with Reeves-Smith and Rupert D'Oyly Carte as his guides. In 1927 he discussed the project of a grand hotel novel with Richmond Temple, publicity chief of the Savoy Hotel group. "In ninety minutes or less he gave me all the ideas I wanted, and I practically decided to write the book."

No other book of his was written under such stress. Following its progress through the unpublished journal pages is like watching the struggles of a swimmer caught in a fatal current. Wave after wave of exhaustion threatens to submerge him. "Utterly exhausted." "Extremely depressed." "Acute nervous exasperation." "Neuralgia flitting all over the body." "Scarcely any desire now to sleep." "Another 1,500 words, despite a ruthless and terrible interruption by Dorothy," whose "*initiative* energy", he notes, "is constantly amazing." "Extremely depressed about everything." "Great household upset." "This book is terrible to do." He wrote to Frederick Marriott on December 4, 1929:

Up till 8.15 tonight I was coming to the Hour of Song. But in the end circumstances were too much for me. Dorothy has just returned from Paris, extremely exhausted and very unwell. The cook has taken to her bed this day. There are 2 new maids in the house who are n.g. Atkinson's (chauffeur) father, mother and sister were all seriously burned today in a fire and are in St. George's Hospital, and I myself last night had about 1 hour's sleep. . . . I regret it extremely. My love to you all.

He was losing money in theatre ventures, some of them backed against his better judgment. A company formed to produce plays at the Court Theatre, Sloane Square, failed after a few months, his share of the loss several hundred pounds. He found small consolations in reflecting that these enterprises of his at least gave employment to people often in need of it. When Hubert Griffith, as dramatic critic,

[337]

remarked of a play which they had seen together that it was hardly worth a mention, Bennett said: "I hope you'll think fit to give it a few lines. Those young girls worked hard. Remember, it's their livelihood. They've probably been rehearsing like mad. It would mean a great deal to them."

Another source of worry was the *New Statesman*. The paper's finances were languishing. There had been a libel action for the settlement of which he had to find, as his directorial share, close on a thousand pounds. Why there was no insurance to cover such a contingency he did not record. He had already put money into circulation schemes and he was being asked for more. He was involved in staff complications. And Clifford Sharp, the editor, was becoming unreliable in matters of policy. Bennett was troubled because he saw nothing for Sharp, whom he had known some time, but resignation or dismissal. "It will be a shock to him." When Sharp was finally dismissed, Bennett noted: "He never argued or protested. It really was a very sad scene. The best thing for me is not to let my imagination work on it at all." Kingsley Martin was a candidate for the succession and was invited to meet Bennett with other members of the board. "He made a favourable impression," but it was agreed to defer a decision until G. D. H. Cole had been interviewed. Meanwhile, the question of new finance was pressing. Bennett was sounded again. "I refused," not necessarily because the paper already owed him money.

Also disturbing was the rumour that Doran was changing his career: much guessing about this between the Pinkers and Bennett. Two years earlier Doran had cabled him enthusiastically about the merger he had accomplished with the firm of Doubleday, which thus became Doubleday, Doran & Company, "making the staunchest and most effective publishing organisation in America," the cable announced. "Crave your benediction." Bennett had cabled back: "May heaven guide you my benediction must be based on further information." Doran cabled again. "Everything going grandly future for us all is brilliant loving greetings." Now his old friend was strangely silent. Bennett was baffled. "Where do we go if the thing is true?" he asked the Pinkers. "It will almost certainly mean finding a new publisher over there and starting new contracts," a possibility which evidently did not appeal to him.

The great economic blizzard was blowing across the United States. A leading New York newspaper-syndicate head, returning home from Berlin via London, wept in a Fleet Street editor's room. When a friend of Bennett's showed him a letter from New York in which the writer, a play-broker, prophesied a complete monetary breakdown, Bennett, said this friend, "looked fearfully gloomy." The reinforcing power of Marcus Aurelius was perhaps in recession too.

The Doran rumour came over more strongly. He could not understand why Doran kept him in the dark. "It all seems very odd," he wrote to Ralph Pinker, adding: "I shall be coming to see you before the end of the month. As I only call at your office about every ten years, I shall regard the event as not without importance. I shall desire to see, in addition to yourself, Mr. Wicken and Miss Pratt, about departmental affairs."

The important visit took place. The Pinkers' distinguished and profitable client was received with deference. F. C. Wicken was manager of the office. Miss Pratt looked after dramatic rights. Wicken was often left in charge and when this happened Bennett made a point of complimenting him on business successfully put through. Their letter exchanges are marked by encouragement and consideration on Bennett's side and by appreciation on the other. After the visit Bennett had requests from members of the staff for his signed photograph. Wicken wrote: "It was a great pleasure to us all to see you in the office and we wish your visits were more frequent." Wicken died, suddenly. Acknowledging Bennett's letter of sympathy, "and the very beautiful wreath," his widow recalled that her husband had told her "that you more than once made favourable remarks about his work. He spoke of it with pride".

(7)

"I failed to recognise three people whom I know well. This is growing on me," noted in his last year, 1930. He assumed it to be an effect of overwork. His past year's total of words had been 340,000. In his journal for the new year he had introduced a new habit, making a daily weather note at the top of each page. Depression and neuralgia were a continuing subject of comment. A new alarm was sounded: "My heart has been beating irregularly now for several days. I think I shall go to see the doctor." "Dorothy's incessant theatre talk" suggests other distractions. "There was no peace the whole evening." Wanting what he called "something biggish" to excite his mind for the novel, which was lagging, he read Balzac's *Interdiction*. For the same purpose he was going to more concerts than for several years.

Schnabel playing Mozart and Brahms. I was next to Margot Oxford. Dame Ethel Smyth right in front of me. Schnabel's piano-playing was very great. His string quartet was simply awful. Dame Ethel Smyth said it made her feel as if she would be taken short.

His old friend André Gide desired to write an introduction for a French translation of *The Old Wives' Tale* which was being done by the Governor of the Tchad, M. Coppet. Roger Martin du Gard was assisting in revisions. "This opportunity of getting a first-class presentation to the lettered French public is almost unique," Bennett wrote to the Pinkers. "There are dozens of writers who would give their heads to have an introduction by Gide, who has spent an immense amount of time on the work, gratis!" It was a much-needed tonic for his self-esteem as an artist.

Jo Davidson, the American sculptor, and his wife dined at Cadogan Square: "they were simply exquisite," a lyrical note rarely sounded in Bennett's appreciation even of his closest friends. He was reading a life of Mrs. Eddy: "marvellous material for a novel." A Christian Science exponent, Mrs. Squire, was coming to the house for talks with him every week. For her services he was paying a fee, later a point of professional argument about whether it might be charged as an expense for income-tax purposes. "I have had her course of treatment for seven months. She has done me good, but not as regards speech." The Christian Science thesis that this is a mental world he said he could accept; some of its other assumptions he could not.

A cheque for 250 guineas from the New York Book of the Month Club for advisory services came as agreeable confirmation of his belief that there was a book club future. As to that, he had conducted himself not entirely becomingly in negotiations for the founding of a book club in Britain. On his last visit to London Doran had asked A. S. Frere of Heinemann's to go and see Bennett. "He has something he wishes to say to you." It was a proposal for starting a book club, to which he announced he was willing to lend his name and prestige. All this provided that Frere would go to work at once and make the necessary financial arrangements.

Taking him at his word, which included a promise to sponsor the scheme generally, Frere went to a great deal of trouble to secure backing. Having finally got it, he heard that Bennett was in touch with the *Daily Express* about a similar scheme. It seemed important to lose no time. Frere promptly registered several likely book club names, secured the interest of Hugh Walpole and J. B. Priestley, and started what became the Book Society, which has had a successful history over the last twenty years. When he next saw Arnold Bennett there was a sharp exchange between them, Bennett protesting that Frere had used *his* idea. Taxed then with having gone back on his word, Bennett said with a lift of his crumpled chin: "I suppose I am at liberty to change my mind if I wish to do so." If this was a wilful deviation from his high standard of personal rectitude one feels that its originating impulse was beyond his control. And he was developing almost pathological obstinacies.

Lunching with Hugh Walpole at 90 Piccadilly, he showed annoyance because cheese was served instead of a sweet. Walpole was known among his friends for being careful, if not mean, in such details. When Bennett asked for a sweet, Walpole said that there was no sweet to be had. "Where's the sweet? I want a sweet," Bennett insisted. Walpole repeated that there was no sweet and that in any event it was now too late to do anything about it. Very deliberately Bennett rose, walked out of the room, took a taxi to the Ritz Hotel three or four hundred yards away, and presently reappeared at Walpole's table. "I . . . I've had . . . a sweet," he said and sat down again.

He had a high place on the invitation list of Lady Colefax, one of the last hostesses in the *salon* tradition. She and Bennett were friends: his journal shows that, like so many others, she went to him for advice. He speaks of her as having "social enemies" and of her "evidently having felt severely some of the things that are said about her". There was one crowded evening at her London home, Argyll House, Chelsea, when very much in the manner of 'the Card', seeing that she had many guests to look after, he said: "Well, I musn't keep you." This notion she brushed aside: "They can take care of themselves." Drawing his attention to the number of people who were in the dining-room, "drinking and munching," she said: "Look! They've got their feet well into the trough!" and Bennett added to his note of it: "Not much brotherly, or sisterly, love at this reception. But much back-biting."

Early in February he lunched at the Caledonian Club with James Bone to meet H. L. Mencken and John Owens, editor of the *Baltimore Sun*. Ivor Brown and Herbert Sidebotham, well-known as 'Scrutator' of the *Sunday Times*, were in the party. "It was highly agreeable. I liked the redoubtable Mencken, and also John Owens, both fundamentally *decent* men." A few days later he supped in the Savoy Grillroom with Alice Duer Miller, famous in the Second World War as

[341]

the author of *The White Cliffs,* and Alexander Woollcott. "Alice Duer Miller is an exceedingly nice woman. I remembered the titles of some articles written by her nineteen years ago and this pleased her. Woollcott was very interesting," which was something less than a compliment to that New York celebrity.

He dined with Robert and Sylvia Lynd, meeting there J. B. Morton, 'Beachcomber' of the *Daily Express*: "excellent, he. Terrific talking the whole time." The next night his hosts were Sir Ian and Lady Hamilton, both put down in the journal as "terrific". And the night after: "To 90, Gower Street to dine with the Duff Coopers. Charming house. One real and two hired menservants. Goodish dinner. Very lively. Lady Juliet Duff, the Harold Nicolsons, Maurice Baring, Desmond MacCarthy. This is astounding: Duff doesn't smoke; hence there were no cigars!" The Bernard Shaws came to lunch at Cadogan Square and the same evening he sat next to Shaw at a dinner given by Wells. "Augustine Birrell, Shaw, John Drinkwater, P. G. Wodehouse, Marie Belloc Lowndes, May Sinclair, J. D. Beresford, and Edgar Jepson. We discussed the row between Wells and the Authors' Society. Opinion was unanimously in Wells' favour and we all decided to demand a special meeting of the Council." Jepson also came to a personal decision, that "Bennett did not at all charm me". He thought him "desperately clever but cheap". Jepson was a small, witty man who played brilliant bridge, smoked highly scented tobacco, and wrote short stories about little girls. Bennett did not care for him, either.

March 16, 1930.—Rheumatism all over the body. We dined at the Savoy. Dorothy carried theatrical talk to excess, so that I had to protest very firmly. I protested throughout dinner. Theatrical talk is a tremendous strain on my nerves. However, she saw the point. Very depressed. Reflected gloomily about D's theatrical financial position. Both bearing up under misfortune.

Before attending the specially convened meeting of the Authors' Society, he lunched with E. M. Forster: "a very reluctant talker. Afterwards: "You never saw such an array of authors. Shaw, Wells, Birrell, Galsworthy, Jacobs, F. Anstey, Anthony Hope, J. M. Barrie, Beresford, Walpole, Priestley, May Sinclair, Marie Belloc Lowndes, Ian Hay, Ashley Dukes, and others. But they made a perfectly rotten show in discussion."

Sir William Rothenstein, the artist, asked him as a favour to read the typescript of his memoirs which he was preparing for publication. Bennett said he would, "simply to be agreeable to him," but it was one more burdensome "chore". The sensation of head tightness had returned. "I had to get up between 3.30 and 5.30 a.m. to obtain control of my mind." After the first night of G. B. Stern's *Debonair* on April 23: "The new young star, Celia Johnson, aged twenty-one, I thought very little of. I got home at 11.50 very depressed."

He was shown over the *Daily Mail* offices and machine-rooms by Esmond Harmsworth [now Lord Rothermere]: "the machinery and organisation there are immense and marvellous." A dinner for American newspaper proprietors visiting London—"Ochs, Scripps, Howells, etc."—gave him an opportunity of meeting the Prince of Wales, "who was late," of sitting next to Nicholas Murray Butler, and of discovering that he "liked Dawes, the American ambassador, best of all". The Prince, meeting him in the lavatory in the course of the evening, said: "I don't know you very well, but may I tell you a story?" Bennett's attitude to royal persons was constrained, sometimes rudely so, no doubt the result of his Methodism, his Liberalism, and perhaps even his Socialism. A distinguished London physician, still with us, had as his guest at the Garrick Club one evening a popular member of the Royal Family. Seeing Bennett dining alone, the host spoke to him, saying that he would like to present him to the Prince. Bennett's response to the courtesy was to draw his napkin across his mouth, turn and stare over the back of his chair at the waiting guest, call out with a casual wave of the hand: "Hullo!" and resume his meal.

May 16, 1930.—Dorothy working up for a nerve storm, being acutely fatigued and worried by her theatre affairs. The fish didn't suit her. She sent down word that she wanted the cook to stay up and cook a supper for her. The cook wouldn't. I went down myself to see the cook, but I immediately saw that there was nothing doing and came back. D. was late for her theatre but, furious, she suddenly at the last minute darted off downstairs to have a row with the cook. Fortunately I caught her at the foot of the basement stairs and brought her back. So I saved the whole evening. In bed at 12.18. D., though exhausted, talked incessant theatre until I left her in bed. These evenings are very disturbing.

That month he wrote 28,000 words of *Imperial Palace*: "best month yet." The same entry includes: "To first Toscanini concert. Simply tremendously beautiful." There were three Toscanini concerts: "the last unequalled, with unequalled enthusiasm. Utterly exhausted. I could not sleep. I probably had an hour in all." At one of the concerts:

I had given seats to Tania [Harriett Cohen and Arnold Bax. Concert terrific, especially the Elgar Variations. I took them to the Savoy Grill for supper. Willie Walton asked if he could join us. Very agreeable. I saw Elgar. He had not been to hear his music. He is a disgruntled old man. I congratulated him on the performance. He said he never went to hear his own music. He is full of affectations, always saying something silly. He said the Variations were composed thirty-one years ago, and people called them silly then. He *didn't* say that that happened to lots of stuff that in the end comes through.

Writing to Dorothy Cheston Bennett, on tour with *Milestones*: "Your letter received this morn was a very good one. I hope you won't expect me to show my feelings too much, because I can't. Each of us has his own way of existing," adding with middle-aged credulity: "although I am young for my years . . ." a claim which the fobs, once again, made incongruous.

There was a Heinemann lunch for Edna Ferber: "I am as thick as thieves with her." They discussed the social side of their lives. "At home she spends two or three nights a week alone, going to bed at 9.30. I spoke of my inability to stand the social racket," from which he appeared to be making no effort to detach himself. Dinners with the Colefaxes, the Laverys, the Sitwells, the Herberts, the Maclagans, with his women friends, Jeanne de Casalis, Ethel Sands, Marjorie Gordon, Harriet Cohen. Suppers at the Savoy with Edgar Wallace, Harry Preston, Sir Denison Ross, A. E. W. Mason, 'Quex' of the *Evening News*. Dancing at the Embassy, at Ciro's, at the lesser night resorts.

"Tania Cohen came to lunch exactly on time. She said she never spent a penny she could save. She looked older and better. Her hair seemed to be in excellent health. She said she loved all the attentions she received. She felt she 'belonged to the public', and seemed at least three-quarters sincere." A supper at the Herberts, 12 Hammersmith Terrace, was "an uproarious evening. An air of picknicking. The Wadsworths and the Eric Kenningtons came in later. Herbert sang. I sang. Mrs. Wadsworth argued too much but seemed quite all right. Gwen Herbert grows more and more admirable and lovable." Meeting Malcolm Sargent for the first time: "Young, clever, vivacious, amusing, interesting. I liked him." An evening with Samuel Butler's biographer was recorded:

> Dined at Henry Festing Jones', 120, Maida Vale. He is getting deaf and has a microphone apparatus for his right ear and a sort of tortoise-shell sounding-box for his left ear. He thus heard fairly well. A simple but admirable meal, as usual. A quiet evening. I was extremely tired and didn't talk till I had been there 1½ hours. The old man (over 80) is as charming and as boyish as ever. He drank our health and Virginia's. He told us that his father was illegitimate. Showed us his fans and books and was quietly expansive. We thought, though, that he must lead a very dull life there all alone. As we went I said: 'Don't come downstairs with us.' He said: 'Yes, I shall. I always do. The time will come when I shan't be able to, but till then I shall continue to take people downstairs.' He stood at the open front door and waved us off.

Mrs. Somerset Maugham's way with taxi-drivers also had to be noted: "it showed her to be a very clear-headed and energetic woman." She had asked him to advise on the suitability of two rooms in her new little house in the King's Road: "would they be quiet enough for Willie to work in and sleep in? She asked me some very intimate questions." Siegfried Sassoon "was in better form than usual" at dinner, but becoming, Bennett thought, "more and more of a solitary."

"The present awful situation in Britain" was the theme of a discussion at the Reform Club, where Bennett joined some of his fellow members in giving a lunch to Sir Josiah (later Lord) Stamp, chairman of the London, Midland & Scottish Railway, and a noted economist. "J. A. Hobson, Arthur Salter, George Paish, Gardiner, Tudor Walters, Spender, Ernest Benn, H. G. Wells."

> I sat next to Stamp, a fattish jolly man of 55 or so, who laughed easily and was generally merry. He gave us one of the most remarkable economic talks I ever heard. Rapid, clear, well-phrased, quite informal. It was so quick I could scarcely follow it. Salter and Hobson were both excellent. All three agreed that the gold problem was the root of the cure and that it must be handled from the world standpoint. Salter argued that if the middle-men's profits could be reduced, the trouble would be almost cured. Stamp pretty well agreed to this. It seems that the difference between wholesale and retail prices was never so great as it is today.

Eric Pinker wrote from New York to report sales of Bennett's short stories at rates swinging uneasily between £50 and £200. The great economic crisis over there, he said, made the book outlook "extremely uncertain". Bennett plodded on with *Imperial Palace*. "In spite of a not-good night, I wrote 1,300 words in two hours five minutes; 8,900 in a week." There was "an enchanting evening" with Frederick Lonsdale at the Garrick Club, where he had dined with his friend Duff Tayler. "Freddie told us the funniest stories. Bed early. Quite a good night up to 4.30. I couldn't sleep after that and felt extremely depressed about everything. Then about 6.45 I must have slept without knowing it, for I felt much better, less tired about the eyes, and less depressed and more *man*ful."

(8)

He showed not only an unaccustomed peremptoriness in taking the flat in Chiltern Court but an odd secretiveness. Having first seen it with Dorothy Cheston Bennett on the recommendation of H. G. Wells, who had taken up residence in the same block, he went back there alone and made various arrangements without mentioning them to anyone else. In a highly predictable man this was not simply unusual. It was abnormal.

The lease at Cadogan Square had run out and could not be renewed. In accordance with the terms of it, Bennett was put to the heavy expense of having it painted inside and out. Dorothy Cheston Bennett had suggested that they look for a house in Richmond or some other quiet outer part of London. He firmly vetoed it. "Too time-wasting, getting to and from." So the Chiltern Court flat was taken, at £1,200 a year for two flats converted into one. The result was a very fine flat and heavily increased expenses with considerable immediate outgoings. His study was a triumph of design, efficiency and comfort. "It became his yacht," Dorothy Cheston Bennett says, "and very definitely a place of his own." He had privately ordered steel bookshelves—"one-eighth of a mile of them," he later boasted to his nephew Richard—to cover the walls, and had commissioned his friend E. McKnight Kauffer, who had revolutionised poster design by his work for the London Tube, to design him a magnificent hand-woven carpet to cover the whole floor and to advise generally on the furnishing of the new flat. Another of his secret arrangements was to order a desk to be specially made for him by a West Country furniture craftsman, S. G. Gilbert. It was an imperative

[346]

of the order that the desk should have "a secret compartment". Wells had his own comment to make on all this magnificence. Talking about it to Osbert Sitwell, he said: "The trouble is, whenever I do a thing, Arnold does it too, but twice as posh."

Arnold Bennett to E. McKnight Kauffer:

> 75 Cadogan Square,
> S.W.1
>
> 18. 9. 30

MY DEAR TED,

   . . . I note about drawers and upright apertures for moods of untidiness. As regards desk fittings; yes, anything attractive and useful. But not a desklight. I have a 'daylight' desk lamp (steel), with which I would not part, and it shall stand on my new desk. I want as little on my desk as possible. . . . I have suppressed the dashboard gadget at the left of the desk, for bells, clock, lights, etc., as I don't need it. The leading idea of my desk is that it is an *expanse*.

> Yours,
>
> A. B.

Not wholly unconnected with his resolve to live at Chiltern Court was his discovery of a letter shute, the kind of practical testimony to human resource that never failed to impress him, who had always been attracted by "gadgets". The thing captivated him. "This is interesting, don't you see? It's the kind of new way of living that we ought to get to know something about."

"*Intensely* tired," he wrote on July 7, after seeing a revival of *The Importance of Being Earnest* at the Lyric Theatre, Hammersmith, the humour of which play he believed "owed much to the influence of W. S. Gilbert". He was experimenting with "a new herb device, hung on the neck", which a London dramatic critic, J. T. Grein, had recommended to him as an insomnia cure. It brought no relief. "Extremely enfeebled, incapable of writing an article." He had nearly finished *Imperial Palace*. "Miss Nerney has read 170,000 words. She told me that she is extremely pleased with it. This gave me great satisfaction."

Two or three days later he was writing: "Curiously, I have no sensation of fatigue after writing 1,800 words; the only fatigue I have felt being the original fatigue due to a very late night. I am working at a tremendous rate and not suffering. I don't understand it." But in two days more: "*Tremendously* exhausted. Tea at Express Dairy."

With a great deal less fuss of preparation than usual, he went to Cornwall for a holiday. Dorothy Cheston Bennett had rented a furnished cottage, not feeling sure until almost the last minute that he would agree to go there. He had never taken a holiday without working through most of it. In 1927 he had been a guest of Otto Kahn, the American banker, in the Duke of Westminster's yacht, the *Flying Cloud*, for a Mediterranean cruise. While the rest of the party was playing bridge or sight-seeing, Bennett as often as not was writing in his cabin. A book, *Mediterranean Scene*, came out of it. On holiday in the Alps with the Aldous Huxleys he wrote large parts of a novel. Visiting Russia with Lord Beaverbrook, Lady Louis Mountbatten, the Hon. Mrs. Norton, and Mrs. Edwin Montagu, he wrote a series of articles, remarking in the journal that he was glad to leave Russia when the time came: "It gets on one's nerves in the end," even on the nerves of a director of the *New Statesman*. His week-ends gave him little respite: he could hardly glance at a house without seeing a story in it. Lady Jones (Enid Bagnold) was walking with him on a late summer afternoon along the cliffs at Rottingdean. "Among the gaudy villas we came upon a little faded octagonal house, apparently consisting of only one room. Its green shutters were closed all round it, the garden gate was locked, the front door was hidden away at the back out of the public view. Weeds grew high in the garden. Arnold Bennett stood and gazed in silence at this queer little abode. He then pretended to see smoke rising stealthily from an iron chimney that rose up behind it. 'She's inside!' he exclaimed. 'She's waiting for him to come down from London. She's cooking. They'll eat it cold tonight. This is a secret meeting place! It's . . . a . . . love nest!' At dinner he elaborated the story of the exquisite run-away woman and the lover who came in after dark by the door at the back, away from the sea. A little later on I passed the house again, thinking of it as 'A.B.' had imagined it, the love nest. Four or five bicycles were piled against the gate. Four or five men came out, mounted, and rode off. The coroner, with his white head, came last. He locked the gate behind him. There had been a suicide from the cliffs and the little house about which 'A.B.' had let his fancy run was the local mortuary building. The iron chimney, I discovered, had nothing to do with the place: it was the ventilating shaft of the main Brighton sewer."

In Cornwall he made "a few notes of strange matters told me by Mason", A. E. W. Mason, and corrected the proofs of *Imperial Palace*, a task which made him "exceedingly tired". There are eighty-eight characters in the book, by his own reckoning, and he was put out by the discovery, in his publishers' office, that one of them named Jack reappeared as Charlie in a later chapter. For him this was ignominy, especially when a cable from New York queried the point. Also, a Miss Cass became 'Mrs.' without benefit of explanation and, adding to his discomfiture, he had wrongly accented a French spelling.

For once he read more than he wrote and found time to make some comments on the work of a writer whose career has been thought by some critics to have been inspired by his own.

Arnold Bennett to Frank Swinnerton:

> Rod Meadow
> Trewoofe
> St. Buryan
> Cornwall

MY DEAR HENRY,   17. 8. 30.
... I have just finished 'Angel Pavement'. The first 100 pages are the worst. I doubt whether Priestley can be justly regarded as quite so negligible as some of us have thought. There are gleams of insight and imagination. I think that the whole chapter, 'Mr. Smeeth Is Worried,' is pretty good—I mean, judged by a highish standard. And there is something to be said for a man who has written a 200,000 word affair of which the second half is better than the first. Unfortunately, the last 70 pages show declension. The general scheme will pass, but the main construction is clumsy.

Not that I shall now read 'The Good Companions'.

Withal, I suspect that if the man could cure his diarrhœa of facile, futile detail, he might one day make you sit up a bit.

> Thine,
> A. B.

"This is not England," he said of the Cornish countryside. He was more relaxed there than he had been for a very long time anywhere. He seemed to fit into the environment, the elemental strangeness of which, he said, made him sure that he could not paint it if he tried. This holiday required of him none of the ponderous display of his existence as a famous man of letters. Gone even was the yachtsman's style and stance. Wearing his old round tweed travelling hat, he would "stroll down the Cove Road, hands in pockets and cigarette dangling, brightly observing the odd variety of inhuman events on either side", quoted from Dorothy Cheston Bennett's remembrance of him at that time.

For her this peaceful holiday was riven by a strange flashing premonition of disaster. "I had a curious vision, like a photograph of the future, in which he was *not there*. I felt that something was going to happen to him." Seeing him refreshed by the new scenes and the change of air, she was reassured. "What we needed at that moment was more of this life, altogether more of it." It was too late. He had paid out a slacker line of contact with the professional side of his career than for many years, but in a matter only of days it had tautened again and was implacably pulling him back to London. "We have had a very great holiday," he wrote to his nephew Richard, "but every share I possess has fallen into a more or less deep pit." It was one of the few references that he made to the personal side of the depression then sweeping across two continents. "*September 1, 1930.*—Third-class up, thus saving £6."

CHAPTER EIGHTEEN

(1)

HIS tiredness of that late summer and autumn can hardly have failed to make him more vulnerable to worry than he would have wished to admit. There is no record of his income for the year. It was greatly reduced. "Finished my short story but it is not good. Too preoccupied with the financial outlook." His American markets had been disturbed by the slump and at home his mainstay had become the *Evening Standard* article, which far from covered his outgoings. Having sold for a thousand pounds the Modigliani for which he had given only £50 a few years before, he heard the next day that he must find almost exactly that amount as his share in more theatre losses. It was a kind of financial frustration which he experienced curiously often in those last years. He compared his position disadvantageously with that of some of his friends, ruefully noting that "Beaverbrook has five millions, and a young brother of his is worth £750,000. Lady Louis Mountbatten, Max says, has an income of £80,000 a year. And V. M.," meaning Mrs. Edwin Montagu, "came into half a million from her deceased spouse."

Domestic tensions were now sometimes still more severe, with hysteria not far away. "Dispute between D. and Miss N. Both these ladies are overworked, over-tired and in a considerable state of nerves." He wrote that "a nerve storm on the distaff side" had driven him out of the house, that he "had grave apprehensions about D's financial affairs", that she complained that if he accepted an invitation to go abroad for a holiday he would "ruin her career". There are journal entries of this time which read as if they were made under hardly bearable mental stress.

Doubts about Doran went on assailing him. "He assured me he had no intention of leaving D. D. & Co. I believed him," and then he heard from the Pinker office that "Mr. Doran has definitely agreed to join William Randolph Hearst". Bennett wrote off immediately to Eric Pinker in New York, asking again: "What publishers are we going to?" Indecision had never been a weakness of his, as it had been of his *alter ego* Richard Larch in *A Man from the North*, but now he had difficulty in making up his mind whether to stay with Doubleday, Doran & Company or to let his books go to another American publishing house; for once he was bereft of resolution. He decided that he had better stay with Doubledays until *Imperial Palace* appeared and then to think out his position afresh. When, that September, Doran arrived in London he asked Bennett to give his future books to the newly founded Hearst book department. Bennett wrote to Eric Pinker:

> I should like, out of pure, absurd friendship, to oblige George if I possibly could. I am fairly familiar with his defects as a man of business, but I like him very much. Still, unless he can guarantee a good sale for a book, and can back his guarantee by an advance to cover it, I shall restrain my friendly feelings. Having discussed the matter with Ralph, I think he agrees with my view that Harpers would be the best people for me.
>
> I am already very keen on my next novel, and the scheme of it is complete. I shall begin it in December and it will be finished—I think—about May. It is based on the plot of the story, 'The Dream', which you sold to some newspaper in Chicago.[1] If I had seen the possibilities of that plot earlier I should never have squandered it on a short story. However, I have turned a short story into a novel before, in 'The Glimpse'.
>
> As to future work, I have not decided anything beyond the next novel.

Imperial Palace was soon to appear. Approaching the publishing date, October 9, he confessed in the journal that he was "nervous about its reception". Hugh Walpole annoyed him by giving it out in the New York *Herald-Tribune* that the novel was about the Savoy.

Arnold Bennett to Hugh Walpole:

75, Cadogan Square,
S. W. 1.

29. 8. 30.

MY DEAR HUGHIE,—It was, I think, an error of discretion on your part to say in the 'Herald Tribune' that my novel is about the Savoy. Even if I mentioned to you the Savoy in connection with the novel,

---

[1] *Dream* is included in *The Night Visitor and Other Stories*. The novel was *Dream of Destiny*, unfinished.

such a private remark was obviously not to be used journalistically, and its divulgation in print might easily lead to trouble with a large number of people. I shall therefore be glad if you will recall your statement in your next article.

It is quite true that I have obtained a very large part of my material from the Savoy people, who were all told that I wanted the stuff for a novel. But the novel is not about the Savoy. It is about a larger and a different hotel, situated in Birdcage Walk, a hotel with a history of its own: The Imperial Palace.

Ever yours,

A. B.

Walpole wrote apologising, making it clear that he had put into print what many were saying. This did not satisfy Bennett, who insisted on a printed retraction, which Walpole made. Their long friendship had never been completely easy on Bennett's side, and his customary 'My sweet Hughie' mode of address in letters seems largely to have been a concession to Walpole's notoriously passionate desire to be liked. He thought Walpole a soft-centred man. Walpole believed that Bennett was jealous of his success as a producer of books which bounded one after the other into the realms of popularity. Bennett had admitted in the journal that he had been jealous of the success and reputation of Somerset Maugham. That was long ago. He had learned to despise jealousy as a base emotion, whereas Walpole was often a prey to it. Bennett wrote to Miss Mary Leonard, who was Doubleday, Doran's representative in London:

The first and most important thing is that *this novel is not about the Savoy*. Mr. Walpole has said that it was and I have written to him to protest and to ask him to withdraw his statement. It is urgent that D. D. & Co. should deny the statement on my behalf. Seeing that nearly all the characters are either directors or employees of the hotel, you can easily imagine the trouble that would be caused if the Imperial Palace got itself labelled as the Savoy. Imperial Palace is an entirely imaginary hotel (in Birdcage Walk) and its characters are fictitious (except one, who is dead). I very strongly object to any mention of the Savoy as being the original of the Imperial Palace. It is true that I got a very large part of my technical information through the great kindness of the Savoy people. If you see Mr. Richmond Temple, the Savoy publicity chief, who is an intimate

[353]

friend of mine, you will do well to explain the matter to him. He is an exceedingly brainy person and could perhaps give you some tips.

I have no idea whether the book is my 'most important' or not. It is the longest. . . . And it is far too short! I have had the idea for this book in my head for years, but I was too frightened by the bigness of the subject to attack it until last year.

This elaborate disavowal was followed by an angry letter to the publishers written out of Bennett's dismay at finding that the jacket for the American edition of the novel contained "an unmistakable picture of the Savoy". He was much upset: "it is absolutely monstrous." He was told that Doran himself had been responsible for commissioning the jacket but he refused to believe it until he had heard direct from his old friend. Cables of protest and appeasement crossed the ocean. "You will guess that I am still not quite calm," he wrote to Doran, and to Ralph Pinker: "I was sitting next to Miss Alice Head"—Hearst's personal representative in London—"last night at dinner. She has always struck me as being a very honest and sincere woman," and they had discussed this business of the jacket for the novel, "and she agreed with my very frank remarks." A note from Newman Flower, of Cassell & Company, who were responsible for the English edition of the novel, assured him that "it is a joy to us all here to work on this book. You've got us all primed up with enthusiasm over it."

"I am working," Bennett wrote to Doran on October 9, 1930. " 'Imperial Palace' appears in England today! Wilson, of Bumpus'," a noted London bookman, "has written to me out of the blue saying that he was immensely taken by it, and that it will be a great success. Well, it may or may not. Wells has written me praising it in the very highest possible terms, and Pauline Smith is enthusiastic. But I have not read any of the reviews."

H. G. Wells to Arnold Bennett:

7 October, 1930

. . . You are the best friend I've ever had. This may colour my vision. I don't think it does. We are also contemporary writers and that alone ought to keep us clear-headed about each other. But this big book of yours seems to me a really great book. I've read it with much the same surprise and delight that I felt about 'The Old Wives' Tale'. It's amazingly complete. It's your complete conquest of a

[354]

world you've raided time after time—not always to my satisfaction. It's an immense picture of a social phase and there is not a character in it that isn't freshly observed true to type and individual—so far as I can check you. . . .

The sincerity of Wells's tribute to their long friendship is not to be doubted. Bennett was unyielding in his admiration for Wells's genius. In one of the last of his *Evening Standard* articles he paid fresh tribute to it. Some of their more intimate friends believed that there was a hardening of feeling between them in the later years, more on Bennett's side than on Wells's. Wells was capable of startling Bennett by the violence of his impatience. He could sadden him by the acerbities of his dealings with publishers and by his ill-tempered flitting from one publisher to another when he had a new book to offer. In his last year Bennett noted: "I found in the post a long typewritten statement by H. G. W. about his difficulties with his collaborators and the Authors' Society in his projected work, 'The Science of Work and Wealth'. I read it all in my bedroom before going to bed. It took twenty-six minutes' quick reading. It makes a rather sad *exposé*, by H. G. himself, of his violent demeanour in writing business letters when he gets cross, ill or worried". It may well have been that in obedience to the course of his inherent invalidism, Wells's temperament became increasingly difficult. Bennett was repelled by difficult temperaments. On Wells's side there was a marked disdain of the social pleasures to which Bennett was surrendering so extravagantly in those years. But it seems that something deeper was at work between them. Bennett said in his last year or so: "The truth about 'H. G.' is that he is a snob." The comment laid bare the gist of the Wellsian passion for the world order in which he and his like were to play an hieratic part. Bennett could accommodate himself to no such conceit. He wanted perfection not for the race but for the individual.

An American critic, Stuart Sherman, discerned in this clash of attitudes the real factor of division between the two men. "Bennett's philosophy," he wrote, "seems to support an altogether decent theory of human conduct"; and as a criticism of Wells, the apologist for moral anarchy with his "loose fluent sensuality", to use Sherman's phrase, it is acutely to the point.

Wells was much moved by Bennett's death; indeed, shaken. It seemed to some who knew both men that Wells thereafter was goaded by a wish to minimise and disqualify Bennett's personal prestige and

[355]

he did not raise his voice to answer disparagements of his old friend and genial rival, the posthumously revealed disorder in whose affairs, those of the high priest of self-management, appeared to give him a peculiar satisfaction. It was hardly consistent in Wells to refer scornfully in print to Bennett's "pseudo-marriage" and that not because in the long ago he had dedicated his contentious novel *Marriage* "fraternally to Arnold Bennett". There was in them a difference of moral quality which became more marked as they moved on into the dangerous zone of middle age. Wells was not without the compassion which Bennett had said was the prime necessity of the great novelist, "but he was almost destitute of love," to quote *The Times Literary Supplement* review of his life and work which appeared some time after his death. That was not to be said of Bennett, who had written in his extra-journal on April 26, 1926: "There is an enormous lot in mere love. I have always known it."

Wells was never thought dull by those who knew him or met him. Arnold Bennett, often muted by his speech defect and by his fatigues, was sometimes thought dull by insensitive acquaintances who did not perceive, either, that he had another social handicap, that of being quintessentially a good man.

(2)

On October 14, 1930, he was one of the thirteen guests invited to lunch by Sir Ernest Benn to meet Henry Ford. "These affairs are futile things. There is no general talk. And Ford is very quiet and shy." Ford's deceptive mildness, he said, reminded him "of a very old lady who lives in the house of her descendants and seems to be nothing at all, but really is the autocrat of the house. I liked him". Through most of the meal Ford had not spoken. When the host mentioned Ford's book, *My Life and Work*, and Bennett had said that he had not yet read it, "Ford at once began to talk and he talked till I left, saying several half-true things." He told Bennett that he had once bought five hundred copies of *How to Live on* 24 *Hours a Day* to give to managers and other people in his motor works.

From that lunch Bennett went on to the Savoy for his first sitting to Jo Davidson, the sculptor, who was doing a series of busts of leading writers to Doran's order at the rumoured price of £1,000 each. "Lincoln Steffens came in. This celebrated American journalist is a quiet, bland, talkative, untidy little man, *très sympathetique*."

On October 30, "J. Thorpe of *Punch* entertained me as an expression of his enthusiasm for *Imperial Palace*." He heard more enthusiasm for the book that evening at the Other Club dinner, a function overshadowed by the death of the Earl of Birkenhead, one of the most conspicuous members. "It was a sort of memorial dinner. Biggest dinner in the history of the club. Nearly thirty people instead of the usual fifteen or sixteen. Churchill spoke well, much moved. Freddie Guest just escaped crying. Home at 11.10. D. in a considerable state of nerves, threatening to run off to Paris, U.S.A., etc."

A well-known caricaturist, Kapp, "called to interest me in two friends of his, authors—Catherine Carswell, whose life of Burns has recently caused trouble in Scotland, and a young novelist, John Collier." He was begged to write a programme appeal for a charity matinée on behalf of Denville Hall, "a home for old players. I wrote it." A representative of the Book League waited on him with a formal request that he would become chairman. "I refused," possibly not for lack of goodwill but because he could not face the necessity of making speeches. "John Roberts, manager of the *New Statesman*, came to discuss the unsatisfactory affairs of the paper." Lili d'Alvarez, the tennis player, "in a most extraordinary letter," invoked his aid in introducing her to a film producer who would encourage her to express herself "on the topmost height of art". He was giving careful consideration to the future of a young relative, Cedric Beardmore, who had written a novel. "I have a nephew (son of my eldest sister), who in my opinion is a born novelist and will certainly make a place for himself. He is twenty-one, and works in an insurance office in the Five Towns. In the last three or four years I have turned down two of his books, and I suggested he should rewrite a third, 'Dod the Potter.' The progress that this boy has made in three years, working only at night, is extremely satisfactory to me."

Another nephew, younger, received some less immediately practical advice. The boy had recently arrived in London to work and had been bidden to dine at Cadogan Square. During the meal his celebrated uncle delivered himself on the subject of investing money. "My advice to you, my boy," he said in his gravest and most authoritative style, "is to buy nitrate shares." Next day this nephew looked up the particular share his uncle had recommended. It stood at 42s., and he was earning, as Bennett well knew, 25s. a week.

A letter from Hugh Walpole pleaded for advice to be passed on to a friend suffering from a health misfortune on which Bennett was presumed to be an authority.

[357]

Arnold Bennett to Hugh Walpole:

75, Cadogan Square,
S. W.

4th October, 1930

MY DEAR HUGHIE,—I do not know any cure for insomnia. I am convinced that most insomnia is due to some poisoning of the system, usually either from indigestion or teeth. Dr. Haydn Brown, of 53 Bedford Square, says that he can cure insomnia, and that he has already cured many cases. So far, he has only begun on my case, so that I cannot speak personally as to results. He is a very interesting man and I have had long talks with him. He has the merit of having got into trouble with the General Medical Council.

I think that a good way of dealing with the symptoms of insomnia (not the causes) is to get resolutely up when one cannot sleep and *do* something—for instance, Hornibrook's exercises, which at once improve the circulation. Also something can be done by going to bed early and quietly, consciously tranquillising the mind beforehand.

That is all I can say.

Ever yours,
A. B.

The reception of *Imperial Palace* was more nerve-trying than he had feared, tense as he already was. Critical opinion was extremely varied in tone and temper. "The editor of *The Times Literary Supplement* has written to apologise for the opening paragraphs of its notice of 'Imperial Palace'." He had also called to account the editor of the *Evening Standard*, in which newspaper his book articles were still appearing: "I expect a general apology for Bruce Lockhart's grossly inaccurate review," which had offended him by "its serious misstatements of fact". To Frank Swinnerton he wrote, alluding to that matter: "There may be some secret history behind the article. If there is I will relate the same for the delight of a few natural hearts." He was perturbed by a statement in the *Newsagent and Booksellers' Review* that "Mr. Bennett's new novel, *Imperial Palace*, is a popular library title, but the sales are disappointing". The novel was priced at 10s. 6d. and the first printing of the English edition was 21,000 copies, of which 14,000 were sold in the first two weeks. Sales on publication in the United States of America, three weeks later, were 11,000 copies, rising to just on 20,000 copies by Christmas. Over there prominent booksellers combined in sending appreciative messages to Bennett.

Richard F. Fuller, of the Old Corner Book Store, Boston: "When I first looked at it with its 768 pages my remark was 'Oh, my Gawd!' Now I wish it were 1768 pages." Franklin Watts of the book department of the W. K. Stewart Company in Washington: "The finest novel I have read in several years." J. G. Kidd of Cincinnati: "For me the best book of the year." Acknowledging these tributes, Bennett said they were "enheartening".

"What am I to do in the clash between my favourite critics?" he wrote about *Imperial Palace* to Frank Swinnerton. "Desmond has no use for Violet, but admires Gracie. You have no use for Gracie, but admire Violet. I ought to tell you that in my opinion Gracie did say quite a few interesting things, and that the Paris affair was intended *not* to be passionate." He wrote to his friend Professor Thomas Bodkin:

> 75, Cadogan Square,
> London, S. W.

MY DEAR T. B.,   16. 10. 30
Your remarks on my Journal 1929 much please me. . . . André Gide was enthusiastic about that book.

'Imperial Palace' is having a good press, but my many critics say that in writing a *big* novel I am imitating Priestley and following a new fashion. Good God! As if the excellent Priestley were not imitating me in this matter. I got 'The Times Literary Supplement' to apologise for their unlawful suggestion that my object in doing Imp. Pal. was to share in Priestley's booty.

We are moving at the end of the month into a huge flat—180 feet long—with 3 bathrooms, and every room a south aspect: 97, Chiltern Court, Clarence Gate, Regent's Park, N.W.1 is the correct postal address, but the place (mint-new) is really over and around Baker Street station. Our moving is a terrific enterprise, for us.

> Yours,
> A. B.

That evening he dined with the Galsworthys and, returning home, wrote in the journal that John Drinkwater, one of the guests, had not shown much vitality but that he, Bennett, had supplied enough for both of them and that the evening was a success. "But John Galsworthy is too quiet (in voice) and afraid to express himself with violence." He was dining out continually and was giving many dinner parties at home. "We have three separate and distinct dinner parties here this week. It will be strenuous for D——," who had to conform to his subtle design for this sort of occasion, that it should consist of more men than women, in the proportion of six to four. His idea was that the women would receive more attention than if each was paired off with a man: "it makes them feel *rarer*," he would say. And the men, according to his theory, had to be at the top of their form in competing for the women's response.

However much vitality he had to spare for these evenings, the journal shows him rising the morning after often quite unfit to face the labours of the day. "After a terrible night" he went out at 6.30 one morning that autumn and caught the first bus he saw. "I had to be alone. I went bus riding all the morning," rediscovering "the instructive pleasures" of bus-riding in London. "I am getting fonder and fonder of bus riding," he noted. There was one day when he crossed the metropolis by bus from west to east and back again. "It gave me numerous ideas. There is a lot to be learnt going about London in this way." He was going also more frequently to the Lyons's and Express Dairy teashops in the King's Road. "I had to be alone" recurs in his notes of these visits. "A woman with parted grey hair and a bun at the back looked tired in a most distinguished way" at the Express Dairy shop. "These places always interest me. I *like* going into them." An urge towards simplifying his living seems to have been upon him. Or a compensatory preface to the expensive new domestic phase on which he was embarking. He had undertaken to bear part of the heavy cost of converting the two flats at Chiltern Court into one. "I had in decency to agree to pay for some of the special alterations I wanted."

Very soon he realised, but would not admit, that he had made a serious misjudgment, that the noises of the Marylebone Road were even harder for him to endure than the servant troubles of Cadogan Square.

(3)

"A French author (excellent), Jacques Chardonne, whom I don't know personally, has written to me to assert that 'I.P.' is the greatest novel of this age, and that I am one of the greatest authors of any age.

[360]

This will do to go on with." Bennett was writing to his nephew Richard. And a cable from his American publishers brought good cheer to him on Christmas morning, 1930: *Imperial Palace only a few hundred copies short of our hoped for sale with book top of best seller lists.* It was a badly needed whiff of success, for in England another novel had over-taken and passed *Imperial Palace* and was rapidly mounting in sales to a point at which they could be called prodigious—*Grand Hotel* by Vicki Baum. This lushly sympathetic story of a Mr. Polly-ish little man braving the lofty splendours of a luxury hotel made *Imperial Palace* seem by comparison a scientific treatise. Against it in the libraries and bookshops *Imperial Palace* could not prevail. Arnold Bennett clung to his hope of a spectacular American success: "Imp. Pal. is at the moment the top of the 'best-sellers' in U.S.A." he wrote to his sister Tertia on Boxing Day. "I am delighted that Christmas is over but I watch the diminishing of your mince-tarts with sadness."

A young Bond Street business man, Trevor Fenwick, much taken by *Imperial Palace*, wrote to Bennett inquiring whether he had thought of the fiction possibilities of "a large modern store", unaware that he had tentatively exploited them long before in *Hugo*. Bennett replied to him:

> 97, Chiltern Court,
> Clarence Gate, N.W.1
>
> 27th November, 1930
>
> DEAR MR. FENWICK,
> Thank you for your letter of the 26th. The idea of writing a novel about a department store has suggested itself to me many times during the past ten years. Mr. Selfridge has offered to place the whole of his establishment at my disposal, and has urged me to do such a novel. But I do not think that I shall ever write it. I have had enough of these vast subjects.
>
> > Believe me,
> > Cordially yours,
> > ARNOLD BENNETT

In his nerve-worn state he was more sensitive to the noises of the Marylebone Road than he might otherwise have been. He had to wear a patent ear-stopping device. "Fred went out and ascertained that the road drilling will stop in a few days." His heart had been "very fluttery". Wells dined with him in the new flat. "We had a great talk, largely about ourselves but also about our friends, including Max." He dined with Lord and Lady Cranborne. "First-rate evening. I liked the Cranbornes." Dined with Jeanne de Casalis, Martita Hunt, and Leslie Hore-Belisha. "Martita Hunt very full of gestures and superlatives and expressions of intense love and admiration for persons and things. I liked her." Dined with Seymour Hicks and Bernard Darwin: with Virginia Woolf—"Virginia is all right; other guests held their breath to listen to us"—and Mrs. Granville Barker and Lord and Lady Esher. With Lord and Lady Dudley, Frederick Lonsdale and the Gerald Kellys. "I had some talk with Gertie Millar (Lady Dudley). She comes from Bradford and told me some Yorkshire stories. A nice unspoilt woman." Dined as the guest of the Epicures Club at the Savoy, where he was presented with a finely bound copy of *Imperial Palace*. "A very fine dinner and very fine wines. Charles Cochran next to me. Went across to the Adelphi Theatre with him afterwards and saw the end of his show *Evergreen*. Talked to Jessie Matthews and Chita." The next day, "up early, not enough sleep. I walked to the Wallace Collection and just sat there." Lunch with Yvonne Arnaud and "Dorothy Cheston B. Yvonne very late and very charming". A Thanksgiving Day party at Claridges, given by the Messmore Kendalls, over from New York, saw him with "Maugham and Arlen, sitting on the floor, drinking Lanson '11. A great evening . . . lasting, unfortunately, till 2.30 a.m."

His old physician friend Griffin examined his heart. "Vagus nerve not controlling it properly. He said it is a common cause of irregularity." A short time afterwards it was decided that in the constant upward stretching involved in arranging his 7,000 books on their new steel shelves he had strained his heart. A rest seemed desirable and even important. "We go to Jo Davidson's on the 29th," he wrote to his nephew, and added: "I'm dining out most nights. I saw Augustine Birrell last night. He stayed later than I did, and seems as young, and he is over eighty," Bennett apparently comforting himself with the thought that this necessarily had some bearing on his own situation. "Total of words for the year, 353,250. Not bad."

(4)

Journal note.—Having left home by the Golden Arrow on 29th December for Paris, I transfer all accounts for the last 3 days of 1930 to 1931. On 29th we dined at Aubers and went to the Casino de Paris. Had oysters at Café du Rond Point at 12.30.

On 30th I felt rotten. I stayed in bed all morning and afternoon. We dined at Versins which was nearly empty, good, but very dear. We met Donald Calthrop.

Wednesday 31st we arrived at S. Pierre des Corps by Sud Express at 1.25. Jo Davidson met us. 28 kilometres to his house.

Davidson had requested final sittings for the bust. "*January 3.*—I sat or rather very exhaustingly stood to Jo D. for over two hours and a quarter in the morning, and about an hour in the afternoon."

Back in Paris three days later, he saw the funeral procession of Marshal Joffre winding through the streets: they had been photographed together during Bennett's visit to the Front in 1915. "A lot of strange sights" at the funeral, he observed, "but I do not feel equal to noting them down; too much fatigue." There had to be another sitting for Davidson at Auteuil:

James Joyce came for lunch. Has grown-up children but seems quite young—slim, tawny. Nearly but not quite blind, can walk about a bit alone. I believe that he only wanted to see me because he wants me to help him with his favourite tenor, John Sullivan. He could not deny that Valery Larbaud had done more for his reputation than any other person, yet he said quite indifferently that he did not read the works of Larbaud.

This indifference of Joyce's may have had a personal meaning for Bennett, who had reviewed *Ulysses* when it was first published in England. He had been astonished, he said, to find the review made the subject of a poster: "Arnold Bennett on Ulysses." He wrote to Professor Bodkin: "It was the first time I had ever seen a *review* as the chief item on a poster," and had added: "Lest you should resent my treatment of 'Ulysses', let me warn you that J. Joyce, whom I don't know, has written to thank me for it."

The next day André Gide came to tea, announcing that he had been ill and was not yet cured. "Then Valery Larbaud came in unexpectedly. I had not seen him for sixteen or seventeen years. Older, fatter, shaken by the death of his mother, but with the same fundamental niceness and knowledge. A great vivacious talk about books." When Larbaud announced that in his opinion Edith Sitwell was the most distinguished

[363]

of the modern English poets, Bennett was in enthusiastic agreement. "Gide said he meant to write a long essay on Richardson's 'Clarissa', but that he had not yet begun to read it!" Exhaustion after that, "all night and all day," recovering sufficiently in the evening to get up and dine at Les Trianons Restaurant with Joyce and his wife.

Admirable food and wine. Mrs. Joyce had to be continually keeping Joyce from drinking. It seems that he drinks too much, but he won't eat enough and a very little drink knocks him over completely and he sinks to the ground. Mrs. Joyce must have a terrible time. They are theoretically poor but they must spend a lot of money. The dinner cost only a little under £6. I had another absolutely rotten night and did not sleep above 2 hours in all.

Rashly, so rashly for him that it was like an enactment of fate, he had drunk water from a carafe in the small hotel where he stayed during that brief Paris visit. Arguing that the stories about Paris drinking water were a popular fallacy, considering the number of citizens who every day drink it without harm, he filled his glass from the carafe with a large emphatic splash. As he did so the old waiter who had been looking after his table spoke quietly, leaning towards Bennett: "Ah, ce n'est pas sage, Monsieur, ce n'est pas sage." Dorothy Cheston Bennett noticed that the reproof made Arnold Bennett look uncomfortable. "He tried to find a place to rest his eyes, avoiding mine."

They travelled back to England in the company of Lady Diana Cooper and Maurice Baring. During the crossing Bennett had "a fearful fit of shivering". Next day he went to bed in the grip of what he and the household supposed was influenza. One of his first inquiring visitors was George Doran, noted as soon as he had gone as "looking a pathetic figure". Aldous Huxley came "and stayed two hours". The next day Bennett felt better, "so much better that I feel a different man. I feel very much better 'in myself';" well enough to note in the journal that "D. was sixteen minutes late for lunch. Last night she was twenty-five minutes late for dinner". But the journal entries now were sketchy. Taxi-ing to the Reform Club on his first day out, he lunched with "the gang", who all thought that he looked better, "while I felt worse."

The following morning, "feeling rather rotten," he was out with Dorothy Cheston Bennett "in the bitter cold" while she did shopping. "I felt very unwell." The same evening he went upstairs to the McKnight

Kauffers' flat. "Sidney Bernstein was there. He said he was thirty-two. This startled me, as he looks older. I said I was sixty-four in May. This startled him, as I look younger."

The last entry in the thirty-two journal volumes was made the next day, February 2, 1931:

> Dull, then sun. Cold. Ernest Griffin took me to be examined by Sir William Willcox, generally. This lasted 11 to 12 and was satisfactory. Afterwards I went with Griffin to his surgery and he syringed out my ears. I got back at 12.30 and then learnt that the book I had written about yesterday for 'Books and Persons' in the 'Evening Standard' was not to be published till the 16th! Terrible. So I had to write another article, on Mrs. C. N. Williamson's reminiscences. Dorothy and I dined in the restaurant, as Fred is away. I began the article at 4.30 and finished it at 6.10. Not bad. Tip at restaurant 1s. 2d.

This was the last article he wrote. In it he quoted an anecdote about life after death. On the same day he wrote his last letter to his sister Tertia, who had been nearer to him in sympathies than anyone else in the family. "I agree about the moral influence of 'flu. I am going to see a physician about my heart and generally. Also, I have only two teeth in my head. Slightly disturbing. Dorothy's illness is nerves and due to overwork and undue worry over nothings. Acting is very bad for her and I shall ban further acting as much as I decently can. When she has a part, she quickly gets infinitely worse, indeed acutely. And she is one of your household worriers. I should like to see you, but not mornings. Tea is the time. I will send you a notelet. I'm doing *no* work, except my weekly article, which I always regard as more lark than labour. But of course I have to keep my correspondence in order. Miss Nerney is marvellous. Fred ditto."

His last appearance as a gregarious man was at a wedding reception at the Savoy Hotel following the marriage of Desmond Flower on February 3, 1931. He said there that he felt "wretchedly ill". He wished he might go home to bed but he had promised to be at a play. When he went to bed that night it was for the last time.

Sir William Willcox, who was an eminent toxicologist, was consulted again. He diagnosed typhoid fever. Hearing details of the patient's health history, he had no doubt that Bennett had suffered a previous attack in 1912 when he had been very ill on the Riviera and weak for months afterwards. "They told me it was inflammation of the intestines," Bennett recalled. The specialist said in an aside to Dorothy Cheston Bennett: "They never speak of typhoid down there—afraid of scaring the visitors."

There were two or three days when it seemed that he had fought through: "a great battle," Willcox said. Symptoms of gall-bladder infection appeared. Atropin injections and hot applications were used to reduce the pain, which at times was acute. For three weeks he hiccoughed, a clownish exhausting affliction that seemed like fate's last piece of facetiousness at his expense. Disquieting new symptoms disclosed that his toxæmia had reached the profound stage. Six doctors and five nurses moved continually about his bed. Drugging became necessary. There was delirium. He would send for Miss Nerney and babble instructions which she could not follow. Sometimes he fancied himself back at Fontainebleau. "How good of you to come all this way!" he said to Coward, his barber from Harrods' who had attended him for ten years. In the temporary absence of a nurse he tried to get out of bed. When Fred, his manservant, found him he was lying on the floor, helpless. He had pulled the quilt over himself where he lay.

His wife arrived from France but could not see him, though she made desperate attempts to reach his bedside. The atmosphere of the flat was tense with fear and hostility and the forces of his disintegration. Old friends called and were allowed fleeting sorrowful glimpses of him, Lord Beaverbrook insisting: "Arnold is the best man we've had since Bonar Law"; Newman Flower overcome by the sight of Bennett's right hand, small and shrivelled, lying on the coverlet—"the hand that wrote *The Old Wives' Tale*." His brother Frank and his sisters stood by in silence, appalled by the terrible mummifying processes of his disease. "I was resolved that Arnold should pass out with his family about him," his eldest sister, the redoubtable Mrs. Beardmore, J.P., wrote in her diary, "and I remained."

In one of his forays of consciousness he plucked at the pleating of the nurse's uniform. "Beautiful," he whispered, smiling his appreciation of the craftsmanship. He asked for Sir Thomas Horder, but not even old friendship could accomplish what medical etiquette did not permit. Each day his weakness became more enfolding. In *Clayhanger* he had described the effects of Cheynes-Stokes breathing, "that rare and awful affliction." Now vengeful time had made him a victim of it, his breathing, loud and harsh and menacing, rattling down the long corridor of the flat. For long hours he clung to Dorothy Cheston

Bennett's wrist. "Everything has gone *wrong*, my girl," he said pitifully to her, scarcely able to whisper the admission of defeat. There were moments in which he tried desperately to speak but could not. Particularly at the end, when he made a supreme, unavailing effort to give utterance to thoughts that remained in the last vestiges of his consciousness. Before that he had clearly been worrying greatly about the future of his child and her mother and about domestic economics and the eclipse of his earning power. Widely publicised stories of his not having left enough money to pay the milk bill the day after his death were untrue and unjust, though the value of his estate was very much smaller than had been forecast.

He died at ten minutes to nine in the evening of March 27, 1931. A sympathetic borough council had allowed straw to be laid over the Marylebone Road outside Chiltern Court to deaden the traffic noises, the last time, it is thought, that this practice of the pre-rubber-tyre era was revived in central London. It was a night of rain. The straw became sodden and slippery. Just after midnight a milk dray skidded and overturned, sending its load of churns crashing along the pavement below the flat in a thunderous din.

*   *   *   *   *

His ashes were taken on an April day day to Burslem cemetery to be placed in his mother's grave, marked by the severe obelisk which bears the names of her people, the Longsons. All around are the "stone-perpetuated names" of other Five Towns folk whom he had known, names which he had written into his account of the funeral of Auntie Hamps in *These Twain*: "the Boultons, the Lawtons, the Blackshaws, the Suttons, the Greenes, the Beardmores, the Dunns, the Hulmes, the Longsons, the Calverts, the Dawsons, the Brindleys, the Baines and the Woods," and H. K. Hales, "the Card," lies with them. The committal words were spoken to the sound of the shunting of an engine at the Sneyd colliery whose pit-mound casts its huge sunset shadow over the cemetery. A civic procession preceded the memorial service in the smoke-blackened church at Stoke.

In London, St. Clement Danes in the Strand was crowded for the service held there in his memory. This was the church which had been faithfully and fearfully attended for twenty years by another celebrated Staffordshire man, Dr. Samuel Johnson, whose statue stands unscathed amid the ruin which later came to the church. When the last notes of

Chopin's Funeral March had vibrated down into the chambers of the dead, there were many men and women in the congregation who walked out into a London that for them would never be the same again. On April 8, *Punch* published its valedictory:

A MAN FROM THE NORTH

Enoch Arnold Bennett, 1867–1931

Here lies a man, from common clay descended,
    Who took the common people of the clay
And from their lives of grime and greatness blended
    Created Life that shall not pass away.

Here lies a child who penned with childish pleasure
    The pageantry before his eyes unfurled,
The pomps and shows, the luxury and leisure,
    The gauds and glitter of the rich man's world.

Yet still could sing, with sympathy unblunted,
    With understanding welded doubly sure,
The saga of the straitened and the stunted,
    The patience and the pathos of the poor.

Here lies a sage who saw in things material
    The outward workings of some cosmic plan—
Each day a chapter in some breathless serial
    Written by Fate for the delight of Man.

Here lies a jester with a sense of duty,
    A master-craftsman in his art engrossed,
A steadfast friend, a worshipper of beauty,
    A kindly critic and a perfect host.

Here lies, in fine, a connoisseur of living
    For whom adventure lurked in every breath;
Shall not his soul go forth without misgiving
    To greet the Great Adventure which is Death?

SOURCES AND ACKNOWLEDGMENTS

(i)

The source I have mainly drawn on are:

(1) Arnold Bennett's journal, covering the years of his career as a man of letters, 1896–1931. Part was published in 1932–33 by Messrs. Cassell & Co. A larger part has remained unpublished, except for extracts used serially in one or two literary publications, and in the present work.

(2) His subsidiary journals and notebooks in which he kept records of his yachting seasons, foreign travel, and miscellaneous experiences collected under the title of 'Some Incidents', but not published.

(3) His novels, particularly those in the Five Towns series, which contain autobiographical matter; *The Truth about an Author*; collected criticisms and reviews; his numerous miscellaneous literary productions, including contributions over many years to newspapers, magazines and periodicals.

(4) His letters, published and unpublished.

(5) *La Jeunesse d'Arnold Bennett*, par Margaret Locherbie-Goff, Docteur de l'Université de Lille (Editions de 'L'Observateur', Avesne-sur-Helpe, France, 1939).

(6) Various published memoirs, and the word-of-mouth recollections of many friends.

(ii)

Before beginning to write this book, I sought the concurrence of Mrs. Arnold Bennett, who lives out the long years of her widowhood in her native France. I wish to acknowledge her most generous response.

From Arnold Bennett's sister, Mrs. Emilie Vernon, and from his brother-in-law, Mr. W. W. Kennerley, I have received much help. It is Mrs. Vernon who has seen to it that her father's reputation as a tyrannical parent has been set in a truer perspective than that drawn in *Clayhanger*, where he figures as Darius Clayhanger, the steam-printer.

Mr. Kennerley has lent me important letters. He has come forward with other documentary materials. He has answered many questions.

I also thank Mr. Richard Bennett, Arnold Bennett's nephew, for lending me the Bennett family photograph album and other useful materials, and for giving me access to letters.

To Miss Dorothy Cheston Bennett I am indebted for the opportunity of studying the thirty volumes of the journal kept by Arnold Bennett, the copyright in which he formally assigned to her; for permission to read certain letters; and for numerous comments and suggestions written by her for my guidance as I approached the final chapters.

My friend Hesketh Pearson first proposed that I should write this book and I have been able to call on him for reassurance as well as advice. Before finally deciding to act on his suggestion I turned to Mr. Frank Swinnerton, who relieved me of a sense of trespass as I contemplated a task for which he, not only by virtue of his close friendship with Arnold Bennett, was better qualified to undertake.

I have had the benefit, too, of the tireless help of a staunch Arnold Bennett researcher, Mr. Thomas Roberts, of St. Helen's. He has given much time and energy to the task of relating persons, scenes and incidents in the Five Towns novels to their author's own local life and experience. He has got together a great quantity of background information which will be useful to future students of Arnold Bennett's work.

(iii)

I have acknowledgements to make in respect of much other help, to Mr. Frank Swinnerton, again, for the opportunity to read and to quote letters; to the H. G. Wells executors, through Mrs. G. P. Wells, for the series of letters exchanged in the course of a friendship which has become part of contemporary literary history, and for permission to quote from H. G. Wells's *Experiment in Autobiography*; the Public Trustee, for permission to use or quote from Arnold Bennett's letters and from his books; and to the trustees of the Hugh Walpole estate, and Mr. G. J. V. Bemrose, curator of the City of Stoke-on-Trent Museums & Art Gallery, for facilities for reading the letters written to Hugh Walpole by Arnold Bennett.

The correspondence between Arnold Bennett and his literary agent, J. B. Pinker, has been made available to me by Messrs. Elkin Matthews, Ltd., and Mr. P. H. Muir. They have also let me see the correspondence between Arnold Bennett and a number of British and American publishers, and the many letters written to Arnold Bennett by George Sturt of Farnham ('George Bourne'). I have been able to quote from the last-named by the kindness of Mrs. H. M. Philipson-Stow, of The Old Vicarage, Farnham, George Sturt's literary executor and treasurer of the Sturt memorial fund. For permission to quote from the Bennett-Pinker correspondence I thank Mr. Eric S. Pinker.

The Countess of Iddesleigh has allowed me to see letters written by Arnold Bennett to her father, F. S. A. Lowndes, and to her mother, Mrs. Belloc Lowndes; Mrs. Wainwright Morgan, notes on Arnold Bennett by her father, Frederick Marriott, and letters written to him by Arnold Bennett; Mr. Paul Herzog, of Washington, D.C., letters written to his mother, the late Mrs. Paul M. Herzog, by Arnold Bennett. I have had other American help in the form of photostats of letters between Arnold Bennett and Frank Harris, sent to me by Mr. Arthur Leonard Ross, of New York, and letters from Arnold Bennett to Mrs. Hilda Hellman, and to Mr. E. McKnight Kauffer, also of New York.

Millicent Duchess of Sutherland found for me the 'apologia' written to her by Arnold Bennett after the publication of *The Card*. Lady Keeble (Miss Lillah McCarthy) has shown me letters which she received from him. It has also been helpful to have seen the letters in the possession of his friends Professor Thomas Bodkin and Mr. Gregory Hill; those written to Mrs. Sidney Marsden and lent to me by Miss Joan Marsden; others in the possession of Mr. James Bone, C.H.; and the unpublished notes made by Mrs. Joll (formerly Miss Eleanor Green).

The Society of Authors has given me permission to print extracts from letters written to Arnold Bennett by George Bernard Shaw.

The letters of Joseph Conrad appear by kind permission of Messrs. J. M. Dent and the trustees of the Conrad Estate.

(iv)

Bulging files of correspondence made necessary by research and consultation fill me with the apprehension that I may have overlooked some claims to acknowledgment of anecdotal reminiscence, factual help given, books lent and presented, or of other practical goodwill. I wish to record my thanks to Mr. J. B. Atkins; the manager, and the staff of the Securities Department, Barclays Bank Limited, 160

Piccadilly, London, W.; Miss Violet F. Barton; Mr. George Beardmore and Mr. John Bennett, nephews of Arnold Bennett; Mr. Archie de Bear; Mr. Frank Belfield; Mr. N. R. Bradshaw; Mr. Collin Brooks; Miss Jeanne de Casalis; Mr. R. T. Chandler; Mr. S. H. Clarke; Mr. A. Egerton Cooper; Mr. Marten Cumberland; Messrs. Gerald Duckworth & Co., Ltd.; Mr. John Dunbar; Mr. J. H. Downing; Mr. Trevor Fenwick; Mr. Kenelm Foss; Mr. A. S. Frere, C.B.E.; Sir Philip Gibbs; Mr. Louis Golding; Mr. Hubert Griffith; Mr. Ernest Hales; Mr. W. D. Hardie (of Messrs. Harrods, Ltd.); Mr. D. Goronwy Harnaman; Mr. Fred Harvey; Mr. D. Macdonald Hastings; Miss Mary Heath; Lord Horder; Lord Inman; the late Sir Francis Joseph, Bart.; Lady Jones; Mr. Alexander Kadison; Miss Gertrude Keir; Sir Gerald Kelly, P.R.A.; Mr. Messmore Kendall; Miss Gertrude Knoblock; Messrs. Le Brasseur & Oakley; Mme Georges Lafourcade; Dr. H. V. Lanchester; The Secretary, The Law Society; Mrs. M. Locherbie-Cameron; Mr. W. A. McWhirter; Mr. Richard Mallett; Mr. Charles Marriott; Mr. Walter Mead; Mr. Frederick Melcher; Mr. Augustus Muir; Mr. Raymond Needham, Q.C.; Miss Winifred Nerney, Arnold Bennett's secretary; Mr. H. Collinson Owen; Mr. John Parker; Mr. A. F. Palmer Phillips; Mr. Eden Phillpotts; Mr. Edward H. Pinto; Mr. Frederick Poke; Mr. Greville Poke; Mr. Arnold Pilbeam; Sir John Pollock, Bart.; Mr. Stephen Potter; Lady Preston; Sir John Richmond; Mr. T. B. Roberts; Miss Berta Ruck; Mr. Geoffrey W. Russell; Mr. Lance Sieveking; Miss Pauline Smith; Messrs. Sotheby & Co.; Mr. W. Spark; Mr. F. R. Steele; Mr. C. A. Stonehill; Mrs. Frank Vernon; Messrs. A. P. Watt & Son; Lord Webb-Johnson; Mr. Frank Whitaker; Mr. Geoffrey Williamson and Mr. Henry Williamson; Mr. Harry Wood.

I add my thanks to the editor of *The Times Literary Supplement* for publishing a letter which produced some of the help acknowledged above, to the editor of *Everybody's* for a valuable appeal in that paper, and likewise to the editor of the *Saturday Review of Literature*. The editors of the *Daily Mail, Daily Express, News Chronicle, Staffordshire Sentinel, John o' London's Weekly*, and *Tit-Bits* kindly allowed me to consult their libraries and files. Acknowledgment is also made to *Punch* for permission to quote the elegiac verses by Jan Struther printed on page 368, to Mr. Ian Winchester for translation help, to Mrs. Madeline Lincoln for her labours with the typing, and to Peter Pound for reading the proofs.

R. P.

INDEX

[Names of persons and places in inverted commas denote characters and places from fiction, or *noms de plume*. The page-numbers in black type that appear after the titles of certain of Arnold Bennett's works give the reference to date of publication.]

[374]

[375]

[378]

[383]

[384]